T5-AGT-448

WORLD OF SEX
VOLUME 2: SEX AND MARRIAGE

Also by Iwao Hoshii (in English)
THE ECONOMIC CHALLENGE TO JAPAN (1964)
THE DYNAMICS OF JAPAN'S BUSINESS EVOLUTION (1966)
JAPAN'S BUSINESS CONCENTRATION (1969)
A FINANCIAL HISTORY OF THE NEW JAPAN (Co-author with T.F.M. Adams, 1972)

PERSPECTIVES ON JAPAN AND THE WEST

THE WORLD
OF SEX

Volume 2
Sex and Marriage

IWAO HOSHII

PAUL NORBURY PUBLICATIONS LIMITED
Woodchurch, Ashford, Kent

First published 1986 by
PAUL NORBURY PUBLICATIONS LTD
Woodchurch, Ashford, Kent.

ISBN 0-904404-55-2

British Library C.I.P. Data
Hoshii, A. Iwao
The world of sex.
Vol. 2: Sex and Marriage
1.Sex——Philosophy
I. Title
306.7'01   HQ21

ISBN 0-904404-55-2

Set in Bembo 10 on 12 by Visual Typesetting, Harrow, Middlesex.
Printed and bound by A. Wheaton & Co. Ltd, Exeter, England.

Contents

17 MARRIAGE AND THE WORKING WOMAN

Foreword

THE POSITION ASSIGNED TO MARRIAGE and the family in the social systems of different societies is not uniform and almost diametrically opposed views on their value have been professed by different individuals. In the West, the family has commonly been regarded as the basic unit of society and it has been the cornerstone of social organisation in Chinese tradition. But in today's society, the family often looks like an endangered species and the trend to do without marriage and family questions their necessity as social institutions.

This book attempts to explore the meaning of marriage and family on the basis of a coherent philosophy of man and to evaluate the fundamental ethical and legal norms that condition the personal character of married life. By way of highlighting the considerable differences in approach to marriage, I have outlined the historical development of some phenomena and illustrated the actual situation by referring to conditions in various countries.

A distinctive feature of this book is the place given to Japan. Japan should be seen not as an exotic country but as a modern nation with the strengths and weaknesses of industrialised countries in a particularly fluid state. I have relied on Japan as the main exhibit, so to speak, in drawing a general picture of the problems of marriage and the family and have made use of Japanese conditions and Japanese law for describing the situation in today's society.

The changes wrought by the sex revolution have also made an impact on Japan but attitudes, behaviour and value systems remain quite different from those in the West. The sex revolution implied a rebellion against responsibility, man's responsibility for his personal destiny but also the responsibility as husband, father and breadwinner or as wife, mother and the guardian of the family's spiritual wholesomeness. While irresponsibility in the affirmation of sex is nothing new, the problems created by this irresponsibility have taken on dimensions threatening the survival of western civilisation.

The most important element in the sex revolution was removing the taboos surrounding sex which involves its 'amoralisation,' and the disregard of traditional norms or even their outright rejection. Basically, the sex revolution repudiated the restraints on sex and asserted the sexual freedom of the individual. The traditional moral precepts and legal rules expressed man's perception of socially acceptable behaviour and its social implications. In the West, the moral as well as the legal rules were largely based on Christian values. As presented by the Church, marriage constituted the only legitimate form of sex relations and the framework of sexual activity.

Although there were important differences in theory and practice, secular society generally came to recognise divorce, and while infringements of sexual restraints by males were widely condoned despite the general prohibition of adultery, female transgressions were severely censured. The basic limitation of sexual relations to the institutionalised form of marriage implied restrictions on individual freedom in favour of social stability. Against this institutional order, the sex revolution raised the question of the foundations and the legitimacy of the traditional restrictions on sex in general and the institutionalisation of marriage in particular.

The basic reason for sexual controls is the uniqueness of man as a personal being. Man and woman are not sexual roles but modes of existence of human beings. The interpretation of sex and marriage must be determined by the image of man as a personal being. The nature of man, the nature of marriage, and the nature of the family form the basis of the ethical rules governing man's life as an individual and as a member of these societies. The variations and discrepancies in the historical forms of marriage and family cannot invalidate the inner meaning of sex and the inherent rationale of the institutions regulating sexual relations nor can they discredit the injunctions and prohibitions postulated by the personality of human relations.

I have emphasised the duties and responsibilities of marriage partners but also delineated what an ideal marriage should be. An ideal, by definition, is something that does not exist in reality. Just as human perfection is not attainable, an ideal marriage remains the object of our dreams, wishes and hopes. An ideal is not a goal to be reached but a beacon that indicates the direction in which we must proceed if we want to overcome what we find unsatisfactory, nocuous or even pernicious. It is a motive to surmount disappointments, to transcend fears and to continue the quest for lovable togetherness despite failures and even betrayals.

That the initial euphoria of newlyweds is followed by a period of frustration and discontent is a very common experience. At such times, the partners must remain convinced that marriage is not a quest for utopia but a human adventure that can succeed and will succeed if they themselves want it. No marriage can be an ideal marriage but every marriage can be an honest and joyful attempt to live up to the challenge of a life in common.

The Japanese counterpart to the *Hite Report, A Nationwide Study of Female Sexuality* (Macmillan, 1976) is the *More Report on Female Sexuality* (Shûeisha, 1983). *More* is the title of the magazine that undertook the surveys. The Japanese subtitle says: 'For the first time, Japanese women talk about sex in their own words.' There is no corresponding work on male sexuality but there have been a number of general surveys on sex.

IWAO HOSHII
June 1986

1

Marriage as Institution and Community

THE WORD MARRIAGE has a twofold meaning; it is used for the act of getting married (wedding) and for the state of being married (wedlock). In the western world, marriage appears as a personal union of love as well as a public and legal institution. An institution is a form that ensures the permanency of social structures and operations. It is not a group in the sense of a number of people but a social frame of order which fixes the order proper to a certain group or regulates a certain kind of function. Society cannot afford to always start from scratch in coping with a certain requirement or fulfilling a certain function. Social tasks which must be accomplished more or less regularly lead to the formation of definite structures or modes of operation.

As an institution, marriage is a permanent and exclusive community of life of two adult heterosexual persons. Marriage and the family constitute an arrangement in which the association of the sexes, the procreation and education of offspring, and the care for the old are regulated. The community of life implies a loving partnership which, as such, is inalienable and non-transferable because the personal assent of the partners includes the reciprocal renunciation of an arbitrary disposal. Marriage is the institutional confirmation and guarantee of a personal decision. The miracle of love can only be experienced by a total and irrevocable commitment. Marriage means a permanent relationship which is established by the marriage contract but whose contents, rights and duties are not determined by the partners. The dissolution of marriage often depends on conditions that are independent of the will of the parties. (In Japan and some other countries, divorce is possible by the agreement of the marriage partners.)

Foundation of Marriage

Marriage has often been called a community of love. Love is not the purpose of marriage but rather belongs to its foundation; nevertheless, the cultivation of love is important for maintaining the spirit of a personal partnership. The meaning of love between man and woman can be expressed in two sentences: 1. Love between man and woman naturally leads to marriage as an indissoluble union of life. 2. Marriage constitutes the perfect union intended in sexual love.

Modern man expects a maximum of happiness from marriage, but the realisation of this expectation is conditioned on the permanency of love. In a lasting marriage, the partners find physical and psychological security together with the satisfaction of their sexual desires. There is no replacement yet for this kind of one-on- one relationship. Only a permanent bond secures the personal integrity of both partners although there is a risk that the duration of the marriage may lead to the disregard of human dignity. In principle, however, marriage is the form of interpersonal relations in which man can experience in the most intensive way that he is esteemed and respected, revered and loved. In this sense, marriage is an eminently teleological institution ordained towards the fulfilment of man's sexuality as well as the growth of his personality. But the durability of marriage requires inner stability which can only be attained by striving for mental and physical equilibrium.

The emphasis on the personal meaning of love is not universal and has not always found suitable recognition. In primitive cultures, marriage is primarily a means of cementing relations between different groups, such as families or clans. Marriages are contracted in con- formity with social organisation and may be based on quasi-political or strictly economic considerations which, however, do not negate the desire for offspring.

In the traditional western conception of marriage as a permanent and exclusive community of life of man and woman, marriage is regarded as a prerequisite of the family. The personal union also requires a bond including material and economic interests. For Aristotle and his medieval commentators, the family coincides with the house- hold and constitutes a natural community for the purpose of taking care of everything man needs for his daily life. The 'house' also forms the basic unit of the political community which represents the organic whole of the primary social uits. First and foremost, husband or wife does not mean a role but the existence as a partner in a community of life — just as male or female is not a role but a mode of existence of human nature. Status is involved in marriage as an institution but is not essential to marriage as a personal union.

In sharp contrast to many modern theories regarding marriage as a scheme that can be manipulated and changed arbitrarily, the Scholastics considered marriage as a 'natural' institution. St Thomas Aquinas speaks of a 'natural inclination' to marriage and explains that marriage is not natural in the sense that it is the result of a natural development occurring with necessity but necessary in the sense that nature induces to marriage. However, there can be no marriage without the free will of the parties. Basically, 'natural inclination' only implies that some form of union of man and woman is natural but is compatible with the view that all actual forms of marriage are the outcome of a historical development. The possibility of marriage is based on the fact that man exists as a personal sexual being. This form of existence is 'natural' and 'necessary' in the sense that the being we call 'man' could not exist in any other way.

A union based on the sexual difference between man and woman is a natural possibility (a possibility not given with human nature but with the mode of existence of man) but it is not a natural or necessary postulate, neither for the individual nor for human society. From a purely biological point of view, the continuation of the human race would also be possible without a permanent union but in view of the personal relations involved in the sexual union of man and woman and the education of the offspring, a permanent and exclusive community of life based on the free choice of the partners appears most suited to the personal character of marriage. This does not mean that all other forms of union of man and woman are 'unnatural' or against the natural law.

Family as a Social Unit

In its essence, the family is a social unit which, as all social units, constitutes a unit of order. Order implies differentiation and integration. The basic differentiation in the family consists in the plurality of its members. This membership admits of a certain latitude. As a community of life, the family may contain several generations. Man and wife already make a family, and in today's nuclear family, father, mother and child or children are its only members. But the large family comprised other relatives and the servants. (In antiquity the slaves were also included, although legally they were not treated as persons but as chattels.)

The second element of differentiation is the plurality of functions. The functions of the family extend to the entire range of human life and include the togetherness of cohabitation, a common household, the procreation and education of children, and the economic functions required for the daily life of the family. In the course of history, the economic functions have undergone deep changes. The plurality of functions involves a plurality of organs and activities. The difference between the roles of father and mother which, in the past, was accepted as natural, has become the subject of heated controversies. The integration of the family is given with its goal which, objectively, constitutes the task of the members and subjectively, demands their cooperation. The goal of the family is the family itself, the common life as a household. This common life results from the fulfilment of the functions proper to the family and realises its proper values: happiness, security, confidence, trust and whatever is included in the love between husband

and wife and between parents and children. As an abstract concept, the common life of the family can be regarded as the same goal but it is actually different for each family.

Her twofold role in the reproductive process makes the wife-mother the centre of the family biologically and sociologically while the legal dominance of the male has been the outcome of his ascent in the public order. Psychologically, too, the relations of the mother with her children constitute a reinforcement of the family which normally also tends to strengthen her bond with her partner. The father's emotional involvement with his offspring is less direct. He may experience a new tenderness when his wife becomes mother but he may also feel displaced as the sole object of his wife's affections.

The family is a form of the social formation that Ferdinand Tönnies called 'community' and distinguished from 'society.' (This is the usual translation of the German *Gesellschaft* but what Tönnies had in mind is something like a 'company.') Society is based on the free will of the parties who conclude a contract for the attainment of a definite purpose. Their relations, therefore, are limited by the purposes for which the contract is concluded as well as the duration of the contract which can also provide for cancellation or the resignation of a partner. Marriage, too, is based on the free consent of the partners but although the will of the marriage partners is involved in the origin of their relations, the meaning and importance of these relations is not fixed by their will. The status resulting from the marriage contract is largely independent of the will of the parties and makes marriage a community of life, love, work, and destiny. There is what might be called a natural framework for the existence and activities of the family which allows wide variations but admits no essential changes.

The family is not an 'agent' of society and neither its existence nor its functions depend on a social mandate. The law may define the groups that are recognised as families and circumscribe their rights and duties but such dispositions cannot change the nature of the family and its inherent meaning.

As a group, the family stands out as a special entity in the consciousness of its members as well as in the view of outsiders. As other groups, the family as such is not an object that can be directly perceived by the senses but is known through the integrating function of human consciousness. The group is recognised as an integral whole, different from its members and something other than the mere sum of its members. The family may have its own mentality which influences the thinking of its members but is also influenced by their thinking. Family affairs are distinguished as 'our' affairs from those of others, and the common experiences of the family are neither 'parallel' nor 'identical' experiences of each family member.

Family Functions

In the social functions of marriage, the togetherness of the partners has often been less important than the status it conferred. Even today, some societies do not consider a male an adult member of the group unless he is married. For the woman, to get married was the proper thing to do also in western society unless she chose to enter religion.

As a community of life, marriage is a community of habitation, the community of 'bed and board.' The social functions of marriage, procreation and education, are the 'natural' outcome of its personal functions. They assure the continuation of the human race for which the family never received a mandate from society and for which it usually is not rewarded. The reason, of course, is that the family is prior to the other social entities that now exist and which could not have come into existence without it.

The preservation of the human race does not only mean the physico-biological maintenance of the species but also the conservation and transmission of its spiritual heritage through the formation of the personality and the education of the children. By this function, the family contributes to the continuation of society as a cultural community.

In caring for the bodily and spiritual well-being of the children, the family fulfils a function that is indispensable for their socialisation and their growth into mature human beings. The educational function of the family has been greatly reduced in modern times but this has not eliminated its necessity and importance. Education means much more than instruction to which it is often abridged. Instruction is mainly directed to intellect and memory while education has more to do with character, dispositions and attitudes. Above all, the development of sympathetic feelings such as love, tenderness and affection demands the protectiveness and security of the family.

Family education is also necessary to accustom children to life in society in outward behaviour as well as inner attitudes. In the family, the child learns the socially acceptable behaviour required for life in society, good manners, politeness, courtesy and decency. The family also cultivates the 'virtues' necessary for the individual's own happiness and his relations with others: sense of responsibility, orderliness, discretion, moderation, selflessness and the spirit of sacrifice. The equality of man and woman can only become a reality if the family fosters the attitude of respect for every individual as a human being.

The case of the 'wolf boy' illustrates the importance of the environment for man's socialisation. The boy, discovered in 1976 in the company of three wolf cubs in a dense Indian jungle died in February 1985 in a home for sick and dying destitutes in Lucknow. During the eight years of his life in civilisation, he never learned to speak.

Through its educational function, the family is the starting point of

man's socialisation in the individual sense of introducing and adapting
the future generation to life in society as well as in the collective sense
of forming human society. Contrary to the behaviour of animals, the
formation of society, although often ascribed to a social instinct, is
mainly the result of rational and voluntary conduct which largely
supersedes instinctive elements. The 'societies' of ants or bees often
regarded as social formations have an essential relation to reproduction,
and in the formation of herds or packs of higher animals (elephants,
wolves, etc.), the strongest male animal usually usurps the role of leader
together with the domination of the females. In human history, not all
forms of society go back directly to the family but as far as social
development can be traced, some kind of family organisation can be
found. The theories on the origin of the family based on psychoanalysis are bold conjectures unsupported by historical evidence. None
of the primitive cultures existing today is without some form of
marriage and family, and monogamous marriage is the decidedly prevailing form. In the cultures in which the origin of social entities is
generally based on biological links, above all descent from a common
ancestor, social organisation is intimately connected with marriage.

There are definitions that inordinately stress the economic aspects,
such as the description of marriage as an arrangement in which one man
is morally and legally entitled to sexual gratification in exchange for
support. Today, the typology of marriage is sometimes based on the
work of one or both of the spouses: marriages in which the wife is the
'professional' housekeeper, marriages in which both spouses have full-
time outside jobs, in which the wife earns a supplementary income or
is a collaborator or associate in the husband's work.

Nowadays, the economic function of the family is often reduced to
that of a unit of consumption but it also remains a unit for the earning
of income and, especially in the country, a unit of production.

Alienation

As a community of life and love, marriage is the natural antidote to the
phenomenon referred to in modern times as alienation. Marx borrowed
this term from Hegel to describe man's condition under capitalism in
which work did not give man the possibility of self-realisation. In
capitalism, as Marx describes it, work is not spontaneous and creative
but enforced and suppressive. Workers have little control over their
work; the product of labour is expropriated by others to be used against
the worker and the worker himself becomes a commodity in the labour
market.

Modern Marxists such as Erich Fromm and Herbert Marcuse find
the fundamental alienation attributable to capitalism in the estrangement of man from himself. In the capitalistic market place, man con-

ducts himself according to ceremonial gestures that are detached from any real inner feelings or capabilities. Proceeding further on the line of thought indicated by Marx, some authors perceive the estrangement not in the split between human nature and the production system, but in the rupture between required activity and subjective experience. Activities that are not experienced as intrinsically rewarding lead to alienation. This conception has been applied by the women's liberation movement to the household chores which deny to the wife her personal self-fulfilment.

Modern mass society has been blamed for the emergence of a general feeling of alienation. The disappearance of the traditional community as a result of industrialisation has isolated man in the anonymity of the urban mass and left him without values and direction. The rationalisation and formalisation of social organisation have reduced personal relations and this disintegration of binding social norms has resulted in an extreme individualism. According to Kierkegaard, the central problem of alienation is the difficulty of attaining an adequate sense of self in a world dominated by purposelessness and despair.

Urbanisation has been held responsible for many of the ills of modern society. This does not mean that urbanisation as well as the anonymity and mobility involved in it can be undone but that the transition from the community pattern of social relations to the living conditions of the vast urban conglomerations has been an important factor in the changes that have affected the family. Until the appearance of the slums housing the proletariat created by the industrial revolution, towns and cities were far better attuned to the satisfaction of man's physical and spiritual needs than the countryside. Western culture has been essentially an urban culture although non-urban settlements such as the monasteries have played a very important role. A phenomenon which revealed the strong attachment of modern Europeans to their cities was the reflux of the city dwellers who had been evacuated to the country into their bombed-out cities after the Second World War.

The situation described by Frédéric Le Play as typical of some parts of Eastern Europe in the middle of the nineteenth century prevailed in Poland until the period between the two wars: the supremacy of the family, submission to the universal mores, religion and paternal authority. After the war, the laicisation of family legislation and factors such as the widespread migration and the beginning of consumerism led to an increase in the number of divorces, a decline in the birthrate and what was called 'moral erosion.' But family bonds remained strong, which was largely attributable to the adherence of the preponderant part of the population, including the young people, to the Catholic faith.

In Germany, the Allensbach Institute of Opinion Research discovered a trend towards stronger social engagement. People join clubs and associations in larger numbers than before. In 1953, only 36 per cent said that they would miss their circle of acquaintances if they had to move; thirty years later, in 1983, 65 per cent expressed the same sentiment, and people are also more interested in their neighbours (27 per cent as against 16 per cent in 1953).

While the nineteenth century slums could somehow function as extensions of the cities, the formation of the shapeless poverty belts surrounding the large cities of Latin America, the so-called *favelas,* can hardly be covered by the term urbanisation. The cities attract the impoverished peasants but cannot integrate them and give them roots.

Today's real problem lies in the growing disappearance of the characteristics of the rural areas. Radio, television and the abundance of machinery available everywhere have fundamentally changed living and working conditions and phenomena such as air and water pollution, noise and traffic jams are common to urban and rural areas.

The followers of Marx consider economic change as the main pre-requisite for overcoming alienation but a restoration of the experience of community is most effectively achieved by marriage. Marriage gives the individual a sense of serious engagement which can overcome the feeling of meaninglessness, isolation and estrangement typical of aliena-tion. The need for security and assurance can create the desire to live in the stream of tradition. People all over the world were unable to cope emotionally with the deep and rapid changes of the post-war era which cut them off from their roots. The political, economic and social upheavals have transformed man's environment to such an extent that old as well as young people feel lost and are searching for an anchor to save them from drift. The desire for relief from the insecurity of the world situation has led to a reappraisal of the past and growing interest in history. But in order to contribute to the rebuilding of the shattered political, economic and social structures, conservative attitudes, values and institutions must have enough cultural, ethical and psychological strength to overcome the present chaos and inaugurate a new social order. That is the basic task confronting marriage and the family today.

Family as Link Between Past and Future

In the past, the family was the link between the ancestors and posterity, so that the main emphasis was on the role of marriage in the procrea-tion and education of offspring. As in other old cultures, marriage appears in the Old Testament as an institution primarily concerned with founding and procuring a family for the continuation of the tribe. In the Roman private cult, the *genius* of the *paterfamilias* (housefather) and the *juno* of the *materfamilias* (housewife) were worshipped. These were the male and female forms of the family's or clan's power of continuing itself by reproduction which were temporarily in the keeping of the heads of the family or clan and passed at death to their successors.

Genius was the creative power that enabled the family to repro-
duce; juno, so named for the goddess Juno, was the female principle of
life. (Genius and juno were at times considered as something like
guardian angels.) In short, the social significance of marriage far
outweighed its role as a source of personal satisfaction and happiness.

Ancestor worship is found in many cultures and in Greece and
Rome, the family implied special religious rites and duties. The Roman
home had a domestic shrine (lararium) in which statuettes representing
the divine ancestors were placed, and the Di Penates, the powers that
ensured that there was enough to eat, were worshipped in every home.

As long as the family remained stable, one of its characteristics was
its linkage with past generations. Naturally, the relation of the living
with the dead is greatly influenced by the ideas and beliefs concerning
death or life after death, and while everything connected with death,
corpse or funeral may be taboo in one society, the dead are buried
under or near the hut of the survivors in another. In traditional societies, death was a public ritual, reinforcing the cohesion of society. In
Christianity, the belief in the immortality of the soul and the resurrec-
tion of the body created a particularly strong attitude of reverence and
piety towards the dead. In the European village, the cemetery adjoined
the church, and attendance at church services was combined with a visit
to the family tomb or the graves of dead relatives and acquaintances.
The connection with the dead strengthened the feeling of solidarity and
the adherence to tradition.

The average Japanese has no clear belief in life after death although
there is much superstition involving ghosts or spirits. But o-bon, the
festival of the dead (sometimes called the Buddhist All Souls' Day, 13–
15 July), when the deceased are supposed to return to the places where
they once lived, each year causes a huge migration. Everyone goes
home to his birthplace or the seat of the family (o-kuni). This
observance, therefore, keeps their rural roots alive in the memory of the
urban Japanese.

In the Confucian scheme of human relations, the wife was completely subordinated to the husband or better, to the lord of the house.
In the feudal system, marriage was not a partnership but a system for
the orderly continuation of lineage for which the wife was but an
instrument. (The Japanese saying hara wa karimono — 'the womb is a
borrowed thing' — expresses the same idea.) Marriage was an arrangement between families rather than between individuals. It was fixed
strictly within the limits of status by official regulations. For the higher
classes, at least, marital negotiations had to be conducted by officials
whose status was commensurate with that of the families concerned.

Changes in Conception of Marriage

St Paul's doctrinal justification of the position of the husband as the
head of the wife and the subjection of the wife under the authority of
the husband (Eph 5,21-29) vested the Roman *paterfamilias* and the
German *muntwalt* with the nimbus of divine ordainment. Marriage as a
sacrament gave religious and moral legitimacy to male dominance in
marriage and the patriarchal form of the family. Just as the religious
legitimisation of the royal power occasioned the doctrine of the divine
right of kings, the paradigm of the Christian household sketched in the
epistles of St Paul made authority an unquestionable personal attribute
of husband and father.

The traditional Catholic doctrine considered marriage as the lawful
union of a man and a woman established by a marriage contract by
which the two partners conferred to each other the mutual, permanent
and exclusive right over their bodies with regard to acts that were, in
their nature, suitable for the procreation of offspring. The Book of
Common Prayer retained the traditional view on marriage. In its
explanation of the purpose of marriage, it stated that marriage was
ordained first for the procreation of children, secondly, for a remedy
against sin, and thirdly, for the mutual society, help and comfort. The
strong emphasis on the legal relations and the generation of children
neglected the personal meaning of marriage. Love between the spouses
somehow belonged to marriage but it was not so essential that marriage
could not be concluded or exist without it. Morally speaking, therefore,
marriage was also permissible for an external purpose, such as
economic security, if the procreation of children was not excluded.
Sexual intercourse was considered morally acceptable only in view of
the possibility of the generation of offspring.

In modern times, views on marriage have changed considerably,
partly under the influence of a transformation of social conditions. The
main factors were the dissolution of the large family, the dissociation
of the family from work and the place of work, the individualisation of
life, the reduction of marriage to a private affair between two
individuals, and the stress on sexual equality.

Partly as a result of these changes, the way of describing marriage
was modified, correcting the primarily legal view of marriage as an
institution based on contract. The strong patriarchal bias in role fixation, the idea of the husband as head of the family and the subordination of the wife to the husband have given way to the conception of
marriage as a cooperative union of equal partners. In the definition of
marriage, the new Canon Law has replaced the consideration of the
'purpose' of marriage by an explanation of the meaning of marriage:
'Marriage by which man and woman together found the community of
the entire life which by its natural character is ordained to the well-

being of the spouses as well as the generation and education of offspring has been elevated by Christ our Lord to the dignity of a sacrament' (c.i.c., can 1055, Par. 1).

In 1958, the Lambeth Conference of the Anglican Church expressed the opinion that the procreation of offspring was not the only purpose of marriage and that intercourse was an expression of the love husband and wife felt for each other. It termed the view that intercourse should only be practised with the conscious intention of producing offspring erroneous.

Instead of speaking of marital rights and duties, preachers now prefer the term matrimonial encounter as the bodily expression of self-surrendering love. Although the Church has not retreated from her condemnation of birth control, responsible parenthood and family planning have found their way into the ecclesiastical vocabulary. Rather than insisting on mutual rights and obligations, marital problems should be solved by the creative moulding of marriage on the basis of the unifying and formative principle of love.

Social Role of Family

Through its functions, the family contributes to social order as well as social and economic well-being. The family forms an important and irreplaceable part of the public order which faces the danger of instability without the stabilising influence of the family. As a cell in the social body, the family does not float as an atom in a vacuum but exists in close connection with the community of the people and shares the ups and downs in the people's destiny. The family shoulders an enormous responsibility since the quality of posterity depends on it; the more stable the family, the more stable will be the next generation.

In its position as a social group, the family fulfils the double function of containing and of protecting the individuality of its members. As against the individual, the family represents a higher authority claiming compliance and subordination. It constitutes a unit to which the individual must conform, expunging the bitterness, strangeness and exclusiveness of individuality so that the individual learns to live together with others. On the other hand, the family interposes itself between the individual and larger groups. The individual is not helplessly facing the 'masses;' he has not only a physical home to which he can retire but also an emotional sanctuary where he feels 'at home' and finds understanding, support, trust and love. The stronger the attachment to the family, the weaker the influence of other groups while a weak identification with the family increases the receptiveness for other influences. The more the individual can experience the family as an extension of his own self, the safer he feels in his own personality.

Many problems of adolescents arise from the present educational system which alienates the young from the family before they have been deeply enough affected by the influence of the home. Conscious and explicit instructions and advice account for the smallest part of family education; its main influence derives from its constant presence as physical and emotional environment and to a certain extent also from its role as a model of behaviour. The influence of school and school-mates is more direct and not only lacks any organic connection with the family but may also be inconsistent and even diametrically opposed to the upbringing in the family.

The Family and its Members

The truly human image of marriage and the family has often been clouded by a distorted representation of their traditional forms in which the husband as head of the family is pictured as wielding absolute authority. Wife and children are totally dependent on him and owe him unconditional obedience. Abuse of power in all forms, from the most brutal physical violence to mental torture endanger life and health of wife and children.

It is certainly true that many societies still recognise a double moral standard for man and woman and apply different norms to their con-duct in sexual matters as well as general behaviour. The one-sidedness in the role attribution of the wife has not yet disappeared. In Germany, the proper sphere of the woman's activities was described by the three 'Ks': *Kinder, Kuche, Kirche* (children, kitchen, church). Adopting the admonitions in the epistles of St Paul, silence, submission and obedi-ence were considered as the typical duties of the wife.

The individual interests of the members of the family had to be subordinated not only to those of the family but also to those of rela-tives and business associates. Autocratic domination was rampant in single families as well as in the 'clan.'

In the traditional role attribution, the father earned the living expenses of the family, took care of its needs and protected it against the outside world. The mother was responsible for all household chores and the health of the family, particularly looking after the sick and rearing the children. The family constituted the community of the pres-ent generation, the cradle of the future and the shelter of the old generation. The family was no purposive association for ensuring rational living conditions but a community of life embracing and connecting several generations. In its role as a community lay the importance of the traditional family.

Supplantation of the Family's Educational Function

In modern times, the social significance of the family has been radically devalued by the state and society. The family has been reduced to the private sphere. Juridically, if recognised at all, it is treated as some kind of voluntary association and not as a unit belonging to the public order. Psychologically, it is explained as an adjunct to man's instinctive needs and it has been deprived of its educational functions. It has become a small group kept together by a few strictly personal needs centered on bed and refrigerator. It continues to exist for practical reasons but the needs which it serves could also be satisfied independently of biological bonds, and this view has been strengthened by the assimilation of 'family-like' associations such as cohabitation, communes and kibbutzim to the family.

Among the trends that have led to the dissolution of the family, the idealisation of emancipation has exercised a strong influence. The individualisation of freedom which disregards the essential ties of the individual, the atomisation of institutions and the autonomy of moral decisions have created the conditions under which 'self-realisation' could be proclaimed as the sole meaning of human existence. The pursuit of a professional career at the expense of womanhood and motherhood could not remain without impact on the family. Although the form of the family may change, its substance remains the same. Fatherhood and motherhood cannot be transformed into interchangeable roles which can be allocated at the discretion of the partners.

The most deplorable results have been caused by the family's loss of its educational function. This loss was not an inexorable fate but the outcome of planned interference by state and society. By identifying education with instruction, the state took over education and made it impossible for the family to fulfil its role in education. Progressive pedagogues supplanted parental authority by representing emancipation from parents as a necessary step in the evolution to self-realisation. The family's authority was sacrificed in order to give adolescents the illusion of 'self-discovery.' States dominated by socialist ideology invented the parent's 'right of caring' which obliges parents to discuss with their children questions of how to take care of them and obtain their consent in accordance with the children's degree of development. What used to be considered a natural way of behaviour or a moral duty was to be transformed into legally prescribed conduct. The state not only fixed the educational model but also made the family powerless in the children's choice of their occupation. It frequently happens that the over-emancipated individuals fall back on their families if they find it impossible to get along in life. The family must be ready to serve as a social clinic in which a meaningless existence can be salvaged or emancipation neurosis cured.

A further step in the devaluation of the family is the manipulation of its role in procreation by birth control, parent substitution and test-tube babies. The family is considered as a freely controllable mechanism.

Divergent Views on Marriage and Family

The traditional form of the family has been under attack from socialists, militant feminists and some social workers. A sign of the opposition to the traditional family was the change from the singular in the appellation of the 'White House Conference on Family' to the plural ('families') which apparently was meant to accommodate phenomena such as cohabitation without formal marriage, one-parent families and unions of homosexuals.

The unity and indissolubility of marriage involves difficult problems. Institutional marriage is a ratification based on public law of a personal relationship of love between two persons but many people consider the ratification alone without the living relationship as a lie and an injustice of which the party who suffers it is equally guilty as the party who causes it. But there may be important and compelling reasons to maintain the institutional façade even after marriage has lost its inner meaning. These problems will be taken up later.

One of the most pernicious attacks on the family is the social insurance system of the modern welfare state. The sophistry of the 'pact between generations' conceals the fact that the legal old-age insurance is no insurance and that its payments are not pensions. A pact with the coming generation is pure fiction. The system provides for a legally imposed redistribution of income from wage or other income earners to those who are no longer economically active which makes it impossible for the family to provide for its own future independently and in accordance with its needs. The system can only function if each generation includes enough active workers whose payments keep the system running. The family, therefore, is necessary and is exploited by the state to rear the next generation of tax-payers and contributors to the social security system.

The negation of traditional values has led to an extremely critical and basically negative view of marriage and the family. Progressionism, which is derived from evolutionism, regards the family as a relic of patriarchy, a group with an unjust and repressive structure in which role fixation leads to parental usurpation of power. From the point of view of evolutionary philosophy, the family does not represent an absolute social structure and always requires new forms. In its adaptation to constantly changing social conditions, it has developed from a husbandless matriarchy through polygeny, rural monogamy and the large family to the nuclear family which, in turn, will have to be replaced by forms better suited to modern conditions.

From a different point of view, social liberalism condemns the limitations on personal liberty inherent in marriage and the family. The individual's right to self-realisation demands freedom from all restrictions and the free arrangement of family relations. The greatest possible freedom of the individual is at the most compatible with a temporary cohabitation as companions or friends. Such a cohabitation requires family planning and the right to abortion because children would obstruct the dissolution of the relationship.

Progressionistic and liberalistic conceptions of marriage were particularly voiced by the so-called partnership theory of marriage. According to this view, the family is only valuable to the extent that it contributes to the well-being and satisfaction of the individual. The family as such has no special task, since it is only the sum of its individual members. If the family does not satisfy the wants of the individual, if it subordinates the wife to the husband or the children to the parents, it must be changed. A family whose members do not enjoy complete liberty is out of fashion. Individuals should be just as free as they would be if they did not belong to a family. The family is only valuable if it fulfils necessary functions better than any other arrangement. But as every other organisation or institution, it is secondary to the personality of the individual and has social significance only to the extent that it contributes to human welfare and individual development.

Feminism and the demand for the liberation of the housewife and mother have been influenced by the liberalistic ideology. This link is apparent in the claim that the woman's innate right to self-realisation cannot be abridged by marriage and family. Sexual equality is appealed to as basis for the postulate of role change because otherwise the independence of the wife cannot be realised. The claim to independence also extends to children; as an essential condition of self-realisation, they must be emancipated as quickly as possible. The right of the freedom of personality requires growth without authority and guidance. This served as foundation for the models of self-determination in schools which proclaimed the principle of anti-authoritarian education.

The dissolution of the family is less noticeable in Japan than in the United States. One of the reasons is the very limited extent to which the emancipatory tenets of feminism have found acceptance in Japan, another the indifference of the average Japanese to any kind of ideological rationalisation of practical behaviour. Psychoanalysis which has strongly shaped American attitudes remains of largely academic interest in Japan. Despite a strong dose of practical hedonism, Japanese society suffers much less from the ravages of licentious sex, drugs and alcohol abuse.

In a different way, marriage and the family have been devalued by collectivism. The position of the collectivity is absolute and demands the complete identification of the individual with society. The welfare of the collectivity is the supreme and only norm. The family is the breeding ground of bourgeois individualism and promotes the cultivation of self-willed differentiation resulting in encapsulation, segregation and separation from the collectivity.

In a speech at a national conference on feature films in December 1981, Hu Yaobang, Secretary-General of the Chinese Communist Party, discussed the love theme in literature and art. While conceding that personal love was important, he stressed that the interests of the country and the revolution should come first. Love between the sexes is a part of life, but it should not be depicted as more important than the revolution. Literature and art should not propagate that love is above everything and everything is for love. The last statement undoubtedly is correct but like other personal values, love is not unconditionally subordinate to country and people and the success of socialism.

In 1982, the Albanian parliament passed a law strengthening the state's right to intervene in family affairs. Commenting on the law, Radio Tirana said that the law does away with 'the bourgeois conception that marriage and the family are private issues or that the state and society need not and cannot interfere.' The law eliminated mutual consent of the spouses as a ground for divorce. 'Organs of the authorities and social organisations are expected to control the development of correct relations in the family,' the broadcast explained.

For reasons of population policy, communist countries have not abolished the family but, on principle, permanent relations are not obligatory and socialist ideology recommends the replacement of the family by communal life-styles. One of the reasons for rejecting the family is the goal of educating the communist man for which the family is not only superfluous but obstructive. The children's collectivistic education is to be carried out in scientifically qualified institutions graded for the various stages of development: baby homes, nurseries, day-care centres, full-day schools, industrial training boarding schools and communes. The experience in the Soviet Union and especially in the German Democratic Republic has shown that the early collectivisation of children achieves the opposite of what it intends; it nurtures egoistic and egocentric individuals recalcitrant to any kind of subordination.

2

Development of the Family

IN KENYA, a wedding can be celebrated in five different forms: as a civil marriage, as a (Christian) church wedding, as a Hindu wedding, as an Islamic wedding, or as a marriage in accordance with African tribal tradition. The first three kinds of marriages must be monogamous but for the last two, polygamy is permitted. Some years ago, a bill was submitted to parliament which would have made adultery punishable with six months' imprisonment. It would also have changed the custom which prevents a widow from inheriting anything at the death of her spouse and makes her the property of the deceased husband's family. The bill was defeated with a large majority. Traditionally, the role of the male in black Africa was waging war, hunting, clearing land and building huts. Women were responsible for gathering wood, fetching water, raising children and harvesting crops. If there was extra food to sell, the women kept the profits.

After independence, men began migrating to the cities to look for jobs, leaving their wives to run the farms. On the farms, male-controlled cash crops like coffee and cocoa were introduced, undercutting the economic power of the women's subsistence crops.

Multiple Marriages

With a few exceptions, women in African tribal societies inherit nothing from their fathers and can be divorced by their husbands without any settlement. They are expected to remain sexually faithful to their mates who are permitted to have other wives and as many girl-friends as they can support. If a woman earns money, it goes to the upkeep of the family but a man can spend his salary on whatever he chooses.

Based on the *Qur'an*, Islamic law allows four wives, and a husband can still say 'I divorce you' three times and send a wife packing to the home of her nearest relative. When Idi Amin was president of Uganda, he issued a decree giving men the option of marrying as many women as they wanted. When King Sobhuza II of Swaziland died in 1982 at the age of 83, he had more than 100 wives. In Indonesia, a Muslim can have four wives but recently, a 28-year-old man was found guilty of polygamy; he had married 128 women but had divorced only 93. A 53-year-old man convicted of fraud and bigamy in Phoenix, Arizona, in

February 1983, had married 105 women in the course of 33 years in 18 American states and nine foreign countries.

In May 1982, the Tibet Autonomous Region People's Congress adopted a regulation which banned future multiple marriages but the law was not retroactive so that Tibetans with more than one spouse were able to keep them. A Bangkok meatball vendor, availing himself of the Thai custom of 'minor wives,' has seven spouses living together with him under the same roof. But to ensure peace, the seven women sleep in different rooms and the husband spends one night a week with each one. Altogether, the family comprises 22 children.

In view of the kaleidoscopic succession of marriage, divorce and remarriage in the entertainment industry, the term 'successive polygamy' gained currency and some of the communes which flourished in the sixties practised 'group marriage.'

Evolution of Marriage

It is clear that monogamy is not the only form of marriage but it can further be asked whether it was an original form or only appeared as the product of a prolonged development. In a more basic formulation, it can be asked whether there always has been some kind of marriage — namely, a regulated form of sex relations, or whether marriage has been the product of cultural progress. This problem actually involves several distinct aspects. First, there is a question of fact, that is, the social conditions or arrangements that exist now or have existed in the past. Secondly, there is the question of origin, that is, how and when these conditions originated and which factors were involved in their formation. Social organisation, however, is not a natural phenomenon which can be observed and described as it exists. The description and analysis of social conditions can be influenced by the ideas the researcher has formed on the nature of these conditions and their causes so that the same social facts may appear in a different light and be interpreted in different ways.

Sir Henry Maine believed that polygeny was the original form of marriage and that it was followed by the patriarchal system from which monogamy evolved. The question of the origin of marriage was first treated systematically by Johann Jakob Bachofen, a Swiss jurist who specialised in the history of law. In 1861, Bachofen published the work *Das Mutterrecht* (it was in the same year that Sir Henry Maine's work *Ancient Law* appeared) which bore the subtitle *Eine Untersuchung über die Gynäkokratie der alten Welt nach ihrer religiösen und rechtlichen Natur* (An Inquiry into the Gynecocracy of Antiquity in its Religious and Legal Nature).

According to Bachofen, the regulation of sexual relations developed in three steps. Originally, promiscuity prevailed — a condition which Bachofen termed hetaerism but which has often been described as sexual communism. There was no regulation of sex relations in general and sexual intercourse in particular and therefore nothing that could be called marriage. Regulation of sexual relations started with the development of agriculture which was invented and carried on by woman. With agriculture, the position of the woman became stable. Woman, Bachofen contended, is by nature nobler and of greater sensibility than man, and influenced by religious inspiration, she forced a regulation of sexual relations. Since the children whose father was uncertain remained with the mother, she became the head of a family which led to matrilineal descent and metronymy; the relation to the mother determined descent, name, property rights and inheritance. Bachofen further contended that hetaerism was replaced by amazonism so that woman became not only the head of the family but also of the political group leading to the matriarchate, the rule of the mothers or all adult women. Some authors who upheld matriarchy as a form of social organisation in which the mother is the head of the family, descent is reckoned matrilineally and the children belong to the mother's clan do not accept Bachofen's theory of the matriarchate.

Matriarchy, a system in which females hold major authority, is clearly distinct from a matrilineal kinship system which simply involves tracing descent through the female line. The latter was and is frequent in primitive societies (probably because, as the Romans said, *mater semper certa est,* it is always certain who the mother is), matriarchy is not. In a society in which descent is reckoned in the female line, women do not necessarily wield greater power. Power can, for instance, be vested in the mother's brother who is the nearest male relative. Although there is a strong link between agriculture and mother goddesses, the latter are not necessarily related to matriarchy. A society can be both patriarchal and matrilineal at the same time. In 1970, an Israeli court upheld an ancient Hebrew law and denied Israeli nationality to children whose father was an Israeli citizen but whose mother was not Jewish.

Bachofen's third stage was patriarchy in which the man takes over as head of the family. Marriage, however, is not necessarily monogamous. Bachofen ascribed the rise of patriarchy also to religion. The cult of Dionysius which revered only fatherhood as divine — the mother was merely a nursemaid — gave the father the first place in the family and state. Children were named after the father and all relations linked to inheritance were determined exclusively patrilineally. The motherless virgin Pallas Athene (according to Greek mythology, Athene emerged armed with spear and shield from the head of Zeus — Pallas: the strong, noble young girl equal to the boy) became the symbol of the rejection of motherhood and gynecocracy. But the final victory of patriarchism was accomplished by Roman Law.

As mentioned above, society implies not only a plurality of

members but also some kind of organisation based on the relations between its members. The relations on which the family rests are the relations between husband and wife, and those between parents and children. While the relation of the father to the child is rather tenuous and sometimes even doubtful, that of the mother is not only biologically but also psychologically strong and pervasive. Nevertheless, birth and nursing do not constitute the only contents of the family and although they seem to make the mother its pivotal member, the functions of the family include the rearing of the children until they can take care of themselves as well as the daily life of the household. Seen in this broader perspective, the role of husband and father appears more substantial so that the formation and functioning of the family can hardly be considered a monopoly of the mother.

It is quite impossible to treat the relations between spouses and the relations between parents and children as two different systems. In the methodology of modern law, the law of marriage and the law of the relations between parents and children constitute two different parts of the family law. But there has always been an organic connection between these parts of the law, and it is impossible to sever problems such as the validity of marriage, legitimacy and inheritance. These relations, therefore, are also intertwined in the sociology of marriage and the family.

The Large Family

Due to its functions as a community of life and a community of generations, the family as household has assumed a variety of forms. In many cultures, the large family has played an important role. In the large family based on kinship, several generations of blood relatives with their wives or husbands live together in the same house or the same neighbourhood. In the large family based on economic cooperation, the household may include more persons not related by blood than the family of blood relatives.

The large family corresponds to a culture in which agriculture is dominant and the family constitutes a more or less autarchic unit of production and consumption. In such societies, marriage is usually based on an agreement between two families which may formally require the assent of bridegroom and bride but on which they have little actual influence. The large family could maintain its position also in societies in which handicrafts prevailed. In the West, the industrialisation together with the political transformation of Europe resulted in the disappearance of the large family.

Theories on the Origin of the Family

A few years after Bachofen, in 1865, John Ferguson McLennan proposed a different sequence of development. He too regarded indiscriminate promiscuity as the original condition of sexual relations. But the insufficient number of women, the result of female infanticide, led to polyandry and a strictly enforced exogamy (with which McLennan dealt extensively in his work *An Inquiry into the Origin of the Form of Capture in Marriage Ceremonies*). At the last stage, the monogamous marriage appeared which was linked to patriarchy.

The development sequence was expanded by Lewis Henry Morgan, an American ethnologist who started from his investigation of the kinship system of the Iroquois. (Morgan's main works are: *League of the Iroquois*, 1851; *Systems of Consanguinity and Affinity of the Human Family*, 1869; *Ancient Society*, 1877). Morgan assumed that unilineal kinship systems exist among all peoples and that all peoples went through the same phases in the development of marriage. Promiscuity represents the original condition of sex relations. Hetaerism which flourished in Greece and Rome at the height of their cultural evolution was not the result of moral depravation but a relic of their barbaric past. The development of the family is determined by the progressive limitation of the members of the opposite sex with whom sexual relations are considered legitimate. The first regulation prohibits sexual relations between parents and children. But blood ties, not marriage, form the basis of cohabitation which leads to the formation of the endogamous family within small groups (that is, sexual relations also occur between brothers and sisters). At the third stage, sexual intercourse between brothers and sisters is prohibited and the so-called *punalua* family (also referred to as group marriage) became the prevailing form of cohabitation.

Punalua is a Polynesian term which signifies tribal moities. According to Morgan, all men of one half of the tribe had free access to all women of the other half, an arrangement which precludes intercourse between brothers and sisters. In his *Bellum Gallicum*, Cesar relates that among the Britons, a group of brothers was married with a group of sisters (that is, every one of the brothers could have sex with every one of the sisters). Morgan regarded monandry (in which a woman has only one husband at a time, also called temporary pair marriage or matriarchal syndyasmic family) as the beginning of individual marriage. This form, however, did not imply an exclusive relationship so that the father remained uncertain. At the following stage, patriarchy appeared which was characterised by the polygamous family. Monogamy developed as the last form of marriage. Morgan attracted the attention of Marx and Engels because he combined the evolution of the forms of marriage with the evolution of the forms of property.

The evolutionary hypothesis of an ascent from promiscuity to monogamy was widely supported in the nineteenth century but also met strong criticism, particularly from ethnologists and anthropologists such as Edward Alexander Westermarck, a Finnish anthropologist (*Origin of Human Marriage*, 1889; *History of Human Marriage*, 1908) who, however, relied much on observations of the behaviour of anthropoids. He remarked that, to a certain extent, civilisation favours polygamy but that further progress restored monogamy. E. Grosse reasoned that in view of the enormously difficult living conditions of primitive man, the monogamous marriage provided the only sensible arrangement. It afforded the best protection for the pregnant and nursing wife and the mother rearing her children and managing her household. A man could more effectively care for one wife and his own children than for several wives and a great number of children. Naturally, such considerations do not decide what forms of marriage actually existed.

The representatives of the *Kulturkreistheorie* (theory of cultural cycles) carried out much research on this problem. This theory which, in contrast to the assumption of a rectilinear development from the simple to the complex maintained cultural diffusionism, was first proposed by Leo Frobenius. After working in museums and building on the observations of Ratzel, Ankermann and Graebner on the similarity of cultural complexes in widely dispersed societies, Frobenius studied the African cultures and expanded the theory into the doctrine of cultural morphology. Much research was done by the ethnologists of the Society of the Divine Word of whom Fr Wilhelm Schmidt in his work on the pygmies (*Die Stellung der Pygmäenvölker in der Entwicklungsgeschichte des Menschen*, 1912) drew attention to societies which remain nearest to man's most primitive conditions.

Together with Fr Wilhelm Koppers, Fr Schmidt set forth the theory that out of primitive culture, three primary cultures arose, characterised by the regulation of marriage and the family: the exogamous patriarchal family, the exogamous matriarchal family, and the patriarchal large family. They contended that monogamy was the oldest and most widely practised form of marriage and that there was no evidence that monogamy generally developed from other forms of marriage. They further pointed out that promiscuity appears only as a secondary phenomenon and usually as a product of decadence of regulated forms of sexual relations. Promiscuity has never been the main form of sexual behaviour in any people which can be historically investigated. Group marriage is not found anywhere in historical times. What has been adduced out of the past as proof of group marriage has a different meaning. The evolutionary scheme which assumes that the simpler is also the earlier and more primitive is an unproven hypothesis and, in many cases, has turned out to be wrong.

Wilhelm Wundt, well-known for his work on folk psychology,

maintained that it was not culture which produced monogamy but that mankind started its cultural development equipped with monogamy as a stable institution. In the most primitive cultures, the monogamous family appears as a primary institution antedating tribe and state.

More precise data for the evaluation of earlier theories can be found in the studies of anthropologists and ethnologists on the social organisations of primitive peoples. Some of the classical works in this field are: Bronislaw K. Malinowski, *The Sexual Life of Savages in Northwestern Melanesia; The Family Among the Australian Aborigines;* Robert H. Lowrie, *Primitive Society;* A.R. Radcliffe-Brown, *The Andaman Islanders;* Margaret Mead, *Coming of Age in Samoa; Growing Up in New Guinea; Sex and Temperament in Three Primitive Societies* (these three works have been brought out in one volume with the title *From the South Seas*). Miss Mead's idyllic description of Samoan sex life and particularly her representation of passage through adolescence without conflicts and crises has been attacked by other anthropologists who think that her preoccupation to prove cultural determinism and the theories of her teacher Franz Boas biased her studies.

These investigations show that the relations existing in a biological family (man-wife, father-son, father-daughter, mother-son, mother-daughter, and so on) are of different importance in different cultures but that the relations between parents and children are recognised in some form in all cultures. However, as Margaret Mead said, there is no institution which can be called 'the' primitive family. It may well be that in some societies and at some stage of development, the family remained merged with the horde or clan but there is no indication that the family arose as a form of social organisation from a condition in which marriage did not exist. There have also been large variations in the functions of the family.

Sociobiology

Professor Edward Wilson, the founder of sociobiology, maintains that there must be some link between man's genetic inheritance and his culture. Sociobiologists equated instinct with culture, but in a later work, Professor Wilson admitted a distinction. In instinct, the genetic rules are very rigid, allowing little or no choice of alternative behaviour. In culture, the rules of behaviour are more flexible, but genetic rules still exist and bias the choice of behaviour. Although there is room for some flexibility, there must be an innate (genetically determined) tendency to filter out certain choices of behaviour. The incest taboo is one of these choices, and the choice of monogamy or polygamy in a given society is also the result of a genetically transmitted bias.

Social anthropologists think that they can dispense with the genes and that the rules a culture makes about marriage are inspired by the advantages to be gained from the social connections created by marriage. Almost all societies encourage marriage outside one's own family, outside one's circle of close relatives and possibly outside one's own village. Marriage widens the group of people from whom cooperation can be expected in securing food and in protecting life and property against enemies.

The trouble with sociobiologists (and some other scientists) is that they have a very biased notion of the human mind. The human mind has its own structure, and although its functions are conditioned by the brain, they cannot be reduced to brain functions.

Cultural Development

Our knowledge not only of primitive cultures but also of the earlier so-called civilised peoples is very deficient. The tacit premise of many authors that evolution is always an upward development has often led to erroneous conclusions. In many parts of Europe, for example, the status of women was higher during the Middle Ages than at the beginning of modern times. In many medieval German towns, the wife was legally equal to her husband. A citizen was not allowed to alienate common possessions — above all, real property — without the consent of his wife. In many local documents, husband and wife are mentioned separately by name as buyers or sellers. Almost all guilds admitted women as members, even the guild of the armourers. The guild of embroiderers was almost entirely in the hands of women. In the documents establishing charitable foundations, husband and wife are very often named together as founders, and on the paintings of reredoses or other pictures, a couple often appears kneeling at the feet of the saint represented in the picture. This is the case not only if the donors were nobles but also if they were burghers. Very seldom, the entire family was represented. The loss of rights of women in Europe has often been the result of the political trend to absolutism and the supersedure of the old law by Roman law initiated by the so-called Reception.

Furthermore, factors that are of minor significance today exercised a strong influence on the family in former times. Among such factors were the high mortality rates of infants and of mothers in or after childbirth, the low life expectancy, and the frequent decimation of populations by epidemics, wars and hunger. Families with children from different mothers (remarriage after the death of the wife) or only one — widowed — parent were relatively numerous. Large families in the sense of members belonging to more than two generations living under the same roof were rare and by no means common. The slow increase in the world population until the beginning of the nineteenth century indicates that offspring could not have been very numerous. (World population: 1650: 545 million; 1750: 730 million; 1850: 1,075 million; 1950: 2,410 million; 1980: 4,415 million. Rate of increase: 1650–1750: 44 per cent; 1750–1850: 47 per cent; 1850–1950: 124 per cent; 1950–1980: 311 per cent.)

The forms of marriage and the family have always developed in the context of the whole culture of a society. Culture comprises the entire man-made environment in which man lives and acts, not only material factors such as nature transformed by man but also moral and religious ideas and attitudes, the knowledge of and views on man, world, and the universe, traditions and aspirations, social institutions, art, literature, science, technology and the economy. It is certainly true that the economic organisation has deeply influenced man's lifestyle at all ages. A combination of hunting (by man) and food gathering (by woman) may have been the most primitive way in which man supported his life. When woman began to cultivate plants, mankind gained not only economic stability thanks to a less precarious method of food supply but also greater local and social stability of which woman may have been the chief beneficiary. An intermediate form between the roving hunter and the sedentary planter was the nomad who raised his cattle and moved, often with the seasons, from pasturage to pasturage.

The law formulated by Émile Durkheim that the family undergoes a continuous contraction in the course of social evolution may indicate the general trend in a given society but the reduction to the nuclear family is by no means universal. The large families as they are described in Homer's *Ilias* or in the Old Testament's narratives of the patriarchs or in the *Book of Kings* were organisations of the public order which provided a rather permanent framework for marriages between individuals and absorbed their children.

It would be misleading to consider today's 'nuclear' family as the prototype and regular form of the family. This is certainly not the case although the nuclear family is not a modern development. In the old Chinese kingdom of Ch'in, the government levied a double tax on every male citizen who was not the head of a household. This led to the breakup of the extended family system. Younger sons were forced to move out and to establish their own households so that the nuclear family became the prevalent form in Ch'in. Han scholars, therefore, attacked the Ch'in system as failing to preserve the principle of filial piety. Ch'in, by the way, established the first unified Chinese empire and the first Ch'in emperor, Shih Huang Ti (221–210 BC) built the Great Wall.

Polygamy

Polygamy is an old and widespread form of marriage. Sociologists distinguish between polyandry (one wife having several husbands) and polygeny (one husband having several wives). Polyandry is very infrequent. It has been found in Polynesia, among Eskimos and Chukchi (in northern Siberia on the coast of the Arctic Ocean), and among the Todas in southern India where the system was said to have been related to the small number of women, the result of female infanticide. A special form of polyandry called fraternal polyandry existed among the Tibetans in the Himalayas where all the woman's husbands had to be brothers.

Polygamy used to be the most common permissible system of mating in many primitive tribes but even in polygamous cultures, many marriages actually were monogamous because of the pressure of the sex ratio and economic factors. In a special form of polygamy called monogeny, only one wife is the wife of status while the other wives are concubines so that this form represents institutionalised concubinage. Polygeny is still common among Muslims and in many parts of Africa. In Benin, Gabon and Equatorial Guinea, for example, polygamy is widespread.

Where childlessness is considered an evil or a disgrace, a barren wife gives the husband the right to take another wife. In the Old Testament's account of the patriarchs, Abraham was asked by his wife, Sarah, who was childless, to sleep with her slave so that she could have children through her. Jacob had children from the two sisters he married as well as from their slaves.

The at least implicit recognition of polygamy (and divorce) in the Old Testament is obviously incompatible with the position that monogamy (and the indissolubility of marriage) is a precept of natural law. St Thomas Aquinas tried to solve the problem by distinguishing between the primary and secondary precepts of the natural law. He asserted that God could give a dispensation from the unity of marriage because it belongs to the secondary precepts (S. theol., Suppl. q. 67, a. 2).

In explaining his solution, St Thomas writes: 'Every action which contradicts the end which nature has in view is called contrary to the natural law. But such an action may be contrary to a primary or a secondary end . . . according as it entirely prevents the attainment of the end or only makes its attainment more difficult or less perfect. Thus, if an act is so contrary to the end intended by nature as to render a primary purpose directly unattainable, that act is forbidden by a primary precept of the natural law; if it prevents in any way the attainment of a secondary end, or makes a primary end more difficult or less perfect in its realisation, it is forbidden, not in virtue of the primary precepts of the natural law, but in virtue of the secondary precepts which are derived from the primary; and in this sense, it is contrary to the natural law. Now marriage has for its principal end the procreation and education of children . . . and for its secondary end, community of life . . . Plurality of wives does not entirely suppress nor even prevent the attainment of the primary end, since one husband can be father by several wives and can educate the children they may bear him. But as regards the secondary end, polygamy, if it does not entirely suppress it, at least places a great obstacle to its realisation, for peace will not easily reign in a family where several wives claim the same husband. . . . Thus it is clear that polygamy is in one way contrary to the natural law, while in another way it is not' (S. theol., Suppl., q. 67, a. 15).

Polygamy was widely practised by the Jewish kings. David already had a number of wives before he became king (2Sam, 3,2-5; 1Chron 14,3) and committed adultery with Bathsheba (2Sam, 11,2-5). Solomon had a harem of 700 foreign princesses and 300 concubines (1Kings 11,1-3). Rehabeam, the son of Solomon, had eighteen wives and 'three score concubines' (2Chron 11,21), and Abia, his successor as king of Judah, married fourteen wives (2Chron 13,21).

The Qur'an limits the number of simultaneous wives to four and this permission is dependent on the condition that justice be done among co-wives. But the Qur'an also states: 'You will never be able to treat women with (equal) justice no matter how much you desire' (Sura 4, 128. On this sentence, modern Islamic theologians base their advocacy of monogamy). When the prophet Mohammad died, he had fourteen wives. Ibn Saud, the extraordinary chieftain who built the kingdom of Saudi Arabia — the only country in the world to be named after its ruling family — fathered at least 43 sons by more than twenty mothers, in addition to some twenty daughters.

The Qur'an enumerates five categories of women Mohammad was entitled to have in his harem: the wives to whom he had given a dowry, the slaves he had obtained as booty, the daughters of his uncles and aunts, both on his father's side and on his mother's side, who had emigrated with him, and every faithful woman who gave herself to the prophet provided he wanted her (Sura 33,49). The Qur'an allowed marriage with Christian or Jewish women but forbade concubinage (Sura 5,7). Intercourse with slaves is lawful even if they are married (Sura 4,28).

At the First International Conference of Muslim Women held in Manila in 1982, the trend of the papers was definitely conservative. Role orientation is the first premise of Islamic social law on which social equilibrium is predicated. Woman's role in society is essentially that of mother and wife. Man's task is to support, care for and defend woman. A Muslim wife is obedient to her husband, not because of any inferiority but because she accepts him as her guardian. Islam does not forbid women from seeking employment if it is necessary or if it is a means for them to express some talent or to serve society. The concept of coeducation is generally rejected. Since girls have spheres of concern different from boys, they must be provided with a different curriculum although this will deprive girls of educational opportunities.

African kings had an unlimited number of wives, and this custom is still preserved by some African rulers. Among the Australian aborigines, the older men appropriated so many of the women of the community that younger men could find no wives.

Mormons

In 1843, Joseph Smith, the founder of the Mormons (Church of Jesus Christ of Latter Day Saints) claimed to have received a revelation confirming the legality of plural marriage. Smith himself had 50 wives; when he was killed by an angry mob in 1844, he was succeeded by Brigham Young who at one time was married to 27 wives and had 17 when he died. The Mormons abandoned polygamy in 1890 as the price for the admission of Utah to the Union (1896) and today any Mormon who practises polygamy can be excommunicated. Despite the legal prohibition and the offical disapproval of the Mormon Church, polygamy is practised in Utah and the surrounding states. Utah authorities estimate the number of polygamists at 10,000 but their number may actually be twice as high. Many polygamists live in large, secretive and often prosperous communes in which all property is owned by the group. Others maintain separate households for the various wives and children. They legally marry only one wife and marry other wives with private rites in their church.

Mormons maintain that polygamy is a matter of religion rather than sexuality. They believe that plural marriage continues in the celestial kingdom — the highest of three Mormon heavens. According to the Mormons' law of chastity, sex is purely for procreation and not for lust. A man may not approach any of his wives except on special command of the Lord or on invitation from the wife when she is fertile.

Among the Yoruba and in Dahomey in West Africa, each family used to have a compound, a group of houses or huts surrounded by a wall or hedge. Each wife had a separate dwelling while the husband had a house of his own where each wife lived with him in turn. The old custom of the Bedouin required that each wife had her own tent or hut — a custom already attested in the Old Testament (v.g., Gen 31, 33).

Harem

The custom of veiling women originally arose as a sign of aristocracy but later served the purpose of segregating women from men. The Arabic word harîm means forbidden and harem refers to the women's quarters as well as the women in an oriental household — who need not be wives or concubines. In her book, 'Harem,' Princess Vittoria Alliata relates that the occupants of Sheik Shakhba's harem in Abu Dhabi were his wife Miriam, his two daughters Gut and Abla, his daughter-in-law Begha, his grand-daughter Fakhra, two Negro slaves and three Pakistani maids. The harem is not an Islamic invention but was taken over by the Muslims after the Turks had conquered Byzantium. Among the Bedouin of the desert, women used to enjoy more freedom and influence than they now have among the affluence of the oil wealth. In his commentary on Plato's *Republic,* the Spanish-born Arabic philosopher Averroës (Ibn Rush, 1126-1198) deplored the position of women in Islam compared with their civic equality in Plato's *Republic.* That women are used only for childbearing and rearing of offspring is detrimental to the economy and responsible for the poverty of the state.

Japanese Family System

It should be noted that monogamy does not exclude pre-marital or extra-marital sex. In many cases, monogamy means that only one wife is the wife of status but that there are *de facto* or *de iure* also minor wives or concubines. In Japan, the family system was closely linked with concubinage; in fact, concubinage and adoption were the two instrumentalities which kept the Japanese family system working. In the Kamakura period (1192-1333), households of the military class constituted closely knit kinship groups controlled by the head of the main family. In the following centuries, feudal relationships gained greater importance but the family organisation characterised by the common surname (only the warrior class had family names) derived from the ancestor and the succession of the eldest son remained strong.

During the Tokugawa shogunate (1603-1868), the feudal order overshadowed kinship relations. Marriages were arranged between families, not between individual persons, and within the limits defined by status. Members of the warrior class were not allowed to marry members of other classes — farmers, artisans or merchants — although in the later years of the Tokugawa era, the impoverished nobility often adopted sons of wealthy merchants as husbands for their daughters. Marriages between residents of different domains were also prohibited, a regulation intended to prevent the formation of power cliques through marriages.

Marriage negotiations had to be conducted through officials whose own rank was commensurate with that of the families involved. For the marriages of *daimyô (feudal lords)* or *hatamoto* (direct lieges of the Tokugawa) with a yearly income of over 10,000 *koku* (one *koku* = 180.5 litres. The revenues of *daimyô* and the salaries of officials were estimated in *koku* of rice; 10,000 *koku* was the lowest income required for the rank of *daimyô*) needed the personal approval of the shogun. Retainers of a *daimyô* of middle rank or above had to obtain the approval of their lord, common warriors (*shibun,* samurai) needed approval by the elders in the local government and other warriors were supervised by inspectors.

The regulation that marriages were only allowed between members of the same class applied even to the outcasts: *eta* and *himin* were prohibited from marrying commoners. (Originally, the *eta* were people engaged in occupations considered unclean by Shinto standards, such as work involving blood or cadavers; in the Tokugawa era, they disposed of cadavers of animals, were tanners, served as executioners or did other dirty work. The *hinin,* 'non-man,' comprised vagabonds, beggars and criminals.)

A special ceremony introduced young men into adulthood at the age of fifteen which qualified them for marriage, but most young men and women were married at about seventeen or eighteen.

The system called *sankin-kôtai* under which the *daimyô* were required to spend every other year in Edo (today's Tokyo) forced them to maintain two residences, one in Edo and the other in their domain. Legal wives and heirs had to be left permanently in Edo. To compensate for the restrictions, *daimyô* and other upper-class warriors were allowed to keep mistresses. In prescriptions written by the founder of the Tokugawa shogunate, Tokugawa Ieyasu, shortly before his death, he designated the number of concubines appropriate to each grade of the *daimyô* and their retainers. (The *sankin-kôtai* system was introduced by the third shogun, Tokugawa Iyemitsu.) The emperor and the court nobility were outside the feudal system but concubinage was a common feature of the social environment. It was only Emperor Hirohito who ended the long tradition of ladies-in-waiting serving as imperial concubines and had 49 such ladies dismissed.

The illegitimate son born of a concubine took precedence over a legitimate daughter in the order of succession as head of the house. Until the enforcement of books Four and Five of the Civil Code (Relations and Inheritance) in 1898, a man could officially recognise a concubine and the children born to him by the concubine (such children were called *shoshi* and were distinguished from legitimate children born in wedlock called *chakushi* and unrecognised illegitimate children called *shiseiji*). Naturally, it hardly contributed to domestic harmony when these children came to live in the father's household. Until the adoption of the new Family Law in 1947, the so-called family system was the legal form of the Japanese family although actually, the small family was the rule, particularly in the cities. In this system, the 'house' (*ie*) was a group comprising a number of spouses or parents and their children with other near relatives under the authority of the head of the house (*kachô*). The first version of the Meiji Civil Code compiled under the direction of Gustave Emile Boissonade and patterned after French law had greatly strengthened the position of the wife and limited the authority of the head of the house. He was not permitted to punish adult children who married without his consent nor punish them for accepting adoption by another family without his consent. Although enacted in 1890, this law was never enforced due to strong reactionary pressure and a revision of books Four and Five of the Code adopted in 1898 reintroduced many of the feudal regulations.

The law separated family headship and parental authority but the head of the house had the right to determine the residence of all family members and his consent was required for marriage and adoption. Anyone marrying without his consent could be expelled from the house. Succession to the headship of the house was limited to males and as a rule to the legitimate eldest son who was not permitted to relinquish the house.

Neither a man under 30 years of age nor a woman under 25 could validly contract a legal marriage without parental consent. When the head of the family died, sons and grandsons took precedence over the wife. She could only obtain ownership of the family property if there were no rightful male heirs. Although the husband did not acquire title to the wife's property, he had the right to its possession and management and perceived rents and profits. On the other hand, he had to bear all family expenses. In many cases, the wife could not perform legal transactions without the prior consent of the husband. The Japanese Penal Code adopted in 1907 retained the discriminatory treatment of men and women. Adultery committed by or with a married woman was criminally punishable but extramarital intercourse by a married man with an unmarried woman was no crime.

The Japanese family system had two characteristics. The first was the authority of the head of the house which extended to all members of the house, including the married couples. A wife married to a man under the authority of the head of the house was subject to her husband and to the head of the house, and their children were subject not only to their own parents but also to the head of the house. The second characteristic was ancestor worship. The ancestors of the family were enshrined in the household. Their cult provided a kind of spiritual foundation and gave the system an ethical and quasi-religious significance. The heir to the headship of the house had to venerate the ancestors, guard the family's genealogical register and take care of the ancestral tablets and the family grave. A relic of the veneration of the ancestors remains in the present Family Law in which Article 897 regulates ownership of the ancestor tables, cult objects and graves. The ancestor cult demanded reverence for the head of the house and submission to the house order. Some houses had their own house law or regulations which contained moral instructions and rules for the organisation of the house and the management of the estate. The house was often divided into the main line (main house, *honke*) and branch lines (cadet families, *bunke*). In the military class, the branch families received their land either from a feudal lord or from the main house, but even in the latter case, they did not owe any special allegiance to the main house.

The pre-war mythology regarded all houses as ultimately derived from the Imperial house which was venerated as the great ancestral house. Loyalty to the emperor and filial piety were two aspects of the same moral principle (*chûkô ichinyô*). This doctrine provided the basis of pre-war nationalism as expounded in the statements of public policy such as the famous *Kokutai no Hongi* (Essence of the National Structure) and *Senji Katei Kyôiku Shidô Yôkô* (Summary of Guidelines for Wartime Family Education) of the Ministry of Education.

Under the old law, marriage implied that one of the partners (usually the wife) would leave the house and would be incorporated into the house of the other partner (this, of course, did not apply to the very rare cases in which two members of the same house married). Marriage required the consent of the heads of the two houses. The presumptive legal heir of a house could not enter into a marriage by which he would become the member of another house. This restriction led to arrangements such as marriage to an heiress (female head of a family) and becoming a member of her family (*nyûfu konin*) and adoption of the husband marrying an heiress (*muko yôshi*). If one of the spouses died, the other remained subject to the authority of the head of the house. If the wife returned to her original house, her children remained in the house into which she had married and she lost all parental rights.

In ancient Japan, a considerable time elapsed from the start of sexual relations between a man and a woman until their cohabitation and marriage. It was a general custom, particularly in rural communities, that a young man would secretly go to the house of a girl at night, but the formal marriage would only be celebrated after the parents gave their consent. A form of marriage called *ashi-ire kon* (stepping-in marriage) began with the young man seeing the girl, and when marriage had been agreed upon, the bride would first stay one night at the house of the groom and gradually lengthen the duration of her stay.

Depending on the situation, the groom would enter the family of the bride or the bride that of the groom. The form of marrige in which the bride went to live in the house of the groom started with the warrior class and became the rule also among the common people in the Edo period. Even if the groom went to live in the house of the bride, a formal marriage was celebrated only after six months or a year had elapsed and no hitch had developed. In many cases, when the groom entered the family of the bride, he would become the head of the family at the death of the bride's father even if the family had a son.

Child Marriages

The Hindu custom of child marriage is said to have originated from the Hindu belief that a woman's menstruation is sinful if she is not married. Usually, the children return to the parental home until they are ready to have their own household. This was also the custom among some Australian tribes and the Toda. Child marriages in India were already banned under British rule in 1930 and the present Child Marriage Restraint Act forbids marriages under the age of 18. But the practice continues, particularly in the form of mass weddings. In the western desert state of Rajasthan, mass weddings sometimes involving as many as 10,000 couples take place each year on an auspicious day known as *Akha Teej*. On this day, Hindus are permitted to perform the marriage rites without the assistance of a holy man who is paid for the function, so poor peasants are able to save money. Unfortunately, children who are not yet physically ready for marriage and motherhood are often forced to submit to intercourse. Death or permanent injuries either from copulation or from pregnancy are the results.

A phenomenon that greatly influenced the development of the family was the extenuation of the family's functions. Until the age of industrialisation, the family actually performed the functions proper to it. In the old days, economic existence, social position, protection, education and religion were linked to the family which formed an important part of the social order. Through the integration of the family with the political, military, religious and economic systems, the family was intimately connected with the social environment and constituted an integral part of the social order. This institutional homogeneity disintegrated chiefly due to the changes in the structure of political and economic institutions. Functions traditionally fulfilled by the family were taken over by the other organisations so that the importance of the family declined.

Family and Economic System

The most notable influences on the forms of marriage in modern times have come from the changes in the economic system. In the course of the industrialisation and particularly the urbanisation connected with it, the family was stripped of more and more of its functions and the small family became its prevalent form. The changes are distinctly reflected in the dwelling. In earlier times, the noble family possessed the ancestral castle or manor. The peasant family owned its farm which had been in the possession of the family for generations. In the towns, where the patrician families owned stately residences, the ordinary burgher lived in the parental home. Today, the dwelling has become a commodity procured on the housing market by either purchase or rent. The home

SM-D

is often no more than a lodging house to which the members of the family, dispersed during the day, repair for the night or what is left of it. Work, recreation, amusement and a large part of the meals are unrelated to the home and often unrelated to the family. For a considerable number of employees, their occupation involves the necessity of moving, and workers who do not want to move often suffer considerable economic disadvantages.

As a result of urbanisation, the supply of goods and services to consumers is often transformed into a public concern. In a capitalistic economy, the supply of food and clothing remains in the hands of private enterprise, at least in times of peace, whereas housing is often publicly regulated. In urban areas, the supply of water, electricity and heat, rubbish collection, street cleaning and transportation are often public services. Depending on the country, the state has a more or less comprehensive monopoly for schools and hospitals, and in the most progressive welfare states, the solicitude for the citizens extends 'from the cradle to the grave.' The physical costs of supplying the urban population rise much more rapidly than the increase in the number of people, and the fundamental tendency indicates a constantly growing per capita consumption. The school can give instruction much more effectively than the family but does not provide the same moral motivation proper to the old family education. The greater material affluence has eroded the spiritual foundation of society, and the social mobility causes stress, scepticism and cynicism.

The defenders of the 'new family' assert that the specialised agencies of the welfare state can provide the necessary services better than the 'old' family. The family's only function should be to give emotional support to the individual but leave education to the school, religious instruction to the churches, protection to the state and the supply of daily necessities to the economy or the state.

Some sociologists are of the opinion that the family as a closed group is not suited for the education of the children. The family should be expanded into the local community and education entrusted to nursery schools and similar agencies. There are cases in which the family is unable or unwilling to take care of its children and society must take over — whether in public institutions or by engaging foster parents is a different question — but such cases are not the norm. They are exceptions and should be treated as exceptions. This is only one of the many problems resulting from the tendency to depend on the welfare state with the shift of responsibility for daily life from the individual and the family to the state. The inordinate increase in the tasks entrusted to society is already causing the collapse of the welfare system.

The capitalistic system was based on the division of capital, management and labour, and its production system designed to meet the needs of a mass market through applied technology (machinery), was fundamentally different from the family economy producing for the actual needs of a fixed group of consumers. This difference finds its most striking expression in the monetisation of the economy and the enormous importance of credit, interest, return, cost effectiveness and investment.

Legal Status of Family

In the old society, the family was the subject of rights and duties, but in modern law, the family has no legal personality. This change is particularly noteworthy in the law of inheritance. Modern law does not recognise family property and family ownership. Roman law and the old German law made family property possible by the device of *fidei commissum*, a form of trust by which property became inalienable and was transmitted in its entirety by inheritance. The family principle found its strongest affirmation in the states organised on the basis of estates (*Ständestaat*) in which family law and the law of inheritance formed part of public law. (It was the *Ständestaat* of the *ancien régime* which was overthrown by the French revolution, and the system is incompatible with freedom and equality. It is mentioned as an illustration of the historical functions of the family.) Land was the essential foundation and pre-requisite of power and both were acquired by a status which was practically based on family law.

In connection with the law of inheritance, the family actually regulated the order of succession. The son of a territorial lord inherited from his father power and property which consisted largely of real estate and comprised the land and the people on it. The noble landlord possessed power and influence because of his status, and even if he lost his material possessions, he retained his status. When the German Civil Code (*Bürgerliches Gesetzbuch,* of 1 January, 1900) was introduced, the Enforcement Law contained provisions recognising the family rights of the former estates of the old German Empire and the family trusts (Art. 58 and 59). Since these provisions favoured only the interests of the large landowners, they were abolished by order of the occupation after World War II. The property and inheritance law introduced by the Civil Code was strictly individualistic.

In today's society, the state constitutes the only independent subject of the public order; all other subjects can act solely under its control and with its permission. The state rules and exercises immediate domination over all persons on its territory, and the family can interpose itself only in very few situations between the state and its members. Basically, the state wields power directly over the mass of atomised individuals who can oppose or influence the state only if they form (legal or illegal) pressure groups. Even the Church can defend her independence only precariously.

An important factor in the decline of the family functions is the possibility given by the present social and economic system to enjoy a relatively satisfactory existence without a family. The individual is no longer dependent on the family for food, clothing, medical care, entertainment and sexual satisfaction. The only function which is generally irreplaceable is the emotional security and protection given by the family. For children, too, the situation is not entirely hopeless without a family, at least in many advanced countries. Although the number of institutions for orphans, waifs or other children without a family is not always sufficient and the quality of the help may be unsatisfactory, help is usually available.

Very striking is the weakening of the role of the family in the field of religion. In families with a strong religious tradition, family prayer, prayer before and after meals, and common attendance of church services were unquestioned practices. In small communities, religious observance of Sunday remains a family activity but very often, the divergent interests of the family members make any common family exercise impossible.

On the whole, the changes brought about by the Second World War have made the family insecure. This insecurity extends to everyday life, the relations of the spouses, the relations between parents and children, the position of the family in society, its economic future and the values and principles on which the family is based. Particularly serious is the insecurity in morality which practically affects all aspects of marriage and the family and threatens not only life in the family but marriage itself.

3

The Rationale of Marriage

The Family in Ancient Greece

THE ACTUAL FORMS OF MARRIAGE and the family as well as the ideas on sex and sexual relations have shown great variations even in the same civilisation. The attitudes to marriage and the family were rather ambiguous in ancient Greece where the *polis*, the political community forming a city, had the highest value and the individual was of significance only as a member of this state and to the extent that his activities were devoted to the state. The state was the whole and its members were parts. This view was expounded in its most extreme form by Plato in his description of the ideal state. The well-being of the state is paramount; the well-being of the individual can be taken into consideration only if it is compatible with the public welfare. All private interests must be sacrificed to the interests of the state. Whatever does not serve the state is diseased and must be destroyed. In Plato's ideal state, the citizens enjoying full political rights have neither property nor family. Both would be obstacles to the unconditional devotion of rulers and warriors to the interests of the community. Women are common property; children are to be educated not in the family but by the state and for the state. Education comprises music, poetry and dance. Weak children as well as weak men are only ballast for the state and must be eliminated.

Plato's ideal state was a utopia but it reflected actual trends. Education, which was a privilege of the upper class, was influenced by the political and cultural attitudes of the *polis*. As a military state, Sparta educated its youth for war. Bodily strength and fitness were more important than spiritual culture and all refinement was rejected. Education was not the task of the family. At the age of seven, the children of the *spartiatai*, the full citizens, entered on the way of life called *agoge*. They lived in dormitories grouped by age, became adults at 20 and gained full citizenship with the right to vote in the city's assembly at 30. As the warrior caste, they observed a communal life-style, living in tents and eating in messhalls. They were forbidden to engage in other occupations; their subsistence was provided by the land allotted to them and cultivated by helots.

In Athens, education had a more artistic and intellectual orientation although sports also played an important role. Family education was at least tolerated.

Christian Ideal of Marriage

Initially, Christianity made no impact on the social structure of the Roman empire but Christian morality influenced not only individual conduct but also the way of thinking on social institutions. The Christian doctrine of redemption and salvation involved the entire man, body and soul, so that sexual behaviour necessarily implied conformity or discrepancy with religious values (see, for example, Rom 6-8). The emphasis on the spiritual implications of marriage in the context of a strict code of sexual behaviour added an entirely new dimension to marriage. The religious interpretation of marriage and the inspiration of family life was reinforced by the important role, the family ('house') played in the early propagation of Christianity. The moral duties of the spouses and the responsibilities of the parents remained paramount in the Christian conception of the family and, together with the spiritual foundation given to the requirements of unicity and indissolubility of marriage, resulted in a considerable strengthening of marriage as an institution in western culture.

Although compliance with the Christian ideal and the canonical rules was never complete in the Middle Ages, the prohibition of divorce and extra-marital sex safeguarded the personal integrity of the marriage partners. Supplementing the precepts and prohibitions showng what was right or wrong, good or evil was the motivation which could not ensure the observance of all norms but achieved a certain degree of moral conduct and kept the consciousness of moral obligaions alive.

Scholastic Doctrine on Marriage

The Scholastics generally recognised the sacramental character of marriage but had some difficulty in applying the sacramental theory to marriage. There was also some uncertainty whether the indissolubility of marriage was the result of its sacramental character or the consummation of marriage. The theoretical exposition of the Christian doctrine was greatly facilitated by the concinnity of the precepts of Christian morality with the essential meaning and tasks of marriage and the family, but the ecclesiastical practice created some difficult problems. While all marriages were considered indissoluble 'by divine law,' the Church claimed that a marriage could be dissolved on the strength of the 'Pauline privilege' (the consummated marriage of two unbaptised persons can be dissolved if one is converted to Christianity and the other will neither convert nor live in peace with the Christian; 1Cor 7, 12-17). A valid marriage which is not consummated is dissolved by the solemn religious profession of either party. (The Justianian Code and Greek Canon Law recognised the dissolution also of a consummated marriage by solemn religious profession.) In both cases (marriage of two unbaptised persons, non-consummated marriage of two baptised or a baptised and a non-baptised person), the marriage can also be dissolved by papal dispensation.

Another problem which greatly bothered Christian moralists was the question of servitude. According to Aristotle, slaves belong to the household, not as members but as 'animated, active and separate instruments existing as human beings belonging to somebody else.' He thought that some men were slaves by nature because their body was strong but their mental faculties were weak and good order required that those who were physically strong but weak in mind serve as slaves. Hence, the Scholastics defended slavery, and even in the twentieth century, some authors maintained that serfdom (serf in the sense of a person attached to the soil and transferred with the land from one owner to another) was not contrary to natural law. This position led to the custom of distinguishing in the family (domestic society) three elements, the conjugal, parental, and servant society, and some authors asserted that the servant society was, at least in some way, a natural society. This tripartite division of the domestic society has been retained in many treatises.

Luther's View on Marriage

Luther, rejecting the sacramental character of marriage, declared that marriage was an external, wordly matter and like clothes, food and house, was subject to secular power. On the other hand, however, the reformers opposed the Catholic doctrine of the pre-eminence of celibacy and therefore declared that marriage was the truly spiritual status, ordained and established by God. Marriage also involved matters of conscience and could not simply be left to be regulated by the state.

Secular Views on Marriage

As in other fields (such as the care of the sick and the poor), the state slowly took over the role of the Church with regard to marriage, family and education. In the beginning, secular law largely followed the provisions of Canon Law, but partly on ideological grounds, partly for practical reasons, secular legislation developed in very different directions. The first outright opposition to the Christian idea of marriage was the provision in the French constitution of 1791 which said: 'The law considers marriage merely as a civil contract.'

The changes in the social structure brougt about by industrialisation and urbanisation led to an increasingly stronger involvement of the state in matters affecting the family and education. But the intervention of the state was basically very different in character from the regulations of the Church. While the Church appealed to the conscience of the faithful in order to ensure compliance with her rules, the state menaces the transgressor of its laws with penalties. In the Church, the pastoral 'care of souls' handles the problems arising from moral precepts and Canon Law. In the state, there is a multiplicity of partly overlapping agencies and jurisdictions but the mental problems and conflicts disrupting the family find only attention if they cause illness or crime.

Kant on Marriage

While anthropologists and ethnologists have mainly been interested in the actual forms of marriage, philosophers and jurists have tried to elucidate its meaning. German legal thought has produced some interesting opinions on marriage and the family (see Diether Huhn, *Der Fall Familie: Recht und Unrecht einer bürgerlichen Einrichtung*). Kant defined marriage as a contract by which two persons of different sex acquire the mutual ownership of their sex organs, but marriage must be consummated for this ownership to become effective. This interpretation assimilates the marriage contract to the contract for the acquisition of the ownership of personal property which is effected by agreement and tradition (delivery). It is amazing how a philosopher like Kant who exalts the autonomy of the human person arrives at such a dehumanising view of marriage but it is the logical result of Kant's myopic approach to this question.

Kant, in his *Metaphysics of Ethics* (1797) starts out by stating that the sexual community is the reciprocal use that one human being makes of the sexual organs and potentialities of another human being. This use can be a natural use (by which a human being can be engendered), or an unnatural (between two persons of the same sex or with a beast). The natural use can be purely according to man's animal nature or according to law. The latter case is marriage, that is, the union of two persons of different sex for the lifelong ownership of their sexual properties. The purpose to beget children is a natural purpose which, however, is not necessary for the lawfulness of marriage, otherwise, marriage would end with the possibility of producing children. Even supposing the desire for the reciprocal use of their sexual properties, man and wife must enter into a contract necessary according to the laws of pure reason.

Explaining the nature of this contract, Kant says that the natural use which one person makes of the sexual organs of another is a use (the German word, *Genuß* means *'usufruct'* as well as 'enjoyment') to which one party surrenders itself to the other. In such an act, man makes himself a thing which is contrary to the right of a human being in his own personality. This can only be justified if the person reciprocally acquires the other person. In this way, the person reacquires himself and his personality. The acquisition of a member belonging to a person is equivalent to the acquisition of the entire person because a member forms a complete unity with the person. Consequently, the giving and receiving of one sex to the use of another is lawful only under this condition.

The equality of possession is only present in monogamy; from the inequality of possession, Kant deduces the illegality of polygamy, fornication, concubinage and morganatic marriages.

Sexuality is the object of the marriage contract, and by basing the satisfaction of the sexual desire of the partner on a contract, it becomes an act involving human freedom. Kant further explains that the acquisition of a wife (or a husband) is not accomplished by the conjugal act without a contract nor by a marital contract without the conjugal act but only by the implementation of the contract in the actual use of the sexual properties.

As a contract, marriage involves equal rights of both partners, and Kant explains the legality as well as the morality of sex on the basis of the contract. Sexuality is made subject to norms but to norms set freely by those subject to these norms. Marriage as such is not moral but the concrete marriage for which the two partners become the reciprocal subjects and objects of the use of sex in accordance with their free will is moral because it does not subject them to a 'heteronomous' norm.

Kant discusses marriage in a chapter entitled 'In a material way personal right,' and distinguishes three kinds of acquisitions: 'Man acquires a wife, the pair acquires children, and the family acquires servants. All this that is acquirable is at the same time inalienable and the right of the owner of these things is the most personal' (Ch. 23). In the Explanatory Remarks in an Appendix, Kant justifies the concept of 'in a material way personal right,' defining it as 'the right of a man to a person other than himself as his own' and explains that 'as his own' does not mean ownership but usufruct of this person — as in the enjoyment of some thing, as a means to an end without prejudice to its personality. This end or purpose must be morally necessary. Only by the marriage contract by which the partners mutually give themselves as persons into the ownership of each other is marital intercourse not 'cannibalistic' because in itself, the mutual use of the sex organs leads to their destruction, the woman by pregnancy and the possibility of a fatal birth, the man by the exhaustion from the repeated demands of the woman.

Kant does not consider marriage as an institution related to a certain social or political order, and marriage is also unrelated to the family. The family is an actual situation existing between minor children and their married or unmarried parents. Kant maintains that the rights and duties of parents derive from procreation which creates the duty of maintaining and supporting the procreated. Children as persons have an original right to support until they are capable of supporting themselves. For Kant, the family seems to be no entity of its own but only a label stuck to a bundle of personal relations, the marital rights and duties and the parental rights and duties of persons living in the same household. Children who remain with their parents after reaching majority are put into the same category as servants belonging to the household on the basis of a contract. Their relation with their parents is no longer that of parent and child but that between the head of the household and a household member. Kant's discussion seems to indicate that he did not consider the family as a basic social unit fulfilling a function essential to the well-being of society but merely as a social fact.

J. G. Fichte on Marriage

Johann Gottlieb Fichte, another representative of German idealism, started from the same basic fact as Kant concerning human sexuality, but he arrived at a different result. Fichte defined marriage as the complete union of two persons of both sexes based on the sex instinct which is its own purpose. He found a difference between male and female sexuality which he deduced by confusing sexuality with the sex act. In the sex act, Fichte said, man is the moving and woman the passive principle. Because he is active, man can satisfy his sexual instinct without losing his dignity, but if woman yields to the sexual instinct, she must suffer for the sake of suffering which is contrary to reason. Woman, therefore, cannot have sexual satisfaction as an objective without sinking below her nature. Woman's sexuality is only a means for the purposes of man. Woman must transform her biologically passive sex role by a moral act which is the act of love. By love, woman fulfills in her surrender to man her own natural desire.

For Fichte, marriage is not a contract and no legal relation. As a moral relation between individuals, marriage must be free of all legal regulations. It is prior to and independent of the legal order. Because marriage exists prior to the state, the only task of marriage legislation is to ensure that marriages are concluded freely, that they are recognised and that they can be dissolved freely if their moral justification disappears. Since the spouses are free to enter marriage, they must also be free to dissolve it. The state has to take notice of marriage and divorce but not to inquire into the reasons.

Prussian Law

A few years before Kant propounded his theory of marriage as a private contract unrelated to any political authority and based on law as the product of pure reason, the codification of the laws of Prussia (*Allgemeines Landrecht,* 1794) defined marriage as a contractual relationship based on public law. The code declared that the principal purpose of marriage was the generation and education of children but that a valid marriage could also be concluded for the sole purpose of mutual support. German jurists generally maintained that the legal definition of marriage should be free of ethical elements and therefore rejected the inclusion of 'community of life' as the purpose of marriage because marriage is legally possible without a common life.

The Prussian code incorporated an order which had just been overthrown by the French revolution, a state based on estates (*Ständestaat*). Civil society (*bürgerliche Gesellschaft*), the code explained, consists of several smaller societies or estates bound together by nature, by law, or by both. One of these societies is the domestic society (*häusliche Gesellschaft*) which is constituted by the union of the spouses and the union of parents and children. Servants, too, belong to the domestic society which, therefore, comprises the relations between man and wife (marital law), parents and children (parental law), and master and servant (servant law). The legitimacy of marriage as a social relationship depends on its conformity with the norms of conduct laid down by the sovereign state.

Hegel

The identification of civil society with and its incorporation into the state was challenged by Hegel. For Hegel, civil society is the opposite of the state. While the state represents the highest form of self-realisation of the mind, 'the reality of the moral idea,' civil society comprises the universality of material living conditions, economic relations, and the arrangements for the protection of property and safety. As a personal union, marriage requires the bodily union as a consequence of the moral union. The community of personal and particular interests follows from marriage.

It was the criticism of Hegel's legal philosophy that led Marx to establish his theory of law and state as superstructures of economic reality. Legal relations and political organisations are not to be explained out of themselves or on the basis of a so-called general development of the human mind but on the basis of the material conditions of society. It is for this reason that all Marxists deny any inherent rationality or independent finality of marriage and the family. The material productive conditions, in legal terms, property relations, determine the form and development of marriage and the family, and these forms change in conformity with the changes in the economic foundation.

Von Savigny

The subjection of marriage to the legal order and the state was justified by Friedrich Carl von Savigny, one of the outstanding German jurists of the nineteenth century. Savigny sees in marriage a double aspect, a moral and a legal relationship. The most important is the moral relationship between the spouses which derives from their free decision. But marriage also includes legal relations, and the legal protection to be given to marriage makes it subject to legislation and judicial procedures. In addition, however, Savigny says, there is a third aspect, the dignity of marriage as an institution which is independent of law as well as the will of the individual partners.

As an institution, marriage constitutes an essential and necessary form of human existence and the indispensable basis of the state. Its claim to recognition is independent of personal choice and opinion. Marriage is intimately connected with the spiritual well-being of the community as well as that of the individual, and in Christian society, monogamy has become the foundation of culture and the elevation of the status of woman. One of the conclusions Savigny draws from his view on the institutional character of marriage is the rejection of divorce by mutual consent (which had been recognised in the Prussian Civil Code).

Engels

Marxism asserts that, as part of society's superstructure, marriage and the family are functions of the economic system so that their development is conditioned by the development of the production structure. Friedrich Engels, Marx's closest collaborator, postulated three forms of marriage corresponding to the three main stages of human evolution. Among the savages, group marriage is dominant, among the barbaric peoples, pair marriage, and among the civilised peoples, monogamy which is supplemented by adultery and prostitution. At the higher stages of barbarism, between the pair marriage and monogamy, the domination of the male over female slaves and polygamy are found. Since monogamy rests on the concentration of a considerable amount of property in the hands of one individual and includes his desire to leave his possessions to his children, the transition from private property to communism will destroy monogamy as well as prostitution. Since the present form of monogamy (monogamous female and polygamous male) is the result of economic conditions, it will disappear together with those conditions. Private households will be abolished and in the communist life-style, society will take over the care for and education of children. Men will be forced to accept a new form of monogamy because women will be emancipated in the new economic system and will no longer be obliged to suffer the marital infidelity of men.

Because marriage, property and the family are the foundations on which the bourgeoisie has built its domination, marriage and the family must be 'theoretically and practically' destroyed. Engels demanded that the education of all children should be carried out in national institutions at public expense starting at the moment the child can do without the initial care of the mother.

Bebel

In a more detailed way than Engels, August Bebel expounded the Marxist views on marriage and the family (*Die Frau und der Sozialismus,* 1879). As other evolutionists, he lets social development start with the horde in which sexual instinct is satisfied without any regulation. Bebel accepted the opinion that in primitive society, women possessed about the same physical strength as men and that the difference in brain volume was smaller than in civilised society. But during pregnancy and in the period of lactation after birth, women become weaker which gives men an opportunity to enslave them. In the beginning of the second stage of social evolution, no permanent individual relationships existed between men and women; the women were the common property of the group and all men could use them. On account of a deficiency of women or the desire of a particular man to own a particular woman or particular women for himself, the third stage emerged at which women gained a certain status. This laid the foundation for private property, the family, the tribe, and the state.

The patriarchal family, in which women and children were the private property of the male, constituted the first form of the family. With the development of the economy, the position of woman changed, but in the patriarchal family as it exists under capitalism, the system of private property also involves a kind of slavery for women. This slavery will only disappear with the abolition of private property. Women will gain equality in the economic system, in the material conditions of life and in intellectual development. A free kind of monogamy founded on the almost equal number of men and women will be possible without any limitation on the personal freedom of both sexes. The state will have no power to pass laws prescribing a permanent sexual union. Only the affection between man and woman will determine their relationship.

Bebel's real intention was to free marriage from all legal restrictions and base marriage solely on love, but his advocacy of 'free love' put him near the utopian sexual communism which is quite different from the strict Marxist interpretation of marriage and the family. Nevertheless, Marxism can be seen as a reversal of the philosophy of history of the old world which placed the 'golden age' at the beginning of human existence when Mother Earth gave to man everything he wanted freely and without effort. Authors like Bebel, Engels, Paul Federn, Erich Fromm and Wilhelm Reich expected a golden age from the overthrow of the patriarchal system by matriarchy. 'The coming revolution is the revolution for matriarchy' (Otto Groß) was one of the socialist slogans.

Fourier

Representative of the rejection of the existing arrangements of sex relations and their replacement by utopia is the imaginary order envisaged by François Charles Marie Fourier (1772-1837). Fourier contended that the system of western civilisation had to be changed if man's inherent greed was to be contained. He proposed that society should be organised in units of 1,600 to 1,800 people living and working in cooperation. These units which he called *phalansteries* would include apartments as well as workshops and wings for social and domestic activities. Fourier wanted to discourage monogamy and in each phalanstery, even the least physically attractive were to be guaranteed a minimum of sex by 'erotic saints' who would make themselves available in private suits set aside for such purposes.

Fourier's sexual utopianism inspired a number of experiments in communal living in the United States of which the Brook Farm Institute of Agriculture may be the best known. Based on a combination of Fourierism with religious ideas was the Oneida Community founded by John Humphrey Noyes which is particularly remembered for its practice of 'male continence' (or Mazdaguan coitus: withholding ejaculation during coitus while making female orgasm possible).

Adler

Alfred Adler emphasised the economic and social inequalities and the differences in status affecting the family. Modern culture suffers from the quest of prestige and the mania for power and the distortions in society are reflected in marriage and the family. The man's consciousness is dominated by his position as the head of the family who provides the material support for the family household. The woman's contribution is undervalued. Children experience the father as the most influential member of the family and many mothers suggest such a misconception by having the father make decisions, administer punishment and settle disputes. The sexual division of labour should not imply difference in status. Socialism will make men more cooperative and reduce the competitive struggle in the family just as it will abolish competition in the economy. In Adler's psychology, the 'feeling of community' is a central theme reflecting his Rousseauistic view that man is good by nature.

Neomarxists have renewed the attacks on the family which they term a 'derivative of bourgeois property relations' — 'private property law applied to one's own child.' The family is to be replaced by an 'elastic family association' which 'in a long-term permanent process' is to develop into a commune.

4

Marriage and the Position of Woman

THE MODERN CONCEPT OF MARRIAGE as a community of life of free
and equal partners implies that marriage does not change the position
of woman as a human individual. But in the actual development of
marriage, the equality which seems a necessary postulate of the idea of
marriage has seldom been woman's actual situation. Equality is a concept extremely useful for demagogic obfuscation but of little clear
content. The sentence 'all men are equal' contains a true meaning
(discussed in Volume I) but in its unqualified generality constitutes a
flagrant contradiction to the obvious facts of reality. The equality
between the sexes must be understood in a meaning that can actually
be ascertained in social reality or recognised as a goal reasonably
attainable.

The most widely discussed problems in the equality between man
and woman concern four fields: legal equality, political equality,
economic equality, and social equality. That woman has been subject to
great inequalities is a historical fact, and marriage has been a factor in
placing or maintaining woman in a position of inequality.

Woman as Property

In many periods of history, woman has undeniably been treated as a
kind of property. The tenth commandment lists the wife among man's
possessions which nobody else should crave: 'Thou shalt not covet they
neighbour's house: neither shalt thou desire his wife, his servant, nor
his handmaid, nor his ox, nor his ass, nor anything that is his' (Exod
20,17; cf Deut 5,21). It is a moot question whether the enumeration
implies an order of value.

A people vanquished in war was reduced to slavery and its women
became the booty of the victors. When Dionysius, the tyrant of Syra-
cuse, had the entire upper class of the city executed, he divided its
property among his followers. In order to replenish the population, he
imported a great number of slaves to whom he distributed the wives
and daughters of his victims. As the legend of the 'Rape of the Sabine
Women' shows, the forcible abduction of women served as a means to
make up for demographic deficiencies. But such events are irrelevant to
the forms of marriage and do not constitute changes in the social
structure. Sexual exploitation of slaves was common and through the

system of household slavery reached into the individual home. In some countries, kidnapping and sale of women remain problems even today, and the same is true for the sale of children.

Views on Woman in Antiquity

The social position of women in antiquity was largely without relation to religious ideas. In the anthropomorphic views on deities, we find male and female gods, gods and goddesses who marry and have children, commit adultery and other abominable crimes. These ideas do not reveal any subordination of the female sex. Female deities were venerated in the old high cultures. Isis was the principal goddess of Egypt, Astarte was the west-semitic goddess of fertility and love and Cybele the Great Mother of Asia Minor. These goddesses symbolised the feminine principle and the never-ending stream of life, woman as the procreatrix on whom rested the continuity of generations. The old patriarchal societies of Greece and Rome had no goddess of woman. The triad Zeus, Hera and Athena, taken over by the Romans as Jupiter, Juno and Minerva, were venerated for the protection of the community. Aphrodite (the Roman Venus) was widely worshipped as a goddess of the sea and of seafaring. Because the Greek word *aphros* means foam (the connection of the originally non-Greek name with *aphros* stems from folk etymology), the legend arose that Aphrodite was born from the white foam produced by the severed genitals of Uranus (Heaven) after his son Cronus threw them into the sea. Her epithet 'Anadyome' (Rising from the Sea) has the same origin. Aphrodite was also venerated as a goddess of war, especially at Sparta and Thebes. Primarily, however, she was a goddess of love and fertility, symbol of the woman as sex object, the apotheosis of woman as satisfying the sexual desire of man.

There was no connection between the sex of the deities and that of their priests. Hera and Athena favoured priestesses while Isis and Cybele were usually served by priests. Appolo inspired the Phytia at Delphi and a priest at Ptoon. Female deities are numerous in Japanese mythology in which Amaterasu-ô-mikami, the goddess of the sun, occupied a central position as the ancestress of the Imperial family.

In the social systems in which woman was legally and economically dependent, marriage implied the transfer of the power over the wife from her family to her husband. Both in Babylonia and Egypt, women enjoyed considerable independence and high esteem. The Code of Hammurabi, King of Babylon, a document which dates from the eighteenth century BC, granted married women a great deal of personal and financial freedom. The bride-price paid by the bridegroom remained her property. Marriage was monogamous although the law fixed certain cases in which it was allowed to have a concubine.

SM-E

Adultery of both sexes was severely punished. The husband could not sell his wife, but he could temporarily assign her as a servant to a creditor. If a wife decided to return to her father or was divorced by her husband, she took her dowry with her. A woman could divorce her husband on the grounds of cruelty or adultery; a husband could divorce his wife at will. The children remained in the custody of her mother who must usually be given adequate means of support. Women could trade on their own account, independently of their husbands, and they could be judges, elders, witnesses and scribes.

The status of women was still higher in ancient Egypt. Woman appears equal to man in all spheres. As goddess, queen, priestess and wife, woman's position involved no inferiority because of her sex. Women owned property, worked in many sectors of the economy, took part in public life and mixed freely with men. In the course of history, Egypt has been ruled by many queens; the New Kingdom reached the height of its power under Queen Hatsheput (1490-1468 BC) who built the terraced temple near Dair Al Bahri.

Women in Greece

In Greece, the status of woman varied from city to city. In Athens, the status of women deteriorated from the free and dignified position of Greek women described by Homer to that of childbearing slaves. Women were subject to the head of the house who, as their *kyrios* (lord), had power over their share in the family estate and was entitled to give them in marriage. The establishment of a marital union was a concern of the families rather than the spouses themselves. The father of the bride or her closest male relative acting as *kyrios* delivered her to the groom after giving her in marriage in a solemn ceremony. The husband became the *kyrios* of his wife and her property.

Wives were secluded in their homes, had no education and few rights, and were considered by their husbands no better than chattels. Female companionship existed only in extramarital relations and was provided by the *hetaerae,* intelligent and educated courtisans, some of whom exerted intellectual and political influence.

In contrast to Athens, women in military Sparta enjoyed near-equality with men, mixing freely with them in public and in sports, including wrestling. Women had a voice in politics and public affairs and were remarkably free of modesty.

In Gortyra (Creta) and some Attic states, where the law was less patriarchal than in Athens, women could own property and be without *kyrios.*

Women in Rome

The old Roman law limited private rights to the rights of the *paterfamilias* (head of the house) who exercised the *patria potestas* (paternal power). The *potestas* of the *paterfamilias* was different from the *imperium* (command) of the state, but originally, it included the right over life and death and extended to the children, all male linear descendants and those adopted into the family. By virtue of the *patria potestas,* the transactions of the *paterfamilias* were those of the house community which was a collective person. The family property did not belong to individuals but to the community of the house as a whole. The disposal of the family property was the exclusive right of the *paterfamilias* who represented the house in all transactions with third parties, concluded all contracts and conducted all civil suits.

Originally, the family property was limited to chattels; land was not individually owned but under the control of the *gentes* (*gens* was a group of families similar to a clan which had a common name, the *nomen gentile.* The *nomen gentile* of Gaius Iulius Caesar, for example, was Iulius, and the Iulii traced their ancestry back to Aeneas of Troy, and over Aeneas's father Anchises to the goddess Venus). But private ownership of land started already prior to the Twelve Tables (fifth century BC). Women were unfit to sign contracts or wills or to act as witness. Nor could they hold public office. Yet despite their legal disabilities, the social status of Roman matrons was high, even in the early days.

Roman Marriage

The old forms of the Roman marriage (*confarreatio, coemptio* and *usus*) transferred certain rights over the person and property of the wife to her husband, not as husband, but as *paterfamilias.* The wife entered the family of the husband if he was *paterfamilias,* otherwise the family to which her husband belonged. Marriage as such did not change the personal status of the wife; she did not give up her family and retained the *nomen gentile* she had acquired at birth. Only the *conventio in manum* subjected her to the power of the husband, made her *materfamilias* (mother of the family) and incorporated her property into the property of the husband. She could have no property of her own, took the position of a daughter in the family and obtained a legal right of inheritance as a daughter of her husband. If the wife had been independent before marriage, she lost her legal status and her property became the property of her husband or the *paterfamilias.*

Roman law distinguished between engagement and marriage. The engagement was a promise which could not be enforced but created an impediment to marriage with somebody else. Breach of the fidelity implied in the engagement by the bride was punished as adultery (this was also the case in Jewish law).

The old forms of marriage gradually became obsolete and marriage with *manus* (that is, subjecting the wife to the *patria potestas* of the husband) disappeared before Justinian and marriage without *manus* became most common. Marriage was a contract without prescribed form which required only the consent of the parties if they were above the age of puberty and the consent of the father if they were under *patria potestas*. Marriage was of greater significance as a social fact than as a legal relation. It was concluded when the partners started to live together with the intention of being husband and wife (*affectio maritalis*). Usually, marriage was accompanied by festivities (*nuptiae*) and the bride was brought to the bridegroom's house (*deductio in domum*) which was regarded as evidence of the will to marry (*affectio maritalis*).

But the existence of the marriage did not depend on cohabitation or consummation. Both spouses had to be Roman citizens or, if one was not, he or she had to have *connubium* (right to a Roman marriage). In a marriage without *manus,* the property of the spouses remained distinct and even gifts between husband and wife were invalid. The bride remained under her father's *patria potestas* and when the father died, under the guardianship of her nearest male relative. The guardian's consent to the disposal of the wife's property became unnecessary so that at the time of the Antonines (second century AD), Roman women enjoyed considerable freedom and the bonds of marriage were greatly relaxed. Sexual relationship of a free woman with a man created the legal presumption of marriage.

Children born in a *iustum matrimonium* (fully valid marriage) were legitimate and heirs of their father and, since the second century AD, also heirs of their mother. Usually, they acquired the status of their father.

Under Augustus, new laws regulated the solemnisation of marriage and divorce (*lex Iulia de maritandis ordinibus*), made adultery a crime (*lex Iulia de adulteriis coercendis*), and promoted marriages by attaching disadvantages to childlessness (*lex Papia Poppaea*) but the effects of these laws were short-lived. Justinian tried to introduce a more formal proceeding for the conclusion of marriage by requiring the upper classes (up to senators) to draft a written contract concerning dowry (*dos*) and matrimonial gifts (*donatio propter nuptias*). Other persons of rank were to declare their consent to marry before an official. This first attempt at a civil marriage was soon rescinded.

In the empire, concubinage was a marriage without dowry which implied a lower status of the woman. Her children were not accepted into the father's family and were not legally their father's heirs. A man could not have a wife and a concubine at the same time. Under Constantine, such children were legitimated by the subsequent marriage of their parents. In medieval times, legitimisation by subsequent marriage was extended to all illegitimate children. Since Romans of rank were forbidden by the Augustan legislation to contract a marriage with women of ill repute (prostitutes, actresses, women who had committed adultery), they resorted to concubinage for their union with women of lesser rank (the emperors Vespesian and Marcus Aurelius used this form of union).

Marriage in Germanic Law

With the penetration of Germanic and Slav tribes into the Roman empire, new ways of thinking showed up in Roman law. One of the changes concerned guardianship over women. According to Germanic law as it appears in the *Leges Barbarorum* (laws of the barbarians, a collection of Romanised tribal laws), the purchase of a wife does not mean the purchase of her body but of the legal power over her. A man who marries a woman from outside his own family makes a payment (*muntgeld*) to the family for the transfer of the *mundium* (responsibility for and power over the woman); in return, there was a settlement on the groom by the bride's family. Marriage was concluded by the transfer of the bride to the bridegroom by the bride's *muntwalt* (legal guardian) and the payment of the *munt* (which later became a provision for widowhood). Essentially, marriage was a transaction between families.

Formally, the consent of both bridegroom and bride was required but it was of little actual influence. The bride was merely the object of the transaction. The man became husband because he acquired the *mundium* over the bride with the intention of making her his wife. It was only in the thirteenth century that the groom did not become husband because he acquired the *mundium* over the woman but he became *muntwalt* because he was the husband. After the first night, the bridegroom compensated the bride for the loss of her virginity by the *morgangiva* (*Morgengabe*, morning gift).

Until the eighth century, betrothal constituted the essential formality of marriage in German law and conferred the right of copulation. The consummation of the union was identified with the act of marriage. The wedding was a subsequent celebration. Prussian law (*Allgemeines Landrecht*, 1794) retained this construction which remained valid until the German Civil Code took effect (1 January, 1900). The betrothed were obliged to permit coitus and the 'stubborn and persistent' refusal of intercourse by one of the partners constituted a ground for the cancellation of the betrothal.

Marriage in Common Law

In the Middle Ages, Roman and Germanic law coalesced. From Roman law remained the principle that a woman who is not married is free but the position of the married woman was governed by the rule of Germanic law that the husband acquired all rights that the woman's family possessed. Canon Law retained the subordination of the wife under the husband and English common law accepted the *patria potestas* in its most extreme form. The married woman, the *feme covert,* was subject to her husband with regard to all rights, duties and legal process. 'Wife selling' has been recorded by Lanfranc (Archbishop of Canterbury, 1070-1089), and reached its peak towards the end of the eighteenth century. Smithfield, an open space in London where the annual Bartholomew Fair was held, was a popular locale for these sales. It was an (illegal) alternative to divorce or annulment practically unobtainable under ecclesiastical law. The *Code Napoléon* adopted the freedom of the wife with regard to property which married women not belonging to the nobility enjoyed in some French provinces on the basis of Roman law. The subjection of the wife under the *patria potestas* survived for a long time in the Scandinavian countries. A similar system existed in India where the mother might have her own son as guardian.

Inequalities in the Status of Women

Even today, the equality of the spouses is not without exceptions. In some cases, the husband is still legally the 'head of the family.' The provisions that the wife must assume the family name and that the husband determines the domicile or residence of the family are found in many laws. In the United States, different treatment of men and women was contained in about 800 federal laws as of 1980. Hundreds of state laws laid down different rules for men and women with regard to inheritance, credit, property and other economic interests. On principle, however, legal equality of men and women is recognised and discrimination on account of sex is prohibited. In many countries, the problem is no longer whether women possess equal rights but whether they are able to avail themselves of their rights in the same way as men.

The political equality of women depends chiefly on their right to vote. Even in the advanced countries of the West, the political equality of women has made only slow progress and the franchise has given women very little practical influence on politics. In all countries, the number of women representatives is relatively small. Women who are party leaders or prime ministers are very rare as the examples of the late Mrs Ghandhi, Mrs Bandaranaike and Mrs Thatcher show.

Of particular importance is women's economic equality and in this field, enormous problems remain despite much progress. Theoretically, most professions are open to women but actually, there are many occupations which women find difficult to enter and in which they encounter even greater obstacles in achieving promotion. The largest percentage of working women is still in so-called pink-collar jobs: teaching, nursing, sales, secretarial work, service jobs in hotels and restaurants. The present economic system of the western world (and even more so the systems in the Soviet Union and the Eastern European countries) is essentially a 'male' product. In their economic activities, women have to contend not only with the male-dominated economic world but also with enormous opposition on the part of the 'system.' Women are subject to severe restraints in the choice of occupation and often meet discriminatory treatment. In all occupational groups, women employees and workers tend to be most numerous in the lowest job categories, they earn less than men doing the same work, their chances of promotion are poorer and their jobs are less secure. Basically, women still suffer under the prejudice that their work is only a sideline for earning some extra money and that women's proper role is marriage and the family.

As a matter of fact, women still stand the best chance of finding satisfaction and happiness in marriage, and preferably in a family with children. Marriage and the family give women tasks that are more responsible and offer greater opportunities for self-development than a career. For men, marriage is unavoidable only in very exceptional cases. It is much simpler for men to remain unmarried than for women, and if a man marries, his life, above all his career, experiences far less changes than that of a woman. In marriage, woman finds a role in which she is equal to man, and in problems of the household and the upbringing of children, her professional knowledge is recognised also by men. In marriage, woman is truly equal although her role is different.

The role attribution to woman as housewife and mother has been branded as in flagrant contradiction to the high-sounding proclamations of moral and political equality in western democratic constitutions. That women are often discriminated against in economic life is an undeniable fact but that there should be no difference in the roles of men and women is a postulate of the absurd egalitarianism of socialist ideology which does not see the difference between 'equal' and 'same.' As human beings, men and women are equal but certainly not the same and it is impossible to replace man and woman by some neuter being. The instances in which ethnology has found the attribution of a female role (in the western sense) to men and vice versa do not negate the 'natural' role of woman as wife and mother. That the wife's activities in household and child care do not find proper recognition in the capitalistic system is a defect which the state should rectify because such a correction is required by distributive justice. The criticism of the present system is valid in as much as a woman must have a real possibility to remain unmarried if she so wishes. But equality does not demand that all women should be able to combine marriage with a career in the same way as men. Woman's double role as mother and breadwinner is not at all socially desirable and to make this double role available to all women is no proper goal of public policy.

Israel's late Prime Minister, Golda Meir, once confessed: 'At work, you think of the children you've left at home. At home, you think of the work you've left unfinished. Such a struggle is unleashed within yourself. Your heart is rent.'

Dual-Career Couples

Nevertheless, dual-career couples have become an integral part of society in western countries. The number of two-income families in the United States is estimated at nearly 30 million, up from 3 million in 1970. A woman's career will not necessarily quash family life, but adaptations both at home and at the place of work are necessary. For American dual-career couples, the greatest concern is the integration of family life and work life with their outside interests and their personal development.

For professional couples, the family is of primary importance, followed by career and outside interests, but many women find it difficult to establish an identity as a wife, mother and professional. In the United States, over 60 per cent of the dual-career couples have a household income of between $30,000 and $100,000, nearly double that of the ordinary households, but life is demanding and the situation is a constant source of stress. Although attitudes towards work and family have changed, behaviour still follows traditional male and female roles.

In the social structure of the West, woman's social position and the position of the family were determined by the social position of the head of the family who used to be the husband. In a society in which differences in status also affected the family, the marriage of a member of the nobility with a woman of lower rank (morganatic marriage) denied the wife and her children any claim to the husband's rank and property. With the greater freedom in the choice of occupation, woman has the possibility of shaping her own career and acquiring a social position of her own. In polite society, the traditional etiquette in the treatment of 'ladies' is still observed but in professional life, the tendency to regard women as 'intruders' is strong and women are often made to feel that they are unwanted and have no business to be there.

Suttee

How little the legal and political equality of women can secure her social position is exemplified by the Hindu custom of *suttee*. In a country in which a woman occupied the highest political office, a wife who loses her husband can contemplate her future only with fear and tribulation. *Suttee* (from the Sanskrit word *sati* meaning a virtuous wife) originally was a free act on the part of the Hindu widow anxious to join her god-husband through the purifying flames. Dressed in a new sari and with bright vermillion daubed across the middle parting of her hair to indicate that she is married, the widow mounted the funeral pyre with folded hands. This self-immolation of the widow had no foundation in the ancient Hindu scriptures but it was a practice often actively urged by relatives ambitious for the prestige of a *suttee* in the family, greedy for her property or wanting one less mouth to feed.

The practice was banned by the British governor-general of India, William Bentick, in 1829 and the present Indian law punishes attempted suicide. When she was prime minister, the late Indira Gandhi stated that her government was opposed to the revival of *suttee*, although even today socio-economic factors often encourage the custom. A widow in a poor Hindu family is unwanted. With the death of her husband, no one is interested in looking after her. Remarriage of widows, although allowed by law, is still to be accepted by orthodox Hindu society.

Suttee is one of the customs that reveal the 'expendability' of women in Indian society. Indian religion venerates female deities but the Indian woman suffers under brutality, murders caused by the demand for dowry, the criminal neglect of female babies, the exploitation of female labour and the general social contempt of women. India has 20 million more men than women, and unlike the situation in other countries, male life expectancy, at 52 years, is one year longer than that of women. Infant mortality is one-third higher for girls than for boys. Amniocentesis for the purpose of ascertaining the sex of the foetus was prohibited in 1981 but this has not changed the social attitude towards baby girls. The preference for male offspring is expressed in the Hindu wedding ritual. In the *saptapadi,* the seven steps around the sacred fire, the bridegroom recites the formula: 'Be my companion. Go together with me for always and ever. Let us generate many, many sons.' The meaning of the Indian marriage is to produce male offspring. Sons increase the family's labour force and they mean support in old age. A pious Hindu can only die in peace if his son lights the funeral pyre when the father's body is cremated.

Suttee is said to be connected with the ordeal by fire of Sita, the wife of the god Ram, related in the epos *Ramajana.* When Ram had recovered his wife who had been abductedby the demon Rawana, he demanded that his wife prove her innocence by fire: 'No man can take back a woman who has lived in the house of another man.' An Indian cartoon, depicting the ordeal of Sitra, lets her recite the following prayer: 'O Agni (the god of fire), it is not that I want to proclaim my virtue to the world. But since Rama demands it, show that I am indeed blameless!'

One theory on the origin of *suttee* assumes that it arose from a very practical consideration. In a society with child marriage, the wife may be much younger than the husband. Since she prepared his meals, she might try to poison him. In ancient times, it happened that many men died suddenly in obscure ways. *Suttee* was introduced to provide the wife with a motive to keep her husband alive as long as possible.

Whatever the origin, Indian society wanted the widow to choose death voluntarily and therefore made life as miserable as possible for a surviving wife. She was not allowed to remarry and was treated like a pariah by her own family. In some localities, the widow was hung upside down on the day of the funeral and her hair cut. For many widows who refused to be burned, prostitution was the only way to make a living.

5

POSSLQ

Extent of Cohabitation

IN 1982, SWITZERLAND SCRAPPED the legal prohibition of concubinage which provided for fines or imprisonment if an order to terminate cohabitation without legal marriage was not obeyed. The change in moral views had made the implementation of the law impossible, the authorities declared. In the last ten years, marriages without marriage certificates have not only become more numerous but have also found a large measure of social acceptance. In the United States, the Census Bureau reported that, as of March 1985, 1.9 million couples were listed as POSSLQ, 'persons of the opposite sex sharing living quarters' without being legally married. Their number had decreased by 5,000 from the preceding year and was the same as in 1981 when 57 per cent had never been married and 32 per cent divorced. More than 70 per cent of these households had no children and in two-thirds of the cases, men and women were under 35 years of age.

The book *Debrett's Etiquette and Modern Manners,* which the publishers of *Peerage* brought out in 1981, advanced the opinion that unmarried couples living together is socially acceptable. 'Respectable' attentions by a gentleman to an unmarried lady need not be directed exclusively to marriage. Living together in unmarried bliss is a legitimate purpose, provided both agree it is what they want. But just 'seeping' into your partner's life, first staying for a weekend, then for a week and finally forgetting to go home altogether is almost never acceptable.

Then there is the problem of the unmarried couple who come to stay. Should they be given the same room? It is courteous to do so, the book says, but if the hostess has strong feelings against it, it is her right to make the rules. In England, however, fewer people were living together without marriage in 1981 than in 1971. 'It's unsatisfactory for the person who really wants marriage,' the head of a survey bureau said. A French survey showed that about 800,000 couples cohabited without formal marriage while the number of marriages dropped to 300,000 in 1983, the lowest figure since 1956. In more than half of the cohabiting couples, the male partner was under 35 years of age and he was over 50 in fewer than one in 25 couples.

In China, cohabitation without marriage is still taboo, at least if a foreigner is involved. In 1981, a Chinese artist who had lived together with a French diplomat who claimed to be her fiancé was condemned to two years detention in a 're-education camp' on the ground of 'incitement to debauchery.' Although Chinese publications warned Chinese girls that they might end up suffering a lifetime of misery if they married a foreigner, be abandoned, sold or reduced to prostitution, the authorities declared that they did not oppose marriages between Chinese and foreigners as long as both were willing and went through the procedures required by Chinese marriage law.

Reasons for Cohabitation

The views, motives and reasons underlying cohabitation without formal marriage vary greatly. Sometimes, the partners have neither the will nor the possibility of entering into a conventional marriage. Young people who have not yet outgrown puberty are hardly mature enough to bind themselves to a definite partner. At 16, the world looks quite different from what it looks like at 20. A choice for life seems out of the question. If the partners agree that they will stay together only so long as they get along with each other, it is simple to separate. Every marriage involves a certain risk. The uncertainty whether marriage is the right thing, whether the present partner is the right choice can never be dispelled and uncertainty is often the reason for hesitation. It seems much better to live together on trial and find out whether it is possible 'to make a go of it.' Partnerships founded on the confidence in the first and only love are usually of very short duration. There are also many pairs living together because one of them had been married but is not legally divorced.

A guide to marriage for couples who want to marry in the Church of England acknowledged without disapproval that sex will not always be a new experience for both partners. But a spokesman for the bishop of London said that the publication (authored by Canon Hugh Melinsky) did not represent the view of the entire church.

In some respects, cohabitation without formal marriage is similar to a so-called common-law marriage. In the suit of Michele Trivola Marvin against Lee Marvin, the plaintiff based her claims on the assertion that she had rendered the services of a wife during their cohabitation. But in common-law marriages, the partners must have the intention to live together as husband and wife, their agreement must be followed by permanent and public cohabitation and their union must be recognised as a marriage by society.

It should be noted that there is no inherent reason why marriage should be concluded with the formalities fixed by Church or state. The only essential requirement is the consent of the parties who are qualified (not legally, but naturally) to contract a marriage. The intervention of some kind of public authority is due to the necessity of protecting marriage and the partners and the importance of marriage for society.

Nai-en

In Japan, a typical form of cohabitation without a legally valid marriage is the so-called *nai-en*. It is an unregistered marriage in which two people live together as man and wife after celebrating a customary (Shinto, Buddhist, or Christian) marriage ceremony. In most cases, the couple intends to have the marriage registered in the family register, but they are regarded as husband and wife also before the registration. *Nai-en* is no mere promise of marriage, and the Japanese courts have recognised it as a quasi-marital relationship. There is no law forbidding the *nai-en* relationship and a customary wedding, although in itself without legal effect, is perfectly legal. But children born out of a *nai-en* relationship are not legitimate children of the father and have no right of inheritance from their father. A promise of marriage or engagement has no legal effect and cannot be enforced although the injured party is entitled to damages in case the other partner repudiates the promise without reason. But the partner in a *nai-en* relationship is treated as a spouse for certain purposes. The Factory Law of 1923 recognised that the surviving spouse of a *nai-en* couple was entitled to compensation, and the phrase 'a person in a situation similar to a marital relationship although not registered' is found in most social security laws (such as the Health Insurance Law, Seamen's Law, Unemployment Insurance Law, National Public Service Mutual Aid Association Law; equivalent expressions are contained in the Labour Standards Law).

Except for *nai-en* relations, cohabitation without legal marriage has not yet found social acceptance in Japan. Actually, there are many couples living together, but in many cases, their situation is rather precarious. Young women, in particular, have to hide their involvement not only from their families but also from their colleagues. It is often easier for college students living away from home to have a liaison than for working women who are supposed to observe the traditional rules of conduct of single women by the people with whom they work.

Cohabitation without marriage may be due to more or less pragmatic considerations such as avoiding or postponing a formal marriage, but it may also be the consequence of a conscious rejection of marriage as an institution. There are people who consider the common life of man and woman as a purely private matter which concerns nobody else. If two human beings have confidence in each other and decide to live together on this basis, it is their own affair and needs no legal regulation. A certificate of marriage and the extravagance of a wedding are unnecessary for marital happiness. A voluntary, unfettered partnership satisfies the need of closeness, tenderness, sexuality, companionship and security. Such people want to protect their personal intimacy against the intrusion of society because a formal marriage implies social restraints. Marriage as an institution involves power and subjection and results in coercion and dependence.

Cohabitation and Life-Style

There are people who deliberately want to live differently from their family and friends. They desire a life of togetherness rather than a common label, to enrich each other without shutting themselves to others, to avoid painful experiences without giving up the longing for deep personal relations. Most important are intensive feelings of affection, spontaneity, openness and life as equal partners without possessiveness and claims to domination. Unmarried couples living together may have an unshakable confidence in the strength of emotional ties and their ability of autonomously shaping their existence without relying on institutional guarantees.

Avoidance of Marriage

In the consciousness of many people, particularly of the young generation, marriage no longer appears as important. Those who live together without marriage consider it as an obsolete and meaningless formality relied on by weak and tradition-bound individuals in need of security. Marriage, they claim, reduces the willingness to make efforts and to take risks, leads to possessiveness and monotonous routine, and results in *isolation au pair*.

The economic conditions of today's society are responsible for many of the difficulties of the family but it would be illusionary to think that the 'liberalisation' of marriage, that is, the recognition of cohabitation as a regular form of marriage (it is nebulous how this could be done without some form of registration) and divorce based on the agreement of the parties could solve any of these problems. In Japan, neither the *nai-en* marriage nor the possibility of divorce by mutual consent has enabled Japanese marriages to cope better with the dislocations and strains resulting from the economic system.

Sometimes, the man does not want a formal marriage because he is afraid of the financial burden and the economic obligations he would incur. 'I don't want to have somebody dipping into my pocket for the rest of my life.' The impossibility or the refusal to assume the economic incidences of marriage indicates that marriage, as an author put it, is concluded for reasons of technical planning. Marriage demands a more or less definite understanding about money, home, occupation, car, and so on. Naturally, such things also play a role when people just live together, but if two individuals agree to get married, these arrangements have to be planned for a longer period and with much more certainty. If a man just lives together with his girlfriend, they need not prepare for the future, they can leave many things undecided or make provisional arrangements.

The technicalities of social security legislation have produced what is called 'pension concubinage.' People live together without formal marriage because one of them would lose his or her old-age, survivor or other pension when getting legally married.

A conventional marriage usually involves a series of outside constraints. The wishes of parents or relatives have to be taken into account, often already in the choice of a partner, then for the wedding, the furnishing of the home or the style of living. Married life is subject to the critical appraisal of relatives or acquaintances. The pressure from outside is so much greater if the young couple has to live with parents or some other relative comes to live with them. The effort to please outsiders may cripple the mutual relations of the spouses. A formal marriage may appear more of a business or utility arrangement than a community of life.

Trial Marriage

The rejection of marriage can be motivated by the rejection of restraints. Partners who are not married can keep their sexual options open. This does not mean that unmarried couples are necessarily unfaithful or in the habit of changing partners but since the relationship is inherently unstable, each partner retains an independence and freedom incompatible with a traditional marriage. Both have the possibility of making a fresh start and trying out new spontaneous lifestyles. A rupture does not entail the same consequences as the failure of a marriage. There is no compulsion to attempt a reconciliation, repair the damage and restore a relationship which may have become unbearable. Each partner can pack up and walk out.

Drawbacks of Informal Cohabitation

Avoidance of a formal marriage and cohabitation relying on mutual trust seem to have a certain plausibility. Some sociologists have advocated trial marriage, marriage on a temporary or experimental basis, because in many cases, the partners simply do not know whether they harmonise with each other or can make their common life a success. It is also true that people change and nobody can be sure how he will think, feel or act in five, ten or twenty years. Ordinarily, sexual attractivenes declines with age and even the deepest emotional involvement does not guarantee a lasting understanding. Marriage is exposed to the development of the partners which may not necessarily be symmetrical and go in the same direction and is also under the influence of external conditions. These and other considerations indicate that a permanent union involves numerous and by no means negligible risks. Nevertheless, a marriage in agreement with the public order undoubtedly gives the union greater stability and regularity, but the problem is whether such stability and regularity are necessary.

Living together without formal marriage is not in accord with the meaning of the union of man and woman. The importance of complying with the legal order can be understood by two basic considerations. First, only the formal marriage imparts to the relations between man and woman the finality consonant with the essential meaning of their union. Secondly, as the foundation of the family, stability and order in the relations between the sexes are indispensable. The procreation of children is not necessarily included in marriage but neither can it be excluded. Although the rights and duties of parents are not without problems, the necessity to clarify parentage is obvious in a society which recognises the natural right and duty of the parents to educate their children. This is only possible if marriage is concluded in a socially recognisable form and could not be achieved if cohabitation would constitute the normal form of sexual relations. The differences in the legal position and social evaluation of an unwed mother or an illegitimate child may be denounced as prejudice, but as a matter of fact, such differences exist and there is no valid reason to expose a woman or a child to the danger of becoming the victim of discrimination. Marriage and the family, therefore, must remain the only legally recognised and thus the regular form of the union and community of life of the two sexes.

In some societies, marriage marks the wife as the exclusive property of her husband. Because the wife is barred from extra-marital relations but the husband is not under the same constraint, cohabitation without marriage has often been represented as an expression of the equality of sexes. The existing marriage and family laws can hardly be said to guarantee the equality of husband and wife in all respects, but the development certainly goes in this direction. The legal regulation of marriage restricts the freedom of the individual; however, in modern times, legal restrictions have been greatly relaxed and in many countries, even adultery is no longer punishable as a crime. In its nature, marriage does not imply a double moral standard and is in itself better suited to protect the equality of the partners than mere cohabitation.

An unwed mother may have valid personal reasons for remaining unmarried but in a society that regards marriage as the normal form of union of the sexes, an unwed mother can hardly expect to be spared social and economic disadvantages.

The legal effects of marriage are neither the only nor the most important differences from cohabitation but they cannot be neglected. In addition to the recognition of the status of husband and wife and the legitimacy of their children, the formal marriage entails specific effects with regard to property, inheritance, taxation and social security (it sometimes happens that cohabitation without marriage is more advantageous for taxation and social security).

Neither the lack of equality in a legal marriage nor the limitations on personal freedom seem to constitute valid reasons for shunning a formal marriage. In societies in which sexual behaviour goes unnoticed so long as it does not involve a violation of criminal law, cohabitation without marriage has lost all meaning as a social protest. It may suit the convenience of partners who want to enjoy sex without assuming any obligations. In this sense, it may be not so much an assertion of freedom than a flight from responsibility. But there may be circumstances beyond the control of the parties (other than an existing marriage) that make it impossible to go through with the formalities of a legal marriage. After all, on the basis of natural law, the consent of the parties able and willing to live as husband and wife is all that is needed, and the legal regulations are of a purely positive nature which may morally be disregarded if there is a sufficient reason to do so.

6

The Unwed Mother

Number of Unwed Mothers

THE FEMINIST MOVEMENT OF THE SIXTIES has effected dramatic changes in the attitudes of society to unwed mothers as well as in their self-image. This change may not be universal but it is too striking to go unnoticed. First, there has been an enormous increase in the number of unwed mothers. A survey of the Japanese Ministry of Health and Welfare undertaken in 1983 found that fatherless households with children below the age of 20 numbered 718,100 (1980: 444,045), almost 2 per cent of all households. In half of the fatherless households, the mother was divorced, and in about one-third, the father was dead, but there were 38,300 unwed mothers (1973: 15,000). Their average age was 41.5 years, and most of them had jobs. In 1982, their average annual income was ¥2 million, less than half of the average yearly income of all households. There were 167,300 households in which a father alone was bringing up children, almost twice the number of such households in 1980 (84,996). His average age was 43.2 years, his average annual income in 1982 was ¥ 2.99 million.

One out of every five American children grows up in a one-parent home. In the United States, the number of one-parent households headed by never-married women rose by 367 per cent between 1970 and 1982.

Of 3,638,933 babies born in the United States in 1983, 737,893 were born to unwed mothers, accounting for 20.3 per cent of all births. The rate of live births by unmarried mothers per 1,000 women was 30.4, the highest since 1940 when this rate was first computed. The highest rate, 42 per 1,000 women, was recorded for unwed women aged 20 to 24, followed by a rate of 41 for those aged 18 and 19. The rate of births to unwed mothers continued to be much higher for black women than whites, although the difference was somewhat smaller than in the past. In 1979, 55 per cent of all black babies were born to unwed mothers, up from 38 per cent in 1970. The percentage of white babies born out of wedlock rose from 5.7 per cent in 1970 to 9.4 per cent in 1979. The rate of childbearing by unwed mothers increased more sharply than the number of women of childbearing age, 6.1 per cent to 4 per cent. The percentage of out-of-wedlock births was particularly high for teenagers, 83 per cent of all births of black teens and 29 per cent of all births to white teens. The birth rate for unmarried teenagers climbed from 12.6 per 1,000 in 1950 to 25.4 per 1,000 in 1978. Among women who were married for the first time during the first half of the 1970s, nearly 11 per cent already had had a child out of wedlock. Nearly one in four of the women who married since 1965 either had already given birth or become pregnant at the time of their marriage, double the proportion of such women in the 1930s and 1940s. Among the women who turned 20 during the second half of the 1970s, 41 per cent of blacks but only 19 per cent of whites had already given birth. Nearly three black births in four in this group were out of wedlock, compared with only one white birth in four.

A survey based on 1,314 single women between the ages of 20 and 29 found that 82 per cent of the women had had intercourse, 53.1 per cent were sexually active, 524 had been pregnant at least once, and out of a total of 1,029 pregnancies, 80 per cent were unwanted. If the national total is calculated on the basis of these data, about 5 million of the 8 million single women in their 20s had sex regularly, and of the 4.8 million pregnancies in that group, 3.8 million were unwanted.

Social Factors

Half of all American girls have pre-marital sex and some start as early as eleven. The difference between flirtation and intercourse has almost disappeared. Having a baby without being married is a kind of status symbol, a sign of maturity. Social and economic conditions are often background factors leading to out-of-wedlock motherhood. Individual attitudes and convictions, the outlook on life and future expectations play a significant role. Teenagers with high aspirations are less likely to have children out of wedlock than those looking for pleasure and an easy life.

In Japan, girls working in occupations such as waitresses, hostesses, attendants at Turkish baths, models and entertainers easily become involved in liaisons resulting in pregnancy; similarly unwed mothers often drift into such occupations. In earlier days, unwed mothers were mostly girls from the economically disadvantaged classes; among them was a relatively high number of feeble-minded and emotionally unstable individuals. Maids, factory workers, telephone operators and waitresses were relatively numerous among unwed mothers but occasionally, schoolgirls became pregnant. Often, the unwed mothers were prostitutes or became prostitutes as a consequence of their 'fall.' Out-of-wedlock motherhood was a social disgrace and the stigma attached not only to the mother but also to the child. In rural areas and small towns, unwed mothers were treated as outcasts and the social ostracism often drove a 'fallen woman' to suicide. In the large cities, illegitimate children were frequently abandoned and in the

nineteenth century and into the twentieth century, the establishment
and management of homes for foundlings was an important part of the
charitable activities of the Church. In places like Shanghai and Calcutta,
the work of nuns and sisters saved the lives of thousands of deserted
infants.

In many instances, couples live together without formal marriage
on account of social conditions, and sexual promiscuity leads to a large
number of illegitimate births. This is often the case in developing countries. In Venezuela, for example, the nationwide percentage of
illegitimate children has been estimated at 52 per cent but in the *barrios*,
the slums of Caracas, the ratio may be as high as 70–80 per cent.

Restrictions on marriage were once partly responsible for
illegitimate births. During the nineteenth century, the legal age of
marriage was high (25 years of age, for example, in some European
countries). In the city of Vienna, an ordinance prohibited the marriage
of 'destitutes.' Such measures naturally encouraged unregulated sexual
relations. Out-of-wedlock births also occurred in the so-called upper
classes but in such cases, the use of abortion was higher than among the
lower classes; alternatively legitimisation by subsequent marriage was
arranged.

There have also been women like Rebecca West (the pen name
Cicily Isabel Fairfield adopted after her model in Ibsen's novels for
writing in *The Freewoman*) who defied society and its moral standards
and took over the entire responsibility for rearing and educating her
child when the child's father (in the case of Rebecca West, H.G. Wells)
shirked his obligations. Dame Rebecca has been called one of the most
intelligent, most courageous, and most undeviating women of the
twentieth century but her son, Anthony West, severely criticised his
mother because his illegitimacy had handicapped his career in a society
which did not share the emancipated views of Wells and West. Maria
Montessori, who settled her affair by accommodating herself to the
prevailing views of society may have chosen a wiser course.

Unwanted Children

Unwanted children are not necessarily born by unwed mothers but a
very high percentage of the children born by unwed mothers is
unwanted. In today's Japan, they may be found dead or alive in trash
cans or department store toilets, and usually dead in coin lockers or the
closets of rented rooms whose occupants have vanished. Those of the
babies who remain alive are taken care of in public or private institutions and in the family register, the notations 'Father unknown,'
'Mother unknown' appear beside a meaningless name and the date of
birth. Some mothers disappear into nowhere leaving their newborn
baby behind in maternity hospitals. Occasionally, a girl expecting a

child may get the father to marry her but girls sometimes do not know who of their lovers or customers fathered the child and boyfriends may be unwilling or unable to assume the responsibilities of marriage. It is not unusual that early in such marriages one of the parties quits. The husband may move out and leave the girl alone with the child or the girl may leave husband and child behind to take up with a new lover. It can hardly be denied that there has been a significant increase in the number of irresponsible mothers but the same can be said of irresponsible males who leave the girls they have made pregnant in the lurch.

Material Conditions

When out-of-wedlock motherhood occurs among the younger age group (say, 10-19), the material adversity of sometimes abysmal poverty is aggravated by mental pressure, solitude and helplessness, desperate fear of discovery before the birth of the child and burning shame afterwards. The situation of the unwed mother was a favourite subject of the social novels of the nineteenth century depicting the disappointment, hopelessness, desperation, rage and revenge of the betrayed women. Homes were established for unmarried women expecting a child where they found refuge until delivery. As a rule, the children were separated from their mothers and given for adoption or brought up in orphanages or foundling homes. For the mother, reeducation was the objective of social protection agencies. For the children, the principle that children were not to be punished for the sins of their parents was gradually recognised and somewhat belatedly, the view prevailed that the unwed mother was not to be punished but helped and that her reintegration into society should be the goal of social policy. This also led to the recognition that it would be desirable to leave mother and child together.

Illegitimacy

The abolition of the distinction between legitimate and illegitimate children was an important objective of the socialist platform in the nineteenth century. As mentioned above, Friedrich Engels predicted that private households would disappear in the future social order and that society would take over the upbringing and education of all children. This would eliminate the distinction between legitimate and illegitimate children. In the new order as envisaged by August Bebel, men and women could have children without being married.

The Second World War brought a sharp increase in illegitimate births and, at the same time, more girls of the upper classes bore children out of wedlock. In the United States, unwed mothers increased among teachers, secretaries and other office personnel. The separation from the family, the aggregation of young people under completely abnormal social conditions, the emotional sympathy with the uncertain fate of the soldiers leaving for the front and the general confusion favoured a kind of conduct that would have been unthinkable under normal conditions.

Defiance of Society

In the West, the attitude of society as well as the self-consciousness of the unwed mother was determined by the traditional morality which regarded the monogamous marriage as the universally valid norm of sexual conduct but connived at deviations from these rules in the upper classes. The social convulsions in the sixties questioned the validity of the traditional norms and particularly branded the hypocrisy, deceit and double morality which ignored the extramarital relations of men. The feminist movement stressed the woman's right in her own body from which it drew the conclusion that a woman could become mother if she wanted but could also decline motherhood which led to the assertion of a right to out-of-wedlock motherhood and a right to abortion. The women who defended this position felt themselves as the pioneers of a new social order and defied the existing society. Independence and self-realisation of the woman were their ideals and they believed above all in the ability of woman to combine motherhood with a professional career.

One of the protagonists of this movement was Bernadette Devlin who had been elected by the Catholic Party of Northern Ireland as the youngest member of the House of Commons and, in a challenge to Ireland's Catholic tradition, announced that she would not marry but bear a child (she later married and was severely injured together with her husband in a terrorist attack). Feminism considered the traditional marriage as a relationship which gave the male a dominant position so that for the woman, marriage meant not only a bond but subjection. On the other hand, motherhood is not only the woman's most proper vocation but also a personally valuable and enriching experience. The relation between mother and child opens to woman physical and emotional possibilities which are unattainable without motherhood. These premises lead to the affirmation of motherhood and the rejection of marriage. 'I want a child but need no husband,' declared Yoko Kirishima. (She had three children out-of-wedlock with a retired US Navy commander, but later married a Japanese twelve years her junior.) Women believe that the traditional form of the family will change. 'In my circle, the number of people has increased who do not live together with their partner but who want to have a child. It seems that slowly people will no longer stick to the family structure in which two parents come to one child in the same house' (Reiko Kishida). This change will also do away with the concealment of extra-marital sex in the upper classes, a relic from the feudal past when the geisha stealthily bore a child to her favourite patron without causing trouble to his family.

Women who want to have a child but only for themselves without being bound to a man naturally are few. To them, a man is indispensable only as a begetter but unwelcome as a marriage partner. There are women who want to demonstrate their generative potential with some kind of euphoria of female freedom. In her book *Mütter ohne Männer* (Mothers without Men), Barbara Bronner describes this type of women: 'They are women who are and must be endowed with a special degree of courage, strength of will, aggressiveness, independence and activity. They are neither feminist fanatics nor haters of men but women who have contested one of man's most cherished privileges, that man alone is competent for the support of children and their integration into society. . . . Women who do not bear a child to a man, women who bear a child to themselves.' The major problem of women without husbands is how to combine a career with the rearing and education of children. They are facing a three-fold task in their roles as housewives, educators and breadwinners.

Not all unwed mothers are opposed to marriage on principle. There are mothers who could not or did not want to marry the father of their child but did not want or were not able to have an abortion. Sometimes, the opposition of the woman's family against the prospective husband or of his family against the prospective bride obstructs a marriage or the man is married and unable or unwilling to dissolve his existing marriage. But in most cases, the unwed mother has been deserted by the father of her child.

There is, however, an obvious discrepancy between the unconditional rejection of marriage proclaimed by a minority of women and the actual conduct of a majority of women cohabiting without marriage. Surveys suggest that free partnership is chosen only for a limited period, above all for the duration of study or training or until a child is planned or born. With relation to children, the prevailing view seems to be that it is important to give up the ambivalence of the relation and to clarify the legal and social status. The partners are less concerned with regulating the position of the mother and attach greater weight to the future security of the child. With regard to the child, the unmarried partners show a greater readiness to recognise social rules and the public significance of marriage. Marriage as an institution is rejected, but the family is acquiesced in as an institution.

Rights of Unmarried Mothers

In some cases, the Japanese courts have upheld the right of the unwed mother to educate her child but in a case in which the illegitimate child of a kindergarten teacher had been taken away from her and adopted by another family without her knowledge and consent, the Osaka District Court dismissed the mother's demand for the return of her child on the ground that she was not suitable for rearing the baby because she had a job. She was told by the court that childbearing by an unmarried woman in an educational post was immoral. The Supreme Court upheld this atrocious ruling.

The Supreme Court of Canada has affirmed the principle that a natural parent, such as an unwed mother, should not be denied custody of her child merely because applicants wishing to adopt the child offer better material prospects of a two-parent instead of a one-parent home. Another opinion maintains that a young unmarried mother is not a suitable custodian of her newborn child and that, therefore, public intervention leading to adoption is in the child's best interest.

Inmates in an Italian prison went on a hunger strike when a prisoner's newborn baby girl was taken away from her. The mother, serving a six-year term for attempted robbery, was taken back to prison from the hospital without seeing her child who had been fathered by her accomplice. The child was placed in an institution after a judge ruled that prison was not an ideal place for rearing a child.

Difficulties of Unmarried Mothers

Education has its special problems for a mother who is alone, particularly if she has to work. The mere fact that she has nobody who can assist her or take her place in looking after her child or children creates a host of problems which grow quantitatively and qualitatively if the children go to school. Difficulties in education and learning are too quickly blamed on the family situation and teachers are not always alert to the needs of a one-parent child. The child has only one person in whom it can confide, and that person is often too busy to give the help the child requires. Everyday life in school, day care centre or kindergarten usually presupposes the normal family. School books speak of father and mother, children have to write compositions on the father's occupation, and classmates tell of family weekends and vacations. The one-parent child's experience that the circumstances of its life are not normal may cause feelings of inferiority, anger or rebellion.

It seems very unlikely that the unwed mother will become a socially acceptable life-style. Japanese society, at least, is far from approving unwed mothers. In a comparative survey sponsored by the Prime Minister's Office carried out in February-March 1981 and covering 1,000 parents with children in each of six countries (Japan, Republic of Korea, United States, United Kingdom, Federal Republic of Germany and France), the western countries' acceptance rate of unmarried mothers ranged from 22 per cent to 50 per cent but was 0.4 per cent for Japan and 3.1 per cent for South Korea.

The way of thinking of mothers with adolescent girls has not changed. They don't want to see their daughters become pregnant before marriage. In the country, the families are very upset when a girl returns with a child, and there are many unwed mothers who have been rejected by their families. The young women who find refuge in a home for unmarried mothers are not going to make a social revolution. Even today, most of Japan's unwed mothers drag out a very miserable existence. If they cannot support themselves, they receive welfare payments which include a child allowance of about ¥£30,000 a month. Recently, the Missionaries of Mary, the sisters of the congregation established by Mother Teresa, opened a home for unwed mothers in Tokyo.

Experts have claimed that unwed mothers bind their children unilaterally to themselves because they lack the partnership with a man. But the danger of emotional pressure from a unilateral mother-child relation is less for children of unwed mothers than for children of divorced mothers. These children often suffer from the solitude with their mother and are psychologically in a bad situation. Nevertheless, unwed mothers feel the problem of the one-sided orientation of the child to the mother and often ask themselves whether their child needs a father. This question can become acute when boys grow older and encounter difficulties the mother cannot cope with alone. The son lacks a partner with whom he can talk about things the way a man experiences them.

Illegitimacy in Japanese Law

Although the social rejection of unwed mothers may not change, mother and child deserve better legal protection. There are no provisions in Japanese law which refer directly to unwed mothers. Indirectly, their position can be deduced from the regulations concerning illegitimate children. (The Japanese text of these provisions does not use the term 'illegitimate' but 'children who are not legitimate.') Legitimate children are those born after their mother acquired the status of wife (this formulation has been chosen in view of the custom of nai-en marriages). The status of wife is only acquired if the marriage is registered in the family register kept in the Family Register Office. Therefore, the question of a legally recognised husband-wife relationship is merely a matter of compliance with a legal formality.

Children of unwed mothers are all non-legitimate children and it is immaterial whether the mother lives in a nai-en relationship, is cohabiting with a man, is a concubine or a prostitute. As in many other countries, the position of the children of unwed mothers remains disadvantageous in Japan. If an unmarried woman gives birth to a child, she must register the birth within two weeks. The birth is registered in the family register of the woman (Family Registration Law Art. 18, Par. 2) and the child receives the family name of the mother (Civil Code, Art. 790, Par. 2). A birth certificate must be attached to the notification for registration. If the mother does not register the child, people living with her, the doctor or the midwife who assisted the birth have the duty of filing for registration (Family Registration Law, Art. 52, Par. 3). The relationship of mother and child can be claimed not only by the parties but also by third parties, and such a claim can be made even if the child is registered as the child of another woman.

The law provides that a father or a mother can recognise an illegitimate child (Civil Code, Art. 779; all following references are also to the Civil Code). The relation to the mother should be beyond dispute, but it happens that a child is registered as the child of another woman. In such a case, a decision or judgement of a court that the relation described in the family register does not actually exist is necessary before the register can be corrected. If a child is not registered, the mother can file a notification of registration even if many years have passed (she may be fined for having neglected the notification).

An illegitimate child legally acquires a father if it is recognised by the father. The effect of the recognition is retroactive (Art. 784) which means that the child is the illegitimate child of the father beginning with birth. The mother retains the parental rights over the child but the father can be given parental rights by agreement (Art. 819, Par. 4 & 5). In the same way, the child continues to have the family name of the mother (Art. 790, Par. 2). In order to be given the family name of the father, the permission of the Family Court is required (Art. 791). The child's guardian can be determined by agreement (Art. 788). The party responsible for the child's support can also be chosen by agreement; if no agreement exists, father and mother will be liable according to their economic resources and other conditions; depending on circumstances, the mother may require compensation for past support.

German Law

In the Federal Republic of Germany, a law regulating the status of children born out of wedlock went into effect on 1 July, 1979. The main objective of the law was to eliminate or mitigate the legal and economic disadvantages of illegitimacy for mother and child. The former expression *unehelich* (out of wedlock) was replaced by *nichtehelich* (not in wedlock). The clause of the old law which declared that there was no blood relationship between the father and the illegitimate child was deleted. The unwed mother who had only 'the right and duty to care for the person of the child' was given full parental rights. The child takes the family name of the mother. According to a decision of the Federal Constitutional Court, the father cannot claim parental rights for himself nor exercise them jointly with the mother. It is up to the mother to determine to what extent the father can visit the child although in exceptional cases, the court can grant visiting rights if this is in the best interest of the child.

In the German Democratic Republic, the mother has full parental rights over her child but the father is responsible for support. The father can file a petition to have the child declared legitimate. The minimum amount of support to be given until the age of 18 is fixed by law.

Because paternity suits are often drawn-out affairs, an American judge introduced a novel procedure. The Circuit Court for Prince George's County, Maryland, allows the blood testing to be done in the court house. Under a contract with the county, attendants from Johns Hopkins University Hospital administer the human leukocyte antigen (HLA) blood test to the parties in each case, mother, child, and the accused father. HLA tests lead to identification in 99 out of 100 cases and also uncover fraudulent schemes when people claim children in the hope of collecting extra welfare benefits.

More important than better legal protection are arrangements to stabilise the economic position of unwed mothers and their children. The most urgent need is for day-care centres which allow the mother to accept at least a part-time job. In many cases, welfare or relief agencies have to take care of single-parent families but the women who consciously reject marriage do not want to live on welfare and need the practical possibility of living according to their convictions without being punished by economic or social ostracism.

There are women who wanted to have a child for themselves without having to accept a husband but then found out that they were unable to cope with the situation alone. After all, to have a child for oneself is a basically wrong way to think of a child. The child exists not for his parents but for himself, and the child's well-being must take precedence over the mother's ideology. Working-class women could not dream of having a child for themselves even if they wanted but women who are economically independent and in a position to afford a child without marriage gradually feel that their situation is not quite ideal. It is not only the pressure of the small things that constitute daily life. Sometimes, the thought occurs that life *à trois* might be more satisfactory. An unwed mother put it this way: 'When my child smiled at me for the first time, I regretted that there was nobody with whom I could share this happiness, nobody to whom it was also important.'

7

Legal Protection of Marriage

AS LIFE IN OTHER GROUPS, family life is not fashioned after legal regulations. Law constitutes the irreplaceable norm of the activities of the state and public agencies which must respect the principle of the supremacy of law but for most people, law enters into their consciousness only when they have broken the law or become the victims of a violation of law. As in other spheres, the law touches only the outside of marriage and the family, their substance depends on the partners. The state has no influence on the quality of marriage and cannot make married life good or bad; it is impossible to enforce by law personal virtues such as love, fidelity or mutual respect. But in modern society, the regulation of the position and functions of marriage and the family seems indispensable.

The legal protection of marriage and the family includes rules for the conclusion, validity and continuation of marriage (restrictions on divorce), but extends also to fields such as education, taxation, social security, housing, and so on.

The Church and Marriage

In western culture, the conclusion of marriage never was a purely private matter but for a long time, it did not involve the intervention of public authority. When marriages were arranged between families, a secret marriage was impossible and the celebration of marriage usually implied a certain *de facto* publicity. The notification (*professio*) of marriage to the Church is already mentioned by Tertullian (ca. 160-230), but in a work written in his Montanist period (*De Pudicitia*). Because of the difficulty of finding Christian husbands of equal rank, Pope Callistus I (218-222) declared that marriages between noble Roman women and slaves or men of inferior status should be considered as true marriages even if no legal marriage were contracted (which would have deprived the women of their rank). He thus created ecclesiastical marriage law.

The participation of the Church in the conclusion of marriage developed gradually. At an early date, the Church imparted a benediction to the engagement (*sponsalia*) which gave it more significance than it had in Roman Law. The special prayers said for newlyweds at the ordinary service finally became a special nuptial mass, but it was only in the ninth century that the exchange of the marriage vows was made part of the ritual. The validity of the marriage, however, did not depend on the church wedding. It was in the Byzantine empire that the ⁻iastical marriage became the only legal form of contracting a ɪge (Emperor Leo in 813).

ᴗntil the time of Pope Alexander III (1159-1181), the Church ᴊased her assessment of the validity of marriage on Roman and Germanic law but gradually, a distinct Church law on marriage developed. The Church assumed sole jurisdiction over marriages, and according to Canon Law, a marriage came into existence by the mutual consent of the parties. There was considerable confusion on account of the distinction between the compact to marry (*sponsalia de praesenti*) and the promise to marry (*sponsalia de futuro*), but if the parties to an engagement had intercourse, it was presumed as a matter of law (*praesumptio iuris et de iure*) that they had the actual intention of getting married and the engagement became a marriage.

The banns, the announcement of an intended marriage, were made obligatory by Innocence III in 1215, but they were not essential for the validity of the marriage. Moreover, no particular form was required for marital consent which made clandestine marriages possible. Clandestine marriages, in turn, created the possibility of bigamous marriages. To remedy this situation, the Council of Trent in its decree *Tametsi* (1563) ruled that a marriage contracted without the presence of the parish priest or his representative and two witnesses which until then had been unlawful, would in future be null and void. But the decree was only binding where it had been published in the vernacular in the parishes, and it was extended to practically the entire Church only in 1907 by the decree *Ne Temere*.

The new code of Canon Law which went into effect in November 1983 provides that, where priests or deacons who could be delegated to represent the bishop or parish priest are lacking, the local bishop, with the approval of the bishops' conference and the permission of the Holy See, can delegate laymen to assist marriages (c.i.c., can. 1112, Par. 1).

Civil Marriage

The Reformation did not immediately create a new marriage law and although Luther considered marriage and the marital state a wordly business, he did agree to have weddings celebrated in the church and the Protestant pastor took over the role of the Catholic parish priest. But legislation concerning marriage became the province of the secular authorities which paved the way for the introduction of a civil marriage ceremony. In 1580, Holland and Friesland, two of the seven United Provinces of the Low Countries made a civil marriage ceremony optional for the Reformed and obligatory for the Dissidents; this regulation was extended to the whole of the Netherlands in 1656. A civil marriage was introduced in England, Scotland and Ireland in 1653 but abolished in the Restoration. England instituted an optional civil ceremony in 1836. In Austria, Joseph II's marriage decree of 1783 made a distinction between the ecclesiastical sacrament of marriage and the civil marriage contract subject to the jurisdiction of the state.

A civil act for non-Catholics was created in France in 1787 and after the Revolution, the civil act became obligatory for all marriages. In countries in which religious marriages were the rule, civil marriage was often introduced for practical reasons.

Secular law controlling marriage largely developed in the nineteenth century, and state legislation generally was non-denominational. Protestant churches usually conformed to the law of the state; from the point of view of the Lutheran Church, marriage as a legal institution is entirely a matter of state law. In the Catholic Church, Canon Law remains the only valid law for Church purposes, but in most countries, Canon Law is not recognised and enforced by the state's tribunals. The coexistence of two systems creates the necessity of two ceremonies — a civil marriage and a Church wedding — in countries where the Church wedding has no legal effects and the civil marriage is necessary for the recognition of the validity of the marriage by the state. This is the case, for example, in Japan, Germany and France. In Germany, the civil marriage must precede the Church ceremony while in England, the civil act takes place immediately after the religious ceremony (usually in the sacristy) if the church or chapel is duly licensed for marriages. In Japan, any kind of religious ceremony is irrelevant to the legal validity of the marriage. In the United States, a church wedding is recognised in many states, but a marriage license is usually necesssary for the lawful solemnisation of a marriage. People who do not belong to a church or do not want a religious wedding exchange the marriage vows before a civil magistrate, such as a justice of the peace. Some states still recognise so-called common-law marriages.

Greece introduced civil marriage for the first time through the revision of the Family Law in 1982. As a result of the Byzantine legislation mentioned above, Russians and Greeks could only get married by a religious ceremony in the Orthodox Church, even when they married abroad. This remained in effect in Russia until the revolution of 1917 and in Greece until the 1982 revision. Greek civil marriage, however, is optional, and the religious marriage retains its legal effects. The new law also provides that civil marriages contracted by Greeks with foreigners outside the country in a way recognised as valid in that country will be recognised as valid which is in accord with the principle that marriage should be contracted in accordance with the law of the place where the marriage is celebrated.

In Israel, the two chief rabbis, one representing the Ashkenazi

(European) Jewry and the other Sephardic (North African) tradition, act as final authorities in most issues concerning family law, including marriage and divorce.

Gretna Green Marriages

The existence of legal rules always leads to attempts to evade their requirements. A famous example in marriage law are the Gretna Green marriages. By the law of Scotland, a valid marriage could be contracted by consent alone without any other formality. When the English marriage act of 1754 rendered the publication of banns or a license necessary in England (which made clandestine marriages impossible), it became usual for persons who eloped to go to Gretna Green, the nearest part of Scotland (in Dumfries, just across the border from Cumberland) and marry according to Scottish law. A sort of chapel was built where the English marriage service was performed by the village blacksmith. In 1856, a law was passed requiring three weeks' previous residence in Scotland, and the wedding traffic was considerably reduced.

Legal Regulation of Marriage

In most advanced countries, the legal position of the marriage partners rests on the recognition of the equality of rights and duties of husband and wife and on the principle of partnership. The equality as legal subjects has no connection with the role attribution in marriage and does not demand the sameness of functions. Nor does the demand of equal legal and social status of legitimate and illegitimate children (such as the Fundamental Law of the Federal Republic of Germany, Art. 6, Par. 5) provide an argument for the legal equality of marriage and cohabitation without marriage.

Legislation cannot change the essential properties of marriage nor the relations and functions inherent in its nature. But the state can determine in which cases a marriage will be recognised as such, which of the rights given with marriage will be protected and which of the obligations enforced by public authority. Marriage law, therefore, generally contains provisions concerning the lawfulness and validity of marriage, the formalities for contracting a marriage, and reasons for divorce or nullity. Family law regulates the inner structure of the family as well as the relations of the family and its members with third parties. The old law provided for the transfer of the woman from her father's family to the power and guardianship of her husband and regulated the economic relations, particularly the property rights, involved in this transfer. Other internal aspects usually determined by law are the relations between parents and child, legitimacy, custody and guardianship.

Right to Marry

The right to marry and the freedom to marry or not to marry are basic human rights which can be regulated or restricted only to the extent that such restrictions are founded in the nature of marriage, that is, facts implying that at least one of the partners is incapable of marriage (immaturity, impotence) or lacks the knowledge or freedom required for marriage (age of consent, loss of reason, deprived of judgement or freedom because of coercion, fear, inebriation, hypnosis, deception or error with regard to essential personal qualities of the partner). In societies upholding monogamy, the existence of a valid marriage makes a subsequent marriage invalid. There is no good reason for allowing the state to prohibit racially mixed marriages while eugenic restrictions may be appropriate.

A private high school for girls in Kyoto, Japan, advised a 19-year-old girl to leave school or be expelled. The girl had married a 23-year-old American with the approval of her father and mother after a two-month courtship but the school authorities were shocked when she reported her change of status. The girl had studied a year in the United States which may have been a contributory factor in her unusual step (for a Japanese). The case was reported on TV and the audience was invited to phone their opinion on the school's decision to the TV station. The results were 50-50 for and against the school's policy. The publicity prompted the school administration to rescind the threat of expulsion and let the young woman finish her senior year but the episode drew attention to the profound differences in cultural attitudes between Japan and the West.

The Catholic Church and a few countries retain the principle of the indissolubility of marriage but most states consider the possibility of a breakdown of marriage and so do most Christian churches. The new German marriage law states that marriage is concluded for life, a rule not contained in the former law. But the law does not say how this rule shall be implemented.

In recent years, there has been a tendency to question the position of the 'normal' family as a generally valid model and to treat unconventional sexual unions, above all cohabitation without marriage, as equally valid forms of sexual relations. The individual may have a right to choose an unconformable way of life but this does not require the right to have a divergent sexual union recognised as a lawful marriage or to demand equal protection with the 'normal' family. From the point of view of public welfare, the state should encourage and protect the traditional form of marriage and the family.

Legal Status of the Family

In the legal treatment of marriage and the family, there are two fundamentally different approaches. It is possible to consider the individuals who get married and found a family, and it is possible to start with marriage and the family as a community and to determine the rights and duties of the members of such a community. The family is not the same as the sum of its members but a unit with its special values, functions, rights and duties. Modern law does not regard the family as legal person, and the family as such has no physical existence. But as a social group, the family is different from its single members, just as the state is a social reality different from its citizens.

As explained above, in the old Japanese law, the position of the marriage partners was unequal. The wife became a member of the husband's 'house.' In this typically patriarchal pattern, the husband occupied a position of authority and dominance while the wife owed obedience and submission and had to rely on the protection by the husband. The husband shouldered the financial responsibility for the common life while the wife had no legal capacity. (A woman could be head of the house but this was exceptional.) The husband managed the property of the wife and acquired the income from her property. For the wife, marital fidelity was a legal duty but no such obligation existed for the husband. The post-war constitution laid down the principle of sexual equality and stipulated 'Marriage shall be based only on the mutual consent of both sexes and it shall be maintained through mutual cooperation with the equal rights of husband and wife as a basis' (Art. 24, Par. 1). This ended the legal disability of the wife so that now each party is entitled to manage its own property and perceive its income. Books Four and Five of the Japanese Civil Code were amended to give effect to the constitutional principle of equality of the sexes and the freedom of consent.

In Japan's existing laws, the old expression 'house' (*ie*) occurs only in the law of inheritance and the words commonly used for 'family' (*katei, kazoku*) are found neither in the Family Law (Book Four of the Civil Code is entitled '*Shinzoku*' — Relations) nor in the law of inheritance; they are also absent in the Family Registration Law. The court competent for domestic relations is called Family Court (*Katei Saibansho*) and the organic law of the court (*Kaji Shinpan-hô*, Domestic Relations Law) states that the purpose of the law is 'to ensure the maintenance of the peace of the family and a sound common life of relations on the basis of respect for the individual and the essential equality of sexes' (Art. 1) but the matters for which the court is competent are all stated in terms of individual rights and duties. The same individual point of view is expressed in the second paragraph of the article on sexual equality in the constitution: 'With regard to the choice of spouse, property rights, inheritance, choice of domicile, divorce and other matters pertaining to marriage and the family, laws shall be enacted from the standpoint of individual dignity and the essential equality of the sexes' (Art. 24, Par. 2).

The difference in approach leads to a difference in priority and emphasis. If the family as a group or an institution is given priority, the interests of the marriage partners are considered relatively and subordinate to the common interest of the family which means that individual wishes in conflict with the well-being of the family will not be recognised.

Qualifications for Marriage

Many of the legal provisions related to marriage concern the conclusion of marriage and regulate who can contract a marriage and how marriage is concluded. The qualifications required for marriage are partly positive (persons who want to marry must have these qualifications) and partly negative (if these conditions obtain, a marriage cannot be contracted). In most laws, the basic requirement, that the persons who want to marry must be persons of different sex, is not expressly laid down but assumed as self-evident. In recent years, however, this requirement has sometimes been challenged by the attempts of homosexuals to have their relations recognised as a marriage.

In one of those 'life is stranger than fiction' stories, a Honduran woman got the surprise of her life when she was told that her husband of nine years was actually a woman — and six months pregnant. The true sex was detected when the 'husband' was killed during a brawl in a bar and doctors examined the body. The only thing the wife had thought odd was that her spouse had always avoided being naked in her presence.

Age

A further requirement generally regarded as a precondition of marriage is a certain age. In some cultures, the institution of child marriage is found, but in most cases, the marriage ceremony does not mean the beginning of conjugal life. In India, the Child Marriage Restraint Act of 1929 prohibited the marriage of girls below the age of 14 and boys below 16. In Egypt, an official certificate of marriage cannot be issued if the bride is less than 16 and the bridegroom less than 18 years of age at the time of the marriage contract.

In common law, the age required for marriage was 14 for boys and 12 for girls. At this age, adolescents have not reached full maturity but biologically, intercourse is possible; however the more important question is whether they are equal to the emotional, economic and social demands of marriage. In some American states, the common-law age requirements had remained in force until recent times.

In Canon Law, the minimum age required for the validity of the marriage is 16 years for men and 14 years for women. The new code empowers the bishops' conferences to fix a higher age for the licitness of marriage and advises pastors to dissuade adolescents from marrying before the age at which marriages are customarily contracted in the region.

The Convention for the Protection of Human Freedom and Fundamental Rights states that with the attainment of the age of marriage, men and women have the right to enter marriage and to found a family in accordance with national laws regulating the exercise of these rights. This, of course, is a very innocuous assertion since it does not protect these rights against encroachments by the state.

The minimum age requirement is of great practical importance both for the future spouses and their children. The rights and duties of marriage are based on the premise that husband and wife are truly mature. The legal marriage age (in Japan, males 18, females 16) silently assumes that the mental and emotional development keeps pace with bodily growth. This assumption seems hardly provable and is in conflict with experience. But society is not in a position to evaluate the inner maturity of a human being and the state has neither the right nor the means to judge the inner qualifications required for marriage. In the past, the consent of the parents has often been made a condition for contracting marriage and while this requirement is sometimes retained for marriages under age, it would constitute a severe limitation on personal freedom and cause considerable practical difficulties if made a general condition. The Council of Trent expressly stated that the consent of the parents was not required for the validity of the marriage.

Modern marriage law generally attempts to reduce the role of the state as a guardian and stresses the personal responsibility of the parties. In this sense, the partners who intend to marry must themselves pass judgement on their own maturity and capacity for marriage in general as well as marriage with a certain partner. It would be preposterous to assume one's maturity for marriage because one has reached the legal age. The capacity for mutual understanding and personal congeniality is much more important for a life in common than the capacity for intercourse, and the problems of education show that the attainment of the legal age for marriage does not guarantee the qualification as educator.

Impediments

Many provisions of today's law go back to Canon Law which, in the western world, was the only regulation of marriage for many centuries. In particular, the prescriptions on the impediments to marriage are generally based on the rules established by the Church. Canon Law distinguished between prohibiting impediments which made marriage illicit and diriment impediments which made it invalid. But the new code of Canon Law does not mention prohibiting impediments. According to Canon Law, marriage is invalid from the start if contracted despite a diriment impediment. German law distinguishes between marriages that are null and void and those that can be challenged. If the nullity of marriage is recognised or the challenge sustained, the marriage is considered void from the beginning. In Japanese law, however, a marriage in disregard of legal prohibitions can be declared invalid, but the annulment is not retroactive. Of the ecclesiastical impediments, some are of a purely religious nature, such as the prohibition of marriage between a Catholic and a non-Christian, holy orders and the public vow of perpetual chastity in a religious institution.

Kinship

Consanguinity and affinity are canonical impediments taken over by secular legislation. The impediment usually extends to affinity by adoption. The new code of Canon Law makes marriage between persons related by legal adoption invalid in the direct line and up to the second degree in the collateral line. The impediment of spiritual relationship (which made marriage between a person who is baptised and the baptiser, godfather or godmother invalid) is not mentioned in the new code. For blood relatives, marriage is prohibited in all degrees between ascendants and descendants and between brothers and sisters as of divine law so that in such cases, a dispensation from the impediment is impossible. In the collateral line, the extent of the prohibition varies. In Canon Law, it extended to the fourth degree until 1918, since then, to the third degree (such as a marriage between persons whose fathers were cousins was invalid) but the new code restored the old rule and made consanguinity in the collateral line up to the fourth degree (for example, between persons whose fathers are second cousins) a diriment impediment. In Japanese law, the impediment of consanguinity extends to all ascendants and descendants and to the third degree in the collateral line (Civil Code, Art. 734). In German law, consanguinity prohibits marriage in the direct line and between brothers and sisters, half brothers and half sisters (Ehegesetz, Art. 4, Par. 1). In the United States, most states prohibit marriages between first cousins.

Affinity exists between the man and the blood relatives of the woman, and the wife and the blood relatives of the husband. In Canon Law, affinity in the direct line is a diriment impediment in any degree; formerly, it also invalidated marriage up to the second degree in the collateral line but this provision has been omitted in the new code. In

Japanese as well as in German law, marriage is prohibited between in-laws in the direct line. Generally, this prohibition exists even if the marriage on which it is based is dissolved. In Japanese law, however, in-law relations end with divorce, and if one of the spouses dies, the surviving spouse can terminate the in-law relationship, but the impediment of affinity remains.

England's Marriage Act of 1949 lists the degrees of kinship by blood or marriage within which marriage is forbidden. The list stems from the 'Table of Kindred and Affinity' drawn up in 1563 and printed with the *Book of Common Prayer*. Kindred whom a man cannot marry include mother, daughter, adopted daughter, father's mother, sisters and daughters of children. Affinity covers 16 relations including wife's mother, wife's daughter and wife's son's daughter. Analogous prohibitions exist for a woman. A panel of the Anglican Church recommended that people connected by marriage should be allowed to marry but the ban on marriages between blood relatives should be retained. The panel split on the question of marriage between step-parents and step-children with a minority opposing marriage with step-children who have been raised in the family since childhood. In a few cases, step-relations have been given dispensation to marry by a private bill.

In the old Japanese Civil Code, a special form of adoption was called '*muko-yôshi engumi*' (marriage of a son-in-law adopted as husband for an heiress), a combination of adoption and marriage. The new Civil Code does not contain this form of adoption but marriage of an adopted son with the daughter of the adopting parents is considered valid despite the seemingly contrary language of Art. 734 of the Civil Code (which exempts the adopted child and collateral relatives of the adopting parents from the prohibition of marriage between blood relatives).

Adultery and Murder of Spouse

Canon Law prohibits marriage between blood relatives in the first degree of the direct line (that is, parents or children) of one of the partners who lived together in an invalid marriage or in public concubinage with the other partners (naturally, the two partners who lived together can get married if there is no other obstacle). The old Canon Law made marriage invalid between persons who committed adultery (that is, one or both were married to a third party when they had intercourse) with a promise of marriage if and when the consort of one or both died, or conspired and caused the death of the consort of one of them, or of whom one (without conspiring with the other) has murdered his or her consort in order to be free to marry his/her accomplice in adultery. The new code has abolished these impediments and made murder of a spouse an impediment. A person who in contemplation of marriage with a certain person kills the spouse of that person or his/her own spouse cannot contract a valid marriage with that person. Likewise invalid is the marriage of two persons who together caused the death of the spouse of one of them either physically or morally (such as by instigating a third party to commit the murder by command, suasion, deceit, and so on; can. 1090).

The old Japanese law prohibited marriage between adulterers if the marriage of the adulterer had been dissolved on account of the adultery or if the adulterer had been punished for adultery. But after the war, adultery was struck from the Penal Code and was also removed from the grounds for divorce. Consequently, adultery was abolished as an impediment to marriage which agrees with the view that adultery is a moral and not a legal concept. Likewise, the prohibition of marriage between persons of whom one had sexual relations with the ascendants or descendants of the other was abolished in the new German marriage law of 1976. The prohibition of marriage between adulterers is found in English law and in some American states.

Bigamy

In all western legal systems, an existing valid marriage is an impediment to the conclusion of another marriage. According to Canon Law, a marriage is invalid if at the time of the conclusion of the marriage, one of the parties was validly married to a third party, but Japanese law considers such a marriage liable to annulment (Civil Code Art. 744). Since Canon Law does not recognise divorce, a marriage with a person who is civilly divorced is invalid (if, however, the previous marriage is declared to have been null and void, a subsequent marriage is possible). There are a few cases of officially sanctioned bigamy in European history. In 726, Gregory II instructed Saint Boniface (the English monk Wynfrith, venerated as Apostle of the Germans) that a man whose wife was unable to exercise the conjugal rites on account of illness should observe abstinence. If, however, he could not practice abstinence, he should marry but should not withdraw his support from the infirm wife unless she were culpable of a detestable crime. Martin Luther allowed Philipp, margrave of Hesse, to have two wives, and Friedrich Wilhelm II, King of Prussia, with the blessing of the Lutheran Church, contracted two consecutive dynastic marriages and, concurrently, two morganatic unions.

In Japanese law, insufficient age, remarriage of the wife before the termination of the legally fixed period after the dissolution of a prior marriage, marriage between relations in forbidden degrees and forbidden marriages of an adopted child can be annulled but again the annulment is not retroactive; the same applies to marriages challengeable on account of coercion or fraud. German law contains detailed provisions for the case that the survivor of a spouse who has officially been declared dead remarries, Japanese law only states the general principle that if the adjudication of disappearance is later overturned, acts performed in good faith prior to the cancellation are valid.

As explained above, polygamy is legal in many countries. This is the case above all in Muslim societies. According to Islamic law, a man may be validly married to four women at the same time. Upon marriage, the husband is obliged to pay his wife her dowry the amount of which is fixed by agreement or by custom. During the marriage, he is bound to maintain and support his wife provided she is obedient to him, not only in domestic matters but also in her general social behaviour. A wife who rejects her husband's dominium by leaving the family home without just cause forfeits her right to maintenance. Polygamy has been abolished in Turkey (which introduced Swiss family law in 1926) and is restricted or discouraged in Tunisia (the Law of Personal Status of 1957 says: 'Polygamy is prohibited'), and other states. In Burma, the Buddhist rules allow a man to have several wives if he can support them. In Malaysia, a Muslim can marry a second wife with the permission of the first. In order to prevent men from marrying second wives in secret, the Islamic Family Law passed by the Malaysian parliament stipulates that a man must obtain written permission from a religious court judge before taking a second wife. A special law prohibits bigamy to non-Muslims and attempts to secure the decent treatment of women in the polygamous marriages of Buddhists. In Thailand, polygamy is prohibited but the institution of 'minor wives' is socially tolerated. A man can keep one or more concubines or register marriage in another district. The children of minor wives are legally illegitimate but are socially regarded as children of their father.

The Indonesian Marriage Law of 1947 stipulates that a man needs the approval of his first wife before he can take another. In an apparent attempt to check the misuse of Muslim law, the Indonesian government issued a regulation requiring all ministers, governors and other high-ranking officials to obtain presidential approval for second marriages. Lower ranking government officials must request permission from their superiors.

In western countries, where monogamy is the obligatory form of marriage and polygamy considered immoral, the legal recognition of polygamous marriages constitutes a difficult problem. Since polygamy offends against the public order, foreigners married to several wives according to Islamic law could not legally maintain their marital life with several wives in a 'monogamous' state. But wives of a polygamous marriage possess the same rights and duties on the basis of their polygamous status and should be treated as having equal rights. Children of polygamous marriages are all legitimate children and all wives (if they meet the other qualifications) have a right to survivors' benefits and other social security payments. All wives and children must also be recognised for the purpose of income tax allowances.

Abduction

An impediment special to Canon Law is abduction. If a woman is kidnapped or detained against her will for the purpose of marriage, the marriage is invalid as long as she remains in the power of her abductor.

For centuries, Kirghiz men have procured their wives by abducting the girl of their choice and the practice still seems widespread. Women are seized in the street and taken to the home of the would-be groom's parents where they are held prisoner until they agree to marry him. Recently, two men were given prison terms after the girls they kidnapped filed charges against them.

Impotence

Canon Law considers impotency a diriment impediment. It means the inability of a person of either sex to have complete sexual intercourse if it precedes the celebration of marriage. Such an inability may be absolute or relative (with respect to a particular partner). Either party can claim nullity of marriage by reason of impotence. It must be distinguished from sterility which is not an impediment. Since 1977, impotency has been interpreted not to invalidate marriages of men with vasectomies and the revised Canon Law requires only the capacity for marital relations irrespective of fecundity. The impossibility of consummating marriage became the subject of a controversy. A man who became paralysed from the waist down and therefore sexually impotent planned to marry his nurse but the chancellor of the Joliet (Illinois) diocese refused to give a dispensation from the impediment. The man insisted that marriage meant many things besides intercourse but the chancellor stuck to the position that the possibility of procreation pertained to the very nature of marriage (theologians generally assert that impotency is an impediment of the natural law). In a similar case, a man who was paralysed from the chest down in a diving accident was denied a church wedding.

In German law, a marriage in which a partner is impotent can be challenged on the basis of a catch-all provision which says that a person can claim annulment of the marriage if, in contracting marriage, he (or she) was in error concerning the person of the other party or personal properties which, in consideration of the facts and a reasonable evaluation of the essence of marriage, would have kept him (her) from concluding the marriage.

A Liberian student at Johns Hopkins University wanted his marriage to a transsexual mate annulled because his wife 'was in fact a man.' He maintained that he had been unaware that his partner had undergone a sex change operation, that she did not allow sex and that the marriage was never consummated. In a written response, the wife claimed that the marriage had been consummated 'in a variety of sexual ways.'

Eugenic Prohibitions

Different from European countries, American marriage laws contain many provisions making marriage dependent on the health of the parties. In the majority of the states, a medical examination and a blood test are required and some states forbid marriage if one of the partners suffers from a contagious disease. In a report released in February 1983, the President's Commission for the Study of Ethical Problems and Behavioural Research stated that genetic screening for disease and defects could be important for improving health but should not be used for achieving a 'genetically healthy society or similarly vague and politically abusable social ideas.' Mandatory genetic evaluation would be justified particularly in cases when voluntary testing proves inadequate to prevent serious harm to the defenceless. The commission endorsed the principle of confidentiality of genetic information but advocated disclosure without consent if the information could avert serious harm to an offspring or other relative (for example, informing a child that he is likely to be the carrier of a disease such as cystic fibrosis even though not suffering from the defect himself).

The eugenic prohibition of marriage which existed in Nazi Germany forbade marriage between 'genetically healthy and genetically impaired' persons. Eugenicists demanded compulsory marriage counselling so as to prevent any valuable hereditary qualities being vitiated by marriage with the offspring of genetically inferior families. The choice of marriage partners should be influenced in such a way that desirable genetic material would be united in as many families as possible. Independently of Darwin's theory of the 'survival of the fittest,' Friedrich Nietzsche had advocated the idea of natural selection. What Nietzsche suggested with expressions such as 'new values,' 'Herrenmoral' and the creation of the superman was amplified by George Bernhard Shaw who reduced the type of the superman to its political and economic origin and maintained that a strictly socialist order was necessary for the systematic selection of a new class of higher men.

There can be no doubt that the presence of hereditary defects in a family imposes a serious responsibility on partners contemplating marriage. Children suffering from hereditary defects or diseases impose a heavy burden on their parents and on society, and life can become unbearable for these children. No responsible person can disregard the possible consequences of hereditary diseases. Although the prohibition of eugenically undesirable marriages restricts individual freedom, such restrictions can be in the best interest of the individuals concerned as well as the public. For the same reason, the compulsory sterilisation of psychopaths seems appropriate.

Racially Mixed Marriages

In countries with a racially mixed population, marriages between members of different races are sometimes prohibited. In Nazi Germany, marriages between 'Aryans' and 'non-Aryans' (particularly Jews) were declared unlawful and 358 Germans were sentenced to imprisonment for 'racial defilement' (marriage with non-Aryans). South Africa classifies all inhabitants on the basis of the 'Race Classification Law' and the 'Immorality Act' prohibited marriage and all sexual relations between members of different races. In 1982, 190 people were prosecuted for violation of the prohibition of sex relations between whites and non-whites, and in 1983, 126 people were convicted of such offences. In June, 1985, however, a law rescinded the prohibition of interracial marriages and repealed Section 16 of the Immorality Act which made sex between different races a crime. This step, although commendable in itself, did not dismantle apartheid and as regards where mixed couples could live and educate their children there was no indication how the problem would be handled.

In the United States, racially mixed marriages were prohibited in 20 states, but in 1967, the US Supreme Court ruled that laws on miscegenation were unconstitutional. Nevertheless, interracial marriages are relatively few. In the 35 states reporting racial characteristics, the proportion of interracial marriages rose from 0.7 per cent of all marriages in 1968 to 1.9 per cent in 1980. Mixed black and white couples numbered 134,000 in 1982. But opposition to such marriages persists. A justice of the peace in Texas refused to marry interracial couples. 'The Lord never intended people of different races to marry,' he said. Two other Tarrant County judges supported his stand.

In Thailand, a government ordinance passed in 1958 prohibited marriages between Thai and Vietnamese refugees but in 1980, a provincial court overruled the ministerial ordinance and declared such marriages valid. Several gulf states have launched 'Marry an Arab' campaigns in order to keep foreign brides out of the Middle East. The carrot-and-stick policy provides financial incentives for those who marry local girls (loans that become grants when the first child is born) and a tax on marriages with foreigners. The exorbitant dowries demanded by Arab families for their daughters have been an important factor in encouraging young men to seek foreign brides.

Marriages between members of different races may imply particularly high demands on love, fidelity and consideration and their children may face social discrimination. But racial differences constitute no reason for state intervention because it is not in conflict with the meaning and tasks of marriage and poses no threat to public welfare. As in other marriages with seemingly serious handicaps (such as differences in age, education and social background), the responsibility should be left to the partners.

A prohibition of marriage based on class distinctions was contained in the Roman Twelve Tables (ca. 450 BC) which prohibited marriages between patricians and plebeians.

Consent

Of basic importance is the freedom of consent. Marriage must be concluded with full freedom of will and complete consciousness. The external manifestation of the will must conform to the inner intention and the consent must be free from error, deceit, intimidation and coercion. The will to marry is essential to the conclusion of marriage. Both parties must declare their will to contract marriage. Consent presupposes that the contracting parties are aware of the object of their undertaking, namely, to view marriage as the union of a man and a woman for a permanent community of life which includes sexual intercourse. According to Canon Law, consent is invalid if the contracting parties were ignorant of the nature of marriage but with the attainment of puberty, knowledge of the nature of marriage is presumed.

Consent is invalid if one of the partners is in error about the person of the other. The corresponding provision in Japanese law says that a marriage is invalid if, on account of an error in the person or some other reason, the parties did not have the will to marry (Civil Code, Art. 742, No. 1). But an error in regard to position, personality, character or ability does not constitute an error in person. Canon Law considered an error concerning the freedom of the partner as an error affecting the person so that the marriage with a person whom the partner believed to be free but who actually was a slave was invalid. If one or both partners lack the will to contract a true marriage, Canon Law considers the consent null and void. This means that consent is invalid if a permanent and exclusive union is rejected or if the consummation of the marriage is repudiated. Juridically, the inner intention is presumed to conform to the outward manifestation but if one or both partners can prove that their declaration of intention feigned a consent which did not exist internally, the marriage is invalid. According to Japanese law, the exclusion of sexual intercourse and the community of life is incompatible with the will to marry, If the parties absolutely reject cohabitation and coitus, no marriage is concluded but if the parties merely intend to postpone cohabitation, the consent is valid. If the parties intend not to register their marriage, the consent required in conformity with Japanese law is lacking and the marriage is legally invalid. But such a consent is sufficient to contract a marriage according to natural law and establishes a *nai-en* relationship.

Consent to marriage extorted by coercion or grave fear is invalid. According to Japanese law, a person inducted to marriage by fraud or coercion can ask the court for annulment (Civil Code, Art. 747, Par. 1). In German law, too, deceit and coercion constitute grounds for annulment.

The rules that marriage must be concluded in a certain form primarily serves the purpose of documenting the marriage in public, although it also includes the declaration of the parties that they intend to marry. One of the purposes of the principle of the publicity of marriage (prohibition of clandestine marriages) was to prevent a man from obtaining fraudulent control of a woman's property.

Formalities in Japan

Theoretically, the provision of the Japanese Civil Code that marriage becomes effective with the notification of registration (Art. 739) is erroneous and in contradiction with the clause of the constitution that 'Marriage shall be based only on the mutual consent of both sexes' (Art. 24, Par. 1). The state can prescribe that consent be given in a certain form which means that the form can be made a *condition* of the validity of marriage but the form cannot be made the *cause* of the legal validity.

In 1981, notification of marriage in Japan was sent to the registry office within one month after the wedding ceremony in 67.1 per cent of the marriages, within one year in 95.8 per cent, and within four years in 98.9 per cent. In the remaining 1.1 per cent, more than four years elapsed before the marriage was registered.

Usually, a new family register is started when a notification of marriage is filed. If the family carries the name of the husband, the register is drawn up in his name; if the family's name is that of the wife, her name appears first in the register. If the spouse whose name becomes the family name already has a family register of his own, no new register is started and the spouse is entered in this register.

The provision that the validity of the marriage depends on its registration creates great difficulties for a marriage between a Japanese and a foreigner. A foreigner cannot have a family register which exists only for Japanese. The validity of a marriage in Japan depends on the domestic law of the man (Law Governing the Application of Laws, Art. 14). For a marriage between a Japanese man and a foreign woman, the name of the woman is not entered in the rubric 'Wife' of the man's family register but under 'Remarks' — only the name of a Japanese national can be entered under 'Wife.' Officially, therefore, the foreign wife of a Japanese does not carry the name of her husband but her name prior to her marriage. She can assume the name of her husband only if she is naturalised or obtains permission of the court to change her name.

Name of Spouse

If a Japanese woman marries a foreigner, the marriage must be legalised according to the law of the husband's homeland (practically, this means a marriage before a consular official). Religious marriages have no legal effect in Japan. The wife's marriage is entered in the register of her family, but the entry, as noted above, consists of an annotation under 'Remarks' that she has married a certain XY and that XY is a foreigner. Legally, she retains her Japanese name and until 1985, could only petition the court to have her name changed. After her marriage, she can obtain a family register of her own which, however, will also be drawn up in her maiden name. Her children will not be entered in her register unless they obtain Japanese nationality.

In order to make her name the same as that of her husband, a Japanese woman obtained the Family Court's permission to have her name and that of her children in her family register changed to Smith. In the family register, the name is written in *katakana,* which makes it Sumisu. When writing the name in *romaji* (which is necessary for a passport), the officials insisted that the *romaji* writing should be Sumisu ('Smith' can be added in parentheses). The explanation of the Ministry of Justice offers a glimpse into the working of the bureaucratic mind. 'Because this name is now a Japanese name, which it must be because it is entered in a Japanese *koseki,* it must be transcribed phonetically when changed back from *katakana* to *romaji.*'

An amendment to the Family Registration Law enacted together with the 1984 revision of the Nationality Law provides that a Japanese spouse can assume the family name of her (his) foreign spouse if a notification to this effect is sent to the registry office within six months from the marriage so that it is no longer necessary to apply to the family court. Upon the dissolution of the marriage, the Japanese spouse can resume her (his) name prior to the marriage by a notification sent within three months after the dissolution of the marriage. As a rule, the partner who changed her (his) name at the time of the marriage resumes her (his) name prior to the marriage when the marriage is dissolved by divorce but under an amendment to the Civil Code passed in 1976, the divorced partner can retain the name she (he) had during the marriage by notifying the registry office within three months after the divorce (Art. 767, Par. 2). When the three months have elapsed, the partner who resumed her (his) old name can change back to the marriage name by applying to the family court (Family Registration Law, Art. 170).

Nationality of Wife and Children

Japan's first Nationlity Law, enacted in 1899, had adopted the principle of patrilineal *ius sanguinis* and the identity of the nationality of husband and wife as well as that of parents and children. The wife acquired Japanese citizenship by marriage with a Japanese man and a Japanese woman lost Japanese citizenship by marriage with a foreign man. The wife also acquired Japanese citizenship when her husband lost it. A foreign man acquired Japanese nationality when his marriage made him a member of his wife's house (*mukoire nyûfu kon-in*). The children of Japanese parents were Japanese.

Through the Nationality Law of 1950, nationality became more individualistic by making the nationality of husband and wife and of parents and children independent. (This was thought to be in accordance with the postulate of equality in Article 21 of the constitution.) A Japanese woman who acquired foreign nationality by marriage with a foreigner did not lose her Japanese nationality but she was subject to the discriminatory treatment pointed out above. On the other hand, the conditions for the naturalisation were less stringent for foreign women married to Japanese men. Ordinarily, naturalisation required five years of residence in Japan (this provision has remained unchanged in the Nationality Law of 1984) but if the applicant was the wife of a Japanese husband, this requirement could be waived (as could be other conditions such as being 20 years of age, legally competent according to the law of her home country and having sufficient means of subsistence).

The International Covenant on Civil and Political Rights ratified by Japan states that all children have the right to acquire citizenship (Art. 24, Par. 3) and the Convention on the Elimination of All Forms of Discrimination Against Women, signed by Japan, requires the abolition of discrimination in the acquisition of and change in nationality, independent nationality of husband and wife and equality of father and mother with regard to the nationality of their children (Art. 9).

In Japan, the legitimacy of the children depends on the law of the country of which the husband was a citizen at the time of the child's birth (Law Governing the Application of Laws, Art. 17). Since the 1950 Nationality Law was based primarily on patrilineal descent, a child acquired Japanese nationality only in the following cases: 1. If the child's father was a Japanese citizen at the time of the child's birth; 2. If the child's father had been a Japanese national at the time of his death; 3. If the child's father was either unknown or stateless and its mother was a Japanese national; 4. If a child was born in Japan and both its parents were either unknown or stateless.

The inequality of women in the transmission of nationality led to serious inconveniences. Two couples of Japanese mothers and American fathers filed suit to gain Japanese citizenship for their daughters. In one of the families, the daughter had American citizenship, but the daughter of the other couple was stateless because her father, a naturalised American, did not meet certain requirements of American law for giving his children American citizenship. (In order to transfer his nationality, an American must have lived in the United States for more than ten years of which at least five must have been beyond the age of 14, a requirement some of the young servicemen stationed in Okinawa fail to meet.) The Tokyo District Court rejected the requests for the confirmation of Japanese nationality of the girls maintaining that the Nationality Law did not contravene the prohibition of sexual discrimination in the constitution. The choice of the principle of patrilineal descent was justified, the court said, in order to avoid dual nationality, and the law allowed the naturalisation of children born to Japanese mothers and alien fathers. The court ignored that the equality of the sexes is a principle laid down in the constitution while the avoidance of dual nationality was a rule chosen by the legislature. It also was prudently silent on the intricacies of the naturalisation procedure which hardly allow the naturalisation of a newborn baby.

Naturalisation in Japan

While the Ministry of Justice persistently denied that the constitution made a revision of the Nationality Law necessary, it admitted that the treaty against the discrimination of women required a change and on 1 January, 1985, a new Nationality Law went into effect. The law provides that a child is a Japanese national: 1. If, at the time of its birth, its father or its mother is a Japanese national; 2. If the father who died prior to the birth of the child, had been a Japanese national at the time of his death; 3. If both parents are unknown or stateless and the child is born in Japan (Art. 2). A child who is legitimated by the marriage of its father and mother and their recognition can acquire Japanese nationality under certain conditions (Art. 3).

The conditions for naturalisation are relaxed for the alien spouse of a Japanese national but the alien must have had a domicile or must have resided in Japan for three consecutive years and must presently be domiciled in Japan. If the alien has been married to a Japanese spouse for three years, a Japanese domicile of one consecutive year is sufficient (Art. 7). The law has detailed provisions (including loss of nationality and choice of nationality) for avoiding or abrogating dual nationality. But without an emendation of the Immigration Ordinance and the Family Registration Law, the legal discrimination against foreigners in marriage matters will not be removed.

As a temporary measure designed to make it possible for children born to a Japanese woman and a foreign man under the old law to acquire Japanese nationality, Article 5 of the Supplementary Provisions lays down the following regulation: a child born between 1 January, 1965, and 31 December, 1984, can acquire Japanese citizenship by sending a notification to the minister of justice between 1 January 1985, and 31 December, 1987, if the child has never been a Japanese national, and if the child's mother was a Japanese national at the time of its birth, is now a Japanese national, or was a Japanese national at the time of her death.

In April 1983, the Kobe Family Court allowed a former Vietnamese, Tran Dinh Tong, to resume his Vietnamese name instead of the Japanese name he had adopted when he became a naturalised Japanese citizen. The Ministry of Justice has a longstanding requirement that any foreigner applying for naturalisation must choose a Japanese name in *kanji* (Chinese ideographs). There is no legal basis for this rule but the ministry considers it necessary for the integration of the applicant into Japanese society. The Vietnamese adopted the name of his Japanese wife when he acquired Japanese nationality but neither he nor his parents liked the loss of his Vietnamese name. The family court ruled that the practice of requiring a foreigner to adopt a Japanese name restricted the freedom of choice at the time of naturalisation. The ruling enabled Tran Dinh Tong to use his name written in *kana* (syllabic script) on any documents. Tran also became the family name of his wife and daughter. The Ministry of Justice has no intention of changing its practice of requiring the adoption of a Japanese name as a condition for naturalisation.

In October 1985, the Osaka High Court upheld the ruling of a family court rejecting the application of a Japanese born as a Korean to change his Japanese name back to his original Korean name. Ryôji Kawato, a 29-year-old high-school teacher, was 15 years old when his parents applied for Japanese citizenship. In accordance with the prevailing practice, the family had to adopt a Japanese name but Ryôji Kawato has been using his Korean name (Chong) since entering college except in official documents. The family court, however, denied his request to change the name in his family register (to make his Korean name his offical name). Ruling on Kawato's appeal, the presiding judge of the Osaka High Court, Shigeki Hiroki, said that the reasons Kawato gave for wanting to change his name did not come within the meaning of 'unavoidable reasons' (*yamu we e-nai jiyû*, Family Register Law, Art. 107, Par. 1) or 'legitimate reasons' (*seitô na jiyû*, ibid., Par. 2) required by law.

In West Germany, the principle of patrilineal nationality was declared discriminatory and therefore unconstitutional and the law was changed.

Britain's Nationality Act

Under Britain's Nationality Act which went into effect on 1 January, 1983, all citizens of Britain, the Channel Islands and the Isle of Man as well as colonies 'closely connected' with Britain are British citizens with the right to live in Britain and pass this right on to their children. (The inhabitants of the Falkland Islands were included by a special provision.) Two other categories of citizenship which confer no automatic right of residence comprise citizens of dependent territories such as Hong Kong, Bermuda, Belize and some other places, and British overseas citizens, mainly Chinese and other Asian minorities who opted for British citizenship when independence was granted to Britain's East African colonies and Malaysia. The act ended the seven-century-old legal tradition of *ius soli* (right of the soil) by which a child born in Britain was automatically eligible for British citizenship.

The nationality of spouses has become controversial in connection with the restrictions on immigration. Until 1 March, 1980, both men and women legally resident in Britain were allowed to bring their spouses or fiancés into the country. Under new rules, a foreign man was allowed to join his wife in Britain if she was British-born or had British-born parents but the entry of the husbands of naturalised women or those of women residing in Britain was subject to restrictions. Three women, foreign-born but settled in Britain, whose husbands were denied entry, appealed to the European Court of Human Rights which found Britain guilty of sex discrimination and ruled that its immigration policies violated the European Convention on Human Rights. But the court rejected the claim that the immigration laws were racist and infringed on the right to a family life.

In Italy, a law enacted in 1983 includes the right of foreign men who marry Italian women to acquire Italian citizenship. The law replaces a 1912 law which enabled foreign women married to Italian men to become Italian citizens. Naturalisation is possible after six months of residence in Italy or after three years from the date of marriage. Men who have been sentenced to more than two years in prison for non-political crimes are ineligible and the minister of the interior can refuse citizenship for security reasons.

According to Catholic doctrine, the sacrament of marriage is administered by the spouses through the exchange of consent but, under ordinary conditions, the ecclesiastical form, that is to say, the presence of the parish priest or his delegate as an authorised official witness, and two other witnesses, is required for the validity of the marriage.

The impossibility of true consent makes the conclusion of a marriage by a mentally incompetent invalid. Canon Law states that persons who: 1. lack sufficient use of reason; 2. labour under severe incapacity to understand the rights and duties of matrimony; and 3. are unable to assume the essential obligations of marriage on account of causes of a psychic nature are incapable of contracting a marriage (c.i.c., can. 1095). Japanese law contains no express provision on this point but in the United States, feeble-minded are often forbidden to marry.

Prevention of Hasty Marriages

A number of rules aim to prevent hasty or fraudulent marriages. One of them is the regulation that minors can only marry with the permission of their parents. No such rule exists in Canon Law and for Japan, the general principle that minors need the consent of their legal representatives for all legal acts applies (Civil Code, Art. 4, Par. 1). The precept that a certain period of time must intervene between the announcement of marriage and the wedding also intends to ensure the soundness of the marriage. The so-called banns prescribed by Canon Law mainly intend to detect impediments to the marriage. The rigorous examination preceding a Catholic marriage generally prevents unions on impulse. In the United States, most states have a rule prescribing a certain waiting period between the issuance of a marriage licence and the celebration of the marriage (usually from three to five days).

Nature of Marriage Contract

Legally, the consent of man and woman essential for the conclusion of marriage constitutes a contract. Different from other contracts, the contents of this contract are not determined by the parties and it cannot be cancelled by mutual agreement in most countries; cancellation is only possible in countries such as Japan which recognise divorce by mutual agreement.

Contracts related to property have specific legal effects concerning the rights and duties of the parties but the contract of marriage basically creates a legal and social status which implies rights and duties of which some are rather explicit and specific but others are more implied and customary. Ferdinand Tönnies has already pointed out the oddity of treating relations essentially based on status according to the rules of contractual relations.

The law does not and cannot define the roles of husband and wife but definite legal effects arise between husband and wife as well as between the spouses and third parties. The basic mutual duty of spouses is the community of life. Japanese law defines the community of life as a common home and mutual help. Japan's Criminal Code provides punishment for violation of the duty of protection (which implies financial support) only in case of failure to take care of infants or elderly persons, sick or disabled (Art. 217-219) but failure to support one's spouse is not punishable.

Family Name

The new German marriage law formulates the right to refuse the community of life as follows: 'A spouse is not obliged to comply with the demand of the other spouse for the implementation of the community (of life) if the demand appears as a misuse of his right or if the marriage has failed' (BGB, Art. 1353 (2) nF). (The failure of the marriage is the only ground of divorce recognised in the new marriage law.) An expression of the marital community is the wife's acceptance of the husband's name but in Japanese as well as German law, the spouses are free to choose the family name of either spouse. The reasons for giving this choice are different. Japanese law provides this possibility in view of the institution of *muko-iri* (marriage in which the bridegroom becomes a member of the bride's family). In Germany, the provision of the old law which made it obligatory for the wife to assume the husband's name was changed. If the couple chooses the bride's surname as the family name, the groom can place his original family name before the new name. In Japan's feudal period, commoners were not allowed to have a surname. Under the old Civil Code, the name of the 'house' (*ie*) was the equivalent of the western surname. For a woman, it may be economically and socially disadvantageous to change her name and, the same as in the West, women, particularly artists and entertainers, writers and professionals, may continue to use their maiden name.

In the Soviet Union as well as in China, husband and wife carry different names. Sweden recently passed legislation which made it optional for the spouses as well as their children which surname they want to adopt. The new Family Law passed in January 1983 by the Greek parliament allows women to retain their maiden name also after marriage. The law guarantees sexual equality, gives women an equal voice in family matters and abolished dowry as a compulsory legal requirement for marriage. The government formed a Council of Equality, a committee charged with promoting women's rights in Greece.

In 1983, the Lower House of the Swiss Federal Parliament revised the marriage laws to give greater equality to women. The family name remains that of the man but the wife can keep her own name if she makes a formal application before marriage. She has the right to choose the conjugal home together with her husband and the house lease can only be cancelled jointly. Both spouses have the right to know the exact income and debts of their partner, the exceptions being lawyers, public notaries, doctors and clergymen.

In December 1980, the California Supreme Court decided in a custody dispute that 'the sole consideration when parents contest a surname should be the child's best interest.' In explaining the grounds of the decision, the court said: 'Nothing in the statutes or constitutions of the United States or California dictates that a child bear the father's surname. Nor, when the parents disagree, is there any command other than in common law that the father's name be preferred.'

Joint Liability

As a community of life, marriage implies a common household and the right of a wife to make purchases and contracts for daily necessities for which the spouses are jointly liable. The present German law extends the right to the husband while Japanese law avoids making one party more responsible than the other. 'The spouses must shoulder the expenses arising from the marriage by taking into account their property, income and all other conditions' (Civil Code, Art. 750). Usually, the spouses are jointly liable to third parties for daily necessities: 'In case one of the spouses has performed a legal act with a third party concerning daily household matters, the other spouse is jointly responsible for the liabilities arising therefrom. However, this does not apply in case the intention not to assume responsibility has been intimated beforehand' (Art. 761).

The new German law stresses the equality of the spouses in deciding the affairs of the family. The rule of the old law that the husband could decide all matters related to the common life has been abolished, in particular the provision that the husband determined the domicile and residence of the family. Both spouses have the right and duty to take care of the common household and both have the right to pursue a professional career. If one of the spouses manages the household, he does so at his own responsibility. In the choice of an outside career, due regard is to be given to the concerns of the other spouse and the family. The law does not attempt to formulate a model for the assignment of the family functions. In the exercise of the parental rights, the former predominance of the father was abolished.

Property Rights of Spouses

Detailed legal norms regulate property and inheritance. Some legal effects of marriage bind the partners regardless of their will but many matters can be settled by the free decisions of the partners. According to Japanese law, the legal property system obtains only if the parties do not stipulate a different arrangement prior to marriage, but against third parties, an agreement between the spouses is only effective if it is registered prior to the registration of the marriage. The basic tendency in modern law is to liberate woman from the legal disadvantages which formerly attached to her position and to secure to her the same rights as man. Under the old legal system, the husband acquired control of the property of the wife; in return, the husband had the duty of supporting the wife 'in conformity with her station.' Modern law is founded on the principle that husband and wife are bound to mutual support and are entitled to a common standard of living. With the decreasing importance of real property and the growing monetisation of the economy as well as the increasing economic independence of women, the basic views on marital property relations have been changing.

In marital property law and in the law of inheritance, the heterogeneity of the legal systems and the reality of life constitutes a difficult problem. The law considers the legal relations between family members as relations between individuals, and the claims against or on the part of third parties are also treated as claims between individuals. The wage claim against an employer relates to the family only in secondary aspects such as family allowances, and has nothing to do with the fact that the existence of a family depends on this claim. The home in which the family lives is legally without relation to the family as such. If the family owns the home, it is legally the property of the husband or the wife or of both as individuals; if it is rented, the lessee is usually the husband. In West Germany, it has become customary for both spouses to sign the lease for the family's home. Children, however, are usually not mentioned even if they are of age, but they are covered by the protective clauses of the contract. If the lessee dies, his spouse or other family members living in the same household have the right to replace the deceased as lessees (BGB, Art. 569 a & b).

The ownership of the car is also in the name of an individual for whose position it is immaterial that he or she is husband or wife or father or mother. Life insurance, fire insurance and similar contracts create purely individual liabilities and claims.

The old law of inheritance was often formed with relation to the family and real property, in particular, was treated as the property of the family or house. In modern law, however, the rights of the family members are generally regulated as individual rights without reference to the family as a unit. In Japan, the revision of the inheritance law in 1947 abolished the institution of family estate and inheritance as head of the family (*katoku sozoku*). In Germany, the system of sole heir existed for agricultural property. Under this system, the agricultural part of the inheritance was exempted from the partition provided for in the general law of inheritance and passed intact to a single individual (usually the oldest son but sometimes the youngest). In many countries, the extent to which the tax laws recognise the family as a household and particularly as a unit of consumption is insufficient. Sometimes, taxation is heavier for married couples if both spouses have independent incomes than for couples living together without formal marriage or couples who are legally divorced but continue to maintain a common household.

Problems of Economic Security

Unsolved problems are how to ensure the support of a family after the demise of the husband, the support of a single woman of advanced age or of a woman divorced after a long marriage. One of the major difficulties which have thwarted attempts to find a solution arises from the fact that a one-person household is relatively more expensive than a household made up of several persons. The costs which correspond to the fixed costs or overhead of a business enterprise (above all housing costs) are not proportional to the number of the family members. After the death of the husband or father, the family cannot manage with half of the former income, and a single woman basically needs the same income as a single man. The solution to give a wife an independent claim to an old-age pension which has often been proposed would necessitate an enormous increase in social security contributions. The double insurance would impose a great burden on the family income whereas the necessity of such a burden is only hypothetical. Just as the income of the breadwinner should be sufficient to maintain the family, his old-age pension should be sufficient to meet the needs of the household after his retirement. The statistical probability of the death of the household head is irrelevant to the actual situation. It makes no difference whether the husband or the wife supports the family. If both are working, the wife can establish an independent social security claim but the benefits she may be entitled to may be insufficient while the contributions greatly burden the family finances. In such a case the spouses should be able to choose old-age insurance for each partner or a pension for the family and the surviving spouse based on the family's total income or a certain part.

In West Germany, a new regulation (effective 1 January, 1986) ensures that the surviving spouse, husband or wife, receives the old-age pension based on his or her own work and 60 per cent of the pension of the deceased spouse. The latter part is subject to certain deductions.

A basic difficulty lies in the fact that today's social security systems (health, unemployment and old age) are run by the state and cannot be adjusted to individual requirements. On principle, the economic system should enable everybody to find an occupation in which he can gain what is necessary for the support of himself and his family and also make it possible to provide for sickness, unemployment, disability and old age. Even if insurance against such eventualities is made compulsory, it could be implemented by private insurance companies with which each insured could make a contract adapted to his needs.

When a wife is divorced after many years of marriage, special provision should be made at the time of the divorce. If the man remarries, it would be unjust if his new wife were to gain all the advantages of the man's life-long work while his former wife was left unprovided. The insurance paid by the husband would probably not be enough to finance two households. Modern law attempts to get away from the principle of guilt in divorce proceedings but the actual reasons for the divorce can hardly be avoided when it comes to settling the property arrangements and regulating the rights and duties of both parties. In most cases, it is not only more advantageous but even necessary for the divorced wife to secure a settlement that is independent of continuous payments.

8

Sexual Awakening

IN MAN, MATURITY MEANS TWO THINGS, first, that he is an 'adult' in his physical and psychic development and, secondly, that he is able to assume his rights and duties as a full member of society. The initiation rites observed by many peoples display the double aspect of the ending of childhood and admission to the tribal community. Initiation belongs to the rites of passage, the ceremonies of social transformation or life-cycle observations. It is not necessarily linked to sexual maturity and has a more comprehensive social and cultural significance. For the initiation, the two sexes are strictly separated and often the young men and women live outside the village 'in the bush.' The initiation rites may include submission to tests and endurance of pain. In many groups, circumcision is one of the ceremonies but it is also administered as a special rite. Instructions on clothing, language, morality and religion and initiation into the tribal traditions and secrets form an important part of the observances which may also include abstinence of certain foods or eating of others (which may contain, for example, hallucinogenic herbs). The initiation prepares for the formation of a family and an independent household although there is no linkage between initiation and marriage.

Companionship Implied in Sexuality

Marriage and family mean a life in common based on the difference in sex. Negatively, this requires overcoming the separateness given with individuality and sexual difference; positively, it demands the formation of a community embracing the entire life and particularly the sphere of man's most intimate relations. In the biblical account of the creation of woman (Gen 2,18-25), the role of woman is not characterised as a sexual being but as a partner because, as the Bible says, 'it is not good for man to be alone' (v. 18), to exist as a single, isolated being. The Hebrew text uses the word *adam* (human being), not the word for male (*'isch*) which appears first after the creation of the woman (v. 23). Woman is man's help like unto himself (v. 18), a role that the beasts could not fulfil (v. 20). And when Adam excuses himself after the fall, he speaks of the 'woman whom Thou gavest me to be my companion' (Gen 3, 12). In the biblical narration, therefore, the help created by God for man is neither help for the procreation of offspring nor for his activities but help to relieve man's loneliness.

R. David Freedman, a biblical scholar at the University of California at Davis, contends that the characterisation of woman in Gen 2,18 has not been satisfactorily expresssed in existing translations. The Revised Standard Version reads: 'It is not good that the man should be alone — I will make him a helper fit for him.' The two key Hebrew words are *ezer kenegdo*. They have been translated as 'fitting helper,' 'helpmate,' 'an aide fit for him.' Freedman thinks that the words mean 'power equal' and that the verse intends to say that Eve was equal in power to Adam. Woman was not meant to be merely man's helper. She was to be instead his partner, he says.

Plato relates the myth of the human pair rent into two halves but reunited by love as man and wife, and in his essay *Beyond the Principle of Pleasure,* Sigmund Freud develops the hypothesis that the drive for reunion must be behind all sexuality. Ludwig Feuerbach expressed the same thought when he wrote that only the union of man and wife make 'the man;' a single individual is not yet the 'true man.'

Ordinarily, marriage is the outcome of a process that creates a link between two persons specifically different from man's general socialness. In the attachment of man and woman leading to matrimony, three stages can be distinguished. Naturally, not everybody passes through these stages as a temporal sequence and they do not describe the only approach to marriage; nevertheless, the three stages of general sexual attraction, personal sexual attraction, and bodily sexual attraction represent an acceptable generalisation of the awakening of heterosexual attachment.

The time between childhood and puberty constitutes a period in which boys and girls become conscious of their own sexuality but remain indifferent or even become antagonistic to the opposite sex. This does not mean that they segregate or avoid all contact with the other sex but that they prefer the company of members of their own sex, particularly for play and recreation. This tendency corresponds to the basic trend of corporal and psychological growth in this period which aims at shaping the sexual peculiarities of each sex. The most enduring friendships between individuals of the same sex are formed during this time and youth gangs recruit new members from boys and girls in this age class. The main significance of this period, therefore, lies in the stronger accentuation of the psychic differences between the sexes.

Puberty as Preparation for Marriage

With the approach to puberty, the attitudes and conduct of adolescents begin to change. Although they are not yet at ease with their own sexuality and the impulse to self-satisfaction predominates in their sexual experience, interest in the other sex begins to stir. This interest mainly takes the form of curiosity related to the body of the other sex, particularly to the sex organs and their function, intercourse and pro-creation. Different from the mere desire of knowledge and information, this inquisitiveness involves an allurement stretching to fascination with the other sex. Adolescents become attentive and receptive to male or female characteristics. The young man begins to admire the typically feminine, woman's gracefulness, litheness, delicacy, tenderness and capacity of empathy; the girl is attracted by man's strength, vigour, self-assurance, calmness and imperturbability. Adolescents are in love not with a definite person but with the opposite sex in general. In their imagination, they portray the partner with whom they would like to live together. The company of persons of the opposite sex is experi-enced as pleasant and desirable but it is not confined to a particular person.

Love in Mother-Child Relationship

The concretisation of the interest in the opposite sex on a definite person constitutes the second phase in the evolution of sexual attraction and results in a state commonly called love. What is love? Psychol-ogists, philosophers, sociologists and theologians have tried to define love, and poets, novelists and dramatists have devoted the best of their talents to exalt or vilify love. Although nobody has come up with a satisfactory definition, the ability to love undoubtedly constitutes one of man's most fundamental powers.

The first emergence of sentiments of love is instinctively involved in the necessities of life of the infant. The baby needs help because it would perish without it, but it can do nothing to secure this help. In its total helplessness, the infant can only manifest its distress, but its first smile woos its mother. It lifts its arms and shrieks with pleasure when its mother happens into its field of vision. This elementary communica-tion forms the indispensable and irreplaceable premise of the later differentiations of love. Biological, instinctive elements predominate in this first intimacy of what is often called a symbiotic relationship in which the need of the infant has been anticipated by the biological preparedness of the mother who is able to provide suitable nourish-ment. The physical disposition, however, is insufficient without the mother's willingness and psychological affirmation of her task. When, in response to the baby's crying, the mother feeds the child and cares for it, she already exercises a psychological influence on the child. Thanks to the mother's solicitude, feelings of belonging and security develop which become the foundation for the child's integration into the family and society.

The reciprocal, almost instinctive biological relations between mother and child which provide the experience of human nearness are not fully replaceable. If an infant awakes from its afternoon nap and finds itself transposed from the world of dreams into a different environment, it starts crying. Adults do not discover any reason for the crying but their soothing words and quieting noises are to no avail; on the contrary, the greater the efforts at pacification, the lustier the tearful wailing. The mother must take the baby into her arms — nobody else. She must hold him very close to her body, hugging him so that he is entirely sheltered in a tight embrace. And she must gently rock him and reassure him by softly singing or humming. The baby's grief gradually dissolves, the sobbing is no longer abysmal. There are short outbursts of renewed crying but soon contentment floats up, first hesitatingly but then more and more cheerfully, and a smile reveals his pleasure of feeling secure.

Children who grow up without the reassuring intimacy of a loving mother are disadvantaged. Another person may provide a substitute for the mother and sometimes this may be necessary. Grandmother, sister, father, other relatives or hired help may have to take the place of the mother, but no impersonal collectivistic system can become the loving object of reference the baby needs.

Analysis of Love

The love between mother and child is only one form of love of which man is capable: love between parents and children, between man and woman, between brothers and sisters, between friends. Something of the first emergence of love between mother and child is contained in all forms of love. On the one hand, quest, longing, coveting to the point of raging passion, while on the other, care, giving, devotion up to heroic self-sacrifice. Man needs somebody to whom he can relate constantly and confidently, to whom he is bound by a mutual personal engagement. Change and separation occur only in emergencies, when the mutual affection cools or the mutual trust is betrayed.

An act of love, Saint Thomas Aquinas explains, always tends toward two things: to the good that one wills and to the person for whom one wills it, since to love a person is to will good for that person. Western thinking on love was always somehow inspired by the idea that 'love is a uniting and binding force' (Pseudo-Dionysius). To quote Saint Thomas: 'For just as when a thing is understood by anyone, there results in the one who understands a conception of the thing understood, which conception we call a word, so when anyone loves something, a certain impression results, so to speak, of the thing loved in the affection of the lover by reason of which the object loved is said to be in the lover, just as the thing understood is in the one who understands' (S. theol., I, q.37, a.1). There is, of course, no real identity; nevertheless, the thing loved is in the lover.

The words related to love in various languages reveal love's many facets. The Greeks used three words: *eros, philia,* and *agape* (there were corresponding verbs only for the last two). Although known as the god of love, Eros originally was a cosmogonic deity which echoes in Aristotle's description of eros as the power that maintains the order and movement of the cosmos and thus keeps the universe together. Plato's eulogy in his *Symposion* has been most influential in shaping the notion of eros as the irresistible yearning striving from poverty to riches, from penury to affluence, from ephemeral to eternal existence. Eros comprises sensual, sexual as well as spiritual, aesthetic love and exalts man's indelible desire for union.

The second word, *philia,* means friendship which is more than sympathy and proves itself in tender care and affectionate understanding. It points to the spirit of brotherhood in which the Quakers gave the name Philadelphia to their city. But *philia* also extends to things and activities undertaken with unselfish interest (philosophy, philanthropy). *Agape* became a key word in the New Testament, used for God's love of man and man's love of God and his neighbour, and *agape* was the meal in which the faithful gathered to commemorate the Lord's supper.

The Latin words *amor* and *caritas* survive in numerous derivations in Italic languages while there are fewer words stemming from *dilectio*. The words derived from *amor* cover almost the entire spectrum of the meanings in which love is used. Different from the intense personal and emotional affection called love, charity connotes the attitude of benevolence and generosity, the wide all-embracing fellow-feeling that takes in the whole of humanity as one's brothers. But *carus,* the adjective, also means 'dear' as in dear friend (similarly, the English 'cherish' and the French *cher* and *cherir*), and the Jesuits use the superlative, *carissimus,* for their novices.

The medieval theologians distinguished between *amor concupiscentiae* (love of concupiscence) and *amor benevolentiae* (love of benevolence). The goal of all desires and the object of love is the good, and whatever is good is of value. The love of concupiscence wants the object of love because it is good for himself; he craves for the good in the beloved in order to make it his own. The love of benevolence loves the object of love for itself; the lover loves because the beloved is worthy of love in himself and without regard to the good accruing to the lover. Strictly speaking, Saint Thomas says, the love of concupiscence cannot be called love because love means to wish good to somebody else, but in the love of concupiscence, man seeks himself.

However, one of the fundamental conditions of human willing and loving is that man can only will and love what in some way is good for him, and in this sense, there is no selfless love. The saying 'Love is an irresistible desire to be irresistibly desired' points to this connection. Love fulfils the yearning of being loved, and love is impossible without faith, trust and confidence in the sincerity and constancy of love.

To the so-called modern man, the word love has lost all value. 'When the children learn to say it, it is already ridiculous' (Bernanos). Sartre asserted that love is doomed to permanent frustration. The need to know others like oneself is matched by its impossibility. Though one needs other people, they can never be other than 'other' people — their subjectivity, their freedom is inaccessible. Man's own existence is absurd but that of other people is hell.

Sexual Attraction

It is true that all human love involves something of a gamble; love can be rejected, misunderstood, misused, or betrayed. Nevertheless, love is man's most precious and most noble endowment without which he cannot attain true maturity and fulfilment. Love brings an expansion of the human ego, it opens new horizons and reveals new aspects of life. The world looks different to a lover. Man's capacity to open his inmost soul to another human being and to give himself from the bottom of his heart is the core of love. Only the generosity of love can overcome man's egoistic narrowness. For the personalness of love, the otherness of the other must be acknowledged as essential to one's own happiness.

In its fullness, love, in the sense of *eros,* implies sensuality as well as spirituality. Love, therefore, is a truly human experience of which, as the medieval philosophers said, 'neither the angels nor the beasts are capable. ' Although containing the sensual desire, *eros* still loves the beloved for the sake of the beloved.

Mystics speak of a purely spiritual love which touches only the soul although mystical experiences also involve the inner senses, but this kind of love which does not unite human beings is beyond the ken of human understanding. The so-called Platonic love is supposedly unrelated to sexuality and remains in the sphere of the spiritual. It is based on the attractiveness of persons as spiritual beings, common intellectual interests and goals, psychic harmony and understanding of the ideals, concerns, fears and disappointments of the partner. Platonic love does not long for union, does not agonise under separation and does not demand exclusiveness of possession. Envy, jealousy and the fear that somebody else could covet the beloved are characteristic of the personal sexual attraction. In this attraction, everything that made the other sex desirable and wonderful is condensed in this one person. This fixation on a single person distinguishes love from pubescent flirtations and infatuations. Why one loves is not susceptible to a rational explanation and such an explanation is entirely irrelevant. As Schopenhauer remarked, human relations are a matter of emotion rather than intellect. No love story can serve as a paradigmatic demonstration of the philosophical or theological concept of love.

Love can be the outcome of a long friendship but it can also flash up in the sudden experience of 'love at first sight.' The desire to be one with the beloved is overwhelming and the thought of separation is unbearable. The lover always carries a token of the beloved with him; a photo is most common but often a lock or some other hair is added. Men sometimes want a pair of their sweetheart's panties which they may use for sexual stimulation.

In today's society, the telephone has become an indispensable means of confabulation between lovers and telephone companies as well as parents of teenagers confirm that conversations exceeding an hour are by no means exceptional. Love yearns for expression; the verbal protestation of love soon becomes insufficient and the urge to escalate tender caresses is often hard to resist. Personal sexual love naturally tends to the third stage, corporal sexual attraction. In its structure and evolution, sexual attraction prepares for the nearness which finds its fulfilment in the mutual surrender in marriage.

Sexual attraction is by no means a phenomenon peculiar to a certain period of human development or necessarily related to marriage. Many men find it easier to communicate with women than with men, and some women make a greater effort to show themselves from their best side when they deal with men rather than with women.

People napping is a common sight on Japanese commuter trains and nappers often lean against the person sitting next to them. Dozing men seem to follow a definite pattern in leaning against another person. If they are sitting between a man and a woman, they will invariably lean against the woman. If they are sitting between two women, they will always lean against the younger of the two or the one who is prettier. Women show no such preferences. When they sit between a man and a woman, they may lean against either one, and whether the man next to her is handsome makes no difference.

Courtship

Personal sexual attraction is not always of the same intensity. It may happen that of two persons who meet, one is ready for marriage and the other is not. They may go together, enjoy each other a great deal and become enamoured of each other, but their goals are different. The young man only wants a good time and has not the slightest intention of getting married whereas the girl has a more serious purpose. On the basis of this difference, a distinction has been made between dating and courtship. The aim of dating is enjoyment, the meaning of true courtship is marriage. The problem is particularly serious on college campuses. Many young men feel that they must delay all thoughts of marriage until they have established themselves in their lifework, but the girls in whom they are interested are little inclined to wait for the realisation of what may turn out to be an impossible dream.

Dating can go on with various partners and is not necessarily on a one-to-one basis; two boys may date two girls. Even when a boy and a girl 'go steady,' it does not exclude other dates. One of the many aspects of dating is waiting for one's date. Women have the reputation of keeping men waiting but in Tokyo, at least, it is often the other way around. A recent survey found that 25 per cent of the girls were resigned to wait up to two hours for their date.

Here is an incident illustrating Japan's teenage sex scene reported by a columnist in the weekly *Sunday Mainichi* which he had been told by a professor at Kyoritsu Women's College. A high school student asked for advice on a personal problem. She has a boyfriend who had been her classmate at junior high school and who is handsome, affectionate and terrific in bed. She boasted about him to a friend who has no boyfriend and thereupon wanted to 'borrow' him. She loaned him to her but the boy became reluctant to spend time with her. She seemed to be hard to satisfy. She wanted to know how she could persuade him to sleep with her again. 'I don't want to ruin my friendship with her,' she said, and added hesitatingly 'and I have already taken money from her for loaning him out.'

The personal sexual attraction is subject to many ups and downs. Partners approach each other not always with full sincerity and unconditional candour. It has been said 'Courtship is a period when the man doesn't mean all he says and the girl doesn't say all she means.' The possibility that the relationship is terminated by one of the partners — sometimes suddenly and without apparent reason — always looms in the background.

The traditional image of manliness may be an obstacle to closer relations. A man is not supposed to show his feelings; he should not weep, at least not in public, and he is expected to be independent and self-reliant. So he is not supposed to feel that he needs a woman.

Conduct during courtship is strongly influenced by social and moral norms for pre-marital relations. Not all societies recognise or permit kissing as an expression of affection. Pre-marital sexual relations are allowed in some societies, and in the western world, the traditional moral barriers against pre-marital sex are frequently disregarded. If the lovers refrain from intercourse, they may indulge in necking and petting. Fondling and kissing of the breasts and mutual titillation of the genitals are widely practised.

In adolescence, young people move out of the family and into different groups, usually peer groups. The value system implanted in the family may be altered or supplanted by the practices of the new environment. These changes may greatly affect sexual behaviour. New opportunities of getting acquainted with persons of the opposite sex present themselves, especially in the context of peer groups. More often than not, the sexual behaviour prevalent in such groups does not square with the notions held by their elders, so that the ideas of what is right or wrong in matters of sex become rather confused.

One of the occasions where the meeting with the other sex frequently has sexual connotations is dancing. Many forms of dancing are presentations of courtship. Group dancing, the same as singing in unison or marching in formation, creates a feeling of harmony and togetherness. Common rhythmic movement can become a deep emotional experience and generate a community of affection and expression. 'What we behold as movement in this environment and thereby sense in its inmost significance, we represent by movement — an alien soul with which we unite ourselves' (Oswald Spengler).

In some of the dances popular with young people at the beginning of the nineteen eighties, two partners face each other and use the body language of dance to communicate mutual attraction, but they may also use each other to show off their individualistic dance style. The action may be centered on the abdomen or hips, or may stress clever footwork or body gyrations, but it is always sexy. Some time ago, partner dancing vanished in disco dancing: 'There are rows and rows of equidistantedly-spaced young Japanese all dancing exactly the same dance, although the complicated pattern of step and hand gestures changes from song to song' (Christopher Mathison). They stare intently into the full-length mirrors surrounding the dance floor, and although their collective body language is not explicitly sexual, it is eminently sensual in an intense simultaneously egocentric and ego-dissolving rhythm.

Instinctive Attraction and Personal Commitment

Sexual attraction naturally contains much of the instinctive and therefore involves the danger that the specifically human element in the personal approach does not keep step with the instinctive allurement. For the stability of the marriage, esteem of the partner as a personal human being is irreplaceable. Truly human love requires mutual appreciation, respect, confidence and reverence. To modern ears, the old hyperbole that the lover adores his beloved sounds fatuous, but the gallant devotion and overpowering enchantment palpable in this expression suggests the nobleness of spirit which must accompany the ardour of the physical desire. Instinct only gives fitful impulses, and the instinctive attraction to one person does not necessarily exclude sexual excitement by others. Only if the mutual convergence of man and woman also embraces heart, soul and spirit can their union gain permanency. Rational calculation is not the strongest bond joining prospective marriage partners; they need an emotional link assuring the credibility of their relationship and the security of mutual confidence.

It is possible to distinguish a sequence of steps in the development of sexual attraction: acquaintance, friendship, endearment, love, attachment, engagement, wedding. Although love at first sight is not impossible, the personal relationship finally leading to marriage usually is formed by an accumulative or intensifying process. The innumerable personal differences cannot be arranged in a systematic classification, but there are some characteristic differences in the attitudes of the two sexes.

Naturally, it would be preposterous to conclude from what is described as the typical conduct of the two sexes to the behaviour of individuals in particular cases, but these generalisations have a certain validity. The man is more aggressive and looks out for a partner who conforms to his inclinations. The woman waits for a man who meets her wishes and expectations. But since the Second World War, women more often take the initiative and 'hook' a man whom they find desirable. Moreover, a woman is not only emotionally more involved but is also led by her emotions. A man whose infatuation with a woman has cooled off may nevertheless continue the relationship because he feels pity for the woman or considers it his duty to marry her. The thought or expectation of marriage may also be stronger on the part of the woman. While the man may sometimes think of marriage as a distant eventuality, the woman regards marriage as the natural fulfilment of the relationship.

9

Sexual Maturity

Sexuality and Human Development

THAT INDIVIDUALS ARE DIFFERENT is beyond dispute and it is obvious that these differences concern not only outward appearances and behaviour but also character, temperament, intelligence and other inner qualities and dispositions. Undoubtedly, individual women differ just as individual men, but a more difficult problem is whether there are typical psychic differences between the two sexes just as there are typical bodily differences and whether and how these differences influence human development.

The old philosophers discussed the question whether there were male and female souls, that is to say, whether men and women had different kinds of souls. The Scholastics' answer was that, as spirit, the soul could have no gender but that this did not mean that man's spiritual functions were not influenced by sexuality. Soul and body are united in man, and spiritual as well as bodily functions are activities of the unit 'man.' Man grows in body and soul. Bodily growth means a change that can be observed by our senses and measured by tape and scales but psychic growth is only accessible through our self-consciousness and can be assessed by others only from our actions (which, of course, also include words). Bodily growth is regarded as more or less natural and automatic although environmental factors (food and other necessities, health care, and so on) are certainly of great importance. The influence of the environment, above all education, is essential for the inception, promotion and direction of man's psychic development.

Education, of course, is not confined to school education but, in its widest sense, comprises everything that contributes to the formation of man by cultivating his psychic and physical powers. Only a small part of what enters into education is experienced as education and often man is unaware of the importance of the influences to which he is exposed. Self-formation and educational influences are seldom directed by a clearly defined image of man and a hierarchical order of human values, and it is scarcely feasible to delineate therein the functions of sexuality. Education is the result of a broad and multifarious stream of experiences which comprise everything that can happen to a human being.

A conscious coordination of sexuality with other human values may be possible in a theoretical model and although its importance may be recognised, the integration of sex into human development rarely occurs in the form of a planned and regulated process. The sphere of sexuality is only too often omitted from general education and specialised sex education oscillates between the extremes of brutal openness which destroys the sacredness of sex and concealment or evasion which rather than covering sex with the veil of mystery fences it off as forbidden, dangerous and immoral.

Man's self-consciousness necessarily includes the consciousness of himself as a sexual being and of his development as a man or a woman. The awareness of his own self implies the perception of his existence as a social being. Man knows that he does not exist alone in this world but together with other men and women. Man's introduction to and confrontation with sex should start in the society nearest at hand — the family. One of the basic functions of the family in sex education is the demonstration of the union of life of persons of the opposite sex as man's natural life-style by father and mother.

Sexual Attraction and Personal Maturity

Sexuality means the possibility of and orientation to a life with a heterosexual partner in a union encompassing the entire human being. While the potential to a life based on sexual heterogeneity belongs to man's natural endowment, the realisation of this potentiality is never a necessary natural process (one of the remarkable differences of man from animals). With the exception of pathological cases (where the 'normal' ends and the 'abnormal' starts constitutes a very difficult problem, particularly in the sphere of sexuality, but in order to recognise a difference between normal and abnormal, it is not necessary to establish an exact boundary line and to solve all borderline cases), sexual activities depend on man's free decision, and the common life as man and wife usually involves the personal choice of the partners. Sexual attraction can bring the partners together and provide the impulse for taking up a life in common, but this life is not restricted to sexual relations and embraces the entire human person. This points to a special difficulty in the progression from sexual attraction to marriage. For most people, sex tends to be overshadowed by the humdrum of everyday life, and the compatibility of man and wife is not assured because they are sexually attracted to each other. The significance of sex and sexual pleasure has been grossly overrated by the media and by popular imagination. Sex life is being considered as an integral part of a 'healthy' and 'happy' life, and the implication is that a life without sexual activity is unhealthy as well as unhappy. Sex is thought indispensable and decisive for achieving man's full potential as a member of the human race. Sex certainly can become an obsession and the 'sex craze' can make sexual stimulation and gratification the purpose and meaning of life. A survey published in *Mademoiselle* magazine in a special section under the title 'Too Much Sex, Too Little Love . . . What Ails the US Male' asserted that the average American bachelor has had sex with 16 sex partners but really wants a loving relationship with one woman. Only one out of five men enjoys one-night stands although two-thirds expect to have sex by the third date and 80 per cent by the fifth date. Once he ties the knot, though, a man likes being married.

The common life of husband and wife involves both as persons, as human beings with all their natural capacities and their physical, intellectual and emotional strengths and weaknesses. Far more important than the prospective development of their sex life is the course their growth as personal beings will take.

Man's growth depends on the reciprocal effects of his natural capabilities and environment. Physical environmental factors are not without significance for his development, but the importance of the social environment is incomparably greater. It would be strange if the interaction between spouses would not play a distinctive role among the social factors contributing to the shaping of man's life. The biographies of great (and not so great) men and women reveal how decisive the support or inhibition by spouse or other intimate has been.

Because sexuality is a natural endowment to be developed and called upon by man's integral growth, sex life does not depend on the strength or weakness of the sexual impulse and physiological qualities but on what man makes of his potentialities. A sex change does not mean that man can add new potentialities or qualities to his powers; it is only an attempt to define uncertainties or ambiguities in his potentialities by deliberate choice. Therefore, that man can shape his own destiny also applies to his sex life. Since sex life cannot be dissociated from man's entire life, it must be assigned a position in accordance with the image of man, the value system and the tasks and goals directing man's existence. It is impossible to find a satisfactory explanation of sexual development without an understanding of the meaning of human life and the basic orientation of man's existence. One of the reasons of the futility of so many attempts at sex education is the failure to see sex life in the overall context of man's destiny and to relate sex to a comprehensive view or philosophy of life.

The sexualisation of public life has buried the essential significance of sex under the garbage of hedonistic sex exploitation. Woman has been degraded to an instrument of sexual excitement and the naked female body to the most effective means of attracting attention. The destructive impact of the commercialisation of sex must be overcome by an affirmation of its inherent value. The partnership model of marriage which forms the foundation of marriage and family therapy requires a positive, integral and hierarchical evaluation of sex as its necessary premise. In order to effect the unconditional mutual acceptance of sexuality by man and woman, the necessary but by no means automatic development of the capacity for love must be incorporated into the growth of man's entire personality. The blending of sexual maturation with the maturity as a personal being provides the indispensable precondition for solving the conflicts which may arise in marriage.

Sexuality, therefore, is a fundamental human endowment of eminently personal significance. It not only shapes the individual in his or her existence as man or woman, but also provides a confirmation of his or her self-experience by the love of the partner. Ackowledgement by others forms an integral part of man's social existence. The individual wins such acceptance and recognition also from friends, companions or fellow-workers, but the most intensive and gratifying endorsement comes from the marriage partner: it is good that you exist. The trust and conviction to be unconditionally accepted by the other makes it possible to give oneself unconditionally to the other.

Marriage and the use of sexuality in marriage depend on man's free choice. It is, therefore, also in man's power not to marry and to refrain from the use of sexuality. Man can do without the companionship of a heterosexual partner. An unmarried life does not mean a rejection of sexuality but renunciation of the use of sex. Man does not become asexual in foregoing sexual pleasure. He cannot relinquish his sexuality nor bar its influence on his existence. An unmarried life can demonstrate that sexuality is not just a matter of sexual intercourse and that the spiritual aspects of sexuality are no less significant than the physical capabilities. Man's entire life is founded on the possibilities given with his existence as a man or a woman but also checked by the limitations included in his sexuality.

Celibacy

A special case of unmarried life is celibacy. The term is usually restricted to the state of people who abstain from marriage for religious reasons. Basically, celibacy has a symbolic meaning. It serves to manifest the holy and sacred, the consecration to God and the separation from the profane world. The sublimation of sexual love to the love of God and neighbour exemplified in the lives of many saints shows the enormous possibilities in man's natural endowment. Celibacy is a testimony to the value of virginity, chastity and purity. The unmarried is to be free from the cares that a family involves and free for the service of God.

Abstention from sexual intercourse often forms the main part of ritual purification. In the religions of early and primitive cultures, sexuality is often subject to negative taboos and sexual activity is forbidden before the hunt, war, or religious ceremonies. In some religions, notably Catholicism and Buddhism, celibacy has been institutionalised.

In the classical civilisations of the West, a well-known example of celibacy were the vestal virgins of Rome who had to remain unmarried for at least the thirty years of their service. Other forms of celibacy were the ascetic philosophers and the priests of the mystery religions. Pythagoras established a small community at Croton in southern Italy whose life was characterised by study, vegetarianism and sexual abstinence. The Pythagoreans may have been influenced by the mysteries of Orpheus. The Neo-Pythagorean Appolonius of Tyana as well as the Stoic Epictetus believed that celibacy would be conducive to the calling of a philosopher. Epictetus considered the freedom from family care as a requirement for performing the task of a teacher. As a celibate teacher, the philosopher would make a far greater contribution to the world than that of bringing into being a few more children.

Celibacy was practised by the priests of the Great Mother cults. The Syrian goddess Cybele was served by eunuchs and sexual abstinence was required for the celebration of the mysteries of Isis. In the cult of Mithras, the god of light and truth and then of the sun, celibacy may have been influenced by Zoroastrianism and, as mentioned in Volume I, the Manicheans required continence of the elect. The Gnostics also associated sexuality with matters which they considered as evil, while the followers of Hermeticism, who believed in the occult and astrology as set forth in the writings ascribed to Hermes Trismegistos and sought to be merged with the One through contemplation, esoteric knowledge or theurgy (the art of influencing gods), had an esoteric circle requiring strict continence.

Celibacy played no role in the Judaism of the Old Testament — only the prophet Jeremiah was not married. The Mosaic law required the priests to abstain from sexual intercourse on the day of their service. Vows of continence were recognised (Num 30,3-16), and the loaves of proposition could only be eaten by those who had abstained from intercourse (1 Sam 21,5-6). There were celibate communities among the Essenes who aspired to live 'in the presence of the angels.'

In early Christianity, some Christians gave up marriage in the expectation of the second coming of Christ and occasionally the position was taken that all Christians should renounce marriage. People already married when they became Christians practised continence in marriage — St Paul already counselled that it should only be done by mutual consent and for a definite time (1 Cor 7,5). Others separated from their spouses from the time of baptism, became celibate after being widowed or practised life-long virginity. St Paul commended virginity (1 Cor 7,25-38) but insisted that he, like the other Apostles, had the right to be married if he so desired (1 Cor 9,5) and the view prevailed that marriage was good but that celibacy was better. St Paul stressed that celibacy was a special gift, a charisma (1 Cor 7,7), and the same idea may underlie the words of Jesus in Matthew, 19,11-12.

Nevertheless, there remained a belief that sexual intercourse was defiling and incompatible with holiness. The view that carnal relations, menstruation and birth cause ritual impurity was widely held and the opinion that sexual activity was wrong for those officiating at the altar may have been responsible for the custom that ordained men gave up sexual relations with their wives but there was no uniformity. The regional council of Elvira in Spain (AD 306) decreed that all priests and bishops, married or not, should abstain from sexual relations but the ecumenical council of Nicea (AD 325) refused to issue such a prohibition. The position of the Eastern churches was sanctioned by the council in Trullo in Constantinople in 691. Bishops must be celibate but priests, deacons and subdeacons could continue marriages already contracted at the time of ordination. This led to the custom of choosing bishops from monks.

In the West, a crisis in the practice of clerical celibacy occurred in the tenth and eleventh centuries from the decline of the Carolingian empire and the invasions of the Vikings. The first and second Lateran councils (1123 and 1139) put an end to the legality of clerical marriages by making higher orders an impediment to valid marriage and vice versa. Celibacy had the practical effect of preventing benefices from becoming private property and being transmitted by inheritance. This was of enormous political importance during the Middle Ages in those countries where the bishops also wielded secular power as territorial rulers.

In today's Catholic Church, celibacy is required for priests and bishops in the Latin rite but in the Oriental rites, priests who marry before ordination may continue married life; bishops, however, must be unmarried. This is also the general practice of the Orthodox churches. Celibacy is also required of the men and women belonging to religious orders and congregations. The Second Vatican Council (1962-65) permitted a married diaconate but the movement to make celibacy optional for priests was strongly resisted. The traditional position, reaffirmed by Pope Paul VI, has been retained in the new code of Canon Law (can 1037).

In his book *Pflichtzölibat,* Heinz-Jürgen Vogels argues that the theology of clerical celibacy involves an insoluble antinomy. Scripture (for example Mt 19, 11-12; 1 Cor 7,7 25-26) describes religious celibacy as a special gift of God, a charisma, but the Latin Church, while recognising that it is a 'peculiar gift of God' (c.i.c., can 247, par.1), considers it as a duty which can be imposed by law and observed by everybody called to the priesthood or emitting the vows of religion.

A Gallup poll conducted in 1983 found that 58 per cent of American Catholics were in favour of and 33 per cent against allowing priests to marry. The proportion of women supporting the marriage of priests, 62 per cent, was higher than that of men, 54 per cent, but young men between 18 and 29, and particularly college graduates, approved of married priests.

The churches of the Reformation (such as the Lutheran, Anglican and Reformed) rejected celibacy as a requirement for church office as well as monasticism. But in the Church of England, monastic orders began to reappear about 1845, and after the Second World War, small Protestant monastic groups were founded.

Celibacy has been practised in many forms in the East. As in other peoples, magical powers were· linked with the abstinence from marriage, the 'Brahma way of life,' in the old India. The Hindu priesthood was hereditary but the *sadhus* (holy men) live a life free of possessions and family obligations. Many *sadhus*, male and female, become celibate early in life, others after marriage and widowhood. The *sadhus* have no organisation and may be devotees of Shiva (called *sannyusins*), of Vishna (*bairagis*), or practitioners of yoga (*yogins*). The *sadhu* has left the world in order to seek *moksa* — final liberation. A life of controlled equilibrium or devotional ecstasy is the goal of the spiritual techniques. Certain schools of yoga teach continence so that sexual energy may be redirected towards tappings centres of enlightenment in the body.

Buddhism started as a celibate group dedicated to the attainment of enlightenment and to this day has monks and nuns. Buddhism and Jainism belong to Indian heterodoxy; both were founded not by Brahmins, members of the priestly caste, but by laymen of the warrior and merchant castes as reactions against the ceremonialism and theology of the priests. Buddha rejected the outward signs of asceticism because they could not purify man's personal existence. But in his doctrine of the four noble truths, Buddha called ignorant concupiscence the real cause of human suffering and characterised the desire of liberation from sensual lust as a right wish.

Buddhist customs vary in different countries. In South-East Asia, young men spend only a year as monks. In Tibet, Tantric monks were married and in Japan, Shinran Shônin (1174-1268), the founder of Jôdo Shinshû, the 'true sect of the Pure Land,' rejected the traditional spiritual ideal of Buddhist monasticism and married. Jôdo Shinshû has been called Japan's Buddhist Protestantism because Shinran taught that man cannot be saved by his works and prayers but only by the mercy of Amida. The aim of his reform was to establish Buddhism as a lay religion.

In South Korea, the efforts of Dr Syngman Rhee, first president of the Republic of Korea, to enforce the celibacy of the Buddhist clergy, resulted in a deep split between the married and unmarried priests and monks. Rhee blamed the decline of Korean Buddhism on the marriage of the clergy which had become the general custom during the time of the Japanese occupation but had also been widely practised before the colonial period. The old Buddhist celibacy law was renewed in 1954 but it met with strong resistance. The unmarried monks are organised in the Cho-ge sect which advocates the eradication of corrupt practices and the renewal of Buddhism.

The Jain religion arose in India at about the same time as Buddhism. Its monastic groups practise severe asceticism, and in one of its schools, those fully initiated go about entirely naked. Jain monks are to avoid even looking at women so as not to be led into temptation.

In China, Taoism had a certain form of monasticism and also believers who remained unmarried. Its monasticism and priesthood were later influenced by Buddhism. Japanese Shinto has no monks or celibate priests but unmarried girls serve at Shinto shrines. Originally, the *miko* seem to have been shamanesses who transmitted messages of the gods and also communicated with the dead. In the large shrines, the *miko* performed the sacred dances, *kagura*.

Celibacy was not one of the original practices of Islam. The *Qur'an* disapproved of monasticism as a human invention (Sura 57,27). But in Sufism (Islamic mysticism), celibacy occurred as a matter of personal spiritual advancement or enthusiasm. Even among members of fraternities, such as the dervishes, celibacy was rare but it was found in some Sufi groups in Turkey and Albania. In the Ottoman empire, the Bektashi brotherhood had a celibate clergy.

Africans in general do not accept celibacy; for an African, it is shameful not to have children.

10

Choice of a Marriage Partner

THE DECISION TO MARRY necessarily includes the choice of a partner. In cultures in which the large family constitutes the usual form of social organisation, marriage only adds a new couple to an already existing group. But in today's society, the changes in social relations connected with marriage can take several forms. The most common pattern may be that two individuals who up to the marriage lived in two separate families leave their families and establish a new, independent household of their own. But either the husband or the wife may stay in the family in which he or she lived so far and the partner joins the household (the 'house' in the old order). Further complications may be involved if one or both partners are divorced or widowed and children of the former marriage still live with their parent or if one of the partners is taking care of an aged father or mother. These diversities may have a certain influence on the choice of partner.

Rarely, if ever, are all circumstances that should be taken into account in the choice of a mate actually considered, because, in reality, a man or woman very seldom establishes an ideal of a spouse and then looks for somebody to meet this standard. Adolescents may form an image of the ideal woman or the ideal man in the period of general sexual attraction to the other sex but this ideal may well be largely based on imagination rather than experience, whereas personal sexual attraction rarely involves a conscious and deliberate relation to this ideal.

Extent of Choice

In the course of history, the choice of a marriage partner has frequently been restricted by external factors. Some of the earliest limitations prescribed to choose the mate from inside or outside a certain group (endogamy or exogamy). Today, legal and religious rules limit the choice and social or economic conditions may narrow the circle of prospective partners. Geographical conditions which used to circumscribe the range of possible acquaintances do no longer operate with the same rigour although local proximity still plays an important role in bringing people together. Employment has become a factor in creating opportunities for meeting eligible bachelors or single girls and modern forms of entertainment and recreation facilitate the search for a desirable mate.

The road to marriage may start either from a long-standing acquaintance or from a casual meeting. Acquaintance leads to dating and if the partners resolve to tie the knot, they become engaged. In such a scenario, the consideration of choice of a partner starts from a certain person and asks whether this person meets the requirements for a marriage partner. Despite the tendency of lovers to idealise the beloved, it is very unlikely that the chosen mate conforms to ideal standards. The choice, therefore, falls on a partner who fulfils the conditions desired in an ideal mate 'more or less.' If it is already certain who the prospective partner is, some allowance will be made in the judgement whether he or she posssesses the qualifications considered desirable. The compromise with reality will result in a choice in which the elect may represent the ideal 'less' rather than 'more.' In other words, it seems very likely that the 'objectivity' of the choice will be impaired and that aspects or circumstances which would dissuade from the choice are not or not sufficiently taken into consideration.

Motives

It could be objected that the entire discussion of the choice of a partner is pointless because such a choice is not made by reason but by the heart and, as Pascal said, *le coeur a ses raisons que la raison ne connaît point.* But even if love is blind, man need not entirely abdicate his reason. Passionate love is a bad guide, and if love becomes infatuation, there is a great probability that love is not founded on the true worth of the beloved.

One of the less reliable reasons for choosing a partner is the so-called 'romantic love.' Romantic love is above all an emotional experience which may or may not be identical with 'love at first sight.' In romantic love, the desire to be loved is stronger than the desire to love. It is a throwback to childhood when most children are cherished by doting parents. It is no coincidence that romantic lovers treat each other like infants and use 'baby' as a term of endearment. For romantic love is a regression to the helplessness of a small child who is entitled to be loved and cared for without doing anything in return. The romantic person demands love not as a reward for good deeds but simply because he exists. The romantic is emotionally immature. As long as two persons remain romantically in love, they do not get to know each other very well. The romantic sees his mate as he wants her to be, and any resemblance between this 'ideal' and a real person is purely coincidental. Many young men and women believe that their love will automatically triumph over impossible financial difficulties, sharp differences in social, political or religious attitudes, or constant clashes in temperament. They believe that 'love will conquer all.'

Love at first sight may not be dangerous in itself, but if it leads to 'instant marriage,' it may invite disaster. 'Marry in haste and repent at leisure,' says the proverb. Like other emotions, love cannot stay at the same intensity for ever. The first enthusiasm of courtship cannot last. The fascination with a beautiful body will not make up for the incompatibility of temperament. It is entirely possible that the choice starts from the heart and begins with an emotional inclination and affectionate attraction, but reason should not relinquish its role as a control organ. People do much what they regret later, but there are differences in the rationality or irrationality of human conduct. It is certainly not advisable to do something a 'normal' human being would consider irrational. It is not particularly astonishing in view of man's weakness for all kinds of nonsense that people rely on horoscopes, fortune-telling or clairvoyance in the choice of a partner or the decision to get married. People unsure of themselves are looking for something to provide the certitude they lack. A person must be sure of himself and know his own mind in order to make a good choice.

Marriage Brokerage

Difficult problems arise from commercial marriage brokerage and the quest for a partner by advertising, acquaintances made through blind dates and catalogues with the description and pictures of women available for marriage. There can be no doubt that marriage bureaux can play a positive role and it is not impossible that two people paired by a computer as mutually compatible actually harmonise and become happy with each other. Marriage brokerage has reached international dimensions. Classified ads in American and Canadian newspapers offer to introduce Asian women to American men by mail. Bachelors who consider American women as selfish, competitive and unfeminine are promised 'loving, devoted and faithful ladies' from places like Hong Kong, the Philippines and Malaysia, and Asian women, stirred by the pronouncements of women's liberation, are looking not only for higher incomes and security, but also for consideration and gentleness, traits, they say, that are lacking in men from their own countries. A growing number of Australians have been advertising in Manila newspapers seeking wives, and Germans, Americans, Canadians and Japanese have also procured 'mail order brides' from the Philippines.

After seeing the 1951 American movie *Westward the Women* on New Year's Day in 1985, 140 bachelors of the tiny Pyrenean village of Plan placed an advertisement for women in a newspaper. More than 500 women in Spain and abroad replied to the ad.

Mail-order brides usually come to the United States on fiancée visas. They have three months to marry the man who sponsored them. If no marriage takes place, they are deported. If they marry, only the husband can apply for the wife's permanent residency status, commonly known as the 'green card.' If the husband does not apply for a green card, the wife's stay in the United States is illegal and she may be deported at any time. If the wife files for a divorce within two years from the date of marriage, the case will be investigated by the Department of Immigration and Naturalisation. What men usually want who opt for a mail-order bride is a supportive and undemanding wife, but what some have in mind is a maid who can double as a concubine.

Marriage to an American citizen is the easiest and quickest way for an alien to get into the United States. The number of aliens entering with visas obtained by marrying US citizens rose from 78,000 in 1978 to 112,000 in 1984. In the Caribbean, marriage brokers supply everything from witnesses at bogus marriages to reusable cardboard and paste wedding cakes for the wedding photo. Some women have been victimised unknowingly but others have been paid for being a willing party to a visa fraud.

In West Germany, the procurement of Asian brides has become a flourishing business. There are about 200 Thaifrau agencies and in 1984, as many as 9,000 West German men married foreign brides picked out of mail-order catalogues. For the price of a one-way ticket from Bangkok (about US$850) and a fee that may come to US$3,000 or more, dealers provide a bride plus a 'marriage warranty' — a guarantee of a full refund if the marriage does not materialise.

Actually, many mail-order brides end up as strippers, bar girls or prostitutes, and some of the bridal brokerages are actually a front for prostitution rings. Even if the foreign women get married, they are completely at the mercy of their husbands who hold their passports. The women cannot speak German, they know nobody and must do whatever the husband demands. If the marriage ends in divorce, they have nowhere to go.

There are marriage ads that are unquestionably serious but there have also been many cases in which the marriage offers were only intended to make acquaintances and set up victims for a possible fraud. Such fraudulent schemes are contrived by men as well as women and prosperous men and women in middle age seem to be the most frequent victims.

Some time ago, the eldest sons of four farming families in northern Japan who were unable to find Japanese girls willing to devote their lives to the hard work of a farmer's wife, 'imported' brides from Taiwan. The men went to Taiwan where they met with eight girls who had shown interest in the project; after a preliminary exchange of information and as a result of personal meetings, four marriages were arranged.

An estimated 9,000 young men on Japan's northern island of Hokkaido are seeking marriage partners, and men running dairy farms encounter particularly great difficulties in finding mates who are not afraid of sharing a life of hard work. The local women prefer the more varied life of the cities. The Japan Youth Centre in Tokyo arranged meetings in which young men engaged in discussions with young women interested in rural life. Following the meeting, the participants listed the members of the opposite sex whom they found attractive and those mutually interested went out together on dates.

A Japanese TV station arranged a meeting between 30 young dairy farmers from Hokkaido and 20 girls chosen from 300 applicants from all over Japan. During the summer, the girls were invited to stay at a Hokkaido village and observe the life of the farmers. Two couples have already been married and five more plan to marry in the near future.

A similar situation was reported to exist in Bavaria where every fifth farmer is looking in vain for a mate. Even the owners of economically sound and attractive properties, where the wife would have to work at most four hours a day and no dowry was expected, find it impossible to induce girls to share their lives.

In the Soviet Union where the ratio of unmarried women to unmarried men is almost 2 to 1, the enormous imbalance makes it difficult to find a marriage partner. In order to help unattached men and women to meet prospective spouses, Singles clubs were set up but the experiment failed. The number of marriages resulting from the contacts provided by the clubs was miserably low while men used them to pick up women so that the clubs had become, as the weekly *Sovietskaya Kultura* said, insulting and degrading for women. Married men regularly frequented the clubs when their wives were away.

The Chinese press frequently mounts campaigns on behalf of miners, mortuary workers and others who have trouble finding spouses. Parents discourage their daughters from romances with men they consider beneath their social status and almost everywhere in the world, the marital prospects of people with 'dirty' jobs are unfavourable.

A Chinese man who had been ostracised as a 'rightist' during the Cultural Revolution spent a quarter of a century in vain looking for a wife. Finally, he persuaded the editor of a Beijing weekly magazine to print a marriage advertisement and was deluged with replies from women all over the country. While the magazine received some protests, the experiment led to the formation of lonely hearts clubs and cut rates for marriage ads.

Mixed Marriages

A great many problems are involved in so-called 'mixed' marriages, that is to say, marriages between individuals belonging to different religions or different races. Religious and ethnic factors inspired the proscription of marriage with 'foreign' wives in the Old Testament. Intermarriage with the Philistines and other inhabitants of Canaan brought the danger of idolatry and apostasy from the worship of the God of Israel. Samson, a folk hero of ancient Israel, came to grief through his marriage with Delilah (Judg 16; Samson had already had bad luck in his marriage to a Philistine woman, Judg 14). Solomon was led astray by his unrestrained lust: 'But King Solomon loved many strange women, together with the daughter of Pharao (see 1 Kings 9,16; 2 Chron 8,11), women of the Moabites, Ammonites, Edomites, Zidonites and Hittites; of the nations concerning which the Lord said unto the children of Israel, Ye shall not go in to them, neither shall they come in unto you: for surely they will turn away your heart after their gods: Solomon clave unto them in love. And he had seven hundred wives, princesses, and three hundred concubines: and his wives turned away his heart. For it came to pass, when Solomon was old, that his wives turned away his heart after other gods: . . . For Solomon went after Ashtoreth, the goddess of the Zidonians, and after Milcom, the abomination of the Ammonites. . . . Then did Solomon build an high place for Chemosh, the abomination of Moab, . . . and for Moloch, the abomination of the children of Ammon' (1 Kings 11,-1-7). Ahab, king of Israel, is censured most severely in this regard: '. . . he took to wife Jezebel, the daughter of Ethbaal, king of the Zidonians, and went and served Baal, and worshipped him. And he reared up an altar for Baal in the house of Baal, which he had built in Samaria' (1 Kings 16,31-32). The prohibition of intermarriage was renewed after the Babylonian exile (Neh 10,31; 13,23-28).

In many states in the United States, 'miscegenation' was prohibited and it was also prohibited in South Africa. Although many legal barriers have been removed, it can hardly be said that such marriages have become socially acceptable. The individuals involved in such marriages face the possibility of adverse reaction on the part of relatives and acquaintances, of diminished career expectations and even of ostracism by the community. A very serious problem is the position of children born of mixed marriages. The fate of the children mostly born out of wedlock in the early years of Japan's post-war occupation is a heart-rending tragedy, and even today, 'halfs' may encounter unpleasant experiences, particularly in their younger years. For individuals, the difference in race and cultural background is no insuperable obstacle to mutual understanding and love, but it would be foolish to deny that intermarriage between people of different race and culture involves special risks.

International Marriages

The possibility of socio-cultural alienation in interracial marriages cannot be denied and the danger of conflicts seems particularly great if one of the partners is a Japanese and the other a westerner. If the couple lives in Japan, discord may arise not from the partners but from the relatives who expect a complete assimilation of the foreigner to Japanese tradition.

In 1980, 7,261 Japanese living in Japan were married to foreigners; 4,386 Japanese men had foreign wives and 2,875 Japanese women had foreign husbands.

Here is how men married to women of a different race think about their marriage: 'The majority of international marriages are not calculated but are affairs of the heart which do not recognise frontiers, boundaries, race, creed or prejudice.' 'I didn't marry my wife because I am open-minded and liberal; I married her because I love her and I want to share my life with her.'

In Germany, a considerable number of marriages have been concluded between Germans and Turks. In 1981, 19,427 Turkish men were married to non-Turkish women and 9,680 German men were married to Turkish women.

Most Japanese men adjust more easily to foreign customs when they are outside the constraints of their own culture. When they return home, they consciously or unconsciously conform to the Japanese way of doing things and their treatment of a foreign-born wife whom they married while abroad may undergo a shocking change.

In the eyes of foreign males, Japanese women are more feminine, more devoted, less demanding and more demure. Generally speaking, Japanese girls are of a pragmatic breed who are careful in their choice of a prospective husband. To them, good husbands are ones who can provide financial security as well as social and emotional compatibility. Japanese in general are educated not to be expressive and open about their feelings, and Japanese women consider it ungracious to be frank and assertive. The difference between Japanese and western women appears in two typical gestures. Japanese women seldom stand with arms akimbo, a favourite posture of western women. When they laugh or are pleasantly surprised, Japanese women put their hands to their mouth, a sign of diffidence and bashfulness.

Among the 'Things Japanese' greatly admired by foreigners is the kimono worn by Japanese women. For many elderly women, the kimono is the only dress they wear and they can put it on in less than five minutes without looking in the mirror. A woman not used to wearing a kimono may need half an hour to get dressed. Special schools and courses teach how to wear a kimono. Younger women like to wear the kimono for special occasions, such as New Year, and for weddings and funerals, most women appear in kimono. It is imperative to choose the right design and colour for the season and the occasion, and to give the garment a straight look around the bust and hip, so as to achieve a high neckline, requires skill. There are over a hundred styles of tying the *obi* (sash). When girls are young and unmarried, the kimono has long sleeves; after marriage, the sleeves become shorter.

Modern women feel more feminine when wearing a kimono. Their steps become shorter, there is more poise to their walk and even their talk sounds more polite than usual.

Some foreign women have a rather low opinion of Japanese men because they do not stand up for women, they ask them their age and they do not compliment them on their beauty. Traditionally, the treatment of women by Japanese men has been one of the more crass manifestations of male macho. Some foreign women, however, think that Japanese men are terrific sex partners. Girls who are working become disillusioned when they get to know their male colleagues better. One girl found the single men she worked with dirty and thriftless. 'Each time they get paid, they spend their money on alcohol, *mah-jong* and *pachinko* (slot machines) — their pastimes when they don't have to work overtime.'

Difference of Religion

Prior to the new code of Canon Law, the Catholic Church distinguished between a marriage in which a Catholic married a baptised person belonging to a different Christian denomination (although it was prohibited to contract such a marriage without proper dispensation, the marriage was valid) and a marriage in which a Catholic married a non-baptised person (without proper dispensation, such a marriage is invalid). In the United States, approximately four out of every ten Catholic marriages involve interfaith marriages, a higher rate than that for Protestants and Jews. But mixed Protestant-Catholic marriages are more likely to end in divorce than either Catholic or Protestant same-faith marriages. In Britain, the percentage of Catholics who intended to marry another Catholic dropped from 75 per cent in 1971 to 42 per cent in 1981. The same development took place among Jews of whom 69 per cent married into the faith in 1971 but only 45 per cent in 1981.

A marriage between two people of different religions poses two basic problems, first, the religious beliefs of the partners, secondly, the faith in which the children are to be brought up. These problems may not have the same degree of acuteness in all cases; there may be differences depending on the fervour or lack of fervour in one or both of the partners. But supposing that both are convinced of their religious beliefs and active practitioners of their faith, the first requirement must be that each respects the other's beliefs. Nobody should expect the other to give up his or her convictions or practices for the sake of marriage, either before or after the wedding. If one is drawn to the other's religion and embraces it of his own accord, this is a personal decision which should have nothing to do with their marriage.

In accordance with her claim of being the only true religion, the Catholic Church used to demand that in a marriage of a Catholic with a non-Catholic, the marriage should be solemnised according to Church rules, that the children be brought up Catholics, and that the Catholic party endeavour to convert the non-Catholic. The practice has become less strict but the basic way of thinking remains the same. Nevertheless, tolerance is recognised as a necessary requirement in a pluralistic society and true tolerance implies respect and reverence for any sincere religious convictions which, however, is not the same as approval of religious bigotry. It is, of course, not always easy to decide where genuine devoutness ends and bigotry starts, but the problem of religion demands the utmost honesty between people before and during marriage.

Religious observances may cause some difficulties when husband and wife worship in different churches, but if they understand each other, they can find ways of accommodating these differences. People may agree before marriage how to handle this problem as well as the question which religion or church the children should belong to and be taught. As many other things, religious education depends much on the actual life of the family although the role of the church or the school may be more important for formal religious instruction.

A problem that may arise in mixed marriages is the reaction of parents or relatives. This question used to be of greater importance in rural areas than in the cities, and it is of more serious concern in countries in which religion still forms an integral part of the people's life than in countries where religion is a purely private matter or is being suppressed.

In order to promote marriages between different castes, the government of the Indian state of Haryana promised a gift of 10,000 rupees ($1,000) to every man or woman of the 'untouchables' marrying outside the caste. Although the Indian constitution makes discrimination against untouchables illegal, higher caste Hindus shun marriages with the harijans.

The greater international mobility leads to conflicts between the customs prevailing in the homeland of immigrants and the social order of the country where they reside. Recently, a 15-year-old girl from the Middle East appealed to police in Lackawanna, N.Y., to stop her father from selling her 12-year-old sister into marriage. She herself had been sold by her father to an uncle at a party in August 1981 and she was forced to marry him under Arab custom. Now, her father was thinking of selling her younger sister in a similar arrangement.

Egocentric Choice

The first question when considering marriage is whether to marry or not to marry. This can mean whether one should marry at all, that is, whether there are reasons which make it prudent or necessary to refrain from getting married or whether marriage at the present time or with a certain partner should be avoided. But the question can also mean whether both partners mean the same when they speak of marriage. it is not always sure that both partners are contemplating the same community of life. Even without the intention of fraud, a person may regard the prospective partner merely as an instrument for furthering his own ambitions. A women may want to use the man's fortune for fulfilling her wishes and a man may covet a beautiful woman only as another piece of furniture for adorning his home.

There is always the danger of an egocentric choice: 'I need you, therefore, you must love me!' A person may want a partner who satisfies his or her demand for security, his craving for domination or his need for prestige. The choice of a partner may never be absolutely altruistic but if the motives are too blatantly self-centred, the marriage has little chance of becoming a partnership.

Oswald Spengler pointed out the difference in the choice of a mate between the 'pristine' man of the country and the emancipated man of the big cities. The peasant chooses the mother of his children; the peasant's wife is mother and motherhood is the destiny she aspired to from childhood. In the 'Ibsen marriage,' as Spengler calls it, marriage becomes an 'artistic task' and the essential requirement is mutual understanding. Instead of children, the women have psychic conflicts.

The basic difficulty in the choice of a marriage partner lies in the impossibility to directly perceive the factors on which a happy marriage depends. As an intimate community of life, marriage is based on man's capacity for intimacy, an intimacy in which the ferocity of sexual lust does not smother the tenderness of personal affection and the devotedness of enamoured attachment does not debilitate the vigour of the instinct. This capacity is different in every human being, and if this difference is too drastic, it will be extremely difficult to reach the sensual and psychic union essential to the marital community. In the last analysis, therefore, the considerations of the choice of a partner should probe whether the intimacy of married life can be realised in a form accessible to both partners.

Personality — the Basic Element in Every Choice

Actually, the problem of the choice of a partner can be regarded as a problem of personality, the interface of the personality of the future husband and the personality of the future wife. Every human being has his own style, his inner shape, his character and mental form which is just as unique and special as his bodily appearance. Both are the result of his genetic inheritance and his reaction to outside influences, and an individual's intellectual and emotional configuration may reflect even more than his body the interaction of his own self with the environment. The assumption of some psychoanalysts that a man's reactions are acquired in infancy under the pressure of external conditions minimises man's plasticity. It is impossible to fathom an individual's personality just by keeping company with him or her for a little while and only marriage will show whether the personalities of the partners are congenial — a recognition which should have been the basis of their choice.

External Considerations

External circumstances may have a great impact on marriage and marital relations, but the effects will depend on the reactions of both partners to these circumstances. Relations between the spouses, relations to their children, and relations to relatives and acquaintances require all those attitudes and modes of behaviour known as virtues, justice, prudence, temperance, courage, self-control, gratitude, generosity and unselfishness. The psychic normalcy of both partners constitutes a valuable asset for a happy marriage. The ability to communicate, freedom from prejudice and a critical attitude towards oneself help to smooth relations. Cooperation will be furthered by understanding, sympathy, patience, tolerance and humour.

For young women who are working, the true motive for getting married may be the wish to escape from their families. This may be the case if the mother is constantly nagging, the father is drinking, and the work unpleasant. What working girls expect from marriage is security, and they spend most of their free time looking for a partner who fits their ideas of a desirable mate. He should not beat his wife, he should not drink, he should not become violent, and should work regularly. Sometimes, the expectations derive from the negative example of their own fathers. Girls want to escape the fate of their mothers.

Disappointment in Marriage

The decision to get married may be difficult for a young woman who has built up a career. If she postpones marriage, she may become too old and finally end up by entering into a not quite satisfactory union. If she gives up her job and the marriage proves disappointing, she will have sacrificed her position and her income for an experience she would rather forget.

A striking phenomenon is the increase in crimes committed by

women anxious to win the good graces of their lovers. Women working in banks or other financial institutions embezzled huge sums to
finance the extravagant tastes (particularly gambling) of their
paramours. Women in their early thirties who saw their prospects of
marriage vanish were particularly prone to such behaviour. A man who
promises marriage after divorcing his present wife may not be an
altogether trustworthy suitor.

In many cases, marriage turns out to be quite different from what
a girl expected but a young woman may be bound to her husband 'for
better, for worse' even if the worse is unbearable. She cannot get
divorced because she will be unable to earn a living, especially if she has
a child. She must lead a life which, at best, is pointless and only too
often hell on earth. But many girls from working families see no alternative to marriage. Marriage seems to offer an escape. The limited
choice of work, insecurity of employment, low pay — all these risk
factors can be evaded by marriage.

Health

Health is one of the basic considerations when contemplating marriage.
This question concerns first of all the individual, which means whether,
in view of his or her health, he or she can safely marry or should give
up the idea of getting married. But it is also a relative question, that is,
whether health and bodily strength make marriage or singleness more
advisable. As mentioned above, many countries require a medical
examination and prohibit marriage of persons suffering from
venereal disease. A difficult problem is relative bodily strength. It
would be an exaggeration to say that an athletically-built man should
not marry a slight woman, but when a man who likes sports and
outdoor activities marries a woman who cannot bear physical exertions
or is only interested in sedentary pursuits, married life may create some
difficulties. The reason is not so much that the husband may find a
more congenial partner in his hobbies than that the lack of common
interests in an important area may become a source of distress. It may
happen that qualifications such as behaviour, manners, speech and
appearance are very important for fitting into the social environment of
each of the partners as well as for their professional careers. If such
factors are disregarded and the choice is made only on the basis of
sexual attraction, the result may be devastating.

Maturity

Besides the legal age necessary for marriage, there can be a question
whether a person is too young or too old for marriage or whether the
relative age of the partners is suitable. Whether he or she is too young

for marriage is less a question of biological age than a question of maturity. Maturity involves a series of conditions, physical and mental, above all emotional maturity as well as economic and social ability to sustain married life. For the man, this usually means the ability to support a family, but this question is relatively simple compared with his aptness to fulfil the role of husband and father. For the woman, her qualifications as wife and mother are essential.

The question of maturity relates not only to the decision whether to get married or not but also to the choice of a partner. For both, man and woman, the capability of managing a household and rearing children are required for maturity. It is difficult to judge one's ability for a job one has never performed and knows only from one's experience in an essentially different role. Furthermore, the handling of this job depends not only one's own talent and efforts but also on the conduct of one's partner who knows just as little as oneself of the demands of this venture.

Marriage can be too early not only physiologically (although in some cases 14- or 15-year-old girls seem to cope quite easily with the tasks of motherhood) but also emotionally. In modern society, the problems connected with marriage and the family have become rather complicated while the simultaneous relaxation of the social structure facilitates the conclusion of marriages diverging from traditional patterns. It is disturbing that in the United States, where about half of all marriages end in divorce, the divorce rate of marriages between teenagers amounts to 80 per cent.

Age Differential

Actually, in the 33 years from 1947 to 1980, the average marriage age of Japanese men rose from 26.1 to 27.8 years, and that of women from 22.9 to 25.2 years. In the United States, the median age of first marriages increased from 20.8 years in 1970 to 22.3 years in 1981 for women and from 23.2 to 29.8 years for men. In Japan, the average marriage age of men was 28.0 years in 1983 and that of women 25.4 years. In 1981, when the average age at the time of the first marriage was 27.1 years for men and 25.3 years for women, 3.3 per cent of the women were under 20 years of age, 50.0 per cent were between 20 and 24, 37.8 per cent between 25 and 29, 6.8 per cent between 30 and 34, 1.3 per cent between 35 and 39 and 0.8 per cent 40 and older.

One reason for the higher marriage age in Japan is the larger number of young people (especially girls) who attend college or university and defer marriage until after graduation. A second reason is the heavy economic burden incidental to the foundation of a family. The increases in young people's wage and salary levels have failed to match the increases in the standard of living, and although parents may shoulder part of the costs of starting a new household, the cost of living may exceed the financial resources of young couples. A third reason is the attractiveness of an independent existence. When young people remain unmarried, they can enjoy many things they would have to give up if they get married.

The Japanese have coined the expression 'singles nobility' (*dokushin kizoku*) for unmarried young people who are enjoying life. In the period between the censuses of 1975 and 1980 (1 October), the proportion of unmarried women in the 20 to 24 age groups rose form 69.2 per cent to 77.9 per cent, and to 81.1 per cent in 1985. Unmarried men represented 60.6 of the 25 to 29 age group in 1985 — up from 48.3 per cent in 1975. The higher marriage age constitutes one of the reasons for the lower birth rate. As part of the programme of the People's Republic of China to control the birth rate, men are discouraged from marrying before they are 26 and women before they are 24.

According to the Swiss Federal Statistics Bureau, marriages are least likely to end in divorce if the husband is between five and ten years older than the wife. An analysis of Switzerland's 1980 census showed the highest divorce rate, 11.6 divorces per 1,000 marriages, if the wife was 20 or more years older than the husband; the rate was 8.3 divorces per 1,000 marriages, if the husband was 20 years older than the wife. The average divorce rate came to 6.9 per 1,000 marriages, if the wife was between eight and twelve years older than the husband and to 5 per 1,000 marriages, if the husband was from eleven to sixteen years older than the wife. If husband and wife were of the same age, the divorce rate was 4.7 per 1,000 marriages, and if the husband was five to ten years older than the wife, the rate was 4.2 divorces per 1,000 marriages. The rate for the last group was low, the Swiss said, 'mainly because women reach emotional maturity earlier than men and therefore seek partners who are somewhat older so as to assure emotional equality.'

Marriage between partners of an advanced age may be less problematic than that between young people if no fraud, swindle or other wrongdoing is involved. In 1977, there were 21,180 brides and 38,820 grooms over 65 years of age in the United States. For 90 per cent of these newlyweds, it was their second marriage. Most of such marriages are not concluded on impulse but are the outcome of long acquaintances. The expectations of the partners are generally lower than those of young people in the enchantment of first love. On the other hand, older peope have more pronounced traits including eccentricities which make mutual adjustment more difficult.

In modern society, the old rule that the husband should be a few years older than the wife is often enforced by economic constraints. In the initial years of working, a man finds it difficult or impossible to earn enough for shouldering the responsibility for a family. This situation has been somewhat modified by the increasing participation of women in the labour force. In many cases, a woman does not give up her job when she gets married. Formerly, a girl often worked in order to contribute to her dowry; nowadays, the wife's pay forms part of (and occasionally the only) income of the family.

Reversal of Age Differential

A phenomenon increasingly observed in recent years is the reversal of the age differential; more men marry older women. In general, women age slower than men, and a woman in her forties can still look very attractive. Psychoanalysts surmise that young men are drawn to older women in order to compensate frustrations experienced in infancy. Another explanation ascribes the choice of an older woman to the man's exceptionally intense and satisfying relation with his mother which he seeks to continue in his rapport with an older woman. For the woman, marriage with a young man represents a relatively greater chance of self-realisation. These women are often single children who grew up under a domineering mother or divorcees who escaped from a hapless marriage with a patriarch. Women in their forties are the last generation still brought up with the faith in the absolute superiority of the male. Many of these women have an occupation which gives them the strength to throw off the shackles of a marriage in which they feel themselves trapped and to make a new start.

The pronouncements of women who married younger men stress the possibility of self-realisation: 'I can finally realise myself.' 'I have become independent because there is no longer somebody behind me giving me orders.' 'I am fond of you because you are intelligent and tender. You have shown me that it is possible to be fully woman and still fully free.'

The higher age seems to heighten the self-confidence and self-respect of the woman, but marriages with younger men are not necessarily more enduring. The difference in age constitutes an additional risk factor, and since the desire for children is weaker in such marriages, they lack a stabilising factor.

It happens that young men who are alcoholics or drug addicts try to find support in an older woman who takes on the role of a therapist. In a reversal of roles, a woman with a drug habit may attempt to give her life a new meaning in the association with a younger man.

The question whether to marry or not acquires an entirely new dimension in the case of remarriage. This choice arises after the death of one's spouse or after divorce; for convenience sake, this topic will be discussed in connection with divorce (Ch. 20).

Marriage Bureaux

The objective conditions influencing the choice of a marriage partner have changed greatly in modern society so that many former restrictions have almost entirely disappeared. It remains true that marriage supposes acquaintanceship but in the mobile society of the industrial and post-industrial age, the opportunities for forming acquaintances are incomparably more numerous than in the agricultural society. Sometimes, demographical factors are important. In regions in which the number of males is much larger than that of females, a woman's chances of marriage are considerably better than in regions with the opposite sex ratio. Moreover, methods such as advertising and marriage bureaux enable people without connections to find suitable partners. As mentioned above, these methods are liable to misuse and deceit but they also offer definite advantages. Computerised marriage brokerage can consider many individual and social factors in matching possible partners. In addition to properties such as height, weight, colour of hair and eyes, voice and age, family, education, profession, income, character, inclinations, hobbies, sports or possible wishes regarding the partner can be taken into consideration. The questionnaire of a firm lists over 160 questions which are used for drafting over 600 computer inputs. The computer makes it possible to weigh concordant as well as complementary factors. Some marriage bureaux have a high reputation for seriousness and reliability, others are accused of frivolity and fraud. There are private enterprises (in Tokyo, for example, there are about 400) and official establishments (in Tokyo, the Metropolitan Government and the ward offices provide marriage counselling). Many large corporations have their own marriage counselling service.

In addition to several books on finding a marriage partner, two magazines specialise in helping women to find prospective husbands. The editors of one of these magazines, all women, view marriage as the antithesis to the career-oriented life-style advocated in the seventies and took advantage of the 'anti-independent women' tendency which came to the fore in 1983.

'Miai'

In Japan, an old method of arranging marriages is called *miai* (literally, 'meeting for looking'). It means a meeting of the partners in a proposed marriage for reciprocal inspection and constitutes an essential step in the negotiations between two families concerning a marital union. Often, the proposal is made by a third party (called *nakôdo*, matchmaker) who also presides over the wedding ceremony. But the initiative can also come from one of the families which asks a third party to look for a suitable partner. The method has the advantage that it is generally in accord with the objective situation of the prospective partners but the personal equation remains somewhat doubtful. It has been asserted that personal affection will develop 'of itself' but such an assertion lacks any solid foundation. In the old Japanese society (as often in the upper classes of western society), the problem was solved by allowing concubines besides a wife corresponding to the husband's social rank or the double moral standard which permitted a man to satisfy his personal sexual inclinations by extra-marital affairs. Today, however, the old customs have lost much of their social acceptability and young people are little inclined to place social considerations above their personal wishes. Even in *miai* marriages, therefore, the consent of the future partners has gained decisive importance.

Miai is used by parents, particularly anxious mothers, for pressing their daughters into marriage when they are getting on in years without finding a suitable partner. 'Girls are like Christmas cakes, they are of no use after 25' is a common saying in some parts of Japan. Relatives, friends and acquaintancess are asked for introductions to families with sons who seem likely marriage candidates.

In order to give young people an occasion to meet marriageable partners, local governments have arranged 'mass-*miai*' (*shûdan miai*) which have only the name in common with the traditional *miai*. A further innovation are video-taped interviews of marriage counsellors with marriageable individuals which can be consulted by people desirous of marriage.

Mass Weddings of the Unification Church

In a completely different category are the mass wedding ceremonies organised by the Reverend Sun Myung Moon, the founder of the Unification Church, in which young people who meet for the first time become engaged or get married. On 1 July, 1982, the Reverend Moon officiated at a wedding ceremony in which 4,150 members of the Unification Church were married, and Moon topped this massive New York ceremony by a monster rally on 14 October, 1982, in Seoul in which 5,837 couples were united in wedlock. The 11,674 brides and grooms came from 84 different countries, and while some had been engaged for four years, others were told they were going to be married a few days before the event. Many of Moon's followers are said to come from broken homes or have broken with their families. They have accepted the life-style of the Unification Church which is shaped by the imposing personality of the Reverend Moon. He controls their thoughts and decisions down to the very personal and intimate decisions of whom to marry, when to marry, and when to consummate the marriage. How well will these marriages develop once the partners outgrow the pressure-cooker atmosphere of the religious community?

The mass marriages of the Unification Church are intimately connected with the Reverend Moon's teaching. The perfect family, he says, is the basis of a perfect society. The world needed a messiah after the fall of Adam and Eve. The first Messiah, Jesus, failed because he was crucified before he could marry and create a perfect family. The Reverend Moon is the second messiah, destined to create a perfect society after defeating communism.

Unification Church law requires newlyweds to wait 40 days to purify themselves before consummating their marriages. Many of the couples participating in the mass weddings live apart while working on church projects and see each other only during the weekends.

In a trial brought by a member of the Unification Church against a professional de-programmer, Moon, who claims to have spoken with Jesus, Moses, and Buddha, testified that decisions on such matters as whom he allows to marry and when were based on divine revelation. 'I act on the divine revelation of God and the theology of the Unification Church,' he said. Moon was denounced for delaying marriage and cohabitation in order to keep his fund raisers longer in the field.

Choice of Mate in China

The *miai* marriages of Japan raise the question of the role of the family in the choice of a mate. Arranged marriages are still common in the Chinese countryside but too many marriages involve money, abduction or other forms of coercion. Trafficking in women is frequent in some parts of China and a Chinese paper accused parents of being greedy and selling their daughters as if they were commodities. The authorities stress that, under the new Marriage Law, engagement or betrothal without the consent of both parties is legally invalid. An article in the *Workers' Daily* called for greater sexual freedom and attacked some of the taboos widely held in the country. 'Some young people are pushed together by arrangement or sale, by swap arrangements between families, by force or trickery or by property deals before they get to know each other, let alone have a chance of falling in love or developing feelings for one another.' In an ideal communist society, the paper said, people would be able to choose their partners with total freedom. 'Sexual liberation is an inevitable historical tendency and implies progress in history.'

Regulations issued by China's Ministry of Civil Affairs prohibit Chinese diplomats, military personnel and security officials from marrying foreigners and virtually make marriage of any college-educated Chinese with a foreigner impossible. The regulations also bar marriage to a foreigner of any Chinese serving a prison term or receiving 're-education' through labour.

Recently, the government organised a dance and match-making drive for which 9,000 Chinese singles, many of them women, crammed into the Working People's Palace of Culture (a former Ching dynasty residence) in Beijing. Participants had to be unmarried or divorced and at least 30 years old. There are large numbers of unmarried people in their 30s with little chance of finding a mate because of the traditional preference for mid-20s marriages. The authorities blame the situation on the Cultural Revolution which deprived people of time and opportunities for romance.

Abuses

In China's Fujian province, arranged marriages involving children, boys as well as girls, as young as eight years old were being celebrated. As a result, an increasing number of girls aged 14 or 15 were giving birth.

A Chinese girl of 16, four years under China's legal marriage age, was liberated by students when her husband-to-be was taking her by train to his home and she told a student of her intention to kill herself if she could not escape. But the girl's parents who had been promised a large sum of money as a betrothal gift insisted that she go through with the marriage and persuaded local officials to falsify papers and list the girl's age as 20.

According to the *Times of India*, women are being kidnapped, sold into marriage, freed by the police and then resold. Women are kidnapped or lured away by racketeers who sell them to waiting grooms. The racketeers later claim to be the woman's guardians and demand that the police free her from the husband who already paid a fee. The girl is rescued with the help of the police only to be sold once again. The newspaper reported the story of a girl who was resold six times before she escaped.

In Islamic Pakistan, marriages are arranged between families, and a family which provided a bride for the son of a family expects to receive a bride for one of its sons in return. Unborn and baby brides are bartered off in deals between families and the law setting the minimum marriage age at 16 is ignored. A Lahore weekly reported that an 18-month-old girl had been married off to a 70-year-old man. Girls aged three and four are married in secret to older men, and daughters are given as concubines to religious leaders.

In some rural tribes, a man unhappy with his wife can declare her an adulteress and throw her out of his house — some tribes even allow murder — and then demand a new wife from the in-laws to replace the 'immoral' daughter they had given him. Parents without another girl promise an unborn daughter or pressure relatives into handing over a niece or a granddaughter.

Another rural custom allows parents to 'marry' a girl to the *Qur'an* and confine her to the house as a virgin for the rest of her life. Land-owners who have daughters but no sons use this custom if they do not want to divide their holdings with a son-in-law.

Village moneylenders sometimes take an infant girl from a poor farmer unable to repay a loan and may keep the girl as a maid or give her in marriage to whomever they choose.

According to Islamic law, fathers have the right to contract their daughters, whether minors or adults, in compulsory marriage. Only when a woman has been married before is her consent necessary, but even then, her father or other marriage guardian must conclude the contract in her name. In Hanafi law, however, (Middle East, with the exception of Saudi Arabia, and India) only under age girls may be contracted in compulsory marriage while adult women may conclude their own marriage contracts. But a woman's guardian may have the marriage annulled if his ward has married beneath her social status.

Reconnoitering of Prospective Bride in Muslim Societies

The *Qur'an* enumerates the persons with whom an unmarried woman may speak unveiled (Sura 33,55) or before whom she can uncover her-self (Sura 24,31). Recently, a committee of Fuquahaa, learned interpreters of the *Qur'an*, decided in Saudi Arabia, that a woman may show her face to her future spouse. If the arrangement for the marriage has been completed, the future bridegroom and bride may meet and the bride may lift her veil. On 25 March, 1981, the Directorate of Fatwa and Guidance declared: 'Islam recognises the legitimacy of proposers seeing their prospective wives.' It also ruled that forcing women into marriage is a 'practice devoid of any religious basis.'

The Ministry of Justice determined that Sharia, Islamic law, per-mits suitors to see and talk to the prospective bride, but this should be done only in the presence of chaperones, a close female kin of the prospective bride or a man unfit to marry her, such as her father, brother or uncle. Islamic scholars insist that the prophet Muhammad himself taught that the bridegroom should see his prospective bride.

Muslim men have to depend on their mothers or sisters to look for suitable wives but customarily they see the face of the woman they take in marriage only at *Jaffah*, the marriage consummation ceremony.

Often, the mother of the would-be groom initiates the process with a visit to the family of the chosen girl. There are a number of stories on the stratagems a mother might use. She offers the girl hard nuts and insists that she crack them with her teeth, to test their strength and ascertain they are not false. She may also pull the hair of the girl to make sure it is natural. And if the mother is glib and clever, she might surreptitiously get a snapshot of the girl and sneak it to her son. If the mother's role proves difficult, a professional matchmaker (*Kathbeh*) takes over.

Attitude of Parents

There are great differences in the attitudes of parents to the marriage of their children and in the role they play in the arrangement of the match. One extreme are parents who want to keep their children for themselves and thus oppose any courtship. For fear that the child will leave them, they treat every suitor as an intruder. This attitude is not restricted to the marriage of daughters but is also found in mothers who think it unbearable to lose their sons (especially if it is an only child). The opposite attitude is to leave everything to the decision of the child which may range from complete disinterest to true respect for the personal dignity of the child. Much depends, of course, on the age and maturity of the child. As long as the child's choice is not an obvious mistake, it will be the correct course not to interfere in the decisions of a 30-year-old man or woman. Some parents look on marriage as a lottery and want their child to hit the jackpot. Parents sometimes entertain fantasies completely unrelated to reality. They talk about the happiness of their children but mean the attainment of their own ambitions.

A relic of Japan's old family system is the *muko-yôshi* (adoption of the bridegroom of an heiress) mentioned above. If the children in a family are all girls, the parents want the young man marrying their eldest (or only) daughter to assume the family name. Legally, this procedure changes the distribution of the inheritance in case of intestate succession but has no longer the significance it had under the old family system. Some young men are unwilling to agree to the change of their family name and regard it as an imposition and an infringement of their freedom while others welcome it because it may give them a higher social status and economic advantages (for example, to take over the business or practice of the father-in-law). The girls are sometimes torn between their desire to please their parents and the love for the man of their choice who refuses to accept what he regards as a humiliating condition.

It is not impossible that parents arrange the marriage of their children, and if the children retain the freedom to refuse, it may not always be undesirable. It happens, however, that parents or relatives use physical force in order to prevent a marriage of which they disapprove. According to a report from India, a father shot his daughter dead because she wanted to marry a man from the caste of the 'untouchables.' The clause in the Japanese constitution 'Marriage shall be based only on the mutual consent of both sexes . . .' (Art. 24, Par. 1) was directed primarily against the custom of arranging marriages between families. On the other hand, young people elope in order to evade the opposition of their families against their marriage. If children get married against the will and wishes of their parents, it can be a traumatic experience for both sides. The parents have the feeling that all their efforts for educating their children have been in vain. For the children, a marriage at which their parents and relatives are not present can hardly be a happy and joyful event and the estrangement may embitter the life of both sides.

Traditionally, Japanese families have been very careful not only about the prospective marriage partner but also about his or her family. It is not unusual for parents to engage private detectives or investigatory agencies to explore the family lineage, economic conditions, health and reputation of their children's choice. Records of physical or mental illnesses, straitened circumstances or socially embarrassing incidents in the family may induce parents to oppose the planned marriage. It is common practice for families to exchange transcripts of the official family register.

In former times, love suicides (*shinjû*) of couples whose parents opposed their marriage took place often enough. The Kegon waterfall at Nikko was (and still is) a favourite spot for carrying out the lovers' death wish.

At a time when economic factors weighed heavily in marriage decisions and the emotional implications were often disregarded, marriages arranged by the families may have been a necessary procedure. When the formal wedding was a social and public matter which had nothing to do with personal affection and the satisfaction of sexual lust was sought in extra-marital relations, the predominance of impersonal factors may not be surprising. Even today, economic considerations cannot be disregarded and in most cases, the balance between economic and emotional elements may not be a matter of either-or but of more or less.

Occasionally, it will be necessary to pay special attention to the family situation of the partners (naturally, this can apply to both sides). There are customs that impose unexpected burdens on one or the other of the parties or their families. In some of Japan's rural districts, the family of the bride is exploited in the most atrocious manner. The girl's parents are forced to comply with totally arbitrary demands on the part of the groom's family in order to protect their daughter from vexation and torment by her in-laws and their relatives.

The role that parents are expected to play in most cases is that of counsellors and friends who are deeply interested in the happiness of their children and try to steer their choice into the right direction. On the basis of their experience (which is not limited to their own marriage), parents can judge whether the marriage promises to be successful or is probably doomed to failure. They can try to influence the choice by advice and guidance without imposing their opinions.

In Japan, the family retains a large role in the formal wedding. The families of the bridegroom and the bride consult on the wedding ceremony and the arrangements for the future household. Unless the parties have their own independent station in life, the announcement of the marriage and the invitations to the wedding are sent out in the names of the parents of the couple. The exchange of presents and the sharing of the costs of the wedding are also primarily a concern of the parents.

As in other questions, a difference in the views of the old and young generation also exists in the attitudes towards relations between the sexes. Parents would normally consider it too young for a fifteen-year-old to think of marriage and therefore oppose dating and having a boyfriend or girlfriend. For young people, dating or generally coming together with members of the opposite sex has nothing to do with marriage. Dating is a relationship that possesses a certain exclusiveness but is not kept up in view of a possible marriage. Association with others is valuable in itself — naturally, young people do not put it this way — and amusement is the main concern.

Basically, this question is part of the general problem of whether youth is valuable in itself, that is, whether youth possesses meaning and significance in itself or is merely a preparation for adult life. The hub of the problem lies in the 'merely.' It is impossible to regard every stage in man's development 'merely' as a preparatory step to the next stage. Adolescence certainly represents a transitional phase in human growth but despite its characteristic immaturity and incompleteness, its value does not depend entirely on its relation and contribution to the future. On the other hand, the relevancy to the future cannot be entirely ignored which, of course, is also true for every phase of adult life. Youth is life and preparation for life. It is difficult to choose what will contribute most to one's future but it is important not to choose what will compromise it. Choices with regard to sex relations are among those most liable to be regretted later.

Engagement

In today's society, engagement does no longer play the same role as in earlier times, but there remains a phase in the preparation for marriage that corresponds more or less to engagement. Dating is usually followed by a period of going-steady which can lead to a regular courtship. But such a relationship is often unstable because it may not have the same meaning for both partners. It admits of an almost infinite variety of intensity and candour. Usually, the woman is emotionally more involved than the man. Both may deceive themselves, be mistaken about their own feelings, or change their views on their partner in the course of the relationship. Since the transition from dating to courtship does not necessarily include a formal engagement, one of the partners may still regard their association as play with no further purpose than mutual enjoyment while the other may seriously think of marriage. In view of the objective factors required for marriage, a young man who has not yet completed his studies may not think of marriage. He must first establish himself in his profession which may require years of special study or professional activities. The immersion in his life's work may make it easier for the young man to postpone the fulfilment of his wish to get married. But if the girl has no professional ambitions, her situation may be quite different. Intellectually, she may understand the necessity of waiting but emotionally, waiting means the negation of her desire for fulfilment without compensation.

Termination of Relationship

A difficult problem is how and when to break off a relationship which is moving towards marriage if one or both of the partners feel that marriage would be a mistake. Recently, a young Japanese woman committed suicide two days before she was to be married. She left a suicide note saying: 'We would be unhappy if we were to marry as planned.'

In March 1983, the Osaka District Court ordered a couple and their son to pay a solatium of ¥5.5 million to the son's former fiancée. The woman had become acquainted with the man shortly after both joined the same pharmaceutical company in the spring of 1975. When the girl told her boyfriend that she belonged to a *buraku* community, he said that he did not care about her family background, and after more than a year of close friendship, the two agreed to get engaged. (*Buraku* refers to people whose ancestors were outcasts because they were engaged in work related to death — particularly the disposal of corpses and tanning — and therefore considered 'unclean' by Shinto standards.) When the young man told his parents that he was going to get married, the parents fiercely opposed the marriage. The father frequently visited the girl and tried to persuade her to give up the marriage. At first, the son was determined to go through with the marriage but tired of the family trouble, he notified his fiancée that he was breaking off the engagement. The court ruled that discrimination against *buraku* people was the reason for the cancellation of the engagement and that the woman was entitled to compensation from the parents and the son.

A 22-year-old girl who had cancelled her engagement was stabbed to death by her former fiancé. The girl had made the acquaintance of the 36-year-old man when, as a college senior, she went to a driving school where the man worked as an instructor. After graduation, the girl who had passed the civil service examination, was hired as a probation officer by the city of Urawa. The families exchanged the customary betrothal gifts but the girl discovered the vile temper and cultural vacuity of her partner who also opposed her plan of continuing her work after marriage. She called off the engagement and returned the betrothal gifts but the man who had had no girlfriend before, insisted on going through with the marriage. One evening, he waited for her to return from work at the railway station, pleaded with her to restore their relationship and killed her when she persisted in her refusal.

As a rule, the development of a relation leads from the initial acquaintanceship over the fixation of the personal inclination to identification, but if the unsettled relationship is protracted, the partners instead of drawing nearer to each other, may grow apart. The convergence of feelings is replaced by their divergence. Marriage after a long acquaintance involves special dangers. Partners may get married because their acquaintances know of their relationship and they are afraid of losing face if they do not get married. The man may feel a kind of pity with the girl and consider it a point of honour to marry her, particularly if they had sexual relations. Until the age of 45, a woman's chances of getting married diminish much faster than those of a man. But it is a serious mistake for both man and woman to marry a partner whom he or she really does not want to marry.

'Realism' in Marriage Decision

In view of the strength of the sex instinct and the many opportunities of having sexual intercourse, it is hardly surprising that there has been an enormous increase in pre-marital sex. Naturally, the prevalence of this conduct does not constitute a moral justification. Virginity is no longer a *conditio sine qua non* of marriage, but the rising number of indifferent marriages because a baby is coming involves a serious problem. Such a union may be concluded without true affection. Pre-marital sex often is a kind of amusement in which young people share and pregnancy is the last thing they intend. In 1979, 4.3 of 1,000 females from 15 to 19 years of age had abortions in Japan but the actual number of abortions may be double the figure of 17,084 cases officially notified by doctors. It happens that girls cannot pay for an abortion or discover too late that they are pregnant and the result are foetuses found in garbage cans, public toilets or coin lockers. There are cases in which the girl does not know who the father of her baby is or has parted company with him. But even if they know the father, girls are reluctant to reveal their condition. In many cases, anxiety, fear, shame and repentance become a painful experience of the young girl.

Confronted with the result of his relationship, a man has the choice of marrying the girl or of persuading her to have an abortion. Where the double standard still prevails, a man may seduce a decent girl but then refuse to marry her because she is no longer a virgin. If an existing union does not make marriage impossible, a man may decide to marry out of a sentiment of chivalry, duty or pity, even if he did not intend to get married before. It may be some kind of fatalistic resignation in face of the accomplished fact — as a man once confessed to his wife: 'I married you not because I loved you but because I had to recognise a reality over which I had no control.' This does not mean that such a marriage is necessarily doomed to failure but neither is it the most desirable motive for marriage.

On the other hand, love or affection may play a lesser role in 'ordinary' marriages than the romanticisation of marriage in the mass media tends to suggest. Girls, in particular, exhibit a realism which often appears almost commercial. Wishes such as '170 cm tall,' 'athletic figure,' 'owner of a sports car' are just pretense to appear choosey before friends. Actually, girls attribute greater importance to a good job than to good looks or to love. In Japan, girls prefer a man who graduated from a prestigious university, has a job with a large company and is not the first or only son of his family — the first son has too great a responsibility for his family. This attitude has sometimes been described as 'girls marry the best possible provider they can stomach.' Men attribute greater importance to the occupation of the girl's father and a certain equality in the status of the two families.

Some recent surveys show that men, too, are becoming more demanding. They want a partner who, first of all, takes good care of their physical needs but is also a sincere woman, affectionate, intelligent, self-confident, sexy and endowed with a sense of humour.

Discrepancy in Expectations

An American psychologist, Dr Clifford Adams, thinks that the difference in the expectations of men and women is one of the reasons of misunderstandings in marriage. In the list of men's desiderata for marriage and their reasons for choosing a marriage partner, sex ranks in second place but it comes only sixth in the women's enumeration. Men place companionship and togetherness first; they are looking for a mate who will be with them on their journey through life. After sex, they want love, affection and tenderness. In fourth place, they value family and home, then they expect a helper who gives them encouragement and consoles them in adversity. Lastly, they desire safety and security. For women, the category love, affection and tenderness comes first, but it is not certain that women mean the same with these terms as men. Secondly, women expect safety and security, then companionship, family and home, and recognition by society. Sex comes last. This order shows how different the expectations and wishes are with which men and women approach marriage. It is not impossible that in this as in other questions, the peculiarity of the female psyche is involved of which Sigmund Freud remarked: 'The great question which I have not been able to answer despite my 30 years of research into the feminine soul is, what does a woman want?'

A Gallup poll carried out in 1982 for a British food company questioned 1,076 people about the values they cherished most and they considered important. Out of 23 choices, 99 per cent of the respondents put health at the top of their list, followed by family life (96 per cent) and law and order (95 per cent). Other highly-rated values were love (90 per cent), money (87 per cent) and a steady job (86 per cent). Sex was deemed important by 72 per cent and success by 70 per cent. At the bottom of the ratings were religion with 46 per cent and politics with 29 per cent. Half of the married people felt they were very happy while only one out of three single people thought so.

Values Influencing Choice of Mate

The old saying 'to marry for health, beauty or wealth' does not state mutually exclusive alternatives and many people would be happy if they could have the three together. The motives or reasons why people resolve to get married and to marry a particular individual can run the entire gamut of human values and often the reasons for which the partners believe or tell others they got married may be quite different from the real reasons. The desire for sexual satisfaction, children, companionship, homeliness, social status and economic security get mixed up with personal factors such as health, age, race, religion, education, erudition, occupation and income. The marriage experience of the partner (divorced, widowed), his family situation and domicile may be of importance for the decision. Personal experiences often modify the elements of the model generally regarded as 'ideal.' Looks and manners are perhaps more important in theory than in the actual choice. Somewhat baffling is that intelligence is not often mentioned as a desirably quality of the woman and that her qualifications as housewife and mother, capable of cooking, sewing, and looking after children, are presumed rather than explicitly demanded. It is not unusual for a man, particularly a man in the liberal professions, to marry a wife who cannot compete with him in intelligence, at least the kind of intelligence characteristic of academe, but it seems undesirable for a wife to have a husband who is less intelligent than she is.

'Getting to Know You'

Disillusionment in marriage is less the result of a discovery of a discrepancy between the qualities of the partner and an ideal and more often the outcome of the experience of his or her true character. If the partners have not known each other for a considerable length of time, the picture they have of each other may be partly based on imagination.

The detection of the partner's true personality does not necessarily result in disappointment, at least not in every respect. It happens that even after long years of living together, a husband or wife finds something good that so far did not seem remarkable or was taken for granted. The real problem is not the choice of a partner — a perfect choice which leaves nothing to be desired may be humanly impossible — but the adjustment in marriage despite disappointments.

Dr George R. Bach, an American psychologist, asserts that conflict in marriage constitutes an important factor for promoting mutual affection and that conflict before marriage is an excellent means for getting to know each other. He thinks that it is just as sensible to have some good fights before marriage — during courtship — as it is later on. In an average courtship, two people con each other; they put on false fronts. They tell each other their life stories generally tailored for the occasion. It would be much better, Dr Bach argues, if instead they had fights. They would learn much more about each other that way. Computer matchmaking is not satisfactory for many reasons, the most important being that good relationships are not based simply on personality match-ups. A few good fights will let a couple know more about themselves than even the most sophisticated computer.

Sociologists discuss a number of situations in which the choice of a partner is influenced by special factors. The image of the parents can induce the wish to find a partner who, physically or by temperament, resembles a loved parent or, negatively, is most unlike a hated parent. The choice of a partner who, consciously or unconsciously, should serve as *ersatz*, involves undeniable dangers. The partner is not chosen for himself and he may be expected to play the role of a double in his entire conduct. It is an unbearable burden if, in the expectation of the partner, a spouse is not allowed to be his own self and his conduct is measured by a model alien to him.

Assortive Mating

A special kind of choice is the so-called 'assortive mating' in which partners with similar characteristics get married. This is a special case of the general phenomenon described by the proverb 'birds of a feather flock together.' Similarities that find most attention are physical or social qualities. Age, height, weight, colour of eyes and hair, general health, physical defects and level of general education are some of the similarities attracting people to each other. Blinds marry blinds and deaf-mutes marry deaf-mutes. Three Japanese deaf-mute men who met three deaf-mute Taiwanese girls when the girls visited Japan kept up the contact by correspondence and the three couples were married in a joint ceremony. Recently, a common wedding ceremony was conducted in a leprosarium in South China for fifteen couples who were inmates of the institution.

One reason for assortive marriages may be that such persons have a better understanding of each other, feel sympathy with each other's fate and want to help each other.

11

Prediction of Marital Happiness

What is Happiness?

WHAT IS HAPPINESS? There is no definition on which philosophers or ordinary mortals agree. The old philosophers discussed beatitude rather than happiness. Happiness was identified with pleasure and the forms of hedonism ranged from the sensual lust of Aristippus and the Cyrenaic school to the 'greatest happiness of the greatest number' of utilitarianism. Many religions teach that perfect happiness is impossible in this world. Even if there were perfect happiness, the certainty of death would always instil the fear of losing it so that it could not be perfect. Nevertheless, the optimists among the philosophers declared that man can always make progress despite his limitations and Leibniz even thought that God had created the best possible world. The pessimists, however, asserted that man is bad and incapable of improvement (Schopenhauer).

Freud thought that happiness in its true sense meant the sudden satisfaction of pent-up intense desires and therefore only possible as an episodic outburst. Because culture is basically inimical to instincts, it suppresses and limits the satisfaction of the instincts which would bring happiness. It seemed not to be ordained in the plan of providence, Freud wrote, that men should be happy. Among the possibilities to forestall pain and suffering from the lack or the depravation of happiness, he listed, in addition to the pathogenic suppression of the instincts, their sublimation (by scientific research) which, however, was only accessible to a few, art (a 'mild narcosis'), religion ('collective fantasy') and, as the 'weakest' form, love and being loved. 'But,' he cautioned, 'we are never more unprotected against suffering than when we love, never more helplessly unhappy than when we have lost the beloved object or its love.'

Japanese surveys questioning women about their views on the relation between marriage and happiness showed a considerable shift in opinion in recent years. In 1984, 30.4 per cent of the women respondents thought that a woman's happiness lay in marriage, down from 39.7 per cent in 1972. The contrary view that a woman could be happy without marriage was held by 24.0 per cent, up from 13.1 per cent in 1972. The belief that marriage was preferable because it contributed to mental and economic security was shared by 21.8 per cent of the women (1972: 20.7 per cent), and 17.6 per cent of the women agreed with the statement that marriage was the obvious thing to do for a woman (1972: 19.9 per cent). The position that it was always possible to divorce if a marriage turned out to be unsatisfactory was supported by 4.1 per cent of the respondents (1972: 2.8 per cent) and 29.0 per cent found this point of view understandable (1972: 18.6 per cent). But 47.9 per cent did not quite agree with this way of thinking (1972: 43.7 per cent) and 14.7 per cent were completely opposed to it (1972: 27.3 per cent).

Marital Happiness

Whatever happiness may be, marital happiness would require that each of the partners be happy and that marriage contribute to the happiness of both. A man is considered happy if he is content but contentment can have a negative meaning. If somebody succeeds in resigning himself to his fate, he may be content but this is hardly what we call happiness and still less what the old philosophers understood by beatitude, 'the perfect satisfaction of all desires.' In western society, the expectation that marriage will bring great personal satisfaction is general and paramount in the thinking of young couples. As human beings, they know that perfect happiness is impossible but this impossibility does not prevent them from expecting that marriage will bring them some kind of felicity that they cannot have without marriage. Naturally, impossible without marriage is the togetherness of the life of husband and wife.

Marital happiness means the largest possible measures of the goods, values, advantages and experiences proper to the community of life as husband and wife. Sexual partnership certainly constitutes an important aspect of their togetherness but it is not the most important element. Only a spiritual union can impart the personal value of human love to the sexual communion, and spiritual, above all emotional, unity is impossible without the unconditional self-surrender in unlimited confidence in the faith of the partner. Marital happiness can only be found if the premises for a spiritual union exist. That does not mean that such a union is required on the first day of marriage but that the partners have the confidence and the will to achieve such a union. Without a certain personal maturity, other than a purely biological maturity, the process of marital interpenetration will not start. It demands the understanding of human values, a feeling for spiritual needs and the recognition that marriage is essentially a personal relationship.

For the marital community of life, the same virtues are necessary that are indispensable for social life in general: patience, self-control, understanding of others, readiness to recognise the other's point of view (not in the sense of agreeing with everything he says but of listening to what he has to say), openness without rudeness, friendliness without weakness, helpfulness without arrogance. But for the common life peculiar to marriage, the qualities concordant with the personality of marriage and the intimacy of marital relations must be stressed. They include tenderness, considerateness and regard for the feelings of others, readiness to accommodate one's own desires to the needs of others, selflessness and the spirit of sacrifice.

People sometimes enter marriage with utopian expectations. Getting married is no foolproof recipe for the instantaneous fulfilment of all wishes but the beginning of a lifelong process of learning and adaptation. Essential for marital happiness is the recognition that marriage is a career that demands the full and unconditional devotion of both partners. As every career, marriage has its rewards and its difficulties and people who are unable or unwilling to share the difficulties of marriage should not be surprised if their marriage fails. Unmixed happiness is not a human possibility; the mere fact that two people live together under the same roof almost makes sure that there will be difficulties.

Basis of Prediction

Sociologists usually discuss the prediction of marital happiness by asking which marriages promise to be successful, that is to say, which constellation of factors is most likely to assure the satisfactory outcome of marriage or, conversely, in which cases can it be predicted with great probability that the marriage would be a failure so that the prospective partners should be dissuaded from going through with their plan. This formulation of the problem shows that the prediction is based on probabilities gained from previous experience. Every marriage is special and every couple is different from all married people who lived before and will come after them. Nevertheless, statistical probabilities can give an indication of the possible and even the likely outcome of a marriage if certain conditions are present.

Happy and Unhappy Marriages

Of basic importance is the personality of the partners. The personal equation seems paramount in the studies of so-called happy marriages, that is, marriages in which the partners considered their marriage a success as well as unhappy marriages, that is, marriages that broke down.

Women in happy marriages were serene, sure of themselves, friendly, kind, warm-hearted, helpful, attentive to detail, reliable in their work, methodical, thrifty, conservative, supporting the status quo in religion, politics and morality, favouring chastity before and in marriage, and advocating religious education. Women in unhappy marriages were nervous, over-sensitive, unfriendly, quarrelsome, restless, unsystematic, wasteful, unconventional, fearful of possible accidents, excitable, short-tempered, suffering from feelings of inferiority, lacking self-confidence, easily flabbergasted, prone to excessive apologies for their faults, piqued if criticised, suspicious of superiors, participating in community projects not for helping but for being complimented.

Men in happy marriages were described as follows: of even temperament, helpful, not self-conscious, polite, patient, kind, on good terms with their superiors, conservative, methodical, treating women as equals, unassuming. Men in unhappy marriages were characterised as nervous, not interested in social activities, prone to fantasies, ill-disposed towards women.

These descriptions touch on character as well as behaviour but in both respects, they only signify that good people have a better chance of achieving a happy marriage than problematic individuals. If all men were saints, earth might become a paradise and there would be fewer problems. The average man does not claim to be a saint, but although he has a number of faults, he also has some good qualities. People seldom form if not an objective, at least a somewhat relevant judgement on themselves. Even more rarely does an individual succeed in fathoming the character of another person sufficiently to arrive at a conclusion on the compatibility of his and the other's character. If a third party (teacher, superior) knows both well, he might be able to make an objective assessment of the chances of a marriage. In the old times when people lived in small communities, some kind of public opinion developed almost automatically on the prospects of a marriage between two parties who were rumoured to be getting married, and the approval or disapproval of the community was sometimes decisive for the consent or disapprobation of the families. In modern societies, such an inquest on the chances for a happy marriage is impossible; nevertheless, the compatibility of the characters of the parties concerned constitutes a question which needs careful consideration.

Basically, character is genetically determined but environmental factors exercise a strong influence on character formation. In this sense, the environmental or objective factors frequently considered in this connection play a certain role. They comprise sibling position, similarity or dissimilarity of the cultural environment in which the partners grew up, economic and social status, education, occupation, religion, and so on. On account of the significance of such factors, parties who both are the youngest or only child are dissuaded from marrying each other. It is difficult for individuals from different cultural environments to understand each other, to communicate and to harmonise. They speak different languages, judge things differently and react differently to the same phenomena.

Personality

Of great importance is the readiness to personal adjustment. Here lies the possibility of a conflict between what the individual regards as essential to his own existence and the requirements of the life in common. A young woman wrote the following considerations on the choice of a husband: 'If my partner demands that I give up something that is of great significance to me, I would not be ready to do it. This would undermine my personality. I want to find out before marriage where our interests, our strengths and weaknesses lie, where it is possible to help each other and where something is beyond me.' There may be expectations that go beyond the potentialities of the partners. A person may possibly be considered as somebody he actually is not and cannot be. Can the partner change and develop his personality through the marriage or despite the marriage? Is it possible to arrive at a mutually satisfactory common denominator? If discords and conflicts appear, the question is whether the parties can live with these differences, whether one or the other can change his or her attitude, or whether the disagreement will be unbearable.

Differences Between Partners

Differences may relate to age, education, intellectual capacity, religious convictions, favoured forms of entertainment or amusement, choice of friends, attitude towards alcohol, preferences in food, desire for or aversion against children, occupation of man or woman, relations to in-laws, use of income and formation of assets. Among these differences, the difference in age can be of considerable consequence. For young people, the possibility of mutual adjustment is much greater than for people of an advanced age.

Attitudes

There are attitudes that are incompatible with marital happiness. Marriage is not the balance of give and take, not a question of 'what must I give and what can I expect from you?' It is impossible to distinguish a sphere of inalienable rights and matters on which a compromise is possible. That both, man and woman, can fully and truly retain their personality and individuality in marriage is one of the essential prerequisites of marital happiness. Equally essential is that both are ready and willing to adjust their attitudes and conduct to the requirements of the life in common. The parties may disagree on what their common life requires but the recognition that the common life is not identical with the fulfilment of the wishes, expectations or demands of one or the other of the partners is indispensable for the success of a marriage.

Although the number of divorces has increased everywhere and half

of all marriages in the United States fail, marriages are more durable
than is commonly assumed. In the United States, 58 per cent of all first
marriages last longer than 15 years, and 52 per cent longer than 20 years;
47 per cent of all couples can celebrate their silver and 16 per cent their
golden wedding anniversary. Naturally, it is impossible to assert that all
marriages that stay together are happy marriages. Spouses may stay
together because they have no other choice or because they cannot make
up their minds to do something else. In many cases, parents do not part
'for the sake of their children.' A marriage may survive crises, fights,
conflicts, disappointments and even mutual contempt. It may last, but
it can hardly be called a happy marriage.

Phases in Adaptation

American psychologists have distinguished four phases in the
development of a marriage. In the first phase, spouses are typically self-
centred, looking only at how the relationship can serve them. At the
next stage, they negotiate *quid pro quos* — a service for a service, a
concession for a concession. In the third period, they begin to appreciate
each other's individuality and make accommodations for the good of the
marriage and each other. When they enter the fourth phase, they have
evolved a set of 'rules of relationship' by which they can avoid or deal
with problems.

What is depressing in this analysis is the prevalence of egotistic
attitudes and the absence of a sense of union, mutual trust and dedication
to a life in common. Actually, there are many things that draw people
together. One of the most important is the birth of a child. The presence
of children does not automatically bring people together but children can
provide a focus of common interest, common concern, common joy and
common anxiety.

There may be partners who present the aspect of a loving and devoted
couple while harbouring deep disappointments, mistrust or resentment.
Partners may remain bound by a mutual dependency while at the same
time loathing each other. But a marriage that is not outright frivolous
at the start has the potential of ripening into a deeper understanding and
affection. Much would be gained if people could preserve their enthusiasm
for marriage. That was Princess Diana's advice to a bride-to-be: 'Married
life is wonderful, so don't worry!' Marriage as a life in common and a
personal union of soul, heart and body is not a myth and not an impossible
dream but neither is it something that happens automatically because
people live together. According to a German proverb, everybody forges
his own happiness. Husband and wife can only forge together, if both
mean the same by happiness.

12

Wedding

Public Celebration

IN MANY SOCIETIES, the contraction of marriage assumes the form of a ceremony. This does not mean that all marriages not concluded according to a certain ritual are considered invalid. But in view of the social significance of marriage and for documenting the position and special status of married people, the matrimonial union is established in a public and usually traditional ceremony. Publicity is an old requirement for the validity of legal acts, and in closed societies, clandestine marriages were condemned as a threat to the certitude of social relations. The publicity of marriage serves to prevent illegal marriages. In many countries, therefore, civil and ecclesiastical marriages are preceded by the banns by which the intended marriage is announced with the exhortation to reveal impediments to the marriage. Banns are unknown in Japan, but patently illegal marriages can be stopped by the refusal to accept the notification of marriages (Civil Code, Art. 740).

In societies with an integrated and uniform order of values, the public celebration often takes the form of a religious rite. The ceremony is an expression of the importance society attributes to marriage. Betrothal is not an everyday happening but a special occurrence. Next to birth and death, marriage is one of the decisive events of human existence. The solemnity emphasises the special bond by which the family is inserted into the group but it also declares the change in the life of the spouses who enter on a new phase of their lives. For the newlyweds, the celebration becomes an emotional experience which makes them aware of their new position and signifies the beginning of a new status. From a religious point of view, marriage means a vocation. The wedding consecrates the spouses for their mission and promises divine assistance for the fulfilment of their task.

Roman Marriage Rite

The relation to the family stands out in the Roman marriage rite. After having acquired the bride by *mancipatio* (originally a form of sale), the bridegroom, in a second phase of the ceremony, asked the bride: *Anne tu mihi materfamilias esse vis?* (Wilt thou be to me mother of the family), to which the bride answered: *Tibi materfamilias esse volo* (I will be to thee the mother of the family). Then, the bride in turn asked the groom: *Anne tu mihi paterfamilias esse vis?* (Wilt thou be to me the father of the family), and the groom replied: *Tibi paterfamilias esse volo* (I will be to thee the father of the family). Iron rings as signs of engagement are mentioned by Pliny, and Roman rings with the representation of two clasped hands have been interpreted as engagement or wedding rings.

The use of rings dates back to the custom of buying a wife. Among the Jews, the ring was the present with which the contract for the purchase of a wife was confirmed. In ancient Greece and Rome, the bridegroom presented a ring, originally to the father of the bride and later to the bride on the occasion of the engagement. In the tradition of the Germanic peoples, a ring given to the vendor of the bride, father, brother or *muntwalt*, acquired the bride. When, in the twelfth century, the bride purchase ceased, rings were exchanged between bridegroom and bride, first, as the sign of engagement, then, as a part of the church wedding.

Church Rituals

The Catholic Church attributes to the marriage of Christians (that is, validly baptised persons) a special sacredness and regards it as a sacrament (namely, an outward sign ordained by Christ to confer grace to the recipient) of which the spouses are the ministers. Since the Council of Trent, the presence of the parish priest and two witnesses is ordinarily necessary for the validity of the marriage if one or both of the partners are Catholics. The essence of the marriage rite is the consent of the parties expressed by their answer to the question of the priest: 'NN, wilt thou take NN, here present, for thy lawful wife [husband] according to the rite of our holy mother, the Church?' The expression of consent is followed by the promise of fidelity: 'I, NN, take thee, NN, for my lawful wife [husband], to love and to hold, from this day forward, for better for worse, for richer for poorer, in sickness and in health, till death do us part.' This promise is not essential for the validity of the marriage. The use of a ring is already mentioned in a Cologne marriage formula of the fourteenth century (which instructs the bridegroom to insert it on the finger next to the little finger).

The Greek Orthodox Church also considers matrimony as a sacrament but stresses the sacramental eternity more than the legal indissolubility of marriage. The wedding is celebrated through a rite of crowning which has its origin in the crowning of the king. The *Canticle of Canticles* says: 'Go forth, ye daughters of Sion and see king Solomon in the crown wherewith his mother crowned him in the day of his espousal' (Cant 3,11). In what has been called 'democratisation,' the crowning of the king (which coincided with his marriage) was imitated in every marriage and the wreath worn by the bride goes back to the crown worn by the queen.

The marriage rite of the Anglican Church is essentially the same as that of the Catholic Church.

The changes in the idea of marriage, particularly of the position of the woman, have occasioned changes in the marriage formula. The bride does no longer promise to obey her husband, and marriage is not described as an antidote to fornication. Whereas Princess Anne still promised to obey Mark Phillips, a commoner, Prince Charles and Lady Diana decided to leave out the 'obey.' The Archbishop of Canterbury asked: 'Diana Frances, wilt thou have this man to thy wedded husband, to live together according to God's law in the holy state of matrimony? Wilt thou love him, comfort him, honour and keep him, in sickness and in health and forsaking all other, keep thee only unto him, so long as ye both shall live?' Her reply was: 'I, Diana Frances, take thee, Charles Philip Arthur George, to my wedded husband, to have and to hold from this day forward, for better for worse, for richer for poorer, in sickness and in health, to love and to cherish, 'til death us do part, according to God's holy ordinance and thereto I pledge thee my troth.' After Charles had put the golden wedding ring on Diana's finger, he said: 'With this ring I thee wed, with my body I thee honour and all my worldly goods with thee I share in the name of the Father, and of the Son, and of the Holy Ghost' (the last clause was changed from '. . . and with my worldly goods I thee endow').

Pomp and Ceremonial

As the public proclamation of the new position in society, the marriage ceremony is adapted to the social position of the contracting parties. This led to the pomp of the marriages of nobility in former times and the competitive ostentation and extravagance of today's Japanese weddings. Because it was a joyful event, the wedding celebration was combined with a banquet. The feast as part of the marriage ceremony is found in old and new cultures and the number of guests invited (such as the entire village) and the duration of the festivities (sometimes an entire week) reflect the significance attributed to marriage.

For the Christian churches, the adaptation of the wedding ritual to the traditions of non-European peoples constitutes a difficult problem. Naturally, this is not merely a question of the ceremonial but also of the concept of marriage as an institution and particularly the requirements of monogamy and indissolubility.

Ius Primae Noctis

Sometimes, the *ius primae noctis* is mentioned in connection with the wedding ceremony. This custom means that the bride prostitutes herself to others than the bridegroom as part of the celebration. Herodotus relates that among the Naramones, a people which lived in what today is Libya, the bride had intercourse with all wedding guests. In other societies, the male relatives of the bridegroom, his friends or the attendants of the bridegroom enjoyed this right. It has been described as the right of the feudal lords to spend the first night with the wives of their serfs or tenants. Such a practice is supposed to have existed in Scotland up to the eleventh century when Malcolm III enacted that the bridegroom may pay a sum of money in lieu. Actually, there is no proof that such a right ever existed, and there are several theories on the origin of such a claim. The feudal lord or guardian in chivalry held the power (called *maritagium* or avail of marriage) of disposing of his infant ward in matrimony. Feudal lords exacted fines on the marriage of their vassals and their children, but these payments were not some kind of commutation for a right of defloration.

The expression *droit du Seigneur* (the Lord's, meaning God's right, which can also be understood as the right of some other lord) was used for the duty of continence on the first wedding night (later extended to three nights) imposed by the Council of Carthage of 398 on the basis of the story of Tobias (Tob 8,4 in the Douay version. This verse is not in the Protestant editions of the Apocrypha). In the Middle Ages, dispensation had to be obtained from the restrictions of the 'nights of Tobias.'

Anthropologists relate that in some tribes, the defloration of virgins is the right or office of certain individuals such as elders or priests.

Civil Wedding

With the secularisation of society in the western world, the state undertook to replace the church in regulating marriage and the civil ceremony was added to or superseded the Church wedding. Usually, the civil marriage is hardly an impressive formality and without deep emotional impact. Social studies often point out that marriages celebrated with a religious rite are happier than those contracted only with a civil act. The reason lies less in the ceremony than in the personality of the spouses who get married with a religious function, in their social and economic position, their education, their convictions and attitudes.

In general, the wedding ceremony has lost much of its public significance and has become an event that concerns only the relatives and acquaintances of the newlyweds. Since marriage has become a private matter, certain formalities are observed in order to secure the legal effects of marriage.

In the Soviet Union, couples marrying for the first time may choose to be married in a 'wedding palace,' usually an ordinary office building which is found in every major town. Otherwise, marriages take place in registry offices. In Moscow's best wedding palace, 40 to 50 couples are married every day so that each wedding can take no longer than 15 minutes; in fact, the ceremony lasts barely ten minutes. For this 'conveyor belt' wedding, the couple and their guests are ushered into a spacious room decorated with a bust of Lenin while a five-man orchestra plays the opening bars of Mendelssohn's *Wedding March*. They hear an instruction on the role of the family in Soviet society, say *da* to the question whether they want to take each other as husband and wife, sign the register, exchange rings, and are then whisked out of the ceremonial hall into a small reception room where guests can congratulate the newlyweds. Alcoholic beverages are confiscated at the cloakroom when the group arrives.

Dowry in India

In most of the new independent African states, marriage legislation often remains a dead letter. Only an emancipated minority perform the formality of a civil marriage whereas tribal traditions are observed by the majority. In India, too, the population adheres to the customary wedding forms. In the Hindu wedding ceremony, the couple goes around a ceremonial fire seven times, each taking a vow to remain faithful to the other and to look after his or her interests. In India (and the Middle East), the custom of paying a dowry for the bride presents a difficult problem. Since 1961, India has had an anti-dowry law but the custom persists. Wedding presents are legal so long as they are not a condition for agreeing to the marriage. Obviously, the difference between a legal 'wedding present' and an illegal 'dowry' is hard to prove in court.

In 1984, the Dowry Prohibition Act of 1961 was strengthened. In the definition of dowry, the words 'in connection with the marriage' were substituted for 'as consideration for the marriage;' also, dowry should be restored to a woman within three months instead of one year, and failure to repay within that time under the revised law is to be punished more severely. Special family courts were to investigate dowry cases.

Dowry-giving began in ancient times when women could not own or inherit property and were not allowed to work outside the home. It was a kind of insurance for the bride. The groom's family was expected to return the money to the widow in the event of the groom's death. Today, in most Indian marriages — Hindu and Moslem — the bride's father is expected to pay a large sum in cash to the bridegroom's family. A marriageable man with a degree from a prestigious college and a good job can expect up to $12,500 from a girl's family for agreeing to marry. Among upper class people in southern India, the dowry has come to include diamond eardrops, a pair of gold bracelets and an expensive necklace. In the northern Punjab, a car, a refrigerator and a stereo set are considered a must.

Many Indian girls complain that boys are more interested in the bank balances of the prospective fathers-in-law than in the wives they are marrying. There have been cases in which parents, unable to raise dowries, have married off their daughters to old, decrepit widowers who treat them more as housemaids than as wives. Occasionally, girls have committed suicide to spare their parents humiliation over the dowry. Newly married women have been tortured or even killed because they did not bring enough cash with them. 'Bride burning' claimed more than 2,200 women between 1979 and 1984, and in New Delhi alone, 258 women died of burns in 1983. Arrests for dowry-related killings numbered just over 100 in the last five years and there were only 12 convictions.

Shot-gun marriages were said to have become a way of finding a bridegroom for a marriageable girl in the state of Bihar. The father hires some local toughs who kidnap an eligible bachelor by inviting him to a picnic or a cinema. The prospective son-in-law is then taken to the bride's place where his future father-in-law apologises and asks him to accept his daughter's hand. If he refuses, he is forced to go through the marriage ceremony with a gun pointed at his back. Once the ceremony is completed, the newlyweds are taken to the boy's home, the bride loaded with gifts. A criminal prosecution puts enormous stress on all concerned and under Hindu law, divorce is a complicated proceeding.

Bangladesh banned the dowry system but the tradition is still widely observed. The Independent Women's Council estimated that several dozen women commit suicide each week so as to escape the ill-treatment on the part of their husband's family because they did not bring a dowry. Recently, a young bride of 18 was tortured and hacked to death by her husband and his family because her father, a poor schoolteacher, was unable to pay the promised dowry of about US$60. In a less gruesome case, a 30-year-old doctor divorced his wife because her father refused to pay an additional dowry of US$1,000.

Japanese Weddings

In the traditional form of the *miai* marriage as well as most of the 'romantic' unions (the ratio of 'love' marriages to arranged matches is about 3:1), the two families entrust a *nakôdo* (matchmaker, usually a married couple) with the responsibility of presiding over the wedding celebration. The old *nakôdo* was deemed to be responsible for the lasting success of the marriage he arranged but nowadays, the *nakôdo* who introduces groom and bride and their families at the traditional wedding reception (*hirôen*) often is a person of the highest social standing the families are in a position to invite. But he may also be an employee of a professional matchmaking service which charges a fee.

April and May, October and November are the most popular months for weddings. The autumn months are favoured in rural areas because the autumn harvest provides ready cash, and the season is also preferred because of the pleasant weather. It is cool but fair so that the bride is more comfortable in her wedding kimono. The heat and humidity deter weddings in the summer months.

The exchange of presents at the announcement of the marriage (engagement), is almost universal. The wedding is usually held outside the home in a wedding hall, hotel, temple or shrine. The celebration comprises a religious ceremony (Shinto, Buddhist, or Christian) and a reception or banquet. The wedding ceremony (which may be omitted) and the reception may be held at different places and at different times, and the official notification of the marriage to the family registry may be sent days, weeks or even months later than the wedding. Generally, the date of the wedding ceremony is considered the date of the marriage, and its discrepancy from the date on which the marriage becomes legally valid bothers nobody. Usually, only relatives and close friends are invited to the wedding ceremony while the guests at the banquet may comprise the relatives of both families, former schoolmates and colleagues of both groom and bride, representatives of the enterprises where they work or worked, and friends, colleagues and business acquaintances of the parents.

The newlyweds may wear Japanese attire (the bridegroom in *haori* and *hakama,* the bride in kimono and wearing the hood called *tsunokakushi*) or western-style formal dress. In the course of the banquet, they change costumes (from Japanese to western clothes or from the white bridal gown to an evening gown). Bridegroom and bride, flanked by the *nakôdo*, are seated on a dais decorated with flowers and set off against a golden backdrop. The guests invited by the family of the groom sit on one side and those related to the bride's family on the other; they are seated in groups arranged according to their connection with the families. The banquet is accompanied by speeches; classmates or colleagues may enliven the proceedings by songs or skits (the yell of the school from which the bridegroom graduated is a favourite act). The representatives of the companies may abuse the occasion may by turning their speech into a PR promotion for their organisation.

The cutting of the wedding cake has become a standard feature and sometimes, in a ceremony called candle service, the newlyweds, holding some kind of taper, go from table to table and light the candles on the tables. At the end of the banquet, the guests are given a souvenir and, under mutual bowing, file past the newlyweds, the *nakôdo* and the parents lined up near the exit. If the newlyweds are young, they change into more comfortable clothes and have a follow-up party with their closest friends.

Weddings have become thoroughly commercialised and are big revenue earners for Japanese hotels. On a single (holiday) day considered propitious for tying the knot, over 30 wedding receptions may be held at any one Tokyo hotel and not infrequently, over a thousand guests are invited to the celebration. If either bridegroom or bride is a well-known personality, the event is turned into a show and featured on television. In 1982, newlyweds spent an average of ¥6.2 million on the wedding ceremony, the honeymoon and furniture for their new home. Of this sum, about half was provided by the couple's parents, the other half by their own savings, money they received as wedding gifts and, if necessary, by loans. The wedding ceremony and reception cost ¥2.01 million (receptions of popular figures in politics, sports and entertainment have cost as much as ¥100-300 million); other expenditures were ¥1.53 million for furniture and appliances, ¥840,000 for the honeymoon, ¥670,000 for the bride's wedding dress and accessories, ¥440,000 for the rings and other gifts, and ¥430,000 for the apartment (key money or down payment).

Usually, the families agree on the portion of the costs each family assumes. Sometimes, a considerable part of the expenses can be covered by the difference between the presents of the guests and the value of the presents distributed in return. Customarily, the family of the bride provides the furniture and furnishings necessary for the new household but many young women who work until their marriage use their savings for their trousseau. A honeymoon trip has become extremely popular, and a 'package' which includes the costs of the ceremony and a honeymoon tour relieves the newlyweds from the trouble of their own planning but also deprives them of the joy of arranging their own kind of celebration and makes the wedding a standardised merchandise. Few couples can afford to spend more than a week on their honeymoon. Overseas trips have been chosen by over half of the honeymooners in recent years, with Hawaii being the favourite destination.

A 1984 survey of the Norinchukin Bank (which serves a largely rural clientele) put the average wedding expenses at ¥6.86 million of which the bridegroom and his family shouldered ¥2.93 million and the bride's family contributed ¥3.93 million. The sums included ¥340,000 in gifts to the parents of the bride and ¥420,000 in reciprocal gifts to the bridegroom's parents. This reflects rural customs and is not representative for the cities. The survey found that the couple invited an average of 84 relatives and friends to their wedding party. On average, each of the guests made a gift of ¥13,000 which reduced the net outlays to ¥1.95 million for the bridegroom and to ¥2.53 million for the bride.

Expensive printed invitations and banquets for wedding guests are prohibited by law in the Republic of Korea. In Thailand, the government supports mass weddings in which 20 or more couples are married in one ceremony. The usual Thai wedding includes a long religious rite conducted by Buddhist monks and ordinarily, many guests show up at the reception held to close the celebration.

In Burma, civil marriage exists but a marriage can be concluded without any formality. No marriage certificate is required and no ceremony is needed. A marriage is valid if a man and a woman of marriageable age agree to live together as husband and wife. If so, they are considered spouses by acquaintances and neighbours. A wedding feast is customary.

In Hong Kong, westernisation has resulted in a decline in marriages arranged by the families. This also has reduced the number of the extremely costly traditional Chinese weddings. Many couples live together before they celebrate an official marriage. But civil ceremonies in western dress at the marriage registry or church weddings may be followed by a Chinese-style banquet.

In the People's Republic of China, the Communist Youth League urged young people to resist the pressure by parents, friends and neighbours for big, expensive weddings. The League warned that such weddings plunge young couples and their families into debt and sometimes lead to crime or suicide. It counselled thrift in buying new furniture and clothing, advocated the elimination of all superstitious elements from the festivities and pleaded for mass weddings. Instead of rowdy celebrations and vulgar speeches, the ceremony should include the planting of two symbolic trees by the newlyweds.

The growing affluence of oil-rich Saudi Arabia has resulted in high marriage fees, excessive bridal dowries and extravagant wedding parties. The religious authorities have criticised the fabulous costs of many Saudi marriages because young men shy away from marriage.

Mass Weddings of Namdhari

Mass weddings are the rule with the Namdhari, a sect of the Sikhs (Punjab). The Namdhari are very religious and make the simple life and the avoidance of any kind of luxury and ostentation a religious duty. Eating of meat, drinking of alcohol and smoking are prohibited and no lavish weddings are allowed. In order to implement this prohibition, no single weddings are celebrated; instead, mass betrothals are conducted several times a year in different localities. The ceremony takes place outdoors. Men and women to be married are clad in white; the only ornaments are strings of white beads. The men squat in rows on straw mats spread on the ground. Then, the brides appear, each puts a strand of white beads around the neck of her future husband and sits down at his left. In the first part of the ritual, *Amrit* (holy water) is given to the couples. This is water sweetened with brown sugar and blessed by the priests. A little *Amrit* is poured into the cupped hands of bride and groom and they sip it slowly. Then, a small fire is lit in the middle of the ground and worshipped. The priests spoon melted butter into the sacred fire to keep it burning.

In the last stage of the ceremony, the scarf of each girl is tied to the long white scarf worn by her husband-to-be, symbolising their union. Inside the scarf-knot is tied the marriage fee paid by the bridegroom. Usually, this fee is one and a quarter rupees, but if a man wants to give more, he can pay up to thirteen rupees at the most, so as to avoid ostentation.

Tied together, the couples rise, form a circle and slowly walk four times around the fire while the priests read aloud from the *Granth Sahib*, the sacred scripture of the Sikhs. After completing the rounds, the couples stand facing the fire and the priests pray for a long and happy married life. The couples then return to their places where the priests untie the knots and take out the money which is used for a simple common meal served to everyone present.

In the afternoon, the couples leave. The bride goes straight to the husband's home, with only the clothes she is wearing, without dowry or presents. She must stay at her husband's home for at least a week before paying a visit to her parents.

Mass weddings of children are celebrated in the Indian state of Rajasthan on the occasion of *Akhateej*, the most auspicious day of the year for marriages according to the beliefs of the people in the region around Ajmer. The rites, a simple Hindu ceremony without the traditional hymn-chanting and the rituals usually observed in weddings, are performed by village elders and about 50 or 60 weddings of child grooms and brides, many of them still infants, are conducted in almost every village of the region. In 1985, about 10,000 children were married on 23 and 24 April in Jodhpur and 40,000 in Jaipur.

Mass Weddings under Alexander the Great

Mass weddings are nothing new. A famous historic example is the wedding of ten thousand of Alexander the Great's Macedonian soldiers with Persian women. This ceremony which took place in Susa in 324 BC was part of Alexander's great design of amalgamating Hellas and the Orient. He and his friend Hephaistion married the daughters of King Darius, Stateira and Drypetis (Alexander had already married Roxane, daughter of King Oxyartes of Bactria) and 80 of his officers were married to daughters of the Iranian nobility. In many cases, the women the soldiers married may have been their concubines. In order to induce the soldiers to settle down in the new Asian cities, Alexander decreed that the Persian wives could not be taken back to Macedonia.

Alexander's attempt to fuse two different peoples and cultures poses the question whether such a policy is feasible, let alone whether it can be successful. To reconcile people by coercion seems morally questionable, to say nothing of the effectiveness of such a method. Can marriage which, at least in today's understanding, demands mutual love, respect, equality and freedom, become the vehicle for political designs?

Cancellation of Wedding

It sometimes happens that a relationship is broken off when all preparations for the wedding have already been made. In Japan, engagements have been cancelled even after the customary exchange of betrothal gifts (*yuinô*). Naturally, there are cases in which objective reasons cause a last-minute postponement of the wedding (such as a death in one of the families) but marriages have also been put off or repudiated outright because one of the parties had changed his or her mind. During courtship, talk of a possible marriage remains largely uncommittal but once the parties have decided to get married, they start to reflect in earnest whether they want to live together with such a companion. The result of such an examination may be negative. The girl may discover that during their courtship, her fiancé had shown all the symptoms of a mother complex, or the young man is posted abroad by his company and the girl does not want to give up her job. The young man may have been agreeable to letting the girl continue her career but then demands that she quit.

In former times, it happened that an informant appeared during the wedding and asserted that an impediment made the marriage invalid, or that the bride answered the question whether she would take the man here present to be her lawful husband with a 'No.' Sometimes, the change of mind is the result of pressure on the part of the families. The young couple may have persisted in their resolve to marry each other despite the opposition of parents or other people but finally realised that the odds against them were too great.

The postponement or cancellation of marriage may sometimes involve difficult financial problems. The Japanese Civil Code does not regulate the promise of marriage or engagement and there are no provisions concerning expenses incurred in view of an intended marriage. But in adjudication and legal theory, rules have been accepted that correspond more or less to the legal provisions in other countries. It is generally held that a promise of marriage or an engagement does not create a claim to enforcement. But the non-fulfilment of a promise gives rise to a claim for damages. The extent of the damage is not restricted to the pecuniary losses suffered as a result of the default but also includes compensation for mental pain. Pecuniary claims comprise the expenses for the announcement of the engagement, presents to the *nakôdo*, losses from the wedding preparations which have become useless and indemnification for having given up a job because of the marriage. Furthermore, betrothal gifts and other presents made on account of the marriage have to be returned.

If the wedding is cancelled by mutual agreement, both sides have the obligation of returning gifts. If one party is responsible for the repudiation of the marriage, this party must return everything it received but cannot demand the same from the other party. Sometimes, however, the courts recognise special local customs with regard to the mutual obligations in case a marriage is not concluded.

The rules regulating the claims for damages in case of cancellation of a marriage also apply to Japan's so-called *nai-en* relationships. Depending on the circumstances of the breakdown of such a union, damages for pecuniary losses as well as mental suffering can be claimed.

A phenomenon illustrating the change in social conditions is the willingness of girls to pay a solatium to their boyfriends if they decide not to go through with the marriage. They admit that it has partly been their fault that they did not discover the shortcomings of their chosen partners for which they renege on their promise. Many girls are financially in a position to pay for their mistake instead of invoking the woman's privilege to change her mind.

13

Conjugal Rites

Consummation of Marriage

MARRIAGE MEANS the community of life of two persons of the opposite sex. Juridically, marriage is concluded by a contract by which a man and a woman confer on each other the mutual, permanent and exclusive right over each other's body with respect to sexual acts. (This definition does not fit countries recognising polygamy.) The 'conjugal rites' form the fulfilment of the vows pronounced by the parties at the wedding ceremony: 'with my body I thee worship.' Juridically and morally, the marriage contract gives the partners a right to sexual intercourse and thereby creates the duty of agreeing to copulation if the partner asks in conformity with his or her right. This does not mean that the spouses are obliged to make use of their right.

Among Catholics, the so-called Joseph marriage combines marriage with virginity. The name is based on the Catholic understanding of the marriage of Mary, the mother of Christ, with Joseph, his foster father. Such a marriage implies that the will to give each other the right to marital union is compatible with the intention (but not with the mutual promise) to make no use of this right. This form of marriage has sometimes been chosen by individuals who, for some reason, were obliged to contract a marriage but wanted to preserve virginity as the ideal of their personal lives. In some cases, the ecclesiastical authorities allowed priests or religious who had contracted a marriage against the provisions of Canon Law and wanted to be reconciled with the Church to live with their partner 'as brother and sister' if serious reasons (for example, the education of young children) made a separation difficult.

From the point of view of social philosophy, the conjugal rites are not based on the contractual relations between husband and wife but on the nature of their union in the community of life established by marriage. Marital intercourse forms an integral part of the togetherness of man and woman characteristic of the state of matrimony.

In Canon Law, the consummation of marriage constitutes a factor which makes the indissolubility of the matrimonial bond final. The *matrimonium ratum et consummatum* (ratified and consummated marriage) is indissoluble with only one exception, the 'Pauline privilege,' which allows the dissolution of a marriage contracted by two unbaptised persons if one is converted to the faith and the other will neither convert nor live in peace with the Christian (see below, divorce). The *matrimonium ratum sed non consummatum* (non-consummated ratified marriage), on the contrary, is dissolved by solemn vows or papal dispensation. A medieval canonist, Hinkmar, archbishop of Reims, taught that the sacramental marriage, and therefore every Christian marriage, is concluded by copulation, and other authors held that consent initiates marriage, and intercourse makes it complete.

Intercourse as Duty

State law referring to the marital community of life is usually interpreted to include sexual relations. Japanese law states: 'Spouses must reside together, cooperate and help each other' (Civil Code, Art. 751, Par. 1), and the new German marriage law says: 'Marriage is concluded for life. The spouses have the mutual obligation to (maintain) the community of marital life' (BGB, Art. 1353 (n.F.) Par. 1). Moral theology considers the marital act also in itself (not as a part of the common life) and inquires into the rights and duties related to what is termed the marital debt. As mentioned above, there is no obligation to ask the partner to have intercourse. Moralists, however, note that there may be circumstances under which it can become a duty to do so, for example, if it is necessary in order to prevent extra-marital relations of the partner, to strengthen the marital union or to restore marital harmony. As a rule, a spouse is obliged to agree to intercourse if the partner's request is 'serious and reasonable.' Juridically, this obligation is deduced from the right to the 'body' and the 'marital act' which constitutes the subject of the marriage contract. Morally, it is a serious obligation of justice which can or must be refused only if grave reasons justify or require such a refusal. The marriage debt is one of the questions Saint Paul discussed in chapter seven of the first epistle to the Corinthians which also contains the 'Pauline privilege' mentioned above.

Refusal of Intercourse

Moralists distinguish between the duty to refuse the marital debt and the right to do so. The duty to refuse exists if compliance (sexual intercourse) would 'in itself' be immoral ('sinful'). According to Catholic doctrine, the sexual act is sinful in itself if it is performed in an 'unnatural' way. Coitus is unnatural in this sense if procreation is intentionally prevented, either by interruption so that the semen is ejaculated outside the vagina (onanism) or by artificial means (birth control by the use of condom, pessary, and so on. The validity of this doctrine will be discussed in Volume 4, Ch. 1). It is also immoral to agree to intercourse if copulation involves the direct danger of death or serious injury or sickness (for example, for mother or child in the last stage of pregnancy or immediately after delivery). A spouse has the right to refuse intercourse if the partner has forfeited the right to demand the marital debt. This is the case if one of the spouses commits adultery (unless the other partner has consented to, caused or forgiven the adultery), lives a criminal or dissolute life or has abused the partner — the same reasons that would justify the suspension of marital cohabitation (*separatio a mensa et thoro*).

If one spouse has committed adultery and the other knowingly and willingly agrees to marital intercourse, the innocent party is presumed to have forgiven the infidelity. Naturally, such forgiveness does not constitute *carte blanche* for further infidelity but after the decriminalisation of adultery, an agreement between spouses that both can have sexual relations outside marriage has no legal consequences. The moral evaluation of so-called 'open marriages' is a different problem.

Japanese law makes 'unfaithful conduct' a ground for divorce (Civil Code, Art. 770, Par. 1, No. 1). The meaning of this expression is more comprehensive than adultery but certainly includes it. Of the other grounds for divorce enumerated in Japanese law, 'malicious abandonment' (Civil Code, Art. 770, Par. 1, No. 2) and 'other serious circumstances making the continuation of the marriage difficult' (ibid., No. 5) would also justify the refusal of marital intercourse.

The West German marriage law provides: 'A spouse is not obliged to comply with the request for the establishment of community if this request constitutes a misuse of his (her) right or if the marriage has broken down' (BGB, Art. 1353 (n.F.), Par. 2). (According to existing German law, the break-down of the marriage is the sole ground for divorce.) Morally, the request for intercourse can also be refused if it constitutes a burden or imposition extraneous to intercourse as such (inordinate frequency, degrading manner — for example, if the partner is drunk or demands coitus in front of others).

Enforcement of Cohabitation

Marital cohabitation can be legally enforced but although cohabitation ordinarily implies marital relations, it is impossible to make coitus as such the object of legal enforcement. On the other hand, deliberate and continuous denial of the marital act would mean the erosion of marriage and justify the suspension of support and an action for divorce. But the use of force for compelling the partner to submit to intercourse is out of the question. Some American states (for example, Oregon, Delaware, Iowa and New Jersey) have enacted statutes which rule out marriage or cohabitation as a defence against physically forcing sexual intercourse upon a spouse (rape). Some years ago, a Belgian court of appeal found a man guilty of rape because he had compelled his wife by force to have intercourse. The man often mistreated his wife and if she refused, he bound her to the bed and forced her to have sex. The court of first instance had held the man guilty of violence but accepted the plea of the defence that the refusal of marital intercourse constituted a neglect of the wife's marital duties. The court of appeal, however, decided that the accused was guilty of rape. 'There is no law that can compel a woman to have intimate relations with her husband against her will. There is no law that accepts violence as an act of sexual persuasion.' Marriage is no excuse for rape. (Unfortunately, this principle has not yet found universal acceptance.) There have been cases in which the husband has been charged with rape after helping a third party engage in sexual relations with his wife.

The old Japanese law made maltreatment or serious insult on the part of the spouse rendering cohabitation intolerable a ground for divorce. This also applied if the maltreatment or serious insult was inflicted by or on linear ascendants of a spouse (old Civil Code, Art. 813, Nos. 5, 7 and 8). In view of these provisions (which are still relevant to the existing legal order), sadism would be a reason to refuse marital relations.

14

The Marital Act

THE MEANING AND PURPOSE of sexuality is procreation. Objectively and in the nature of things, the continuation of the species is the reason for the existence of sexually differentiated organisms, sex organs and the activation of these organs. (As mentioned above, there is also asexual propagation.) The continuation of the species is so intimately connected with the existence of its specimens that in some cases, fertilisation brings the death of the organism. By transmitting life, the task of the organism has been completed and the meaning of its existence exhausted. Also in cases in which fertilisation is not a single unrepeatable act, it is regulated in such a way that the survival of the species is assured (as in seasonally-regulated mating involving spring birth when conditions for survival are most favourable).

Sexual Activity as a Human Act

In man, existence is not tied in an indissoluble way to the continuation of the species. As a spiritual being, man can find meaning and value in his life regardless of his sexuality and without activating his sexual potentialities. Man's sexual activity is not a purely physiological process but includes sensitive and spiritual elements. The Scholastic philosophers distinguished between an act of man (*actus hominis*) and a human act (*actus humanus*). As a material being, man is subject to the laws of physics, as an organism, he breathes and digests food, as an animal, a sentient creature, he experiences sensations of hot and cold, but all these actions are beyond man's conscious control, they are acts of man (something which happens to or occurs in man); but not human acts. There are also spontaneous, indeliberate reactions of man's will of which he is not master. To the extent that man is master of his actions and controls them by his knowledge and free will, his doings assume a specifically human character. These are voluntary acts for which man is responsible.

Sexual intercourse necessarily involves a physiological process, but the meaning and purpose of this action is not limited to man's biological life and his bodily functions. There are, of course, involuntary motions of the sex instinct such as nocturnal emissions and unintentional stimulation of the sex organs which may lead to erection and ejaculation.

If a man has to remain at the same place or in the same position for a long time, the fear produced by the expectation of not being able to go to the toilet may result in erection and ejaculation. But even in such cases, the activation of the sex organs is different from purely physiological processes such as breathing or digestion. It not only is an intermittent activity but also conditioned on specific internal or external stimulation. All the more so the marital act is no purely mechanical process. Both partners are involved with body and soul and their sensitive and spiritual cognitive and emotional faculties. There are enormous differences in the manner in which the partners engage in sexual relations, even apart from situations such as rape and prostitution.

Differences in Sex Experience of Men and Women

Physiologically as well as emotionally, intercourse means a very different experience for man and woman. For man, the main aspects are erection, penetration and ejaculation (orgasm). They constitute the most visible manifestation of the swelling tension of vital energy and the excitation of the physiological and sensual powers inseparable from intercourse. Because the physiological processes are accompanied by strong sensitive impressions, they dominate the consciousness but as such, the physiological acts are rather localised. In the male, sexual desire often induces the erection of the penis. Suggestive written or pictorial representations of sex and sexual fantasies as well as touching the sex organs, self-stimulation or excitation by others will bring about the erection of the penis. Physiologically, the mental or physical stimulation acts on the nervous system which causes the inflow of blood into the glans and the cavernous bodies while blocking its discharge. The indirect process of erection explains the possibility of psychological obstruction of intercourse. The purpose of the erection of the penis and its concomitant hardening is the insertion into the vulva, one of the numerous teleological aspects of sex. The mucous secretion which may accompany sexual arousal apart from erection also serves to facilitate penetration.

Foreplay

For woman, the foreplay is of much greater importance than for man. One of the most common complaints of women mentioned in the various sex reports is the insufficient attention of their partners to the preliminaries of intercourse. The male thinks only of his own satisfaction and believes that the insertion of the penis and the piston movement will automatically bring satisfaction to the woman. Women want more kisses and more fondling, more embraces and more sweet talk. They want to be excited by caresses titillating their entire body, but especially breasts and nipples, thighs and sex organs. Kissing is almost universal as foreplay, but the kissing of the woman's breasts is less common than touching and fondling with the hands. Many women experience erotic arousal if their breasts are caressed which may even lead to orgasm.

It happens that women have orgasm when they nurse their babies. Nevertheless, woman's sexual arousal does not necessarily depend on foreplay. As mentioned above, a woman's sexual desire responds to the same internal and external stimulation as a man's and the expectation of intercourse is also effective in women. Her sexual excitement is less concentrated on the sex organs and affects her entire body, but there is an influx of blood into the clitoris which makes it more receptive to stimulation and the mucous excretion of the vagina prepares it for the insertion of the penis.

It may be just forgetfulness that men sometimes neglect the foreplay. Intercourse has become some kind of routine, and foreplay appears less and less important. Men have little difficulty in getting ready if they are in the mood for sex play, and because they usually take the initiative, they feel no need for foreplay. But if a woman is not in the right mood, she may need time to respond or find difficulty in getting aroused although the greater variety of erogenous zones in the female body should facilitate sexual arousal. Women may have to overcome their reluctance to talk about the mechanics of sex and let their partner know how they feel, where they like to be touched, how long and the kind of touch they find most exciting. If men are left to their own devices, they may have great difficulty in pleasing their mates. A heart-to-heart talk when not making love and a gentle hint now and then when in bed together may make the marital act more satisfactory to both.

Male Initiative

In the structure and function of the sex organs, the initiative of the male is programmed which does not mean that the female cannot take the initiative. In the ordinary form of coitus, however, the male appears as active and the female as passive. The 'mounting' position of the male, the insertion of the penis and the rhythmic movement mean that the male conquers the female, makes her his own, takes possession of her. The female appears to submit, to yield and to surrender herself. The man embracing the woman and the woman clinging to the man express these basic tendencies. But the outward appearances do not reveal the real relations of the sexes. It is the woman's right to attract attention, to arouse passion and to be wooed. The interplay of desire and being desired, of coveting and being coveted, of lusting and being lusted after which marks the unfolding of the attraction of the sexes is repeated over and over again in the sex act. Woman is the centre of sexuality. To the delight of the male in conquering the female corresponds the delight of the female in making the male her own. Before surrendering her body, the woman has subjugated the man. Spiritually, emotionally and voluptuously, the man belongs to her. Many women are not aware of the hold they have over men but those who do usually know how to make use of it.

Orgasm

Ideally, sexual intercourse should end in the simultaneous orgasm of man and woman but it often does not. Unless there is some interference, the sexual stimulation of men usually leads to ejaculation but to many women, intercourse does not bring orgasm. In pre-war Japan, many women did not experience orgasm before the birth of their first child, and some women never reached orgasm. The reports on women's sexuality emphasise that for women, orgasm results from the stimulation of the clitoris rather than the stimulation of the vagina, and although the movement of the penis stimulates labia, clitoris and vagina, it often seems insufficient. Men tend to think that their penis plays the most important part in intercourse and that a large and stiff penis enhances sexual pleasure. Some women like the stimulation from a large, hard penis but others find the insertion of the penis unpleasant and even painful, particularly if lubrication is insufficient (which may be the case if the woman is not ready or the man has drunk). According to Shere Hite, 70 per cent of the women surveyed could not achieve orgasm through intercourse alone and she concluded that the vast majority of women experience orgasm from clitoral, not vaginal stimulation so that intercourse leaves them unsatisfied. She suggested that women should stimulate themselves while in bed with their partners.

A report on sex in East Germany asserted that 70 per cent of the women almost always achieved orgasm during intercourse, up from 26 per cent in the 1950s. In West Germany, coitus brought orgasm to 40-50 per cent of the women.

Of the women answering the More survey, only 10 per cent always achieved orgasm through intercourse while 40 per cent could always induce orgasm by masturbation and 76 per cent always or nearly always. Many of the women, therefore, combined masturbation with intercourse, some masturbated by stimulating the clitoris before, others during or after intercourse. Many women concealed their masturbation from their sex partners — some for the same reasons that women often feigned orgasm: so as not to disappoint their partners, be considered as frigid, or because they were reluctant to talk about their sexual needs. But over half of the women asked their partners to stimulate the clitoris — usually manually. The stimulation of the clitoris means nothing to the male.

Most women noted a difference between the orgasm procured by masturbation and the orgasm experienced in intercourse although they found it difficult to describe it. Orgasm resulting from masturbation was said to be narrow or shallow although focused sharper on the genital region while orgasm from intercourse was deep, wide, diffusive and affecting almost the entire body. Many women noticed the emotional difference. Masturbation, although bringing excitement and pleasure, leaves a feeling of emptiness, loneliness and estrangement. Some women like the feeling of their vagina enveloping the penis as an expression of their hold on their partners.

The assumption that intercourse should produce an orgasm can create much unhappiness and anxiety because some women never experience orgasms and about one in five women has orgasms only occasionally or irregularly. Women should realise that the lack of orgasm is neither unhealthy nor a sign of sexual insufficiency. But the failure to achieve orgasm may be the result of an insufficient understanding of the sex act which underlines the necessity of adequate sexual instruction before marriage. The failure to experience satisfaction may make intercourse an annoyance rather than a pleasure.

Importance of Orgasm

A woman describing her first intercourse remarked that it was quite different from what she had expected. She did not dislike it when she felt 'this thing' going into her but it wasn't automatic pleasure. Other women were disappointed because orgasm did not bring the ecstasy often described in pulp magazines. For couples with good or at least normal marital relations, intercourse becomes a joyful affirmation of their togetherness. The full delight of coitus is only experienced if the partners become not only 'one flesh' in their carnal union but also one heart and one soul in the shared sensation of excitement. Naturally, the satisfaction of the sexual desire is not a common experience. In the marital act, each partner ideally derives full sexual enjoyment in the acme of sexual lust but this is felt by each partner individually and is not in the strict sense a shared experience. Nevertheless, intercourse is only satisfactory if it renews and strengthens the consciousness and certitude of belonging to each other, the deep conviction of 'I am yours and you are mine.' Women want sexual satisfaction, but the majority of women appreciate tenderness more than clitoral stimulation and the experience of nearness and intimacy is more important than orgasm. To the question 'Would you be content to be held close and treated tenderly and forget about "the act"?' columnist Ann Landers received about 90,000 answers of which 72 per cent wanted less emphasis on the act and more loving togetherness.

In a half-humorous riposte to Ann Lander's survey, columnist Mike Royko invited men to write to him whether they preferred sex with their wives (or other companions) to bowling, fishing, golf, watching TV or sitting at a bar with their pals. The result: of about 10,000 men, 66 per cent opted for sex, 22 per cent chose bowling, drinking, golf, cuddling or something else, and 12 per cent couldn't make up their minds. While many men complained that the lovely girl they married had become a cold, dull and fat inadequate — slovenliness and unresponsiveness were the most often voiced discontents — others, even men in their 60s and 70s, extolled the happiness of married life and the satisfaction they found in sex. Unhappy sex relations, a man wrote, should not be blamed on frigid wives but on inconsiderate, ignorant and boorish husbands who neither know nor care about the sexual needs, responses and desires of their wives. Women want to make love, not make sex, and feel unhappy if they don't get it.

Nevertheless, intercourse brings the feeling of oneness, security and confidence, the confirmation of being loved and desired, and it will always remain the ultimate manifestation of mutual affection. The naked embrace is one of the most satisfying expressions of togetherness — whether it leads to intercourse or not. The feeling of bodily warmth from the contact of the naked bodies is not just a source of sensuous pleasure but the reassurance of being sheltered and protected, of having somebody to cling to, to trust and love. Being united in love forms the essential premise for making intercourse the most precious personal experience of the partners.

Sex symbols can cause both positive and negative reactions. A woman who compares her husband with the current film idol will be turned off, but if she fantasises that her partner is the perfect lover portrayed in the movies and dreams about it during the day, she may prepare herself psychologically, emotionally and physically for satisfactory sex with her partner. The same is true for the male. He can be depressed by the impression that his wife cannot measure up to the sirens on the screen but he can also imagine that he is embracing the voluptuous body on TV or in the latest issue of *Playboy* that aroused his passion.

Emotional Involvement

The bodily contact and the awareness of the partner's sexual arousal form part of the sensual pleasure felt by each partner, and although the impulse to satisfy one's lust is the main stimulus to continue intercourse until orgasm occurs, it does not exclude the concomitant feeling of affection for the partner. The absence of any emotional involvement ('man only wants to masturbate inside a vagina') denies the essence of marital intercourse. Women feel miserable when forced to have intercourse with somebody they do not love and their reactions range from disgust to horror. Even prostitutes need time to overcome the aversion and get used to offering their bodies without any involvement.

The separation of physical sex from emotions results in the dehumanisation of sex which makes intercourse empty and meaningless. In the traditional view, intercourse has its place within the framework of the most intimate personal relations, but in some circles, copulation is regarded as a just somewhat more sensuous expression of affection than a kiss. Theoretically, Platonic love may be compatible with marriage but such lovers usually end up in bed together.

Sex partners feel great satisfaction from simultaneous orgasms but this synchronism is hard to achieve. In the early years, man's ejaculation often occurs before the woman reaches orgasm while in later years, it takes the man longer to come to an ejaculation. Usually, the orgasm is short, only a few seconds, and it is followed by a period of relaxation. Even if sexual stimulation continues, the male is unable to respond to it. A woman may experience a series of orgasms and some women reach a climax twice during intercourse. Younger men can have erection and ejaculation again after a short interval but this becomes impossible in later years. In a book entitled *Extended Sexual Orgasm*, Alan and Donna Bauer claim to offer a method leading to deep, continuous orgasm of ever-increasing arousal lasting 30 minutes to an hour or more. A combination of tantric sex with pop psychology is said to create conditions for pleasure which not only overcome resistances but also ease a variety of ailments.

A hilarious (at least for the bystanders) episode was reported from Nairobi. A man and his married mistress had a rendezvous at the woman's home but when the time came to part they found themselves inseparably locked in their amorous embrace. Terrified, they put aside their disgrace and screamed for help. Neighbours hearing their cries thought they were being robbed and were more than startled to find the pair in their passionate and compromising position. Since the neighbours' tugging failed to uncouple the two, the police were called. Their efforts were also to no avail and an ambulance brought the couple, loaded on a single stretcher, to the hospital where it took the staff six hours to separate them.

Over Emphasis on Orgasm

The sex revolution has created the trend to stress the techniques of intercourse, to attach the greatest importance to the pleasure derived from sexual relations and make the frequency and intensity of orgasm the measure of marital happiness. It is one of the instances in which, as Harvey Cox has formulated it after van Peursen, modern man is concerned with the art of loving rather than with love. The identification of happiness with sexual prowess has created a perverse exaltation of the purely physiological capacity divorced from the meaning of sex as a personal union and in disregard of the unity of body and soul characteristic of human sexuality.

Sexual intercourse is being made an end in itself and the meaning of marital life reduced to physiological sensations. As a result, the quest of sexual happiness becomes intertwined with the fear of losing it. It is impossible to always feel the same pleasure or to derive constantly increasing satisfaction from sex. The pleasure experienced in intercourse is influenced by many factors some of which cannot be controlled at will. While intercourse is an important element of marital life, it constitutes neither its highest value nor an indispensable part.

The notion of virility and masculinity popularised by the pulp magazines has made the capacity for orgasm the measure of success in sexual relations and reinforced the tendency of men to demand intercourse regardless of the condition and the mood of the woman. Japanese women usually comply even if they feel no inclination themselves. The traditional attitude of regarding the husband as their master and the fear to offend him make women consent even to unreasonable requests. This submissiveness is very pronounced in women cohabitating without formal marriage because they are afraid of losing their partners. Men tend to break off coitus as soon as they have ejaculated, often leaving the woman unfulfilled and empty. Very few Japanese women talk to their sex partners about coitus. They are too shy to explain what they feel, want or miss or how coitus could become more satisfactory to them. If they did, the partner might think that his technique were bad. Sex still is a subject 'nice' girls do not talk about and women are loath to mention.

This is one of the reasons why women very seldom propose sex. They consider it improper to ask because they are supposed to be passive. They do not want to tell their partners what to do because the male should take the lead. A woman who feels lonely and despondent and desperately wants to be embraced, caressed and reassured of the love and affection of her husband does not utter a word to draw her husband's attention to her longing for sympathy.

Sexual Satisfaction

Only a partner whose sexuality, including tenderness and eroticism, is mature and who is conscious of his (her) own acceptability and lovableness can give him- (her-) self as an independent as well as an indigent being, and only if his self-love meshes with that of his partner can he experience himself as freely accepted, coveted but also respected. Otherwise, the partner will be nothing but a lustfully 'used' object, serving a limited purpose and interchangeable at will (Heribert Wahl).

As the affirmation of one's own self, the marital act includes the conquest of the partner as well as the surrender to her or him. It is impossible to take without giving at the same time, and the key to marital happiness is to extend the give-and-take beyond the body and the sex organs to the give-and-take of affection and personality. The emotional and spiritual involvement distinguishes marital intercourse from the lechery of the libertine who only wants a woman because her body has a cavity which he can penetrate with his penis or the readiness of the whore who thinks about hooking the next customer. Sexuality must be understood as a value and task of the whole person, and sexual intercourse should not be reduced to merely genital satisfaction.

If approached properly, making love is a ritual — the oldest and most cherished ritual of mankind — by which young lovers seal their fresh and sweet union and grandparents still enjoy the best moments of human existence. Some people experience orgasm as an ecstasy of voluptuousness while others find the description of the pleasure connected with sexual satisfaction highly exaggerated. Nevertheless, orgasm brings a unique sexual gratification different from all other forms of sensual enjoyment. Ancient mythology may be irrelevant to modern man but the feeling of awe and wonderment at man's creative power ringing in some of these myths conveys the irresistible fascination sex has exercised over all generations. In Indian mythology, coitus is a repetition of the creation of the world, the spiritual moment in which the self acquires heavenly bliss. The union of masculinity and femininity in the process of enlightenment represented in tantric Buddhism by the ecstatic sexual embrace of male and female deities implies the transcendence of the sameness of man over the diversity of sexual distinctions.

Doctors report that the number of people biting other people has been rising in recent years and in some of these cases, the bites result from too much passion between lovers. They may bite each other's earlobe or bite the partner's lip, nose or nipple.

For Plato, the sexual union was the symbol of every kind of satisfying happiness, and marital intercourse should be the apogee of joy in a personal relationship. In Sartre's view, sexuality is an essential aspect of man's existence but cannot possibly be the basis of an intersubjective relationship. Sexuality, Sartre maintains, fluctuates between sadism and masochism; either the other person or oneself is merely a thing, not a person. While Sartre's analysis may be relevant to sexual brutalisation or prostitution, it is entirely wrong when sex is an expression of mutual love in which the desire to possess is inseparable from the yearning to belong.

Adjuncts to Copulation

Customs surrounding sexual intercourse vary greatly. Many people, particularly women, prefer love-making in the dark, many restrict coitus to the evening or night. Among younger people, complete nakedness seems to prevail which facilitates foreplay (the common or mutual undressing is in itself a very effective foreplay) and is undoubtedly conducive to greater sexual enjoyment. But the prudishness fostered by the association of sex and nakedness with sin or indecency induces many couples not to remove all clothing and to copulate under a blanket. It is said that Robert and Elizabeth Browning, despite their romantic runaway marriage and their ardent love poems, never saw each other naked. At the beginning of the twentieth century, prostitutes demanded extra payment if they were asked to undress completely — not because of the trouble but because it was considered perverse to look at a naked woman. A 1984 American sex survey found that a high percentage of men as well as women preferred sex in the nude.

In Japan, living conditions may often not afford the privacy desirable for marital intercourse. Parents may not have a separate bedroom, and even if they have a room of their own, the sliding doors between rooms are more symbolic than real partitions. The walls between apartments are almost paper-thin so that neighbours can guess what is going on next door. For many women, intercourse becomes an unpleasant burden. At the end of the day, when she has been busy with countless small things necessary for the household, a woman is tired and worn out. Many Japanese 'salarymen' come home late and their wives have to serve supper at any odd time between seven and midnight. If a wife has to take care of small children or if she is working, she wants nothing more than to sleep and is hardly in a mood for sexual adventure.

It sometimes happens that husband and wife have divergent preferences; he may like to have sex at night while she is too tired or he may find it more enjoyable to have intercourse in the morning when the wife is still sleepy and her senses dull.

Eroticism and Moral Consciousness

For the entire sphere of sexuality and particularly for sex in marriage, the basic thinking on sex and the recognition of its true meaning are of the greatest importance. The attitudes towards sex prior to marriage and sex education necessarily influence behaviour in marriage. People whose views on sex equated sex with sin may experience a feeling of guilt about sexual activities even after marriage. Women may feel discomfort with sexuality partly as the result of parental admonitions and partly on account of the association with the excretory system. Having been told in their youth that sex was 'bad' and sinful, women's conscience reacts to sex as to a violation of moral standards and sexual gratification may be accompanied by uneasiness. They learned to consider sex and the sex organs as something unclean, dirty, shameful and immoral, something to hide and neither to think nor talk about. Some women retain this detractive attitude towards sex later in life, others resume it when they become involved with a partner whose sex they find distasteful. Some women find the seminal fluid horrible, others gladly swallow it in oral sex. Men, especially adolescents, may also be under the sway of damnatory attitudes towards sex which may take on various forms, from mere indifference and complete lack of interest in sex to fear and revulsion. The Old Testament exemplifies the association of sexual intercourse and ejaculation with uncleanness and defilement in religious thought (for example, Lev 15, 16-18; 22,4) and the *Qur'an* allows the use of sand for the ablution required after intercourse (Sura 4,46; 5,9).

Many people confuse conscience which is a judgement on the conformity of one's actions (comprising 'thoughts, words, and deeds') with binding moral norms and bodily feelings of anxiety caused by the fear of doing something unacceptable by social standards. Because today's society is highly ambivalent concerning standards of sexual behaviour, people have become insecure in their judgements on the morality of sex.

Many girls think that masturbation is bad when they discover it as a means of pleasure because they have been warned not to touch the sex organs, but they change their way of thinking when they get used to self-gratification. When a woman marries, the household chores tend to dominate her thinking, and when she becomes a mother, the satisfaction of the physical needs of her child relegates most other concerns to a place of less importance. She feels herself more as a mother than as a wife. As a mother, she must be a 'decent' woman and decent women do not have sex.

Anxiety

A woman may be dominated by fear, fear of surrendering herself, fear of succumbing or fear of becoming pregnant. This fear often dampens woman's enjoyment of sex. Not only unmarried but also married women who do not want children feel concern whether the method of birth control she or her partner uses will work. This anxiety often makes it psychologically impossible to achieve orgasm. This kind of psychological blockage can be particularly strong in women who have had an abortion. The emotional trauma left by their frightful experience and their wish to never again undergo an operation become a conscious or subconscious obstacle to the unrestrained abandonment to sexual lust. Women should know their bodies and bodily functions, be able to determine 'safe' periods and have effective means of birth control for other days. They will be unable to enjoy sex unless they can be sure that it will not lead to pregnancy. Frigidity requires medical help.

Women are not the only ones having difficulties with sex. In Japan, the number of so-called 'wedding-night divorces' has been growing. Usually, these failures are due to the inability of the groom to consummate the marriage. It has been theorised that the excessive protection of boys by their mothers has created a 'mother complex,' and when a young man marries a girl who either was chosen by his mother or resembles her, he feels unable to carry out the marital act. A specialist in this field reported that nearly 80 per cent of the cases of male impotence had no basis in any physical abnormality, indicating that it was caused psychologically.

The cases of 'honeymoon' impotence showed high percentages of eldest sons, youngest sons, and only sons — males most likely to be the victims of motherly over-protection or subject to parental pressure and the stress attributable to Japan's highly competitive society. Primary impotence often results from excessive nervousness or ignorance about sex, and each failure compounds the problem by increasing the individual's anxiety. Their partners sometimes make the situation worse by openly criticising or ridiculing the unhappy male. Secondary impotence is also growing among Japanese men, especially those under stress in their jobs or having problems with their wives.

Impotence and Infertility

American researchers suggested that male distance runners who cover more than 60 km a week may experience a reduced sex drive due to a significantly lower (about 30 per cent) level of testosterone. In the same way, women distance runners have shown a noticeable drop in the level of prolactin (luteotropin), sometimes causing the women to stop menstruating. In adolescent girls, heavy training can delay the onset of puberty.

A number of developments are exploring remedies for infertility. In women, blocked Fallopian tubes are a common cause of infertility. Research is under way to construct an artificial Fallopian tube from super-smooth polymer plastic developed to line the first permanent artificial heart. Another possibility under study is the transplant of natural tubes from one woman to another. In Japan, a device has been developed for distinguishing psychological impotence from impotence of purely physical origin. It is based on the fact that a patient suffering from psychological impotence can have an erection during the light sleep period characterised by rapid eye movement (REM). Sex therapy can be effective in psychogenic impotence while medication can sometimes cure physical impotence. If drugs cannot help, impotence may be overcome by penile implants.

A Chinese doctor claims to have developed a successful acupuncture treatment for male sterility and impotence. Since 1976, Dr Wang Yizhi of Jinan University in Canton (Ghuangzhou) has clinically treated over 400 cases of male sterility, including complaints such as low sperm count, impotence, non-ejaculation or premature ejaculation, with a success rate of over 60 per cent.

The Beijing newspaper *China Daily* reported that Chinese doctors had developed a concoction of 11 medicinal herbs which restored sexual vitality to men and was also effective against lumbago, lethargy, palpitation and difficulty in breathing.

Freud maintained that infantile taboos could only be overcome and sexual normality achieved if a man could imagine having intercourse with his mother or sister (a woman with her father). Everybody examining himself with regard to this demand, Freud wrote, will discover that he condemns sex as something debasing, something which soils and defiles, not only bodily.

Freud was unable to fathom the true meaning of sex because sex can be adequately understood only in the context of man's spirituality and personality. Sex forms part of man's innermost self and is inextricably linked to his maturity and personal fulfilment. To reduce the sex act to a merely physiological function deprives it of its meaning as an expression of mutual love and joyful intimacy.

Sex — During Menstruation and Pregnancy

Taboos against intercourse during the woman's menstrual period are found in many cultures. The Mosaic law fixed the death penalty for those having intercourse during menstruation (Lev 20,18) but contains also a simple prohibition without a penalty (Lev 18,9) and a clause declaring a man impure for seven days having intercourse with a woman during menstruation (Lev 15,24). From a medical point of view, coitus during menstruation involves no particular danger, and this period certainly is the safest for avoiding conception.

The problem is different for intercourse during pregnancy. An American pathologist expressed the view that sexual intercourse during pregnancy may be more dangerous to the unborn child than the combined effects of alcohol use and cigarette smoking. Sex with a pregnant woman increases the chance of infection from bacteria in semen. The infection attacks the placenta, the life support system for the embryo that transfers food, oxygen and protective chemicals from the mother's blood to the baby's. Intercourse increases the risk of miscarriage and may cause developmental problems in the foetus, particularly in a surviving infant's nervous system. These risks may start early, certainly at the beginning of the fourth month of pregnancy. Other paediatricians and gynaecologists, however, maintain that, where there are no special circumstances, a couple may continue having intercourse throughout the pregnancy of the woman.

According to American doctors, normal sexual relations are permissible and may sometimes even be beneficial for people with heart problems under proper medical supervision. They should avoid sex after meals or the intake of alcohol but otherwise, three-quarters of the cardiac patients treated by a heart specialist were able to return to sexual activity.

Frequency of Intercourse

The frequency of sexual intercourse is a problem each couple has to solve on a case-by-case basis. The sexual desire of one partner may urge to have sex five times a day while the other may rather opt for five times a year. It is impossible to fix beforehand a definite schedule and only mutual tenderness which enters into the feelings of the other partner can find the time when both partners are emotionally inclined to make love. It would be basically wrong to fix a certain number as normal for a marriage, or to determine a maximum or minimum. It would also be a mistake to designate certain days or hours for marital intercourse. 'How much sex is necessary to make a marriage happy' is a meaningless question. Spouses who love each other and are happy with each other, for whom the marital act is the supreme expression of their love and happiness, will have intercourse when they are in the mood to affirm their intimacy in that way and any kind of schedule would simply be irrelevant.

Shere Hite asserts that American society, by identifying manliness with sexual activity, pressures men into having as much sex as possible, but she rightly concludes that nobody can say how often a man 'ought to have' sex. American housewives are said to have sex twice as often as career women.

A Japanese study covering male salary earners found that over 30 per cent had sex once or twice a month, 30 per cent once a week, 19 per cent twice a week, and less than 10 per cent twice or more often a week. Many men in their thirties had intercourse twice a week while the majority of those in their forties settled for once a week and those in their fifties for once every two weeks. A woman cited in the More Report found it impossible to stay with a partner who wanted sex seven times a night while another woman complained that her husband ignored her sexual needs. 'I want to be recognised not only as a mother and housekeeper, but also as a wife and woman,' she wrote. Soviet researchers reported that men often overestimate a younger woman's desire for sex while they underestimate that of older women. Males are most potent in their late twenties, while women manifest a maximum interest in sex by the age of 30 and often maintain it until the age of 60.

Aphrodisiacs

In all ages and in all civilisations, people have used aphrodisiacs, naturally not necessarily in the form of drugs. Many of these means or methods are nothing more than superstition or quackery but sexual desire can certainly be stimulated by drugs. P-chlorophenylalamine seems to reduce the amount of serotonin in the brain, a substance considered to inhibit sex. Of other drugs, pargyline, while stimulating sex, has undesirable side effects.

An American medical team reached the conclusion that hallucinogenic drugs have aphrodisiac qualities and may contribute to multiple orgasms. They listed as sex stimulants in the order of potency: cocaine, lysergic acid diethylamide, mascaline, marijuana and hashish.

An American gerontologist, Dr Panayiotis D. Tsitouras, found that older men's sexual vigour is not enhanced by injections of the male sex hormone testosterone and that there is only a minor association between the level of the hormone in a subject's blood and the degree of sexual potency. Researchers detected no significant influence of coronary artery disease, muscle mass or smoking on testosterone levels or sexual activity. Alcohol stimulates the sexual desire of women but the same is not true for men and alcohol may even blunt their sexual potency.

Scientists have detected that smell can act as a sexual stimulant. In the animal world, the females of some species (such as the cat family) attract males by their smell, in other species, the roles are reversed (the male of the Oriental fruit moth emits a chemical that smells like lemons and contains methyl jasmonate, known in the perfume world as the 'queen of aromas'). Among humans, the so-called pheromones (hormonal substances) which smell like vinegar or rancid butter are more likely to excite males than perfume.

Whether man or woman derives most pleasure from intercourse is a question about which the Greek gods have already quarrelled. In a dispute with her husband Zeus, Hera, the queen of the Olympian gods and the goddess of marriage, had contended that women had less pleasure in love than men. But Teiresias of Theben, who had been both man and woman — he had been turned into a woman when he killed the female of two coupling snakes but regained his own sex when he also killed the male — told her that love gave women nine times more pleasure than it gave men whereupon Hera, enraged, blinded him. As can be expected, psychological findings are inconclusive.

Japanese Survey on Sex

In a Japanese survey commissioned by Kyodo News Service in late 1981, a research team from the Faculty of Medicine of Tokyo University had questionnaires distributed to 10,500 management-level employees or their wives, a control group from the general public (5,800 men and women selected at random from electoral rolls), a group of 1,000 men and women staying overnight in hospitals and 800 men and women in rural areas. There were great differences in the response rates (managerial group 8 per cent, general group 11 per cent, hospital group 29 per cent, rural group 54 per cent).

The average age of the respondents was 45 years for men and 48.2 years for women. Married couples had an average of 2.2 children. Only 16 per cent of the managerial group were living in a three-generation household (usually with one or both of the husband's parents) while the proportion was twice as high in the population at large.

Sex was considered important by 67 per cent of the men and 50 per cent of the women. Four out of five women believed that their husbands understood their physical needs and over 40 per cent of husbands and wives said they could discuss their intimate feelings with their partners. One-third of the women, however, had inhibitions discussing sex, 24 per cent faked orgasm, and 33 per cent quietly resigned when unfulfilled in intercourse. While 62 per cent of the men always achieved orgasm with their marriage partners, only 45 per cent of the women were equally satisfied.

Sexual intercourse was initiated by the husband 'always' according to 60 per cent of the women and 'mostly' in the case of 36 per cent. The average couple made love 1.2 times a week, taking a little over 20 minutes. The rate was lower, 1.1 times, for the managerial group than for the general group (1.5 times). By age classes, men in their forties had sex 1.36 times a week, women 1.05 times; men in their fifties 0.87 times, women 0.71 times; men in their sixties 0.86 times, women 0.62 times.

Managers considered their free day or the night before a holiday as the best time for having sex, and managerial couples took more time over sex and indulged more in foreplay than the general group. Overall, 80 per cent had foreplay 'always' or 'often' and the proportion was almost 90 per cent for couples in their forties. The favourite forms of foreplay on the part of men were caressing the woman's genitals (70 per cent) and breasts (70 per cent) and kissing her nipples (60 per cent) and mouth (50 per cent). Most of the women fondled the man's genitals (70 per cent) but the proportion of women kissing the mouth of their husbands decreased sharply for women in their fifties and sixties. Nearly 30 per cent of the husbands practised cunnilingus and about 20 per cent of the wives fellatio. Managers were more concerned about their wives' satisfaction than men in the general group, but the proportion of wives experiencing orgasm was the same in both groups (31 per cent).

Reflecting Japan's housing conditions, 60 per cent of the husbands and 70 per cent of the wives were 'always' or 'usually' bothered by the thought that children or others living with them might be aware of their intercourse. Customarily, a separate set of *futon* (bedding) is spread for each person sleeping in the same room, and only about 20 per cent of the couples slept together. Over 60 per cent of the respondents preferred just enough lighting to distinguish things, and while only 7 per cent of the husbands and 4 per cent of the wives in their forties (only 5 per cent of the husbands and none of the wives in their sixties) were naked from the start, over half shed their clothing in the course of the act.

The survey found a strong correlation between the custom of sleeping together, having intercourse relatively often, naked and with the lights on, practising oral sex and a high rate of orgasm of the wife.

Overall, three out of five wives had had abortions — the proportion was four out of five in the 50 to 54 age bracket. Since 30 per cent of the women had passed menopause, 40 per cent of the couples were not practising birth control. Among those who did, the main forms were condom (about 75 per cent), rhythm method (about 25 per cent) and coitus interruptus (about 15 per cent).

In the managerial group, one out of four men and in the general group, one out of five suffered a 'fairly continuous' period of impotence at some time or other which 33.8 per cent ascribed to stress, 38.2 per cent to domestic worries and fatigue (including trouble with the wife, 10.6 per cent) and 10.1 per cent to illness.

Marital Infidelity

Twice as many men as women (58 per cent to 22.6 per cent) had been attracted to people other than their marriage partners. Of the men in their forties, 60 per cent were emotionally attached to a woman other than their wife; the ratio was 57 per cent for men in their fifties and 47 per cent for those in their sixties. An affectionate inclination to a man other than their husband was felt by 27 per cent of the women in their forties, 12 per cent of those in their fifties and 19 per cent of those in their sixties. One in five men (20.5 per cent) had actually been unfaithful over the past year (the proportion was slightly higher for the managerial group). Infidelity was rare among women in general (2.5 per cent) but twice as high (5 per cent) among wives of managers. Most of the wives gave 'close human contact' as the reason for extra-marital sex while most of the men were motivated by the desire of a 'fresh sexual experience (34.6 per cent) or drawn into it 'on the spur of the moment' (39.2 per cent). Men found partners for their extra-marital affairs in amusement establishments (56.9 per cent) or among business acquaintances (31.8 per cent) while business acquaintances were the most frequent extra-marital partners of women (40 per cent), followed by former schoolmates and acquaintances from hobby or education classes or sports activities (both 33.3 per cent). That women very seldom acted 'on the spur of the moment' seems to indicate that their extra-marital affairs are more deliberate.

Men still adhered to a double moral standard. Marital infidelity was regarded all right for men if it did not interfere with the family by twice as many men as those who thought it permissible for women. Of the men in their forties, 56 per cent had had pre-marital sexual relations with a person of the opposite sex other than their marriage partner (men in their fifties, 64 per cent, in their sixties, 68 per cent). Only one per cent of the women in their forties had had such relations but 9 per cent of the women in their fifties and sixties. Roughly half of both men and women would condone pre-marital sex by their sons but disapprove of it for their daughters. Over 80 per cent of the respondents rated their spouses highly both as sex partners and as understanding and loving companions but 11 per cent of the wives (twice the ratio of men) had 'seriously considered' terminating their marriage.

More Report on Female Sexuality

In a survey modelled after the Hite Report a team of eight women on the staff of the Japanese magazine *More* undertook to explore the sexual experience of Japanese women. The magazine was started in 1977, a year after the publication of the Hite report on female sexuality and was aimed at women in their twenties. The editors were greatly influenced by the Hite Report and Erica Jong's *Fear of Flying* — the expression *tonde iru onna* (flying woman) meaning an independent woman, came into vogue around that time.

More's research team included no sex specialist and no man because it wanted to be free from the prejudices and biases often found in the studies on women's sexuality published by male experts. To questionnaires containing 45 mostly descriptive questions, 5,227 answers were received, and a second questionnaire in which some questions were changed drew 348 answers. The respondents were women aged between 13 and 60, with 74 per cent belonging to the 24-29 year group. The report, published in January 1983 under the title 'The More Report on Female Sexuality' contains three chapters. The first reproduces 60 complete answers, the second chapter gives a selection of the answers to 35 of the 45 questions, and the third chapter brings comments by the editors. The More Report has a didactic purpose; it wants to help women to understand and enjoy their sexuality by interpreting sex from the woman's point of view.

The readership of the magazine constitutes a somewhat special group which cannot be considered a random sample of the female population. It is greatly skewed because of the preponderance of younger women with what might be called liberal persuasions (Women below the age of 24 accounted for 57.6 per cent of the respondents to the first survey and for 66.4 per cent of those who answered the second.) Nevertheless, the surveys provide valid insights into the attitudes towards sex and sexual behaviour. The surfeit of questions on masturbation and orgasm produced a certain repetitiveness in the answers whereas the personal aspects of marital relations received little attention.

The findings of the survey are not too different from those of the American surveys and the Japanese survey mentioned above. Sexual awareness of Japanese women is similar to that of their sisters in western countries and on the surface, their sexual attitudes and values are not too different. Basically, however, they retain a rather passive attitude towards sex. Almost all women experience sexual desire but do not initiate sex. Girls have their first sexual experiences at about the same low age as in western countries. They engage in sex because their partners want them to although curiosity also plays an important role. Women refrain from initiating sex because they have been taught that it is a dirty and shameful thing.

More women reach orgasm by masturbation than by intercourse and about 70 per cent of the women fake orgasm during copulation. Their partners end sex when they reach orgasm without caring about the woman's satisfaction. Women have been conditioned to be passive and compliant and pretend to be fulfilled so that their partners do not get the impression that they are frigid.

About one-third of the respondents to the second survey had been sexually abused by relatives or close friends when they were young. Japanese men still retain the double standard on sexual morality, going on sex tours or otherwise engaging in pre-marital or extra-marital sex but regarding it improper for women. In their choice of a wife, men spurn the liberal women they would welcome as lovers and choose a woman they expect to be docile and submissive.

Below are a few of the findings of the surveys in statistical form:

Women who had submitted to cunnilingus accounted for 87 per cent of the respondents to the first survey; 27 per cent had disliked it but 64 per cent had no inhibition. Fellatio had been practised by 83 per cent of whom 32 per cent had felt repugnance but 58 per cent had been at ease. Of the women who had experienced intercourse, 46 per cent had had sex also during the menstrual period; 47 per cent of these women had it with reluctance, only 33 per cent had no objection.

Of the 5,067 women answering the first survey, 4,619 had sex partners; 3,700 (80 per cent) had a single and 919 (20 per cent) several sex partners. The sex partners were lovers (2,463), spouses (1,148), friends (654), fiancés (317), cohabitants (189), others (409).

The second survey (involving 348 answers) asked at what age the respondents had begun to masturbate and when they had their first heterosexual relation: 41 had started to masturbate in infancy, 26 between the ages of 7 and 8, 31 between 9 and 10, and 44 between 11 and 12; 17 were not sure of the exact age but had started during elementary school. Intercourse with the opposite sex had been experienced by 8 respondents between the ages of 10 and 14, by 11 at 15, by 31 at 16, by 40 at 17 and by 44 at 18. Of the respondents who had experienced orgasm, 63 per cent had achieved their first orgasm by masturbation, 22 per cent by intercourse, 10 per cent by petting or oral sex, and 3 per cent by other methods. Of the respondents to the first survey, 7 per cent reported that they often felt no emotional rapport with their partners, 48 per cent said that this happened sometimes but 43 per cent did not have this problem.

There was a certain difference in the role of masturbation in the More Report and the Kyodo News Service survey. According to the first survey of the More Report, 21 per cent of the respondents masturbated frequently, 46 per cent from time to time, and 30 per cent seldom. The second survey found that 92 per cent of the respondents masturbated and 6 per cent did not. The Kyodo survey asked about masturbation after marriage and of the women in their forties (for whom the frequencies were the highest), 2 per cent masturbated frequently, 9 per cent from time to time, 35 per cent very seldom, and 51 per cent never.

15

Sex Life in Marriage

A RIGHT UNDERSTANDING OF MARRIAGE can only be gained if the role of sex is not confined to the marital act. From the point of view of time, intercourse takes up only a small fraction of the common life of the spouses. It would be a fundamental misinterpretation to regard the partner only as a sex object and copulation as the essence of marriage but it would also be a serious shortcoming if the spouses would behave in daily life as if two asexual beings shared the same dwelling for reasons of utility. A satisfying sexual relationship in daily life forms the indispensable premise for the marital act to become the spontaneous and joyous expression of marital togetherness.

False Ideals of Sexuality

The image of sexuality created by the media exalts the physical attraction exuded by the virility of the male and the glamour of the female. Men as well as women regard sexual attractiveness as a personal trait that enhances their individual value and their standing in society. Sexual impressiveness is considered the foundation of marital relations and the lack of sexual gorgeousness a severe handicap to marriage. Not every man can be an Adonis nor every women an Aphrodite. There is no reason why everybody should be measured by the norms applied to movie stars, beauty queens or advertising models. Very few people correspond to these fallacious ideals of sexuality but the constant representation of married life as conditioned on the conformity with what is billed as the typical man or woman has created completely superfluous inferiority complexes. The obsession with the merely physical and external attributes of sex induces people to neglect the aspects of their personality that constitute their true and most valuable assets and their best qualities for achieving success in marriage as well as in social life.

Manliness does not require macho attitudes or behaviour, and femininity does not consist in 'ideal' measurements or a smooth complexion. There may be men who regard tenderness, caring, affection and dependency as incompatible with masculinity. A rough rind may hide a sweet fruit, but why should a man try to appear less approachable to his wife (and children) than he really is? She will not hold him for an easy touch if he shows the gentleness that is his real character. Marriage partners have no need to conform to sexual stereotypes; they cannot afford to judge each other on the basis of external appearances. While sexual attractiveness is a legitimate element in the choice of a marriage partner, it cannot be the reason for the choice. Neither can it be made the sole rationale of the life in common. Marriage certainly is the community of two persons of whom one is a man and the other a woman, but it is their commonness as human persons rather than their masculinity or femininity that makes marriage possible. The sexual diversity constitutes the specific difference distinguishing marriage from all other human communities and therefore the *conditio sine qua non,* the indispensable premise for marriage. But its existential foundation is the fact that man and woman are in the true and full sense human beings. In a personalistic view of marriage, sexual attractiveness forms only one aspect of the personal attractiveness which leads to marriage and supports its continuation.

Commonness and Individuality

As a personal community of life, marriage can only be meaningful if the intimacy of the togetherness involves the entire human being and embraces its spiritual capacities as well as the sensual-bodily aspects. Obviously, commonness does not mean renunciation of one's own life; on the contrary, the intimacy with the marriage partner brings a richer, fuller, and more satisfying life, not as if the enrichment of one's own life were the purpose of the life in common but because togetherness achieves a mutual fecundation which a single person does not experience.

Nor does the commonness of marriage negate or truncate the individuality of each of the partners. Each retains the right to his or her own personality, his or her individual inner life which also includes the psychological elements of sex life. The life in common does not mean that the partners renounce their separateness and unicity. Normally, only something that can be revealed in some external manifestation can become common, although it is precisely in marriage that harmony and understanding may require no words. Nevertheless, it is humanly impossible to open one's entire inner life to somebody else, and a large part of the inner sexual life will remain the individual experience of each partner. In every human being, the sensual-spiritual sex life will retain a very individual form, from sexual fantasies and desires to the satisfaction of sexual lust. The preservation of the individuality of one's inner life cannot be equated with selfishness but constitutes a necessary condition of the union of two persons.

Practical Aspects of Togetherness

Togetherness requires more or less equal progress in the development of spiritual, emotional, sensual and bodily intimacy so that the personal nearness will not be rent by inordinately large inequalities. It may happen that the starting points of the partners are quite different and such a discrepancy may put some strain on the marriage. In this sense, marriage is a problem of communication, not in the narrow sense of verbal-conceptual exchanges but of a living union in all spheres of human existence. This again is not a question of reflexive-conscious accommodation but of the spontaneous-natural behaviour of two persons who belong together in the depth of their personalities. Sex life is nothing special or extraordinary but an integral part of the daily life in common. The separation of sexual relations from the totality of life endangers marriage. The secret of a happy marriage consists in giving the entire life the atmosphere of a loving sexual communion.

Such intimacy, warmth and snugness of the life in common may appear as an ideal impossible to realise in the desolateness and amid the frictions of everyday life but it should be the beacon for shaping marital relations. Spouses cannot afford to neglect anything that could enhance their union. There may be valid reasons (such as health) for sleeping separately but this involves the renunciation of a symbolically and practically important part of marital intimacy. Not only in intercourse, but on other occasions, too, the contact of the naked bodies can be a trustful manifestation of bodily-sensual rapport.

Different from western customs, the Japanese way of bathing favours the common bathing of husband and wife although the tradition passed down from feudal times disposes otherwise. Great constraint on the manifestation of affection, not only in public but also in private is characteristic of Japan. The young generation feels no inhibitions in this respect but one cannot escape the impression that for young couples the outward display of tenderness seems to end with marriage. Thereafter, every sign of fondness becomes superfluous.

The mutual respect and esteem of the spouses does not require ceremonious rigidity or cringing obseqiousness in their relations but the reverence for each other should prevent the show of affection from making the partner a plaything.

Intercultural Marriages

Special problems are posed by so-called bi-cultural marriages, such as the marriage between a westerner and a Japanese. Naturally, marriage is first of all a relation between two human beings and not two citizens of different countries, but it is also true that the difference in cultural backgrounds can become an obstacle to the understanding and harmony of husband and wife. This is particularly the case if the cultural differences imply different attitudes to sex and different approaches to sex life. The differences in the manifestation of endearment may already create a problem in mixed marriages.

A western woman expects a far greater measure of tenderness, caresses, and physical expressions of fondness than Japanese husbands are used to bestow on their wives. In the west, kisses, embraces or fondling of the wife's hair, ears or hands seem natural adjuncts of communication between spouses, and if foreigners married to Japanese men do not receive these tokens of affection, they may feel insecure, lonely and unloved. Westerners married to Japanese women freely kiss or embrace their wives in public which sometimes embarrasses them. In Japan, physical contact does not form part of the etiquette of salutation. To shake hands is no longer frowned upon and is generally practised with foreigners.

Young people hold hands, embrace each other and are very unconcerned about showing affection in public. Still, generally speaking, physical touching, caressing, kissing and other signs of affection are more comfortable for westerners than for Japanese. Westerners married to Japanese expect a greater manifestation of affection than is common in Japanese marriages. Western women, in particular, may feel the need for touching and showing affection, being kissed and hugged and generally giving and receiving physical expressions of warmth and love.

Japanese are not less sexual or physically intimate in sex relations than westerners but it may well be that Japanese men, particularly those of middle age and deeply engrossed in their work, do not meet the expectations of occidental women with regard to the demonstration of love and affection. Japanese men have the reputation of being poor lovers and unresponsive to the sexual needs of their wives. This may not be generally true but western women have complained of the lack of sexual intimacy and the unresponsiveness of their Japanese husbands.

The scarcity of the demonstration of affection between Japanese spouses is illustrated by a letter a housewife sent to the family page of a Japanese newspaper. She relates her embarrassment when quizzed by her children about her marriage. 'Mama,' asked her three-year-old daughter, 'why don't you marry papa?' and she was amazed when told that they were married. After a while, the older girl, a first-grader, renewed the questioning: 'Mama, have you ever kissed papa?' — 'Me? Kiss? Oh no, God forbid I should kiss him!' was her automatic reply.

Sexual Frustration

Sexual frustration is very unpleasant to live with day by day, year after year, for a good woman who would never think of sleeping around. It makes her bicker with her husband, yell at the kids, eat sweets endlessly or lose her appetite, get an ulcer, waste time daydreaming instead of doing her work. Intercultural marriages have their problems but these problems are not unsolvable. This supposes that the marriage was not a hasty and irresponsible lark but a serious personal engagement, and that both partners are mature enough to distinguish essentials from accidentals.

Essential to marriage is the mutual belonging, the will to a common life as husband and wife. The expression of affection, the manifestation of intimacy, although important, may take on different forms and change with the development of the marriage and the moods of the partners. It is largely a question of mutual understanding, personal tact, the ability to sense the mood of the partner and to respond to his or her feelings without long debates. Basically, the partners have to find a style of intimacy satisfactory to both and flexible enough to meet the changing requirements of everyday life. There is no reason in the world why cross-cultural marriages should not be successful.

Shortcomings of Japanese Men

The lack of affectionateness is not limited to occidental women marrying Japanese men. Basically, Japanese men are unprepared to recognise women as equal partners in sex relations. Japanese mothers continue to indoctrinate their sons with the notion that they are the lords of creation. The boys imbibe the attitude of absolute male superiority with their mother's milk. This goes together with an extraordinary intense emotional relationship with their mothers. Hence, there are two basic expectations of the Japanese male, motherly catering to his physical needs and gratification of sex impulses. In both ways, a woman does not interfere with the self-centredness of the male; it requires no emotional involvement and leaves his feeling of superiority intact. As a foreign woman put it, Japanese men want to relegate women to two simple positions, on their backs or at the sink. In this way, the male can feel safe.

Generally, the Japanese are less oppressed and inhibited about sex than people in the West, but this is largely on the physiological level. Psychologically, Japanese men seem to find it difficult to relate properly to the other sex. They lack the respect for the personal worth of each human being which has become an integral part of the western tradition — although, unfortunately, it is often disregarded, even on a massive scale. Frequently, they are not polite to women and fail to show even the kind of appreciation considered elementary in western society. According to a western lady, Japanese men treat women like housemaids. In marriage, therefore, men often fail to relate to women on equal terms. They do not experience marriage as a personal union of two equal partners. The man can relegate his emotional demands into the background by his ambition to succeed in his job and his absorption with his work while the woman's desire for love, affection, sympathy and understanding is frustrated.

I have always been struck by the lack of terms of endearment in the Japanese language and the rude way in which gentlemen address their wives. There is no fixed way in which Japanese couples address each other. After the war, 'papa' and 'mama' have become popular to which *otô-san* and *okâ-san* are frequently substituted. Younger people call each other by first name (with or without *san*), but even today, the domineering *oi* and the submissive *anata* are still used and the unmistakable undertone of arrogance in *oi* (which pre-war policemen used for calling people) reflects the lack of inner reverence for their spouses.

In a typical Japanese movie, the woman manages nothing more than *Anata, ai-shiteru* (I love you) at the height of a love scene. Still more difficult for the Japanese male is the recognition that women are intellectually his equals and entitled to female pride and enjoyment of their loveliness.

To foreign observers, the Japanese marriage seems to involve a minimum of physical comfort and a maximum of psychological discomfort. But, as I said above, in this field generalisations are difficult and with the growing number of marriages supposedly based on love, mutuality not only in sex but also in eros, in personal friendship, intellectual cross-fertilisation and loving care should grow. Japanese couples seem to become more affectionate with age. It may be that men lose some of their aggressive assertion of male superiority and become more receptive to the motherly affection of the wife who has taken care of him uncomplainingly through thirty or forty years of marital indifference. With their children grown up and the man no longer bound to the company, the wife becomes a companion — what she should have been right from the start of the marriage — and a partner in common life.

It remains, however, what a foreigner once observed: 'Japanese husbands don't have to worry about being in love (with their wives) so much. Neither do they have to worry about cultivating affection.'

A 1985 survey to which 1,128 American women pursuing executive, professional or entrepreneurial careers ranging in age from 25 to 45 with a median income of $39,000 responded showed that most of the respondents liked to have sex often but half of them managed to make love just once or twice a week, 18 per cent enjoyed sex three or more times a week but 30 per cent had to be content with two or three times a month. Fifty-five per cent had made love with co-workers. More than 70 per cent of such encounters were with men on the woman's corporate level, 26 per cent with men from levels above them and 3 per cent with subordinates.

Opportunities for sex diminish and the quality of sex relations may suffer from the presence of children. Unrestrained sexual freedom becomes impossible and spontaneous sexuality is limited unless the parents act on the conviction that there is no reason to hide sex from children. The situation is particularly delicate when children grow older but still sleep with their parents or in adjacent rooms. There is a period when young children experience fear and want the assurance that father and mother can see or hear them when they are sleeping. Children may use the fear of sleeping alone as a pretext for creeping into their parents' beds, and a mother who takes or allows her son into her bed when her husband is absent may be motivated by the sensual-sexual pleasure she derives from the bodily contact.

There is always a peripheral fear of having the conjugal privacy invaded but couples will have to learn to cope with this risk and take advantage of the situation when the children are 'out of the way.'

Erosion of Eroticism

A threat to marital harmony and even to marital fidelity arises from the tendency of some men to dissociate tenderness and sexuality. They display tenderness only when they court a woman; as soon as they have 'conquered' her, their tenderness vanishes. The woman is like some kind of object in a game to be pursued and captured. Once the chase is over, the interest is gone. A woman whom a man possesses offers less cheer to his self-conceit than a woman who denies herself to him. The conquest of another woman feeds his ego; his feeling of superman depends on proving his prowess in subjugating any woman who challenges his sexual appetite. It is not necessarily a sadomasochistic urge to degrade or desecrate but it reveals a basic contempt for women.

A marriage may be even so happy it cannot escape the possibility of being endangered. The danger may arise suddenly but can also be the effect of a long process of decay or erosion. Marriage can be jeopardised when it becomes shallow. Sooner or later, husband or wife or both may become bored with their marriage and particularly with their sexual relations. They get along with each other but there is no excitement. Their relations concern merely external affairs and their communications are reduced to banalities and platitudes. Sex with another woman (or man) would be great but he (or she) is just not interested in making love to his wife (her husband). In such a situation, the experience of sexual attraction to a third party may become devastating. But the same experience can also break up a marriage that so far had shown no sign of deterioration.

Sexual Fantasies

It cannot be helped that married life settles into a routine in which sex, at least in terms of time and attention, becomes marginal. Making love with each other is nothing new. It lacks the fascination of the forbidden fruit and the piquancy of probing an unexplored body. Although many moralists condemn it and the partner would be shocked if she (or he) learned about it, but there is no obstacle to indulging in sexual fantasies while having intercourse and letting one's imagination free play in the satisfaction of one's lustful desires. To commit adultery in one's fancy is still preferable to actually committing adultery.

A French study found that sex plays a dominant role in dreams and fantasies. Men's most common fantasy is a woman naked under her dress; the next best thing to nakedness is a soberly-clad woman with sexy lingerie underneath or a lady in leather. French women dream of physical love in nature, making love in the sea or carrying on an arousing conversation on the beach. Love in a railway car is a fantasy of over half of French women while two-thirds of the men fantasise about making love driving their own car with their partners in the passenger seat. Love with a movie star is a fantasy of about half of each sex but unusual sex such as three-way sex, sadomasochism or voyeurism ranks low in dreams and fantasies.

Extra-Marital Affairs

According to an American survey on male attitudes undertaken in 1977, the answers to the question 'what do you consider the ideal sex life for yourself?' were as follows: 'marriage with the wife being the only sex partner' 50.5 per cent; 'marriage but also outside sex activity' 19.9 per cent; 'living with one woman but without marriage' 10.6 per cent. The correspondents' actual sex life showed the following pattern: 'married and no adultery' 49.5 per cent; 'married but relations with one or two other women' 28.5 per cent; 'married and relations with many other women' 13 per cent; 'relations with other women with the consent of wife or steady' 5.5 per cent.

Sexual fidelity was the chief characteristic of the French marriage, but about 30 per cent of the men and 10 per cent of the women admitted that they had been unfaithful. Of young Italian wives, a quarter confessed that they had betrayed their husbands, but of those who had remained faithful, about one-half had done so because they had had no chance of extra-marital sex. According to Italian women, Italian men are disappointing as lovers, overbearing as husbands, and phantom fathers; they are negligent, unprotecting and adulterers. Italian wives complained that sex was just another household chore which had to be performed for the convenience and pleasure of the husband. Naturally, these responses may indicate certain broad trends in a given society but they cannot be relied upon as representing actual conditions.

Menopause

Extra-marital affairs have often been linked to what has been described as a mid-life crisis. A pronounced form of such a crisis can appear as the result of the woman's menopause. The menopause is an inevitable and unpreventable part of aging which is seldom life-threatening but may still be very uncomfortable. For many women, the physical and psychological effects are very real. The menopause brings the cessation of menstruation and the end of a woman's reproductive ability. It used to occur in the late forties but with the increase in life expectancy and improved health, it may now occur after 50.

The first sign of the menopause is the irregularity of the menstrual periods. Physiologically, the menopause involves a deep drop in the production of female hormones, particularly estrogen, by the woman's aging ovaries. For some, the decline in estrogen supply is gradual, for others, it is sudden and creates more serious disorders. Nervousness, irritability, insomnia, depression and circulatory problems are some of the more common symptoms. Other complaints are dizziness, numbness, nausea, sudden flushing, heart palpitation, skin spots, backaches, dry mouth and brittle bones. By 55, a woman runs ten times the risk of bone fracture as does a man of the same age. Most vulnerable to fracture are forearms, hips and vertebrae. The reason for this condition is the lack of estrogen which causes the bones to lose density, turn brittle and collapse.

The progressive thinning of the bones called osteoporosis can leave the skeleton too fragile to withstand even minimum stress and the bones of the spine can become so papery that they collapse. When the disintegrating vertebrae are compressed, the patient experiences waves of heat and night sweat; tingling in the toes or fingers often accompanies the hot flushes. Five vertebrae may fill the space normally filled by three, causing a protuberance known as 'dowager's hump.' Normally, the body forms new bone tissue as the old bone is broken down in a process called resorption. Estrogen helps regulate the rate of this remodelling. If the hormone is deficient, bone is not replaced as quickly as it is removed. Smoking, poor diet and lack of exercise increase a woman's chances of developing osteoporosis.

At puberty, people require 1,200 mg of calcium a day; post-menstrual women require 1,500 mg to offset the resorption process. Attempts have been made to balance the loss of estrogen by estrogen replacement therapy (ERT; originally called HRT, hormone replacement therapy). But the estrogen pills may bring an increased risk of cancer of the uterus lining, gall bladder problems and hypertension. The likelihood of endometrial cancer is reduced if progesterone is added to estrogen. Another treatment combines sodium fluoride with calcium.

Which phenomena are attributable to hormonal changes is not entirely clear. The wrinkling of the skin seems to belong to the general process of aging, and the tendency to grow more facial hair may be the result of the higher rates of male hormones due to the loss of estrogen. This deficiency also causes the thinning of the walls of the vagina which may make intercourse painful and lead to troublesome infections.

According to some scientists, the unpleasant symptoms of menopause are a modern artefact because early hominid women nursed their last child well into their forties, and since nursing suppresses the distasteful effects of menopause caused by wild swings in estrogen levels, these early women entered middle age without discomfort. In view of the low life expectancy of primitive man, this theory does not seem very plausible.

The emotional problems connected with the menopause have often been exaggerated. There is no mental syndrome typical of menopause. Many women feel that things are over for them once they are menopausal and that they are 'too old for sex.' This attitude is nonsense. A physician who tells a woman simply to knit and not be disturbed is making a mistake. The menopause is not a trivial experience. Many women feel more sexual which can involve just as much danger for an existing marriage as the sexual apathy of other menopausal women.

Some sociologists maintain that the time before the menopause, around 35, is already a critical period for women. Events with a deep emotional impact occurring at that time, such as the death of the husband, divorce, or separation from children, are said to be one of the main reasons of alcoholism among women.

For men, there is no physiological development similar to the menopause, although there is a regression in the ability of having intercourse and in later years in the ability of erection. Two researchers at San Francisco State University surveyed more than 200 men and women between the ages of 80 and 102 and found that sexual intimacy remained an important part of the lives of the elderly. Elderly men seemed more interested in sex than women. While 62 per cent of the men were sexually active, only 30 per cent of the women engaged in sex 'sometimes' or 'often.' Of all the retirees questioned, 47 per cent said they had sexual intercourse, 33.9 per cent had oral sex, 56.1 per cent masturbated and 73 per cent touched and caressed the body of their sex partner. Cessation of sexual activities was more likely the result of the restrictions of living conditions than diminishing sexual desire.

An American couple (Morton and Joan Walker, authors of *Sexual Nutrition*) asserted that poor diet was the leading cause of loss of libido. Good nutrition would heighten sexuality, they claimed. Foods rich in phosphorus can increase sex drive, zinc enables males to perform, garlic and chamomile relieve symptoms of pre-menstrual syndrome, and ginseng helps restore vitality.

Mid-Life Crisis

In man's emotional development, there may come a mid-life crisis, sometimes called the 'Grey Itch' or the 'Gauguin syndrome.' It may comprise phenomena such as job-hopping, extra-marital affairs, divorce, and sometimes suicide. More often than not, the conflict between job and home is at the heart of the problem. The man has been too absorbed in his work for too long to the exclusion of thinking about his family or even about his own feelings. For the corporate man, work is the only focus in his life. Up to a point, he is carried on by his desire to succeed, to climb the professional or social ladder, to get into the driver's seat. But then he realises that he is not going to make it to the top or that the position he sweated so hard for and finally got isn't all he expected. He feels disappointed, his work is no longer satisfying. At home, his wife may have grown away from him and have found independent pursuits — she may have become 'liberated' and discovered her own 'identity.' His children have also gone their own ways. Such a situation may create a feeling of loneliness or disappointment, the desire for a new 'companionship' or the need for comfort and motherliness.

Some women in middle life have little or no interest in sex, some may even hate making love. For some, sex has lost the attraction it once had, for others, the repression of passion and eroticism they practised in childhood reasserts itself; still others may be angry with their husbands or so taken up with the chores of daily life that they consider sex a troublesome nuisance.

It may also happen that the husband loses interest in sex. While the loss of sexual drive may often be the reason for a woman's negative attitude to sex, it seldom is the real reason why a man becomes turned off. Occasionally, overwork, ill health or bodily and emotional fatigue induced by other causes may interfere with a man's physical or psychological capacity for sex but this is not often the case.

Sex can be used as a weapon by both partners. Dissatisfaction with one's spouse may find expression in the attitude to sexual relations, and the reasons for displeasure may relate to all aspects of married life. Naturally, the absorption of sexual interest by another actual or potential sex partner cannot be ruled out.

In short, there are many reasons for a negative attitude towards sex and the worst thing is to leave it there. It is impossible to turn back the clock and to restore the passion felt by young lovers. A solution must be forward-looking, that is to say, to find a form of sexual intimacy that satisfies both partners without imposing a physical or psychological burden on either of them. This supposes that they talk without any inhibition — which may be the biggest hurdle to overcome.

For both men and women, the mid-life crisis may bring a reassessment of values. They may feel that the promises that life held out have not been fulfilled and now want to get something out of life before it is too late. Extra-marital liaisons may appear as a way of affirming their worth, continued attractiveness and youth. Marital relations may have become stale and meaningless, the partners may have lost sexual interest in each other and they may have become sexually incompatible. One or the other may be overwhelmed by the entrancement of a 'new-found' love. The situation is made worse by the inability to communicate with each other, to confess their problems and discuss their relationship.

Liaisons

Men are inclined to engage in extra-marital affairs because they feel that they have nothing to lose by cheating. The availability of women to cheat with adds to the lack of restraint, and some men try to rationalise their infidelity by asserting that men are biologically polygamous. But many unfaithful men struggle with the feeling of guilt and sneakiness and experience rueful anguish when their wives find out about their affairs. On the other hand, their ego is hurt when they are rejected by their extra-marital partners.

Mistresses are not concerned about the morality of sleeping with married men and don't take marriage very seriously. Some career women choose married men as sex partners because they want to avoid closeness. They may be terrified of committing themselves and prefer married men because such men do not make too many demands on a woman. All these women want from a man is tenderness, relaxation and sex. But even highly independent women who enter an affair with the intention of avoiding a permanent relationship may get more deeply involved and finally want the man to leave his wife for her — which he is not likely to do.

The high divorce rate adds to the number of women willing to have affairs with married men because they find it difficult to acquire a new spouse. For both men and women, mobility at work and discretionary work time contribute to cheating. People working in free-lance professions or jobs with flexible hours, for example, have more opportunities to engage in extra-marital affairs than people in routine jobs. People with high verbal skills find it easier to hook up with somebody and marital trouble may provide the incentive for seeking happiness outside marriage.

The question how much extra-marital emotional, sexual or erotic interest a marriage can endure admits of no general answer. Patient, understanding or tolerant husbands or wives may forgive occasional infidelity and sometimes a husband or wife may put up with a habitually unfaithful partner. But the quality of the marriage will deteriorate and it may break up sooner or later.

Rationalisation of Infidelity

Not all marriages face the trials and tribulations of Beverly Hills bedroom manners where a young wife may find her husband in bed with her mother. Women generally are more faithful than men. The reason is at least partly the different position of the satisfaction of the sexual instinct in the emotional structure. In men, the desire for sexual satisfaction is rather loosely connected with feelings such as tenderness, attachment, surrender or infatuation. The sexual urge makes itself felt like a biological impulse, independent of psychic inclinations. Men deceive and betray their wives without any admission of guilt because they tell themselves that their heart was not in it and that it was just a fleeting affair and nothing but relief from an irresistible compulsion.

For a woman, sexuality is so much more interwoven with her emotional life. Usually (if she is not a prostitute) she needs trust, devotion, affection and sympathy and sex is a manifestation of her emotional inclination. She goes without sex rather than engage in sex play for which she feels no psychic attraction and she does not want to risk the security of a satisfactory emotional relationship for the sake of sexual adventure. It may happen that a wife gets fed up with the infidelity of her husband and retaliates by having an affair of her own. There are also women who enjoy their dominance over men and want to prove that they can get any man they find desirable. But women are generally more afraid than men of the personal and social consequences an extra-marital affair might have and even today, the fear of an unwanted pregnancy still represents an important restraint. The demand for equality seems to have had little influence on the attitudes to marital fidelity and relatively few women try to pursue total equality with men.

Some psychologists have advocated 'permitted' adultery, 'vacation' from marriage, partner swapping and sex parties as ways of overcoming the boredom of marriage. Open marriage was to do away with the possessiveness of marriage. Marital fidelity has been called the strait-jacket of marriage and jealousy has been ridiculed as a neurotic or infantile reaction. In the United States, clubs for extra-marital sex are not popular despite much publicity. Most husbands and wives feel possessive of their spouses and are little inclined to sexual tolerance. A wife may feel desolate when she learns of the unfaithfulness of her husband but a man will fly into a rage when he thinks that 'his wife had been opening naked thighs' to another man. Wayward behaviour contributes nothing to solving marital difficulties and only creates new ones. Marriage without complete mutual trust, openness and faith in the integrity of the partner becomes an empty shell.

There may be some special reasons why men form extra-marital liaisons. Affairs with secretaries are common because this relationship assumes many features associated with marital life: physical nearness, common interests, personal understanding, emotional involvement. For the corporate man, divorce is undesirable because of the effects it would have on his career, his social standing or his children. But the daily encounter with sexually attractive females constantly stimulates his sexual longings for which he finds no satisfaction at home. Emotional immaturity may be solaced by the adoration of a lover who is willing or can be pressured into sex with seemingly no further consequences.

Some men experience what is called the 'madonna-whore' complex. They put their wives on a pedestal of undefiled womanhood and act out their sexual lusts with other women who give them sensual thrills and sexual pleasure.

How to Deal with Unfaithfulness

There is no universal rule for dealing with the unfaithfulness of one's spouse. In most cases, conjugal infidelity of men is not caused by the wiles of an 'adulteress.' A man does not seek or maintain an on-going affair because of the evil intentions of a lover. The problem usually begins at home, and the reasons may range from sexual incompatibility to plain boredom. Most women as well as men know when their partners are unfaithful. In such a situation, the crucial issue is why it happened. Instead of looking for a scapegoat, the betrayed spouse should try to understand the factors that contributed to the dissolution of the marriage. This may be of major importance for deciding on how to handle the problem.

A wife who faces an uncertain future in case of separation or divorce will sometimes be inclined to feign ignorance and try to go on as if nothing had happened. Psychologically, this may be nearly impossible and there is no guarantee that patience and forbearance will win back an errant spouse. In the long run, it may be inevitable to confront the unfaithful partner, and if it has to be done anyhow, it may just as well be done sooner rather than later. But then, there is always a chance that the disloyal spouse will come to his or her senses and recognise what he or she is losing. Walking out is the end, and before taking this decisive step, a re-examination of one's priorities may suggest that a compromise is better than a rupture. Forgiving and forgetting are not easy but it is not absolutely impossible to make a new start.

Theoretically, there seem to be three options. The first is to agree to what has been called an open marriage. Husband and wife can have sexual relations, either ephemeral or somewhat permanent, with other partners, freely and openly. The proponents of this form of sexual arrangement claim that the 'possessiveness' of exclusive sex between husband and wife prevents the full development of man's sexual capacity. But tolerance or rather sexual licence is at variance with the personal meaning of marriage in a monogamous society. Polygamy, and the various forms in which men have freed themselves from the limitation of one sex partner, are based at least on the practical inequality of women. The open marriage recognises the equality of man and woman but negates the meaning of marriage as a personal union. It is true that there are no absolute rights and duties among men and no absolute bonds, but the intimacy of the personal oneness of husband and wife is lost in an open marriage. The freedom from 'possessiveness' and 'exclusivity' does not lift marriage into a 'higher' and more 'fulfilling' dimension.

The second alternative for solving the conflict created by a new love is divorce. This implies the judgement that the new liaison is more valuable than the existing marriage. Divorce may affect not only the couple being divorced but also their children, and it may involve not only one but two families. The marriage partner may be resigned to divorce as the only possible solution or may be unwilling to continue a relationship that is no longer viable. Once the mutual trust has been destroyed, it is difficult to save the marital union.

The third choice is renunciation. In the conflict between duty and desire, responsibility and yearning, self-discipline and concupiscence, no solution is possible without sacrifice. The third choice is only feasible if it is based on the conviction, shared by both partners, that their existing marriage is worth saving and that it can be saved by common effort and common commitment. It must be based on a frank discussion of the situation, the recognition of the past shortcomings and a pledge of mutual understanding and help.

American research seems to show that there has been an increase in marital infidelity on the part of women. A 1983 *Playboy* survey (of singles in their mid-twenties and married people in their early thirties) reported that 45 per cent of the married men and 34 per cent of the women confessed to marital infidelity, and the percentage of young wives was higher than that of men. The reasons that women give for their extra-marital entanglements point to a basic deficiency in intimacy and communication in marital relations. Some women state that infidelity enhances their marital sex but they acknowledge that it weakens the emotional bond of marriage. Many unfaithful women contend that they are not primarily interested in sex but in the relationship, in holding, caring and romance. In some cases, revenge on an unfaithful husband was the motive but more often, it was out of loneliness and isolation. They do not feel married; psychologically, they feel single and unattached. They cannot commit themselves entirely to their spouse. Basically, the urge for sexual loyalty is a powerful and omnipresent female yearning; a wife's affair is a signal that the marriage is over.

16

The Marital Community

WHAT MUST A MARRIAGE BE LIKE if it is to deserve the name of marriage? The statement that a marriage should be happy only makes sense if one knows what happiness is, and in view of the enormous differences in opinion on the meaning of happiness it seems impossible to find a satisfactory answer. Some psychologists are of the opinion that man seeks the fulfilment of four basic wants: power, affection, security and excitement, while political scientists regard money, power and fame as the basic values of today's society. The desire for power would rather imperil marriage but some kind of power seems involved in all human relations. An American researcher maintained that 'intimacy and power' were the crucial factors in the success or failure of marriage. Some experts believe that most couples settle their contest for power by confrontation and that the power struggle constitutes the critical phase which determines who takes the leadership role and who has the higher status. But, as in politics, power is a poor substitute for reason. A system of shared power need not be the outcome of a struggle and a fight is certainly not the best way to decide who should do what.

Uniqueness of Marital Community

Affection, security and excitement may not be specific concerns of marriage but they play an important role in marital relations. Marriage can greatly contribute to the fulfilment of these needs as a community of love and reverence, sexuality and intellectual communication, education and sociality, and generally as a union combining progress with continuity. Marriage is an uncertain venture in whose development the partners can draw nearer to each other but also drift apart in divergent directions.

Every human being is unique and singular and distinguished in his individuality from every other human being. Every pair of human beings, therefore, is likewise unique and inimitable, so that every marriage possesses an individuality that is exclusively its own. The partners form a combination that will never be duplicated in human history. The 'you and I' of each marriage can exist only once. Each partner develops his own personality and in an ideal situation, each partner will enhance the growth of the other although the degree of support will not necessarily be the same. The common life, therefore, will reflect the mutual help, or the succour given by one and the obstruction by the other, or the undesirable case of mutual inhibition.

Probability of Success

Given the preliminaries of marriage, the chance that marriage will cultivate mutual inspiration should be better than the possibility that their togetherness will remain without influence on the spiritual and emotional development of the partners. It may be that man's quest for a stable, secure and radiant reality is, as some existentialists maintain, intrinsically doomed to failure and that his attempt to fuse his own aspirations with the destiny of another person will only confirm the absurdity of his endeavour to overcome the limitations of his individuality.

Like human life, marriage is preordained to end — 'until death do us part' — and the end will not depend on the success or failure of marriage and cannot be conditioned on the attainment of the happiness husband and wife promised to give each other. Nevertheless, marriage can achieve what Schopenhauer considered genuine liberation: breaking through the bounds of individuality imposed by the ego to true compassion, selflessness and human kindness. In marriage, one human being feels the sufferings of another human being as his own, and although this may not be the abnegation of the will to life as Schopenhauer understood it, it can create a partnership that enables two human beings to face up to the 'horrors of existence' and bear them together through the whole gamut of human possibilities from the ecstasy of jubilant communion to the abyss of hopelessness and despair.

One of the reasons for the failure of marriages is the exaggerated expectations raised by the contemporary clichés of the ideal husband and wife. People imagine that the marriage partner can be 'educated' to live up to the ideal arbitrarily set up by the other partner. Naturally, nobody can change his personality, his character and temperament; there are limits to the changes he or she can make in favour of matrimonial harmony. It is unreal to demand that husband and wife should accept the likes and dislikes, the preferences or aversions, the tastes and antipathies of the partner. On the other hand, marriage cannot have as its purpose 'to live one's own self.' If this were the essence of marriage, the partner would be degraded to an instrument of ego satisfaction, and if both partners seek the adulation of their selfishness, any partnership will be doomed.

Progress in marriage depends on the progress each of the partners makes, and unless both partners are willing to learn, it will be difficult to develop the potential of the marriage. Too many couples do not know what is important in marriage and what is not. Different things are

considered important by different people but there are some basics such
as understanding and patience without which the marital union cannot
exist. Marriage certainly has utilitarian aspects which may be expressed
as 'I take care of you and you take care of me,' but this reciprocal
engagement cannot be reduced to a neat bargain in which both sides give
and receive exactly the same. Their common life requires different things
from each partner, and especially when children arrive, marriage cannot
be reduced to a bilateral exchange of equivalent services.

Married Life and Environment

The relations inside marriage are complicated by influences from outside,
above all influences from other people and from living conditions.
Practically all men live within a certain cultural group, and the mutual
influence and harmonisation of the spouses is inseparable from the effects
of the social, cultural, spiritual, moral and religious (or areligious)
conditions of the milieu, economic circumstances and standard of living.
The composition of the family can greatly affect marital life. The most
notable phenomenon in Japan's post-war development has been the
emergence of the nuclear family as the preponderant form of household.
According to the 1980 national census, nuclear families constituted
21,594,000 households, 63.3 per cent of the total of 34,106,000
households, and 75.4 per cent of the 28,594,000 kinship families.
Households made up of unrelated persons numbered 62,000 and one-
person households 5,388,000 (15.8 per cent of all households).

External factors can contribute to making marriage an ever new
experience of love and trust, or letting it decay into purely superficial
and meaningless cohabitation, to stifling boredom and forlorn despair,
to a prison suppressing every free movement, to a life of grating and
exhausting tension, to physical and mental pain, conflict, revolt and
fighting.

A consideration of the actual situation of existing marriages in a
given community can hardly show what marriage should be. An analysis
of the idea of marriage must be based on the end and purpose of marriage,
the common life of husband and wife. By their decision to choose
marriage as their form of life, husband and wife are bound to the common
end and are responsible for the attainment of this end. The end is the
foundation of their rights and duties. The meaning of marriage, however,
does not consist in the assertion of rights and the fulfilment of duties but
in the life for which these rights and duties constitute the external
framework.

Legal Duties of Spouses

In its regulation of marriage, modern law attempts to define the rights
and duties of the marriage partners. The Japanese civil code enumerates

cohabitation, mutual cooperation and assistance as duties of husband and wife (Art. 752). These duties also extend to minor children living with their parents. Under the old civil code, the husband was the head of the conjugal community and had the right to determine the place of cohabitation. The post-war revision of the family law intended to apply the constitutional principle of the equality of both sexes to marital relations. This essential equality must be recognised in the selection of the domicile (Art. 24, Par.2), but the law is silent on the way in which the choice is to be made if the partners cannot come to an agreement. Neither the family courts nor the district courts are competent to fix the residence. The work of husband and wife, the health of the family members, the education of the children and the financial resources of the family are some of the considerations entering into the decision. These are also reasons why husband or wife may temporarily live apart. In Japan, this problem often arises in connection with the transfer of employees, particularly their assignment to overseas posts. (This question is discussed in Volume 3.)

The old law recognised that the husband's right to choose the family's domicile was not absolute and that the wife was not obliged to live at the place chosen by the husband if the choice constituted an abuse of his right. The unjustified refusal of cohabitation, however, constitutes a ground for divorce.

Cooperation

Cooperation supposes that husband and wife fulfil different functions but that these functions are complementary and coalesce into the common life. In the typical form of division of labour underlying the concept of cooperation, the husband worked outside and his earnings provided the financial means for supporting the household while the wife took care of the household and the children.

In today's society, the accent has shifted from the basic financial needs of the family to the husband's help with the household chores. In the vast majority of households, the old role attribution persists but the husband is expected to show a greater degree of cooperation with the duties of housekeeping. The most common expression of this cooperation is 'doing the dishes' and with regard to this particular activity, a survey has established illuminating differences between some representative countries.

	DOING THE DISHES			%
	Husband	Wife	Children	Family
Japan	0.8	88.6	3.2	3.5
United States	6.8	64.0	7.3	20.6
Federal Republic of Germany	4.4	72.0	2.8	17.5
United Kingdom	14.9	55.9	3.4	20.2

Japanese husbands don't help in the kitchen and still less with the dishes. Some men, however, are proud of their culinary skills and want to demonstrate them. Young couples often share homework and child care. Many Japanese wives, however, are used to their husbands coming home late from work, not because they have been particularly busy but because they dawdle at a bar, a *pachinko* (pinball) hall or a *mah-jong* parlour. Middle-aged Japanese men seem not to mind the lack of togetherness; they are content to live in their own world and are not interested in the world of their wives. They may display an indifference bordering on cruelty if, for example, the wife gets sick or has a baby. The father may show affection to the baby but not to the mother. In a typical case, the foreign wife of a Japanese listed as her major problems the relation of her husband with his mother (who seemed to replace the wife in the affections of the husband), the husband's long working hours and the husband becoming non-communicative at home.

According to a survey of the Allenbacher Institute for Opinion Research covering the households of 1,200 working wives in the state of Baden-Württemberg, West Germany, less than 20 per cent of the husbands of working wives get their hands wet in the sink. Over 80 per cent of the working women between the ages of 20 and 60 said that they received little or no help from their spouses. In households in which the father helped, more than half of the children helped, too. If the father failed to join in, the number of children doing some of the household chores fell to 20 per cent.

Daily life is made up of trivia but that does not make it trivial. The small things of everyday life are important. A Japanese survey found that wives missed their husbands most when some heavy work had to be done around the house. They also missed their husbands when they had nobody to talk to and felt lonely. Some wives were apprehensive of their safety and wanted their husbands with them as bodyguards. A minority, however, did not mind the absence of their mates and some felt happier when their husbands were not at home. In Japan, young couples often shop together on Sundays, but the ordinary Japanese housewife clings to the custom of daily shopping for the evening meal despite refrigerators and a wide selection of frozen foods.

Middle-aged and elderly women often feel that they have nothing in common with their husbands once the children grow up — at least until grandchildren arrive. A wife who was looking for something other than their offspring to share with her husband became interested in baseball and found that the discussion of the technicalities of baseball brought a rebirth of communications and saved her from boredom.

The old Japanese family law stated explicitly that the wife was responsible for housekeeping, but the present law avoids any reference to specific functions and merely lays down the principle that the spouses are jointly liable for the ordinary household expenditures (Art. 761). If the spouses adopt the legal property system, the wife becomes co-owner of the assets acquired by the husband in his own name during the community life and a certain percentage is reserved to the wife.

If the common life is terminated, for example, by the death of the husband or through divorce, an accounting must be made. In a settlement necessitated by divorce, the difference between the assets of the partners at the beginning of the marriage (net assets, or subtracting liabilities) and the assets at the termination of the marriage is calculated. The total increase in assets is halved, and the party whose assets grew less than half of the total increase can claim the difference from the other party. In the case of death, one-quarter of the increase in assets of the deceased partner is given to the surviving spouse as a special share of the inheritance. The law also provides for an accounting and settlement while the marriage continues in a number of special cases, for example, if the spouses have been living separately for at least three years, if one of the spouses is recklessly remiss in fulfilling his or her economic duties or refuses without reason to inform the other party of the economic situation.

While the parties can appeal to the courts for enforcing financial obligations, it is practically impossible to have recourse to the law for compelling the performance of the duty of cooperation in other cases.

The third duty imposed by law is assistance. The obligation of mutual aid between spouses is similar to the duty of support among relatives (Art. 877 & 881). It does not mean some kind of conditional or supplementary help but the duty to provide everything required for the community of life of the spouses and their minor children. It includes the essentials of food, clothing and shelter as well as medical expenses (including childbirth), funeral expenses, the educational expenses for minor children and also social expenses. The duty to support relatives only arises if some relatives are well off and others destitute but spouses must contribute to the costs connected with married life in consideration of all their assets and revenues.

These legal provisions are concerned with the external, material and financial conditions of marriage but their purpose is the security and stability of the community of life. The law aims at an equitable sharing of the duties and burdens of marriage by both partners, but in order to achieve this goal, the partners have to come to an understanding of what these rules mean for them. Husband and wife will have to reach at least an implicit agreement on the monetary management of their household. A husband who trusts his wife will leave her a free hand in household spending. After all, when he married her, he must have thought that she was a competent housekeeper. If he finds out that her spending habits are ruinous, he should try to teach her the essentials of household budgeting, to keep expenditures within the ceiling of revenues. In practice, however, the behaviour of husbands ranges from the scoundrel who doesn't give his wife a penny for living expenses, and even steals the money the wife earns herself, to the dreamer who takes no interest whatever in worldly affairs. There are penny pinchers who make their wives ask for money for every purchase, and generous or irresponsible souls who allow their spouses to run up debts they will never be able to repay.

Finances in Japanese Families

Here are some of the ways in which Japanese employees, commonly called 'salarymen,' provide money for household expenses. Salaried employees used to bring a pay envelope home every month and receive bonus payments twice a year which, together, amounted to five or six monthly salaries. Some gave the pay envelope unopened to their wives and received a fixed sum, say between ¥25,000 and ¥50,000 as pocket-money for their own expenses which commonly included lunch (in large firms, employees eat at the company cafeteria and the costs are deducted from their monthly salaries), cigarettes, coffee, drinks, magazines, gambling (pinball, *mah-jong*, races) and golf. Now, many firms transfer salaries and wages into the employee's bank account, and besides having the passbook, the wife has one or more credit cards and a card for automatic cash dispensers. Some husbands used to take out what they wanted to use for themselves before they gave their wife the household money; now they sometimes have a certain part of their salary paid in cash and not transferred to their bank account.

Many families have to repay loans or pay for goods bought on credit (in many instances, these payments are withheld from the salary, with larger deductions from the bonus payments) so that the cash available for household expenditures may be insufficient. Some husbands retain all their overtime pay or a certain percentage of the bonus payments, and the sly ones used to resort to cheating by replacing the pay slip in their envelope by a forged one showing a lower amount.

Of 650 housewives in the metropolitan area polled by Fuji Bank, 70 per cent stated that their husbands worked overtime and over 60 per cent thought that the household budget would be tight without the husband's overtime pay. More than 55 per cent used the extra money to cover part of their household expenses.

Husbands' Spending

In recent years, wage increases have failed to keep pace with the real rate of price increases and many Japanese husbands have been forced to cut back on their spending because their pocket-money did not go up sufficiently to continue their former style of leisure activities. Sometimes, husbands jeopardise the economic security of their families by their outlays for recreation. Golf can be very expensive; club membership may cost up to a couple of million yen and greens fees are high so that a day of golf may set the family back by tens of thousands of yen. Even more aggravating is gambling. Local bodies can authorise races (horse, bicycle and motor-boat races) and the law allows betting on these races. But there is much illegal gambling in which losses are much heavier than in the legal betting. While the races are instituted by local governments, the actual arrangements are in the hands of private organisations of which the Japan Motorboat Association, controlled by Ryôichi Sasakawa, is known for its immense financial resources.

A more sinister form of gambling are the gaming sessions organised by gangsters, the so-called *bôryokudan*. The presidents of small companies and other small businessmen are the main victims of this highly disreputable pastime, but managers and 'salarymen' also get involved in this gambling. Since the stakes are high, the participants very often incur debts, and when they borrow from the moneylenders known as *sarakin*, their financial situation becomes desperate. Gambling, therefore, constitutes a real threat to Japanese family life. Its least pernicious effect is pressure on the family budget, but in many cases, it leads to crime and 'family suicide.'

Women's Use of Free Time

A common problem of married women is how to use their free time. If they have young children, they are fully occupied but when their children start going to school or if they have no children, they want to do something that gives them satisfaction. Many choose to work outside, resume the career they abandoned when they got married or work at least part-time. But for many, outside work is no viable solution and in order to avoid boredom or frustration, they pursue a variety of hobbies, attend courses or lectures or engage in social work. Some women become overly concerned with their health, even to the point of developing hypochondria. They may spend innumerable hours in beauty parlours or fitness centres, or they may become uncontrollable shoppers or bargain-hunters for everything from clothes to oriental art.

The basic problem is that these women need something to fill the void left after the routine household chores have been taken care of, something that keeps away boredom, dispels the sense of uselessness and provides a feeling of achievement. This problem did not exist when families had large numbers of children and the oldest children got married and had children before the youngest children grew up. It is a problem related to the prevalence of the nuclear family and the economic system in which the place of work is separated from the home. Hence, there is no real solution to this problem and whatever can be done is not much more than an anodyne. Nevertheless, husband and wife can apportion the tasks of their common life in such a way that there is a more or less satisfactory balance of responsibilities and the wife feels that she is truly a partner and not a housemaid.

Women and Aging

Although aging creates problems for both sexes, women may face particularly difficult changes when they advance in years. Men experience a decline in sexual drive and potency but they are usually less concerned with their physical appearance. Coming on top of the changes connected with the menopause, aging threatens the self-esteem and self-confidence of women. Appearance counts much in the consciousness of their worth, and to enhance beauty by cosmetics and clothes seems elementary for women in the advanced countries. This works as long as women are young but when they reach the end of the forties, the aging process catches up. Unless a woman is able to adjust the standards by which she judges her own value, middle age may cause emotional insecurity.

Since women generally live longer than men, wives often outlive their husbands. In 1984, the average life expectancy of Japanese men was 74.54 years, that of women 80.78 years. There were 3,110,000 households comprising men over 65 and women over 60. Of the people aged 65 and over in September 1985, 5,085,000 were men and 7,320,000 women. Nationwide, people over 65 living alone accounted for 9.8 per cent of the people over 65 but in Tokyo, the ratio was 12.4 per cent. In 1983, 63.4 per cent of the men and 82.6 per cent of the women aged 65 and older were living together with their children (in 1960, the percentages had been 80.3 per cent of the men and 82.6 per cent of the women), 30.7 per cent of the men and 13.0 per cent of the women lived with their spouses. 114,054 women and 58,015 women lived in nursing homes; 51.4 per cent of the inmates of these homes were bedridden.

Working husbands provided the living expenses of 49 per cent of the women over 50 years of age, 41 per cent received support from their children, 34 per cent worked themselves, 25 per cent received pensions and 5 per cent had income from property. Women, therefore, run a greater risk than men of being alone in old age and of needing financial assistance.

In the West, separate households of parents and their grown-up and married children are the rule, and most of the elderly do not want to become dependent on their children. Some governments expect an easing of the problems of social security from the restoration of the multi-generation family, but this kind of family solidarity may often result in unbearable physical and emotional burdens for both sides. Needs, interests and conditions of the old and young generation differ greatly which may easily cause misunderstandings and conflicts. The young find it difficult to accept the often whimsical behaviour of the elderly who, in turn, dread tutelage by their children. The physical and mental regression which takes place also in healthy individuals and reduces cells by almost half affects their character and conduct. They may be under the influence of the basic fears of old people: fear of indigence, fear of starvation, fear of dependence, fear of failure, and fear of dying lonely and unmourned.

Too often, people are unprepared for life after retirement, not only as far as living conditions are concerned but also with regard to activities and the way of giving life meaning and direction. Old age is not just waiting for death but a new period of life with its own problems as well as opportunities.

Privately operated homes for the elderly offer residence and also care and support while safeguarding a certain amount of personal freedom, but relatively few old people are able to meet the financial requirements of these institutions. In Japan, some homes accept applicants who transfer their property holdings to the institution.

A woman growing older needs to find self-respect and self-confidence in who she is and not in how she looks. More than anybody else, her husband can help her to retain her sense of worth. He must reassure her that his affection remains unchanged and that he enjoys living with her because he still loves her and wants her and needs more than ever.

Depression

One of the threats to the stability and integrity of marital life is depression. Depression may involve psychosomatic disorders and can be associated with a variety of psychic states. It may be a manic-depressive or any other endogen, neurotic or reactive disorder. Symptoms of depression are changes in sleep patterns, low energy levels, loss of interest or appetite, difficulty in concentration, lack of motivation, anxiety, irritability, agitation, feelings of inferiority, low self-esteem, loss of self-confidence and difficulty to function in a normal routine. People find it impossible to communicate; they have nothing to talk about and may spend many hours brooding alone. Suicidal tendencies or drug dependence may appear.

Depression can disrupt social and business life as well as relations with spouse and children. It is not a question of intelligence and in most cases treatment requires more than medication. Recent research has shown that the so-called neurotransmitters — substances transmitting a stimulus from one nerve cell to another — play an important role in the genesis of depression. It seems that a disturbance of the balance of these substances (also called biogenic amines) triggers depression.

According to psychologists, depression affects more women than men which reflects psychic and hormonal differences. It may, of course, also involve men's unwillingness to seek help for psychological problems which they consider a blot on their manliness. Women, it is said, are more susceptible to depression because they cannot be happy without a strong emotional attachment which means that women want love. A woman's problem, therefore, is 'does anybody really love me?'

A study undertaken by the University of California at Los Angeles found that women are twice as likely as men to suffer from depression. Housewives are the most vulnerable because of loneliness and frustration. Married working women do not handle the pressures of job and family as well as men with both roles, but cope with stress better than housewives. Men find the combination of marriage, work and children manageable, but the same situation can cause role conflicts and severe depression for women, especially when career pressures and family responsibilities labefy a woman's satisfaction. Depression can often become very severe for unmarried women who lack the strong social support offered by marriage.

On the whole, however, Japanese women seem to be better able to cope with the trials of life than men. Only half as many women commit suicide as men (1984: suicides of men 16,246; of women 8,088).

In her book, *Pressure Points in the Lives of Women*, Maggie Scarf has traced the connection between depression and the stages in a woman's life. For teenagers and women in the early twenties, separation from parents is the chief cause of depression. In the late twenties, the conflict between career ambitions and the commitment to husband and children becomes a source of depression. The overwhelming concern of women in their thirties is their marriage. The reality of their marriage does not accord with their expectations, causing self-doubts and insecurity. In their forties women reflect on missed opportunities and realise that there is no second chance. The exclusive role of wife and mother is no longer highly valued by society. She suffers from an anxiety syndrome because she possesses no identity outside marriage, she has the feeling of being nobody.

Loneliness and isolation depress many women. People have become unable to communicate. In the morning, nobody has time. In the supermarket, the housewife collects what she needs, pays and leaves. In the high-rise apartment buildings, neighbourliness is latent. When the family is together in the evening, conversation is limited to occasional comments on the television programme. Still, married women are more fortunate than single women who, overburdened by career, household and child rearing, can find nobody in whom they can confide.

The emotional issues troubling women in their fifties are twofold. For some women, the adjustment to the loss of the children leaving home constitutes the main difficulty. For others, the loss of attractiveness results in despondency. A woman who never had confidence in her basic self-worth and lovableness but could rely to a degree on her good looks finds life without that crutch intolerable. Women in their sixties and seventies are depressed because they cannot cope with the deaths of their husbands and best friends and feel terribly alone.

There are many positive sides to the position of middle-aged women. They become free to take outside jobs and engage in activities for which they had no time when the children were young. They can devote much of their time to their grandchildren without being tied to their care. They may manage the family finances, take up new hobbies or sports or enter local politics. In some societies, middle age brings women greater prestige, authority and freedom. When in-laws are no longer there, the wife becomes more self-assured, assertive and independent. She has a freer hand in running the household.

Wives of Expatriates

Life in Japan is not always smooth for foreigners, and expatriate families may encounter special difficulties. Corporate executives sent over by their organisation are generally well taken care of materially, but the emotional problems, usually different for the different members of the family, are sometimes devastating. Adolescents of school age may be able to adapt themselves most easily, particularly in the large cities where they can attend schools for foreigners. They may also succeed in learning some Japanese which gives them considerable freedom of action. The husband and father can keep himself occupied with his professional duties; he has a circle of business acquaintances, may belong to a club, pursue a hobby, play golf or do whatever he likes. The situation is most difficult for the wife who is often left with much free time and a great void to fill. Social or charitable work, hobbies and leisure activities are palliatives at best. Few of the things she can do give real satisfaction and often only increase the sense of frustration and aimless boredom. Her circle of acquaintances is restricted and social gatherings may become a strain on the nerves. The difficulty of finding contacts with Japanese society is felt most poignantly by expatriate wives.

A wife who gave up her own professional career so that her husband could accept the offer of an overseas assignment may regret that she agreed to the transfer when she experiences the loneliness, emptiness and constraints of the lives of expatriate wives. The worst thing she can do is to let her feelings pull her away from her husband instead of working out a solution acceptable to both.

In some cases, the wife may find a job. (The legal aspects of working in Japan are too complex to discuss at length here.) Basically, the applicant for a working visa must be sponsored by an employer in Japan and show that the job cannot be filled by a Japanese (for example, a job for which a native English speaker is required). The number of foreign women working in Japan has increased in recent years and many encounter the same difficulties experienced by Japanese women. A few employed by foreign firms receive the generous expatriate benefits, including housing, food and educational allowances and transportation supplements given to male executives transferred by their companies. But western firms have few openings for non-Japanese speaking local hires, even for those with previous business experience or advanced degrees. Women cannot find positions that are directly related to their previous job experience and must accept positions at a lower level of responsibility in a related field at a lower salary.

The majority of foreign women working in Japan are not business professionals but English teachers, or editors or writers of English publications, and many women professionals who work for Japanese companies are asked to devote a great portion of their office hours to writing or correcting business documents. An American who worked for a major Japanese trading company received a salary 66 per cent lower than that of her male predecessor although she had more experience than he had. Japanese firms often hire foreign women because it gives them the prestige of having a foreigner with the abilities of an English speaker at a very low cost. Although some foreign women have been very successful, the Japanese business world is not ready to integrate foreigners in general, not just foreign women.

Difficulties of Expatriates

For men, the stay in Japan may likewise bring complications. The Japanese system with its emphasis on work and achievement also enwraps the foreign business man or journalist. The exigencies of work seem incompatible with family life and the desire to be home in the evening with wife and children is often thwarted. For men in responsible positions, the job not only keeps them away from home in the evening, but may also require days and even weeks of absence. Then, there is the 'falling in love with the Japanese secretary' problem which has wrecked many marriages.

The balance between personal and professional needs is never easy, and the pressures are heavy in overseas jobs. Men are working to provide for their families only to discover that their efforts have cost them their families. They do not have the time to enjoy the years when their children are growing up and instead of gratitude, they may encounter anger and resentment on the part of a family from which they have become estranged and alienated. Men do not want to be relegated to the role of provider and financier but find it practically impossible to be with their families for common relaxation.

A strange situation may arise when one of the spouses finds Japan congenial and the other hates it. Such a discrepancy of perceptions may develop if one of the foreign couple is an Asian and the other a westerner, but it may also be the outcome of differences in character and nervous system. Tokyo's noisy restlessness may appeal to an enterprising temperament but scare a contemplative type. With patience, luck and money, everybody can find a place that suits his or her tastes but the simultaneous satisfaction of divergent or even opposite preferences requires an art of compromise beyond the capabilities of many couples.

Domestic Contract

Some years ago, an American feminist group drew up a domestic contract designed to achieve an understanding between husband and wife concerning their rights and duties. Three principles were considered basic to such an agreement. They were: '1. We reject the notion that the work which brings in more money is more valuable. The ability to earn more money is a privilege which must not be compounded by enabling the larger earner to buy out of his or her duties and put the burden on the partner who earns less. 2. We believe each partner has an equal right to his/her own time, work, values, choices. As long as all duties are performed, each may use his/her time any way he/she chooses. 3. As parents, we believe we must share all responsibility for taking care of our children and home — and not only the work but also the responsibility. . . . Sharing responsibility shall mean dividing jobs and dividing time.'

Love

It should be clear that the mere external observance of some rules is insufficient for a happy marriage. Marriage depends not only on what the partners do (or do not do) but also and sometimes even more on the spirit in which they do it. The most necessary and most characteristic factor of marital life is marital love. Conjugal love is the most perfect kind of love among men, a love which loves the partner as one's own self. Conjugal love as the essence of the personal union embracing heart and body is only possible between two beings fully, irrevocably and exclusively bound to each other. Love between husband and wife involves intimacy as well as reverence. Reverence, respect, veneration elevates this love from the level of passionate selfishness to the height of personal devotion. Respect without intimacy can be cold as ice, and intimacy without reverence sordid as mud.

Love is characterised by objective and subjective elements, what I love and the way in which I love. The subjectivity of love comes out in St Augustine's explanation that love cannot be seen: 'Some libertine and debauchee loves a very beautiful woman: he is attracted by the beauty of the body but internally the quest is for the mutuality of love. For if he learns that she hates him, would not that ardour and impetuosity for the beautiful limbs cool off and would he not as it were recoil from what he craved? He is offended and even begins to hate what he craved? He is offended and even begins to hate what he loved. Has the form changed? Is not everything there that allured him? It is there, but he burned in what he saw and demanded from the heart what he did not see. If, however, he becomes aware that his love is reciprocated, how passionately inflamed will he be? She sees him, he sees her, nobody sees the love, but what is not seen is nonetheless loved . . .' (Serm. 34).

Building on the Greek concept of the world as cosmos, an orderly, harmonious system, St Augustine expounded the notion of an 'order of love.' Only God as the *summum bonum*, the highest good, is absolutely and unconditionally lovable for His own sake. All other things are lovable only to the extent that they participate in God's being, goodness, intelligibility and beauty. Thus, the objective order of being becomes a norm for man's love, his desires and his conduct. A higher good should not be sacrificed for a lower good, the love of a person not placed below the love of money. The order of love is based on the inherent gradation of things, and orderly love must conform in its nature and intensity to the nature and dignity of the object of love.

The essence of love is not mutual giving. To impart from what one possesses is only an expression of love, but not love itself. Love is the surrender of one's self to the unity with the beloved, the common being of the lovers whose love makes them one. Love which is not requited by the beloved and does not create a union of love is benevolence and sympathy rather than love.

In a broader interpretation, love is the most exquisite form of communication and communication is essential to love. Intimacy and communication are irreplaceable aspects of married life. There are enormous differences in degree but an attempt to get along with a minimum of one or the other can only end with the demise of the marriage.

Naturally, communication cannot be reduced to verbal communication but, under normal circumstances, verbal communication is the most adaptable vehicle of love. Love can create unforgettable moments of silent togetherness, but love must also be able to sustain the chit-chat of everyday life. As long as people love each other, they will have something to say to each other.

Conversation between married couples will seldom or never concern deep philosophical or religious problems; it will usually be small talk, the children, the weather, prices, the cost of living, shopping and even TV programmes or baseball (soccer) games. Occasionally, there will be subjects of greater concern, purchases, trips, a new job or moving. But the ability to talk if there is nothing to talk about is just as important in marriage as it is in business.

Companionship

The companionship a wife expects from her husband may mean conversation or regular diversions such as eating out, dancing or other entertainment. But a husband coming home from work may not be in the mood to listen to the wife's detailed account of the day's happenings and fails to show interest in the wife's stories. Man's capacity of sensing another person's moods is in itself much weaker than woman's and men are very awkward in feigning emotions they do not feel.

Emotional Love

M. Scott Peck, in his book *The Road Less Travelled,* emphasises that love is not a feeling but a sustained pattern of action. It is volitional rather than emotional. The romantic notion of love implies that love is an overwhelming sensation but real love is the thoughtful decision to exert one's self to nurture one's own and the beloved's spiritual growth, the proper goal of life. Marital love as well as parental love is not spontaneous and easy, it is not a simple natural welling-up of passion. There is no love without effort.

Nevertheless, emotional love has been a favourite theme in western culture. In their songs and poems, the troubadours idealised courtly love by exalting the perfections of the beloved, but the love of which they sang remained a highly stylised and formal fantasy. In seventeenth-century France, love became passion and was analysed in paradoxical terms of imagination as pleasurable pain and sweet martyrdom. The individualisation of love is achieved in romantic love. The idea that love desires the other person as a unique individual generates the possibility of a love marriage and the fusion of a marriage for love and permanent marital love. It also established that love is its own justification and needs no other reason.

Religious Interpretation of Love

In the Christian tradition, love has an eminently religious meaning. 'God is love' (1Jo 4,16) is the epitome of the Christian message. The love of God constitutes the prototype of all true love so that the love of God forms the model and motive of all love. The first Epistle of St John makes the love of man the touchstone of the love of God: 'If anyone says, "I love God," and hates his brother, he is a liar. For how can·he who does not love his brother whom he sees, love God whom he does not see?' (1Jo 4,20). This text also suggests the fundamental difficulty in connecting the love of man with the love of God. The love of God is not based on experience but on faith while some kind of experience is essential to the love of man. Emotional elements are not excluded from the love of God — 'Thou shalt love the Lord thy God with thy whole heart, and with thy whole soul, and with thy whole mind' (Matth 22,37). Affections form part of the experimental knowledge of God's presence in mystical experiences which do not necessarily involve psycho-physical phenomena such as visions or ecstasies. This direct experience is not the effect of human endeavour but a free gift which induced Michel de Molinos, the founder of quietism, to assert that perfection consisted in the complete passivity of the soul. Basically, however, the Christian tradition has stressed the active and volitional aspects of love which St Paul already stated in what has been called the 'hymn of love': 'Love is patient, is kind; love does not envy, is not pretentious, is not puffed up, is not ambitious, is not self-seeking, is not provoked; thinks no evil, does not rejoice over wickedness, but rejoices with the truth; bears with all things, believes all things, hopes all things, endures all things' (1Cor 13, 4-7).

The greatness and uniqueness of marital love can only be preserved by the exclusiveness and indissolubility of the monogamous marriage, and marital faithfulness is an indispensable postulate of love. Conjugal rights and duties are of a strictly personal nature, they cannot be transferred or ceded. Adultery, also with the approval of the partner, is incompatible with the personal meaning of marriage and irreconcilable with the spirit of marital love.

Conjugal love must guide and inspire the cooperation and mutual help in fulfilling the tasks of marriage, in carrying the common burden and relieving the partner's pain. The marital community is necessarily a community of fate. In the old English wedding ceremony, the spouses promised mutual faith with the words 'I take thee for my lawful wife (husband), to have and to hold from this day forward, for better for worse, for richer for poorer, in sickness and in health, till death do us part.' As a community of fate, marriage is exposed to all the perils of human life, not only to the calamities threatening life and limb or property and possessions but also to misfortune, failure, disappointment and mistakes. It may happen that wrongdoing makes it impossible to preserve the marital community but guilt and forgiveness are inextricably interwoven with a community of fate.

Conjugal love provides the basis for solving conflicts between the community and the individuals belonging to it. As in every community, there can be no conflict between the true good of the community and the true good of the individuals; the problem is that it is often difficult to recognise what the true good is. Everyone naturally considers everything from his own point of view and often is blind to what the other regards as evident. A lover who loves his beloved as his own self should be ready to acknowledge the demands of the marital union even if they require the sacrifice of his own interest and the renunciation of his wishes. It is love which enables man to give up his own self for the sake of the beloved and to find his own happiness in the happiness of the other.

Mutual Trust

One of the most essential requirements of marital life is mutual trust. The intimacy of conjugal relations is impossible without trust, but trust between spouses may lead to conflicts. The law recognises the priority of the trust between spouses by giving a spouse the right to refuse to testify against the other spouse in civil as well as in criminal procedures (Code of Civil Procedure, Art. 280, No. 1; Code of Criminal Procedure, Art. 147, No. 1; the same applies to other relatives). In daily life, the solidarity of the spouses against third parties should be beyond doubt. Before appealing to third parties such as relatives, friends, acquaintances or superiors, spouses should try to compose their differences by themselves; only if their own efforts fail should they call upon outsiders.

Marital solidarity also requires that spouses do not discuss their intimate relations with others. There are cases in which a doctor, psychiatrist or clergyman should be consulted, but to disclose the details of conjugal life on a TV talk show is more than bad taste, it is a prostitution of marital intimacy and a debasement of the trust spouses should be able to place in each other. On the other hand, people often have great confidence in friends they knew before getting married and are inclined to talk to them about their marital problems.

In a Japanese survey answered by somewhat over 2,000 households, nearly half of the wives said that they consulted their parents when marital problems arose and almost 40 per cent would seek advice from their friends. About 30 per cent of the husbands would not talk about difficulties in marriage with anyone while 35 per cent would talk them over with their friends.

There are psychologists who think that marriage should allow for separate activities of each spouse. The question is not one of occupational or other special work each partner does alone but of leisure and recreation, sports and entertainment. These psychologists reason that resentment will grow to the extent that couples attempt to monopolise each other's time and that the desire for freedom will increase. As mentioned above, the advocates of an 'open marriage' consider extra-marital affairs as an appropriate expression of the personal freedom of spouses.

Separate Pursuits

The idea that husband and wife 'monopolise each other's time' reveals a basic misunderstanding of marriage which, after all, is a community of life. The notion that husband and wife live at the same address but that each goes his or her separate ways is incompatible with marital togetherness. Nevertheless, there are many pursuits that do not involve the rejection of the life in common and that each of the spouses can take up alone. In Japan, the custom that husband and wife are invited together to social functions is less firmly established than in the West. A married couple is invited together to weddings but there are numerous occasions, above all in the business world, on which the marital status of the guest is considered irrelevant. Japanese wives do not expect to be invited with their husbands to social affairs but foreign wives regard the omission as a slur. The lack of a common social life makes it difficult for wives to have common friends with their husbands.

By traditional standards, socialising would be an occasion to demonstrate marital solidarity, but in a society in which career women are no exceptions, even a couple with no marital problems may engage in respectable recreation separately.

A wife should not be taken up so completely with household chores that she has not a single moment for herself. The need of 'free time,' 'alone time' or privacy may vary according to temperament, education and interests. Some of the leisure activities of the wives of middle management employees in Tokyo were: hobbies, such as needlework, going out with friends, seeing movies, visiting theatres, concerts or museums, shopping in department stores, watching TV, reading newspapers or magazines, playing golf and exercising for health. As of 1981, 13,760,217 Japanese women had a driver's licence, 30.6 per cent of the total of 44,973,064. At the end of December 1982, about 60,000 women held a captain's licence for small craft (such as motorboats). There were few women pilots.

A controversy on the family page of a popular magazine over the wife's right to go out at night led to a survey in which 10 per cent of the respondents answered that women should be allowed to go out freely at night and 46 per cent thought that they should be able to go out at night once in a while for relaxation. But 46 per cent asserted that housewives should stay home at night for the sake of the family. Here are two typical views: 'Why shouldn't a housewife be allowed to have her own private time and get rid of stress? To make the home a place for real rest, the housewife has to work. . . . For her to be a dynamic, lively woman, she should be allowed the freedom of staying up drinking till 2 am once in a while' (28-year-old housewife). — 'How can a housewife be allowed to go out in search of freedom or to get rid of stress and fail to greet her husband when he comes home exhausted from a day of hard work?' (61-year-old housewife).

One of the separate activities that has come into vogue in the United States is separate vacations. Dual-career couples who are used to being independent and have more money may find separate vacations a practical way of avoiding the shuffling of complicated schedules which, however, may also become a scheme for escaping from each other. For couples with completely different tastes of recreation, separate vacations may solve a dilemma, but only if they are not a pretext to take advantage of one's partner. It is better than a fight that one party wins or a compromise that leaves both unsatisfied.

Marital Conflicts

Although most married couples protest that they love each other, they have to admit that marital tensions can exist and that quarrels do occur. Intimacy contains the seed of conflict. Marital disagreements are a universal experience; it may happen that a marriage does not survive the first night or the honeymoon and a marriage may break up after forty years of happy togetherness. Squabbles between husband and wife may be and often are about trifles which, on second thought, a mature person would find too ridiculous to argue about. Minor maladjustments can be magnified until it seems that the marriage is hopelessly compromised. It so happens that domestic quarrels often erupt at night, and if they lead to shouting, the exchange of threats or the smashing of furniture and china, the whole neighbourhood may become witness of the disagreements. Besides ruining the reputation of the family, such clashes may cause irreparable emotional damage and their repetition may make the break-up of the marriage almost unavoidable.

Monogamous marriage necessarily involves the polarity of being bound to one partner and the desire for freedom and change. In the course of married life, the struggle for power and domination may go on parallel with a deepening of companionship which makes the two indispensable to each other and keeps them together despite their conflicts.

There may be material reasons for disputes, food (the wife's cooking), clothing, home and furniture, amusement and recreation or the lack of it; there may be mental reasons, character, habits, tendencies, customs; there may be conduct and attitudes in general or towards each other; it may be everyday life or some extraordinary event. The choice of a mate is greatly influenced by the character of each of the partners, and marital difficulties may be due to the clash of personalities. Diffidence, insecurity and fear may be just as destructive of marital relations as jealousy, envy, ambition, vanity, aggressiveness and arrogance. Men sometimes want to feel their power; they think that their position depends on asserting their strength and therefore contend with imaginary competition. Psychiatrists think that jealousy is a dangerous state. 'Othello's syndrome,' they warn, is not uncommon. Wives often feel flattered by their husband's jealousy because it makes them feel attractive but eventually they may be accused of having an affair. A jealous husband may inflict grievous bodily harm on a wife he suspects of being unfaithful and he may even become a killer.

In many marriages, the life-style is a compromise between the requirements of a job (or two jobs) and the needs of married life. One-sided perspectives are normal in human beings. Each of the spouses may have his or her point of view on everything from the kind of house they should live in to the brand of coffee for breakfast. Conflicts may result from differences in age, education, intellectual interests, religious beliefs, want or dislike of children, the children's education, relations with in-laws, choice of friends, occupation of husband or wife, allocation of income, forms of investment, attitude towards drinking, food, and so on.

Family Meals

While the wife's cooking often is the object of entirely frivolous complaints, it may happen that her dislike of the kitchen poses a health hazard to the family. Japan's Ministry of Health and Welfare warned that the growing use of pre-cooked and frozen foods might deprive the family of essential nutrients. In a survey that covered 6,000 families, the ministry found that 10.3 per cent of the families had pre-cooked foods three or four times a week, and 32 per cent once or twice. In 13.2 per cent of the households, cooking took less than 30 minutes, in 32.2 per cent, less than 45 minutes. According to the ministry's dietitians, meals may lack nutrients such as calcium or vitamin A and B, if cooking takes less than 45 minutes or pre-cooked food is served twice or more often a week.

In the United States, the term 'grazing' is being used to describe an eating revolution sweeping professional classes, typically people aged 28 to 50 with husband and wife each making more than $25,000 a year. These busy Americans have given up family meals; they don't have scheduled meal times, don't eat three square meals a day but nibble a little bit here and a little bit there 10 or 15 times. Certain types of food are kept in the larder or refrigerator and family members go in and take a snack. Since more than half of all married women work outside the home, they have little time or inclination to prepare traditional meat-and-vegetable meals. The art of serious cooking is being lost with a mere 30 per cent of American meals being the old-fashioned home-cooked kind.

A British scientist counselled that all married couples, whatever their age, should look to their diets if they wished to achieve a congenial partnership. The quarrelsome mate quite likely is one whose nerves are starved of protein. The love and harmony of marriage are severely strained by 'on-edge' nerves — often caused by poor nutrition. Powdered skimmed milk is not going to cure all the ills of a marriage, but with more than half of all people losing their youth before they are forty, it seems logical to safeguard personal happiness by making certain that the nervous system is well fortified by protective foods.

Escape from Marriage

Couples may be unaware of the real causes of their unhappiness. When people don't understand each other, they may fear each other. Sometimes, the reaction to difficulties is to conceal or repress them rather than to solve them. There are, therefore, covert differences besides overt conflicts. Instead of facing up to the problems, people try to escape. Escape may take on various forms, drinking being one of the most frequently used means for fleeing from reality. There may also be day-dreaming, outside activities such as sports, clubs, social work or travel. In more difficult situations, husband or wife may seek extra-marital relations and look to other people for the understanding he or she does not find at home.

One form of escape is actual physical disappearance. In 1981, the Japanese police received 104,624 requests to search for missing people of which 53,953 (51.6 per cent) were women. Of the total number, 44.6 per cent were teenagers, and the requests were more numerous for girls (27,400) than for boys (19,257). Family troubles caused relatively more disappearances of men (21.7 per cent) than of women (13.6 per cent) and more men vanished on account of the other sex (19.9 per cent) than women (13.8 per cent). Many men (11.5 per cent) absconded for economic reasons, particularly because they could not repay their debts.

It used to be a very common experience that the wife made the major adjustments, most frequently when she married into an 'old' family. Nowadays, women are no longer willing to be subordinate and self-sacrificing. If one of the marriage partners dominates, there may be outward submission but inner rage. Rage is usually destructive because emotion obscures reason. There must be a safety valve for allowing pent-up emotions to be aired. In an ideal situation, there should be willingness on both sides to discuss whatever discontent either of them harbours and to make whatever adjustments are needed without expecting anything in return. Such a discussion supposes that the parties do not only hear words but seriously try to understand what the other really wants to say.

The greatest difficulty in understanding the other is the lack of self-understanding. Only a man who knows what he is and why he is what he is can be in a position to understand another person's reaction. Each of the partners must earnestly and sincerely try to understand himself as well as the other and be willing to accept the help of the other in understanding himself since self-understanding is the essential prerequisite for mutual understanding.

How to Settle Quarrels

No quarrel can be settled without mutual respect. Many men do not respect a woman as a person. Too often the male is still dominated by the idea that he is going to make all the decisions and he does not really believe that his wife has brains enough to bother with. On the other hand, there are women who have little respect for their husbands. They have learned to be devious in expressing their thoughts or in getting what they want. Because they can get away with their dissembling, they think of their husbands as stupid.

The Chicago Cana Conference drew up a set of rules for keeping domestic quarrels manageable. They were: 1. Keep little things little. 2. Keep it a discussion — a difference of opinion need not turn into an argument. 3. Keep your tongue and temper. 4. Keep it fair — don't insult or insinuate. 5. Keep it to yourselves — two are enough for a good fight. 6. Keep it current — don't rake up the past to support your present position. 7. Keep talking — the silent treatment is deadly and defeating. 8. Keep it short — never let the sun set upon your anger (Eph 4,26).

In Washington, DC, a psychologist, in cooperation with an actress puts up a play treating marital problems and then discusses problems presented by the audience.

Some psychologists find a development syndrome in marriage passing through the stages of childhood and adolescence to maturity. The childhood stage repeats the symbiosis in which the child is totally dependent on the mother whereas in the adolescent phase, the desire for independence leads to a power struggle. It seems impossible, however, to discover a fixed development pattern in every marriage and there is no mechanism which could determine such a pattern. When people get married, they should be sufficiently mature to talk to each other as adults, without shouting or screaming or other infantile tantrums.

Drinking Problems of Women

The modern economic system which usually forces the husband to go out to work in the morning and, particularly in Japan, keeps him away from home until late at night, has played a major role in turning housewives into alcoholics. Women in their thirties without an occupation or hobby who devote their entire time to housekeeping are most likely to seek relief from boredom or mental depression in drink. A study based on a rather small sample found that 88.6 per cent of male alcoholics started drinking between the ages of 16 and 30, while only 46.5 per cent of the female alcoholics began drinking during these years and 22.8 per cent took to drink between 36 and 40. Of the women alcoholics, 54.4 per cent were housewives, 18.4 per cent were supported by their parents, children or common-law husbands, and 17.5 per cent were working women. 47.4 per cent had worked as bar hostesses or in similar occupations. Of the women, 28.9 per cent were divorced against 17.4 per cent of the men.

Of the women covered by another Japanese study on alcoholics, half were housewives, 11.1 per cent worked in offices or were involved in a trade, 10.0 per cent were self-employed, 7.8 per cent were in the service industry, 6.6 per cent were managers, and 4.4 per cent worked in bars, cabarets, snack bars or other *mizu shôbai*. For twice as many women as men, 68.9 per cent, a particular event triggered their recourse to alcohol, the death of parents or other relatives, infidelity of the husband, divorce or separation from children. One out of three alcoholics had attempted suicide.

A study of the family background of alcoholics showed that in the families in which alcoholics lived up to the age of 18, the father had been a drunkard in one out of three cases, three out of ten came from families that had suffered economic hardship, and for one out of five, the family had experienced some kind of trouble. About half of the alcoholics thought drinking was bad when they were young (15-18 years old), one out of four thought that women should not drink, and women who had not drunk until they were 30 believed that drinking was morally wrong. Again, twice as many women as men, 65.7 per cent, thought that it was bad to drink alone but drank stealthily at home. Women suffering from psychoses or depression who took up drinking accounted for 35.2 per cent of the female alcoholics in their thirties and for 42.2 per cent of those in their forties. It is the age when children are older and begin to grow up, the husband is completely absorbed by his work and women feel lonely and disillusioned, unable to find any meaning in their lives.

In Japan, the ratio of women drinkers has risen from one in five women in the sixties to one in every two in the seventies. According to government statistics, the percentage of housewives in the drinking population increased from 18.3 per cent in 1968 to 46.6 per cent in 1977. Women alcoholics accounted for 6.7 per cent of the more than 2 million alcoholics in Japan. Most women start drinking after reaching the age of 35 in order to forget their worries about their social and family life. The number of women drinkers has also been rising in the 40-59 age group when women feel abandoned by their children or worry about their change of life.

Police find drunken women drivers harder to deal with than male offenders. Unlike men, women very seldom admit that they are in the wrong. They deny that they have been drinking, refuse to submit to a test, and finally start crying pleading to be let go. In 1983, Gumma police stopped an average of two drunken women drivers every night, most of them office workers.

Alcoholism

In the USSR, alcoholism has increased more among women than among men. On dairy farms, it happens that the cows are not milked because the milkmaids are on a drinking spree.

An American researcher who studied adopted children contended that inherited tendencies as well as family environment played a part in alcoholism. The study distinguished two types of alcoholism, with different symptoms and different probable causes. Type 1 alcoholics who begin drinking in their mid-twenties to thirties develop medical problems such as liver damage around middle age; they are said to have a genetic as well as an environmental predisposition. Type 2 alcoholics, mainly men, rarely have medical problems but often are criminals; the study found inherited tendencies decisive and environmental influences unimportant. When the natural father was an alcoholic, 22.9 per cent of the sons and 3.5 per cent of the daughters became alcoholics. When the mother was an alcoholic, 26 per cent of the sons and 10.3 of the daughters were alcoholics.

American women who have taken over many jobs once held by men have also adopted the drinking habits of men. In 1962, only 29 per cent of the liquor store customers were women; in 1984, women accounted for 51 per cent of the clientèle, and they were buying liquor with a sort of prestige macho image. Women make at least half of the decisions as to what brands to buy for the home, and in bars, women want to present a more assertive image by ordering the same kind of drinks their male associates are drinking.

Alcoholism as such is not an inherited tendency but the inherited personality traits predispose to the misuse of alcohol. In many cases, alcoholism starts as a response to stress, anxiety, depression, despondency or unhappiness. Some people become hostile, others become withdrawn. Women sometimes hug the comfort of their beds rather than face the world.

In Britain, the general household survey of the Central Statistics Office of 1980 found that 23 per cent of men were heavy drinkers, while among women, 41 per cent were light drinkers. The presence of children in the home influences drinking patterns. The younger the child, the less likely is it that the mother drinks. As children grow older, the number of drinking mothers rises. Among married women aged 18 to 24, 62 per cent of those without children were frequent drinkers compared with only 37 per cent of mothers with children up to the age of four.

Alcohol can have harmful effects on the health of everybody, but it is particularly injurious to women and young people. Women develop cirrhosis of the liver faster than men. An American study found that women have much less tolerance for drinking than men and liver degeneration can be caused in women by only a third as much alcohol as in men. The metabolism of alcohol in women can be affected by the menstrual cycle and the use of oral contraceptives.

Women and Smoking

There may be habits that one partner can or will not give up and the

other finds objectionable. Smoking used to be a major irritant of
housewives before women took up smoking. The ashes strewn on rugs
and furniture and the stench of tobacco fumes adhering to curtains were
more unpleasant for many housewives than smoking itself. A Japanese
study found that wives of cigarette smokers ran an increased risk of
developing lung cancer. This study has been dismissed as erroneous, but
an American study showed that cigarette smoking is a major cause of
cervical cancer. The strongest association was in female smokers between
the ages of 20 and 29; women in that age group who smoked were 17
times more likely to be afflicted by cervical cancer than non-smokers.
For women of all ages, smoking increases the incidence of cervical cancer
three times. In Japan, 13.5 per cent of all adult women were smokers
(1983).

Women took up smoking as a badge of liberation and many women
remain hooked because they fear that they will gain weight if they quit.
The American Cancer Society reported that smoking has become the
single greatest threat to the health of American women. For the first
time, lung cancer will kill more women than breast cancer, the Society
said. Young women in their teens and 20s are now smoking more than
young men and the health statistics begin to bear out the warning of
Joseph Califano, then Secretary of Health, Education and Welfare that
'women who smoke like men, die like men.' So-called 'male' diseases
now claim a growing number of victims among women and add to the
specific threats smoking creates for women and their babies: stillbirths,
sudden infant deaths and miscarriages, lowered fertility and danger of
strokes and heart attacks in smokers who take birth control pills.

Of the 23,301 persons charged in Japan with abuse of stimulant
drugs in 1983, 3,974 were women and among them were 497 housewives.
A police survey found that about 70 per cent of the housewives, half of
them in their 30s, had started taking drugs out of curiosity or for a thrill,
and most of them had continued using drugs for three years before they
were caught. Only seven women had been forced to start using
stimulants.

Since no man is perfect, spouses may have cause for finding fault
with each other. But criticism should always be constructive. It is
insufficient to point out a shortcoming; the way of correcting it must be
explained at the same time. If one partner feels unhappy about something
but does not know what can be done about it, a discussion of possible
solutions is in order, otherwise, a smouldering atmosphere of discontent
may poison relations.

Family Violence

The most deplorable development in a marriage is the occurrence of
physical violence. Together with child abuse, wife beating represents a

tragic perversion of the intimacy of family life (in the seventies, husband beating also became a more frequent event). The greater attention given to sociological research on family violence in the sixties and seventies revealed that it was a disturbance of frightening proportions. Violence may involve all members of the family: violence of husband against wife or vice versa, maltreatment of children, including sexual abuse, sibling abuse (both physical and sexual), parent abuse and finally abuse of the elderly. In the United States, estimates of the number of victims of family violence, children, wives, husbands and parents who got struck, stabbed, beaten up, punched or kicked at least once a year ranged between 8 and 28 million (1975). In the category of extreme violence, a study concluded that there were at least 4.7 million badly battered wives in the United States, or about 10 per cent of all married women. Again in the United States, one out of every six couples will have some kind of physical altercation — ranging from slapping or throwing things to using a knife or a gun — at least once a year. In addition to the deaths resulting from physical abuse, there are planned and wilful murders of children and spouses. Abuse of the elderly often takes the form of tying up those who need constant watching (for example, to the bed) in order to get them out of the way for shopping or house-keeping, or by using excessive amounts of alcohol or sleeping pills to keep them under control.

Most of the calls received by telephone counselling services come from wives, typically in the morning, when the husband has left for work and the children are at school. 'My husband beats me and the kids almost every day. What shall I do?' Calls tend to be particularly numerous on Monday mornings and on the days following a holiday. Experienced consultants try to find out whether the woman only wants to talk away her grief or is looking for a way out of the misery of a failed marriage. Some women may want to save their marriage but others have given up hope and are anxious to terminate an unbearable situation.

The family's everyday life brings numerous occasions for disagreement and because the family members live in constant physical nearness, there is a built-in factor for escalating every trivial squabble. Much of the physical violence between spouses starts with verbal altercations or abuse, and, as is the case in many other situations, people have recourse to their fists when reason fails. In a similar way, family quarrels tend to become noisy. The verbal jangle reaches higher and higher decibels; mutual accusations and threats are reinforced by breaking crockery and furniture or hurling assorted missiles at each other. The whole neighbourhood is entertained by this real-life melodrama. The police are loath to get involved in marital disputes and neighbours prefer to stay out. But the reputation of the family is ruined and the children may have to pay with shame and embarrassment for the unrestrained outburst of parental discord.

Alcohol is an important contributing factor in the abuse of children or spouses. In the United States, 70 per cent of all family violence is related to alcohol. The brutalisation of women by drunken husbands is an all too common phenomenon, but violence resulting from rows over meals, money and extra-marital relations is also frequent. The increase in alcoholism among women has also been responsible for the rise in marital violence.

In Japan, wife beating is said to be particularly prevalent among the so-called intelligentsia. Husbands take out their frustrations in the office and business on their wives. Responding to the question whether she was happily married, the 33-year-old wife of a company employee replied: 'I have been married for eight years and beaten 56 times by my husband. Do you call this happy?'

Recently, a 15-year-old girl was arrested for killing her father. The father, owner of a steel factory in Higashi Osaka, habitually beat up his wife after drinking, and the four children had tried in vain to stop their father from punching their mother. When the father came home drunk Saturday night and started trouncing his wife, the girl became angry and stabbed her father with a kitchen knife.

Although wife beating is common in Japan, the issue has not received enough publicity to influence public opinion. Violence has been condoned so consistently in the country's past that it only becomes a problem when it attracts the attention of special interest groups. Otherwise, brutality is taken for granted. While foreign studies have often discussed the excesses of the Japanese military, the subject has been almost taboo in Japan. The Japanese government and particularly the Ministry of Education have done their best to prevent a national soul-searching and the glorification of violence in the comics and on TV has given the stamp of approval to macho brutality.

In South Korea most husbands who abuse their wives are high school or college graduates. A Korean counselling organisation found that about half of all Korean wives were habitually beaten by their husbands and many wives were also abused by their mothers- or sisters-in-law. The leading motive in men's brutality is their desire to demonstrate their authority. Women put up with this treatment because they would find it difficult to support themselves after getting a divorce.

Wife-beating constitutes a serious problem in China where it is a vestige of the country's feudal past. Under communism, women theoretically have equal rights but Chinese women are often afraid to challenge their husbands and in many cases tolerate beatings because they consider it a disgrace to seek help. China has no refuge centres for battered wives who must rely on the neighbourhood welfare committees, the local branches of the state-run Women's Association or the courts. In order to educate the public, the government publicises particularly vicious cases. In January 1984, the newspapers reported the execution of a minor official in the city of Hebi (Henan province) who had raped three women and sexually tortured his wife with cigarettes, electric shocks, needles and belts. In another case, a woman doctor was punched and kicked in the face, stomach and limbs because she refused her husband's demand for a divorce, and her mother-in-law tried to get her evicted from the hospital.

Mao Zedong once wrote that Chinese women should free themselves from feudal China's 'four thick ropes' — the authority of men, political oppression, religious rites and obedience to family.

In Kuwait, the High Court of Appeals granted a woman's plea to leave her husband because he beat her up. The court ruled that, under Islamic law, a husband can beat his wife provided she suffer no injury. The husband has the right to beat his wife, the court said, but not to maltreat her.

In the United States, some women who killed their husbands have won acquittal from a murder charge by basing their defence on the 'battered woman's syndrome.' To prove self-defence when the killing did not occur in an actual altercation, the wife has to demonstrate that it was reasonable for her to perceive that her life was in danger. To kill the husband must be shown as the only way open to the battered woman to escape from her situation. When it can be proven that the husband was a bully who deserved what he got (or got what he deserved), the wife will not be convicted.

A Florida woman fired both barrels of a double-barrel shotgun at her husband, emptied each of three 38-calibre revolvers into him and finally discharged a single-barrel shotgun. She was acquitted when the evidence showed that prior to the shooting, the husband had threatened to kill his entire family and himself and that for years, he had severely beaten his wife and sexually assaulted her and his oldest daughter. A woman who hired a 'hit man' to kill her husband went free when her lawyer proved that she had been abused for years. But prosecutors and some judges object to such testimony on the ground that it is prejudicial and puts the victim on trial instead of the defendant.

Sadomasochism also occurs in marriage, and sadistic husbands seem to be much more numerous than masochistic wives. A masochistic partner unswervingly clings to the sadist consort.

Japanese doctors have invented the term 'wife-pathogenic disease' for phenomena induced by the behaviour of wives against their husbands. They list the following instances: husbands who refuse to go to work — just like children who do not want to go to school; husbands who, instead of going home after office hours, hang around in *pachinko* parlours or go to the movies because they fear the sexual demands their wives might make; lack of initiative; impotence due to psychological reasons; refusal to have marital relations as a means of punishing their wives.

Shelters for Battered Wives

In many countries, special 'safe' houses give temporary shelter to women who flee from domestic violence. In feudal Japan, women could return to their families if life with their husbands became unbearable or they could escape to what were called *kakekomi-dera* (refuge temple) where they found shelter. Since women had no right to ask for a divorce, the temple would negotiate with the husband. These temples, therefore, were also called *enkiri-dera* (divorce temple); the best-known was Matsugaoka Tôkeiji. The wife who wanted to stay permanently at such a temple would have to become a nun.

There are public as well as private shelters for battered wives but, generally speaking, there is too little understanding of and concern about family violence. One reason is that the family has decreased in size and visibility and that the inside story of the family is often distorted. Even physicians may fail to recognise the seriousness of the threat to the health and life of women. It is understandable that women who have been brutalised by their husbands regard all men as beasts but that does not make this opinion correct. On the other hand, a husband should never, absolutely never and under no circumstances, beat his wife. Naturally, if physically attacked, he can defend himself, but striking one's wife first is inexcusable for any husband.

Illness

Besides marital conflict, the common life of husband and wife can be endangered by illness and is broken up by death. Illness of one spouse can bring forth heroic proof of affection but also the coldest show of indifference. In many women, the illness of the husband evokes what are often called 'motherly instincts' — the special capacity of women to care, nurse, cherish and caress. Compared with women, men are less capable of demonstrating their emotional involvement with the pain and suffering of their spouses which should not lead to the conclusion that men are unfeeling and callous.

In the old times, the care of the sick was one of the common functions of the family; people were taken to a hospital only for communicable diseases or if they had no family. In many primitive societies, women were entrusted with the art of healing and were the repositories of whatever medical or pseudo-medical knowledge the group possessed. Medicine men were believed to wield supernatural powers which could influence the elements or human events but in matters affecting health and human life, women played the more important role. Although there are orders and congregations of men for the care of the sick (such as the Alexian Brothers who manage hospitals for the insane, epileptics and inebriates), most of the congregations serving in hospitals are those of women.

Most wives want to be informed of the exact state of health of their spouses, particularly if they suffer from illnesses such as cancer or heart trouble. Even more than physical illness do emotional disturbances require the understanding and sympathy of the spouse. Problems such as feelings of hopelessness, depression, alienation, alcoholism or drug abuse can create the danger of suicide. In such situations, emotional support and comfort by the spouse can make the difference between life and death while insensitivity can become a decisive factor for giving way to a suicidal inclination.

Death of Spouse

The death of the husband may be a more wrenching experience for the wife than the loss of the wife to the husband. In the traditional role allocation in which the wife devotes most of her time and energy to the household, the wife is, as a rule, more emotionally involved in the marriage than the husband. To take care of her husband and children gives meaning and direction to her life (an attitude vehemently opposed by the women's liberation movement). Nevertheless, the loss of his wife can deeply affect the emotional life of a man who is also deprived of the loving care for his everyday needs. For both, the loss of the sex partner and companion in whom he or she could confide, whom he could trust, on whom he could rely and who shared joys and sorrows, success and failure, the sweetness of love and the anxiety of parenthood, this loss intimates the constraints of man's existential limitation. Lasting happiness is beyond man's experience, and the happier the marriage, the more heartrending the agony of separation. Religious faith in a future life may instill the hope of a reunion in a better world but the emotional trauma left by the crushing grief of the parting from the beloved may fundamentally change the outlook on life.

An American study reached the surprising conclusion that the surviving spouses in unhappy marriages grieve far longer for their lost mates than do the survivors of loving partnerships. Anguish is also more likely to linger for years if a spouse dies unexpectedly. The sudden death appears senseless, causes bewilderment and refusal to accept a world in which tragedy occurs so arbitrarily. The spouse left behind protests: 'It makes no sense.'

Extreme dependence on a mate complicates recovery from his or her death. If one spouse relied on the other for everything from keeping the house to making outside friends, he or she may find it impossible to function autonomously.

The anticipation of the death of the husband plays a major role in the concern women feel about their future. According to a recent Japanese poll, women are worried about how they will fare in their old age, concern about their health and their economic security being the most prominent reasons for their anxiety. Women fear that their husbands will die before them, or that they will become disabled and will have nobody to take care of them. More than half of the women covered by the survey hoped to live with children when their husbands died. More women would depend on their daughters-in-law than on their daughters if they were confined to a hospital — only 3.7 per cent expected their husbands to look after them. Over half wanted to go on working as long as they could. Benefit payments from pensions together with savings or income from a job were expected to provide the means of existence in old age; only 10 per cent counted on help from their children.

Some time ago, people started to refer to retired old men who stayed home doing nothing and were a nuisance to their wives as *sodai gomi* (bulk garbage). That such an expression could gain currency is a sad indication of the lack of understanding of the functions of the family but also of the widespread failure of Japanese men to make a positive contribution to the work of the household.

Suicide of Elderly

Old people account for a disproportionally large number of suicides. According to the National Police Agency, the total number of suicides in Japan in 1985 amounted to 23,599, 15,624 men and 7,975 women. The suicide rate was 19.5 per 100,000 population (men 26.3; women 13.0); 3.2 per cent of all deaths were attributable to suicide. The number of suicides declined in the last two years (1984: 24,334 cases, suicide rate 20.5; 1983: 24,985 cases; suicide rate 21.1) but the rates were still much higher than the post-war low (14.2 in 1967). In recent years, however, the highest suicide rates were among old people. In 1985, suicide of people aged 65 and older numbered 5,580, 23.6 per cent of all suicides and corresponding to a suicide rate of 45.0. Although, generally speaking, suicides of men are double those of women, suicides of women over 65 years of age were more numerous than those of men in this age group (men: 2,731, 17.5 per cent of all male suicides; women: 2,849, 35.7 per cent of all female suicides) but the suicide rate of men (50.1) was still higher than that of women (41.1). The highest suicide rates were among people over 80.

Suicides in Other Age Groups

A notable development has been the increase in the number of suicides of men in middle age. In the post-war years (1947-1972), the suicide rate of men aged 35 to 39 was 19.3; it was 19.2 for men between 40 and 44 and 24.0 for those from 45 to 49. In the years from 1973 to 1982, the rate was 25.4 for men from 35 to 39, 28.9 for those from 40 to 44 and 30.5 for the 45 to 49 age group. In 1985, suicides of men aged 40 to 49 numbered 3,678 (suicide rate 42.0), and those of men from 50 to 59 was 3,487 (suicide rate 46.0); these two age groups accounted for 45.9 per cent of all male suicides (suicides of men between 30 and 39 numbered 2,510; suicide rate 25.2). More women than men in the old generation (65 and older) kill themselves because of illness (2,125 cases, 74.6 per cent of all female suicides of that age group, against 1,927 men, 70.6 per cent of the male suicides). Altogether, 10,009 suicides (42.4 per cent of all suicides) were attributed to illness (men 5,880 cases, 37.6 per cent of the male total; women 4,129 cases, 51.8 per cent of the female total); other apparent reasons were nervous breakdown, alcoholism or other psychiatric disorders (4,091 cases, 17.3 per cent of the total; men 2,387 cases, 15.3 per cent; women 1,704 cases, 21.4 per cent), economic difficulties (2,684 cases, 11.4 per cent; men 2,418 cases, 15.5 per cent of the total for men), problems at the place of work (1,148 cases, 4.9 per cent; men 1,082 cases, 6.9 per cent of the total for men) and sex relations (833 cases, 3.5 per cent; men 540 cases, 3.4 per cent of the male total; women 293 cases, 3.9 per cent of the female total). Suicides of old people were relatively numerous in rural areas, and with 1,255 cases, suicides of farmers and fishermen constituted the largest category of suicides by occupation.

Of the 23,516 suicides over 14 years of age, 12,654 (53.8 per cent) were married (men 8,880, 57.1 per cent; women 3,774, 47.5 per cent), 5,025 were unmarried (21.4 per cent; men 3,792, 24.4 per cent; women 1,233, 15.5 per cent), 3,664 (15.6 per cent) were widowed (men 1,248, 8.0 per cent; women 2,416, 30.4 per cent) and 1,521 divorced (6.4 per cent; men 1,116, 7.2 per cent; women 405, 5.1 per cent). Significant was the difference between the sexes of unmarried and widowed suicides.

While the suicide rates of the older age groups have been rising, those for the younger generation have declined. In the 1947 to 1972 period, the suicide rate of young men between 14 and 19 was 17.8; it was 42.0 for the 20 to 24 group and 33.9 for those aged 25 to 29. In the 1973 to 1982 period, the rates were 11.3, 25.0 and 25.6, respectively. In 1985, the suicide rate of young men between 15 and 19 was 7.1, that of men between 20 and 24 19.9 and for the 25 to 29 group, it was 24.6. The suicide rates of girls and young women in the 1973 to 1982 period were also much lower than in the post-war (1947-1972) era (females 15-19 years of age: 6.1 as against 13.9; 20 to 24 years: 13.8 as against 29.3; 25 to 29 years: 13.4 as against 20.3). In 1985, the suicide rate was 3.3 for young women between 14 and 19, 8.7 for those from 20 to 24 and 9.8 for the 25 to 29 age group.

The increase in the suicides of middle-aged men has been blamed on job problems, such as transfers to positions necessitating the separation of the employee from his family, the stress of long commuting hours in the large cities, heavy workloads and intense competition for management posts. Moreover, financial difficulties, often arising from the burden of loans for the purchase of a house but also from imprudent borrowing for gambling and problems of the children's education were given as reasons for the high suicide rates. The official reports of the Ministry of Health and Welfare listed poor health as the main reason for suicides, followed by alcoholism and mental problems. Poor health may be the main reason for suicides of the aged. Suicides among teenagers are lower although the stress of entrance examinations has become much greater than in earlier years.

Different from Japan, the suicide rate of teenagers has gone up in the United States. In 1982, the rate for 15-to-24-year-olds was 12.1 per 100,000. This was somewhat lower than the overall average — 12.4 — but much higher than in former years (1950: 4.5). The suicide rates for most other age groups have stayed the same or have fallen but they have risen for old people. Those over 60 represent 12 per cent of the US population but are responsible for 25 per cent of all suicides. Statistics show a decrease in suicides among those over 60 since 1960 but Professor Nancy J. Osgood contends that there is an accelerating suicide rate amongst those over 75 and that women aged 85 and over commit suicide at a fairly high rate. Generally, men commit suicide three times as often as women in all age groups but the ratio rises to 10 to 1 at 75 and higher and to 12 to 1 at 85 and higher. Marital status is one of the most crucial factors for men. The rate is much higher for unmarried men and highest in the first two years after being widowed or divorced.

A not quite ordinary threat to married life comes from brushes with the law. Japan's old civil code provided that punishment for a heinous crime or a prison sentence of three years or longer for any other crime entitled the other spouseonger for any other crime entitled the other spouse to ask for a divorce. This provision has been deleted in the new civil code but such an event may cause the breakdown of the marriage and thus lead to divorce. Even minor crimes can disrupt marital life but depending on the nature of the misconduct, the effects on the relations of the spouses may vary. People who love each other do not easily give up and will stand by each other through both the sweet and bitter experiences of life.

Concubinage

An institution that owes its existence to a warped view of marriage and a disregard of morality is concubinage. Concubinage has existed in many forms. It was a substitute for marriage for Roman slaves who were legally incompetent to contract a marriage. As explained above (Ch. 4), concubinage gained importance following the matrimonial legislation of Emperor Augustus. Until the reform of Pope Gregory VIII (1073-1085), concubinage was widespread among the clergy in the west and Canon Law considers the marriage in which at least one partner is a Catholic and which is not concluded in accordance with Canon Law as concubinage. Until the Second World War, many people in the upper classes of western society kept mistresses; since then, the old aristocracy found it too expensive to set up a mistress in a separate establishment as in former days. Mistresses still exist, but mostly on company expense accounts. In Japan, the keeping of a mistress by those who can afford it (and by some who can't) raises few eyebrows. In China, the revolution did away with the custom of taking concubines but there have been reports that the practice has reappeared.

Mistresses

When concubinage replaces marriage, the relation between the partners may not be different from that between spouses. But if a mistress is kept in addition to the 'lawful wife,' something is wrong. It often means that the legal marriage has been made into a social arrangement separate from the personal relationship between husband and wife and is based solely or mainly on social, economic or political considerations. The sex life of the husband (and in many cases, also of the wife) is a different matter. Extra-marital affairs with prostitutes, which the 'double morality' acknowledged in some societies also condones, are temporary irritants but keeping a mistress creates a permanent disorder in married life and represents a constant source of friction.

In her book *The Making of the American Mistress,* Melina Sands, foundress of 'Mistresses Anonymous,' opines that the capacity to listen is the main asset of a mistress. 'Men have mistresses because they have needs that they are unable to fill in their other lives.' Men have the need to communicate — sexually, verbally and tactily, but these needs remain unfulfilled at home because husbands see their wives at all the wrong times, when they are tired or early in the morning when both are at their worst. Affairs are almost always discovered, but they last because they are addicting and lure men by their melodrama, sexuality, risk and heightened feelings.

The Book of Royal Lists (Cray Brown and Lesley Cunliffe) gives the names of 16 English kings known to have had mistresses and the 79 illegitimate children they sired. Not many wives will be so understanding as Queen Alexandra who, after the death of King Edward VII, sent back to Lily Langtry a neatly laundered pile of handkerchiefs the famous beauty had forgotten in the royal bedroom. Different from prostitutes, a mistress is supposed to be faithful to her patron. Virginie Oldoinin, mistress of Napoleon III, refused all enticements until, in 1855, British Lord Hertford offered her 1 million gold francs for one night. His lordship must have got his money's worth for Mlle Oldoinin spent the next three days recovering.

The influence of royal mistresses on public affairs was notorious under Louis XIV and Louis XV. Although Louis XIV planned and supervised the execution of his own policy, he was greatly influenced by his mistresses, Louise de la Vallière, Mme de Montespan and Mme de Maintenon whom he married after the death of his wife, the Infanta Maria Theresa of Spain. Louis XV fell entirely under the influence of his mistresses, Mme Pompadour and Mme du Barry.

The boundary line between an 'affair' and a 'mistress' is somewhat fluid. In Japan, in particular, 'natives' as well as 'expatriates' get 'involved' and such relations may be of considerable duration. The arrangements vary from the patron taking complete care of all the needs of the woman (providing for her even better than for his own family) to the woman footing the bill for the affair. The first reaction of a wife who discovers the unfaithfulness of her husband will be 'that woman or me.' The husband, when being found out, tends to look for excuses. But there are men who are unwilling to give up that relationship and there are women who prefer the security of a nominal marriage with its mixture of freedom and emptiness to the uncertainty of a divorce.

According to tax investigators, the payment of allowances to mistresses is one of the personal purposes for which family companies are often misused.

In the Indian state of Gujarat, an arrangement has become popular which is a cross between bigamy and keeping a mistress. Bigamy is banned in India, but a married man who desires a new relationship without divorcing his wife signs a so-called 'friendship agreement' with a single woman. The man sets up a new household with his 'friend' while maintaining his legally wedded wife and children. Some of these contracts are even registered but legally they are not binding. The divorce laws are very strict in Gujarat state, making it almost impossible for a spouse to obtain a divorce unless the other party agrees, but there is no law that says you cannot keep a mistress. Because the friendship agreement is no marriage, there is no bigamy; because the relation is open, there is no deceit; and because the husband retains his wife, there is no abandonment. The contract offers a 'cloak of legitimacy' to the woman who signs it and some women are unaware that it is not a marriage at all. The woman has no recourse if the man walks out on her; she has no claim to maintenance and cannot ask for a share in his property.

17

Marriage and the Working Woman

Woman's Functions

THE PROBLEMS CONNECTED WITH WOMAN'S POSITION in society and her role in the labour market acquire a new dimension when considered in relation to marriage and the family. Logically, the position and functions of man also change with marriage but these changes seem to involve far less problems than the changes that marriage entails for woman. These changes are mainly ascribable to the role attributions which, it seems, differ in different societies and in different periods of history. In western society, the married woman fulfils three basic functions inside the house: she is wife, mother, and mistress of the household. These three functions usually go together, although with different emphasis. Outside the family, women have played leading roles in public life and religion. In primitive societies, the role of women in public life was usually related to the tribal organisation and in some way an extension of her role in the family, but in the West, the activities of women as political or religious leaders were and are without link to her family functions. Naturally, when a woman accedes to the throne in monarchies in which succession is not restricted by the Salic law she does so as a member of the dynasty but this has nothing to do with the role of woman in the family. Today's career women are also outside the traditional scheme of the role of woman.

Of the three functions, woman's role as mother constitutes her most basic part. It is the foundation of her status and her most secure position. There hardly is any society in which the importance of propagation is not recognised and nowhere is the continuation of the race considered as a matter that could be changed by popular vote. The mother is the centre of the family; she and her children form the core of the family as a social unit. The emotional attachment between mother and child is mutual. Although the mother is usually separated from her children when they found their own families, she still remains their mother. Woman's role as mother is in no way the result of a historical development; it is the role for which she is destined by her physiological and emotional disposition. Mother is sexually less restricted than wife. Wife necessarily carries the connotation of a male partner but a woman can be the mother of sons and daughters and she can be mother to children she did not bear. The term mother is susceptible of wider analogous use than the word father and occasionally all elderly women are regarded as mother figures.

The function of mistress of the house is closely associated with that of mother. The household chores and child care in the modern nuclear family give only a very inadequate idea of what mistress of the house really means. In Homer, the household appears as a large and complex organisation. Penelope, the faithful wife of Odysseus (this, anyhow, is the common interpretation), does much more than weaving the shroud for Laertes which she then unravels at night to stave off her suitors. The praise of the wife in Proverbs (31, 10–31) is concerned exclusively with her external occupations, her care of the household, her economic activities, her circumspection and her acquisitions. Not a word is said about the emotional and spiritual relations between her and her husband. Not every culture reaches a point at which man's inner life finds adequate attention and the relations between the sexes are explored also in the claims that marriage makes on the minds and hearts of the spouses.

As suggested by the passage in Proverbs, the function of woman as mistress of the house is the starting point of woman's economic activities. Generally speaking, the status of women is low in hunting and nomadic tribes but is relatively high in groups which depend for their subsistence on agriculture. In numerous primitive societies, women were responsible not only for preparing the meals but also for providing the things required for sustaining the family, from gathering firewood to making clothes. Many sociologists maintain that women started planting in order to secure regular crops. Women may also have been the first to barter or sell their surplus produce. Selling farm products remains the function of women in many communities in South-East Asia where local trade is largely conducted by women. The husband may carry the load to the bazaar; he then returns home to take care of the children and prepare the meals. This inversion of roles comes from activities which originally were an extension of the work of the household but there are also instances in which women took up work as an independent activity. In pre-war Japan, peasant women carried products to the city (this is the case even today in very rare instances) and women peddled the wares made at home. The work of women divers gathering abalone, oysters or pearls seems unrelated to the family, as was the very different kind of work in factories and mines which developed with the industrial revolution and separated women from their families.

The most explicitly sexual role of woman is that of wife. Apart from the very exceptional case of polyandrous societies and polygamous cultures, marriage is a one-woman, one-man relationship and this aspect has received special emphasis through the modern accent on marriage as a partnership. In the old times, a man married to found a family; the family was the essential purpose of marriage. In the modern way of thinking, the 'boy-and-girl' pattern prevails but even in western society, the concept of the 'home' remains important. In today's Japan, 'mother' and 'homemaker' overshadow 'wife' in the common evaluation of the role of women and the wife's 'motherly' care for her husband is more appreciated than that of a sex partner. Nevertheless, the Japanese wife's submissive behaviour towards her husband in the presence of third parties is no indication of her real status. The wife is the undisputed mistress of the house, and this position implies that she is in charge of finances, at least of day-to-day expenses, the style of living, the education of the children and the relations of the family with the neighbourhood. Although the wife controls the purse in many households, an increasing number of men seem to hand their wives just the necessary amount of money for daily expenses, and in some families, the presence of the mother-in-law weakens the wife's position.

Women's Readiness to Work

A survey conducted by Japan's Prime Minister's Office in October and November 1983 showed that 59 per cent of the 2,418 respondents, women between the ages of 20 and 60, had some kind of job. Of the working women, 38 per cent had continued work without interruption, while 45 per cent had resumed work after quitting for marriage and childcare. The main reason for working was economic; 72 per cent worked in order to meet household expenses. Complaints voiced by 19 per cent of the women workers concerned low wages, long hours or menial work, but 75 per cent were satisfied with their jobs. Half of the women who were not working would like to have part-time jobs but they were deterred by bad working conditions, age restrictions, and the difficulty of getting their old jobs back after retiring for raising their children.

A poll that covered 1,000 office women aged 20 to 29 in Tokyo showed that 69.7 per cent intended to work after marriage, about 25 per cent planned to quit upon having children but seek reemployment in the future, 24.5 per cent hoped to continue work after having children, and 19.4 per cent wanted to postpone retirement until they had children.

After marriage, 52.6 per cent intended to work outside the home to the extent that it would not inconvenience husband or children while 42.8 per cent thought that they should devote themselves primarily to running the household and raising their children. Many office workers were dissatisfied with their present jobs and 42.5 per cent wanted to quit and become designers, copywriters, illustrators or journalists, and 80 per cent sought opportunities for acquiring professional qualifications.

In a survey conducted in 1984 by the Prime Minister's Office on the attitudes to the combination of work and marriage, the preponderant opinion was that women should stop working for marriage and childbirth but could resume when the children grew up (women 45.3 per cent, men

36.1 per cent). More women were in favour of continuing work also after marriage and childbirth than men (women 20.1 per cent, men 15.7 per cent), but more women thought that women should cease working when they got married (women 11.1 per cent, men 16.4 per cent) or had their first child (women 10.6 per cent, men 13.9 per cent). Only a small minority held the view that a married woman should not have an outside job (women 6.1 per cent, men 9.8 per cent).

Woman's Place in the Home?

Nevertheless, the view that the place of woman is in the home is still held by the vast majority of Japanese. In another survey conducted by the Prime Minister's Office, the question 'Do you agree with the statement that the husband should earn a living and the wife should stay at home and take care of the family?' was answered with 'yes' by 83.2 per cent of the women and 83.8 per cent of the men. In another survey, only 5.8 per cent of the women opposed the traditional role attribution outright but 17.8 per cent were more against it than for it. How strong the traditional sex roles are embedded in the value system of the people is also apparent in the answers to the question 'What makes life most meaningful?' The answers of women: children 52.6 per cent, family 13.2 per cent, occupation 9.0 per cent, husband 2.7 per cent. The answers of men: career 43.8 per cent, children 28.8 per cent, hobbies 15.9 per cent, wife 4.8 per cent. Noteworthy is the enormous preponderance of the role of mother over that of wife and the low value of the marriage partner in the answers of both sexes.

Japan is not the only country where the traditional role attributions remain strong. A West German commission reporting on 'Measures for the Implementation of the Social and Legal Equality of Women' stated that almost all proposals were based on old role models. Despite the fact that millions of women were working, the association man-job, woman-home was not only prevalent in daily life but also assumed as evident in textbooks and known to three-year-olds.

In a poll commissioned by Virginia Slims cigarettes questioning 3,000 women and 1,000 men, 51 per cent of the women said that in a choice between a family and a career they would opt for outside work. On another question, 42 per cent of the women wanted housewives to receive a weekly salary from their husbands for staying home and running the household but 65 per cent of the men opposed this idea. The survey found that 49 per cent of the women and 51 per cent of the men thought there were more advantages to being a man than being a woman, compared with 31 per cent of the women and 42 per cent of the men holding that view in 1974.

Value of Household Work

Women justly resent the view that housework is considered less productive and less constructive than an outside job. A housewife wants recognition for her function which is essential for the entire family. Her work demands not only sacrifice but also more ingenuity, effort and self-reliance than many jobs held by career women. As one woman put it: 'A housewife is not a dependent in the true psychological sense of the word just because her name is put in the 'dependent' box of the income return.'

The work of the mother has its own value, and her work deserves the same social security and recognition as outside work. Human society needs values that are anchored in the culture of the family, such as love, naturalness, fidelity, renunciation, solicitude and care for the future generation. Such values are tied to the work of the mother.

'Housewife' should be recognised by society and legislation as an occupation much more necessary and much more difficult than many professional jobs. In industry, factors considered for job classification are the conditions under which the work has to be performed and the independent decisions it involves. A housewife has little data on which she can rely for making her decisions. She knows the maximum amount of money she can spend, but how she allocates it to the various spending categories and how she arranges that the money lasts through the month are entirely up to her ingenuity. There are innumerable books on the care of infants and the education of children and a never-ending stream of TV programmes on every aspect of her work as mother and housekeeper, but nobody can tell her what she should do under the actual conditions of her family. If decision-making is one of the main attributes of management, the housewife's work can certainly be characterised as a managerial occupation.

In our society, monetary compensation is not only the reward paid for services but the amount of money a person earns is often equated with his or her worth. Since the housewife receives no cash remuneration, she often feels that her work is not recognised. According to the Economic Planning Agency, the work of an average Japanese housewife was worth ¥63,000 a month in 1978, and in 1981, a British insurance company put the value of a housewife's work at £200 a week. According to the American magazine *Family Circle,* a housewife does 22 different jobs and another survey found that a housewife has 69 different types of work to do. *Family Circle* stated that at 1981 prices, the work of a housewife was worth $793.79 a week or about $41,000 a year. Cooking alone would come to $62 a week or $3,162 a year; cleaning the house $22 a week or $1,122 a year. Taking care of the children would cost an average of $9,000 a year and acting as hostess or maid $3,000.

Many of the things undertaken out of a false ideal of equality have led not only to a decline in the birthrate but also to the loss of contentment and happiness and made women more susceptible to psychoses. The problem does not require a new role attribution but a change in society's traditional measures and concepts of values. Women's capabilities and activities such as the work connected with the household, the education of children and the care of the family must be given greater social recognition.

How to Combine Family and Career

At the same time, however, the combination of a career with marriage and family must be established as a valid pattern of a woman's life. At present, many women who do not fit into the traditional role of a Japanese housewife are miserable. Women are expected to be completely loyal and devoted to their families in return for receiving a lifetime guarantee of security free from any real threat of divorce. If they seek a career, they have to sacrifice marriage and children. If they try to do both, they have two full-time jobs. Nobody quite trusts them as a mother. Nobody trusts them as a professional career woman, either. It can hardly be said that the problems involved in the work of women have been solved. While outside work may not interfere with a woman's role as wife, it often imperils her functions as mother and housewife because today's economic system makes adjustments for the multiple demands of work, household and children difficult. It can hardly be expected that the economic system will become more accommodating to the needs of the family in the near future but neither will women stop working outside the home.

Many working women could be helped if more enterprises were to adopt flexitime or the more ambitious scheme developed by a German firm called 'individual working time' system. Under this programme, a contract is drawn up between the employer and each employee stipulating the minimum number of hours of work per year. Actual working time is arranged by each department on a weekly basis. Each employee has a time account controlled by a computer which operates like a bank account. The 'flexiyear' plan allows employees to arrange the week so that they can take care of their personal business.

In Japan, the law guarantees maternity leave before and after childbirth and many European countries have similar regulations but there is no general rule providing this kind of protection to pregnant women in the United States. Many feminists think that their movement should have placed more emphasis on improving conditions enabling women to combine work with having children and raising a family.

From 1960 to 1980, the percentage of married women in the American labour force rose from 32 per cent to 51 per cent, and in 1980, the number of children with mothers who worked (31.8 million) was larger than the number of children with mothers at home (26.3 million). The ratio of single earner households declined from 49.6 per cent in 1960 to 22.4 per cent in 1980. Many Americans seem to agree with the view that in today's economy, two wage earners are needed to support a family. Although the influx of women into the labour force has grown uninterruptedly and the US labour force comprised 46.9 million women in 1981, women were still working largely in less remunerative jobs and were paid less than men in similar positions. Only 5 per cent of the executives in the top 50 American companies were women and 80 per cent of all women who worked held down 'pink-collar' jobs and got paid about two-thirds of men's pay. Women accounted for 70 per cent of all classroom teachers but they made an average of $3,000 a year less than their male colleagues.

Feminisation of Poverty

The most alarming phenomenon in the United States has been the 'feminisation of poverty.' Female heads of households form a disproportionally large group of people in poverty. In the United States in 1984, there were 10 million households maintained by women with no husband; 35 per cent of them lived below the poverty level. In 1959, 25 per cent of poor whites and 29 per cent of poor blacks lived in female-headed households; in 1984, 42 per cent of poor whites and 68 per cent of poor blacks did so. The increase in the number of separations, divorces and children born out of wedlock was blamed for the situation, and the failure of 75 per cent of the absent fathers to pay child support was an additional factor.

In Britain, 54 per cent of the mothers with dependent children were working in 1980, 17 per cent of them full-time. Of the full-time women workers, 6 per cent worked more than 40 hours a week compared with 34 per cent of men (16 per cent of the men worked 51 hours a week or more).

Motherhood and Work

According to a West German survey carried out in 1982, the majority of young women between the ages of 15 and 19 placed a professional career at the top of their future goals but they also wanted to have a family. Only 6 per cent did not want children but 10 per cent rejected marriage on principle. Forty-seven per cent intended to remain at home as long as their children would be young but wanted to resume their professional career later. Only 5 per cent planned to devote themselves entirely to the upbringing of their children. Part-time work was favoured by 23 per cent in order to reconcile job and family.

If the children are grown up, an older woman can find work outside the home and take up a full-time job if her husband is cooperative. Young women with a good-paying full-time job will often be reluctant to get married if it means giving up their work irrevocably and assume household duties for ever. It seems unfair to force a woman into long and onerous training for a profession and then make it impossible for her to exercise it later. Some kind of accommodation seems necessary which would enable a woman to resume her professional career once her role as mother demands less of her time and efforts.

Obstacles to Outside Work

Nevertheless, difficulties or trouble may arise in families with teenage children when the mother starts or resumes working. The children are used to having their mother available for their needs or requests at any time of the day or night. This very convenient situation changes when the mother is absent for the best part of the day: just as the husband must adjust himself to the changed circumstances, the children must also get used to doing certain things for themselves.

Women forced to interrupt their professional careers on account of their duties as mothers or their work as homekeepers find the resumption of their professional work particularly difficult in occupations in which constant progress is being made, such as science, technology or law. This is one of the reasons why even in fields in which women predominate such as education and health service, the leading experts are men.

A woman who starts working after having lived only as mother and housewife may experience a distressing upset in her life rhythm. As a mother, she lives the whole day with her child and her life is shaped by her care for the child. The child's feeding needs, its sleep, play, moods and health determine the daily routine of the mother. The ordinary household chores, cooking, cleaning, laundry and shopping, are adjusted to the needs of the child. When a mother starts working, her day is no longer controlled by the care of her child but by the hours of work. The child is deprived of its hold over the daily life of the mother who has to cope with an inorganic and artificial schedule.

The development of the nuclear family has been responsible for some of the difficulties hampering the outside work of the mother and housewife. If grandparents live in the same house or in the neighbourhood, it is much easier for the mother to be absent for some time without much damage to the children. Children remain in their accustomed environment and are less hurt by the absence of the mother when they are with somebody they trust.

Many working women find the housework a burden. Working women living alone or husband and wife without children may put off much of the housework until Saturday or Sunday but this is impossible if they have children. Surprisingly, Japanese working women rely little on frozen, pre-cooked or instant foods. These types of food make up 37 per cent of the purchases of women working full-time, 35 per cent of those of part-timers, and 37 per cent of the foods bought by ordinary housewives. Women prefer to buy fresh fish and fresh vegetables. Social expenses may be as high as 64 per cent of all expenses of working women, as against 38 per cent of those of women without jobs. Working women spend more on entertainment or meeting with friends and on handbags than women who do not work.

Woman's engagement in professional work has created some social incongruities. Girls are encouraged to prepare for a career by study and professional training but then find it difficult or nearly impossible to combine professional work with having a family. A mother who lives entirely for her family must bear with financial and social disadvantages but the double task of mother and career woman overburdens her and she is held responsible for eventual shortcomings in the education of her children. In professional life, what counts is performance and success, not attitude or ethos. 'I meant well,' is no excuse in business. The mother is held principally responsible for the emotional security and the feeling of togetherness in the family which, however, is entirely irrelevant to the computation of her pension claims.

Women's Aptitude for Heavy Work

Professional activities of women, above all work outside the home of married women, has been opposed as a matter of principle and considered irreconcilable with woman's role as mother and housewife. The engagement in outside work is disapproved for particular reasons, such as woman's constitution, the unfavourable working conditions for women, and the situation of the economy. Woman's body structure and her bodily strength make her the 'weaker sex.' Ergometric studies have shown that, on average, woman's strength in lifting and lowering loads, carrying, pushing and pulling is only 68.6 per cent that of man. Woman's endurance in continuous work is only 67 per cent of man's power of perseverance. The high accident rate of women installing electric cables has become a classical example for the unfitness of women for certain kinds of jobs. Pregnancy severely limits the bodily exertions of women. Until today, women have not been accepted as being fully able to compete with men and this bias has obstructed their training and professional education so that they have been handicapped in their ability to perform even before they start working.

The increase in the number of working women has been cited as cause of the decline in the birth rate. The larger participation of women in the labour force has resulted in later marriages; because women continue to work after marriage, the first birth is postponed and the average number of children born during the fertile years of women has decreased.

Reconciliation of Career with Motherhood

A British survey found that one-third of the mothers who remained career women after having children admitted to guilt feelings because of the limited time and attention they were able to give their children. A small percentage of the women said they had put off having a family in making a career for themselves until it was too late. Some regretted their earlier decision not to have children.

Soledad Becerril, wife of an Andalusian marquess and minister of culture when Leopoldo Calvo Sotelo was prime minister, became impatient when she was asked: 'How do you square your political career with your family life?' 'The same question,' she retorted, 'could be asked of a man but nobody gets the idea.'

Motives for Working

Why should a housewife or a mother with children want to work? The most obvious motive, of course, is money. Women may have to work because they have to earn a living. The economic motive admits of many degrees, from sheer necessity to the desire of having some extra money to spend. In one-parent families, the mother may be and often is the only adult and the only breadwinner. Economic necessity may also be the reason when the father is not able to earn enough and the mother must work to contribute to the financial support of the family. Economic reasons were cited by most of the women respondents in a 1981 survey of the Prime Minister's Office for taking up part-time employment: living expenses (60.3 per cent), educational expenses (12.6 per cent), repayment of loans (5.9 per cent), recreation, pocket money (5.4 per cent), saving for old age or sickness (4.2 per cent), use of free time (7.9 per cent), use of skills (2.1 per cent), other (1.7 per cent).

In Sweden, almost 80 per cent of the women of working age are gainfully employed. A majority of women would prefer to stay at home with their children but many of these families would fall below the Swedish poverty line if they did. The number of pre-school children entrusted to public day care centres has risen from 20 per cent to 64 per cent in the last 15 years. A woman who stays at home will receive a minimum from the national health insurance and other public insurance systems because such compensation is based on her earned income.

According to a survey undertaken by Dai-Ichi Kangyo Bank, asking 500 single women between the ages of 18 and 27 working in the Tokyo offices of large companies about the motives for working (multiple answers possible), 46.0 per cent wanted to save money, 28.2 per cent hoped to find a husband, and 25.9 per cent wished to live an independent life. The main reasons for saving were preparation for a future wedding (72.2 per cent), foreign travel (51.2 per cent) or other leisure activities

(48.1 per cent). Their work allowed them to purchase fashionable items such as clothing, shoes and handbags, and to spend money on music and magazines. Their average monthly take-home pay came to ¥113,900 of which they used ¥50,200 for pocket money and deposited ¥34,000 in their savings accounts. As of August 1984, their average savings amounted to ¥1.02 million.

Although women's pay is lower than that of men, the amounts earned by women are by no means negligible. According to a survey of Tokai Bank covering housewives in Tokyo, Osaka and Nagoya, 56 per cent of the respondents held jobs — the percentage was 67 per cent for women without children. The average annual income of the working housewives (of whom 33.9 per cent were part-time workers) amounted to ¥1,241,000 which contributed 23.4 per cent to the household income. 49.2 per cent of the working housewives began working to help their families and 42 per cent gave saving for the future as their prime objective for working.

Funds in the savings accounts of working housewives averaged ¥4,186,000 but 11.7 per cent owned balances exceeding ¥10 million. Some 9.6 per cent of all housewives and 8.9 per cent of all working wives kept savings of over ¥2 million of which their husbands knew nothing. The average secret savings of all housewives amounted to ¥ 612,000, those of wives with jobs to ¥570,000. Of the working housewives, 47.3 per cent said they needed their hidden savings to make ends meet at home, and 44.8 per cent of the non-working housewives used them for buying things for themselves.

A special class of working women are mothers of families of which the father has died or is permanently disabled. Although such families usually are entitled to some kind of financial assistance, their income may be insufficient and the mother must work to support the family. The living standards of such families may be low and children may have to give up higher education in order to work.

In countries with a high divorce rate, for example, in the United States where about half of all marriages end in divorce, or in West Germany where one in three marriages breaks up, women are beginning to realise that they must be able to support themselves. But mothers also work because they do not want to give up a career they started before their marriage, or because they find more pleasure and satisfaction in a career than in housekeeping. Few working women seem to suffer from the pressure of two roles and college graduates who are housewives find their lives less rewarding than college graduates who have outside employment. Married working women who went to college but stopped short of obtaining a degree often end up with clerical jobs they find unsatisfactory.

Satisfaction from Career

Some of the satisfaction professional women get from their jobs may come from their consciousness that they work outside and beyond the role traditionally assigned to women. All work can be accompanied by a feeling of accomplishment and the satisfaction of fulfilling a useful role but success in a self-chosen career for which the obstacles of bias and prejudice had to be overcome may be particularly gratifying. The challenge of professional involvement, the prestige of a high-paying job, and the 'sweet smell of success' can give an enormous emotional uplift.

Some women like to have outside work because it gives them an opportunity to meet other people, including other men. In Japan, about the only contact of married women with men other than their husbands are shop clerks and salesmen, and the conversation usually ends when the housewife says: 'No, thank you.' Middle class families rarely make or receive social visits, and while young people may arrange 'parties,' this is practically impossible for the ordinary family. Many Japanese men limit the conversation with their wives to monosyllabic hums feigning attention to the wife's utterances.

Independence

There has been a change in the motivation of working women, especially in their work after marriage. Economic necessity may still be the main reason for working and many young women want to save in order to get married. But for many women, the desire to be independent and to be able to take care of themselves without anybody's help has become the dominant factor. Almost 80 per cent of all working women say that they want to become self-supporting and able to stand on their own feet. Over 40 per cent of all women having a full-time professional job give as reason for their work their determination to be self-reliant and to depend on nobody, and 30 per cent of all women working part-time say the same. Women who worked before getting married think that marriage is no reason to stop working. Their husband should be self-supporting, and they want to be so, too. If they would have to give up their job, they would become a mere adjunct to their husband. A woman who does not work has the feeling that she has become the victim of her marriage. Outside work, young women think, enables them to meet other people, widen their horizon and have a 'progressive' view of life. Married women who cannot work outside feel that they can only live because they are married. They are dissatisfied because they believe that their role as mother and housewife does not make their lives sufficiently meaningful.

Contribution to Family Economy

Not only agriculture, but also many small businesses used to involve the work of the entire family. The modernisation of the retail trade has forced many 'pop and mom' shops out of business. It sometimes happens that the wife helps her husband to build up a business but when the enterprise grows, she is eased out to make room for hired professional help. Nevertheless, in many households, the wife's work either supplements the family income or contributes a substantial part. In 1981, the average monthly income of Japanese households amounted to ¥367,111 of which the head of the household earned ¥307,533 and the wife ¥26,207. But the average conceals that in some families, the wife is the only breadwinner or that the household actually needs two wage earners.

Factors already mentioned such as the greater employment opportunities for women, the increase in work requiring less physical strength and the lighter burden of the housework have facilitated the entry of women into the labour market but the most important reason for women to augment the family income by seeking employment may have been the larger financial needs of many families. Japan's living standard has risen rapidly in the post-war era, and although wages and salaries have gone up, too, the greater affluence has created demands that cannot be satisfied by the ordinary earnings of the average employee. The desire to acquire their own home has induced many families to go into debt, and the repayment of loans imposes a much heavier burden on the family budget than originally anticipated. Many home buyers do not sufficiently realise what it means when, month by month, they have to divert 25 to 40 per cent of their income to the repayment of a loan, and this for 20 years. The desire to give their children a higher education also leads to greater financial burdens and concern about the future induces many families to accumulate savings to supplement their prospective old-age pensions.

If husband and wife are both working, they often keep separate accounts. They agree on the percentage or the sum each contributes to common expenses and use the rest of their incomes as they please. Or they open a common account to which both contribute and from which expenses such as gas, electricity, water, telephone and television are settled automatically. In still another method, they have a common account into which both deposit their earnings and agree on how much is to be used for living expenses, how much for savings, and how much each should get for his or her personal needs. Very often, the wife takes over the accounting, makes the ordinary purchases by herself but discusses major outlays with her husband.

Effects of Wife's Work on Conjugal Relations

It may be unavoidable that the relations between husband and wife change when the wife works and her income becomes equal to that of the husband. It also strengthens the expectations of the wife that the husband assume a greater role in the education of the children and the housework. But a German study found that only 16 per cent of the men in families in which both husband and wife worked helped with the household chores after coming home from work whereas 72 per cent of the wives did housework in the evening. The shorter workday has not brought any significant change. Many men seem to be allergic to certain types of work (cleaning, laundry) but young men have less inhibitions in this respect than the older generation.

Most Japanese women in part-time positions find that their work does not interfere with their roles as mothers and home-keepers, but many Japanese wives think that the long working hours of their husbands greatly reduce the role they can play in assisting in the education of their children and in helping with the housework. Many Japanese men are not convinced that the work of their wives is important and do not want to hear anything about it when they come home.

Effects on Children

The opponents of the work of women emphasise the adverse influence of the absence of the mother on the upbringing of the children. Contact with the mother is the most important requirement for the sound growth of a child. A criminologist estimated that the danger of becoming a criminal was 7.5 times greater for children who were deprived of their mothers in their first years than for children who were sheltered by the presence of their mothers. Psychologists and sociologists have expressed similar opinions and confirmed the correlation of negative social indicators (criminality, suicide) with outside work of the mother. For the mother herself, too, her concern about the children she cannot take care of in the way she would like to constitutes an enormous emotional burden. Some scholars assert that it is an erroneous view of reality to think that women can be, at the same time, both mother of a family and career woman.

The National Research Council of the American National Academy of Sciences reported in August 1982 that more than half of the children growing up in the United States had working mothers. As of 1980, about 53 per cent of all children under 18 years of age had mothers who were employed or seeking employment. The proportion of two-parent families with mothers in the labour force nearly doubled between 1960 and 1980.

The study contended that taken by itself, the fact that the mother works outside the home has no universally predictable effect on children but conceded that under certain conditions, maternal employment appears to exert a certain influence depending on the age and sex of the child, the family's position in society, and the nature of the mother's work. It may have a salutary effect on girls but exert a negative influence on boys.

Data collected by the US National Centre for Health Services Research suggested that children of working mothers are no more likely to get sick and stay home from school than children whose mothers do not work outside. A survey of households with 5,538 children between the ages of 1 and 11 found that 71.4 per cent of the children whose mothers worked full-time were sick at least one day per year; if mothers worked part-time, 74.5 per cent got sick, and if mothers did not work outside the home, 71.9 per cent. The proportion of children who spent at least one day sick in bed was 58.4 per cent if mothers worked full-time, 62.7 per cent if they worked part-time, and 59.4 per cent if mothers did not work outside the home. The proportion of children who were taken to the doctor at least once a year was 74.7 per cent if the mother worked full-time, 78.1 per cent if she worked part-time, and 78.0 per cent if she did no outside work. The study also found that the ratio of children whose families made phone calls to the doctor was virtually the same whether the mother worked or not.

According to an older survey (1977), 62 per cent of the children whose mothers were working at jobs away from home were left with day-care centres, fathers looked after 10 per cent and mothers took 5 per cent with them to work. The remaining 20 per cent were taken care of by grandparents or other relatives, friends or baby-sitters.

An Indian woman expressed these thoughts on the subject: 'Due to economic factors, many Indian mothers have to work, but they are always eager to return home and spend the rest of their time, by choice, with their families. If the children are convinced that their mother is working out of necessity, they feel sympathy for her and try to make her happy by behaving themselves, especially if they see the father respecting their mother. But children also get angry if their mother after office hours seeks her own pleasure and leaves them alone. Children never forgive this because the need for warmth and security is greatest at that age. In India, the children are taken care of by the elder child when the mother is at work. For some reason, children's expectations of fathers are of a different type.

'In short, a non-working mother of a self-centred and pleasure-seeking nature will do more harm to her children than a working mother who really cares for them. In the same way, children whose fathers take an interest in them are happier. Children who do not receive warmth will always suffer emotional frustration and become destructive.'

A sign of the growing fragility of the family is the number of households in which the father is left alone with young children. According to the 1980 census, there were 119,700 Japanese households in which the father was alone with children below the age of 18. The reasons for this situation were: disappearance of the wife 36 per cent, divorce 35 per cent, death of the wife 26 per cent, separation 3 per cent.

If the father does not have the means to hire a housekeeper, he is entitled to the services of a social helper 8 hours a day, 5 days a week.

The Japanese Ministry of Labour planned to organise 'mutual assistance groups' with the help of the National Federation of Regional Women's Associations. Under this plan, married working women are to help one another with general household chores such as cooking, baby-sitting, laundry and care for sick persons if the need arises. The groups would not take over the work of professional housekeepers or visiting nurses. The plan may run into trouble because of a court decision which held neighbours responsible for the accidental drowning of a boy left in their custody.

18

The Dissolution of Marriage

Marital Crisis

THERE IS NO PARADIGM for the development of marriage which could claim universal validity. Each marriage is an adventure, and the outcome of this adventure depends on so many internal and external factors that it is impossible at the beginning of the marriage to predict how it will end. In some cases, the partners anticipate or, in a more cynical attitude, calculate that they will separate. In provisional or experimental marriages or cohabitation, which can be called off at the pleasure of the parties, separation is programmed from the start and causes no surprise. But in other marriages, both parties had the sincere intention to live together "til death us do part.' They were firmly convinced that they were made for each other, that they loved each other, and that no power on earth could divide them. Man's psychic development, however, is even less predictable than his corporal growth, and more than convictions, man's feelings, inclinations, preferences, aversions, expectations and fears can change.

The closest togetherness offers no guarantee that two people will develop in the same direction. A spiritual and, above all, an emotional divergence can endanger a marriage, and the more sincere, honest and open the partners are with each other, the more destructive will be the impact of their dissociation. In itself, such a discontinuity involves no moral qualification. In retrospect, the parties may detect many things they could have done differently but such hindsight does not reverse the development. Marital crises may be noticed too late and the conflicts may worsen by wrong behaviour. Mutual misunderstanding and defensive attitudes may exacerbate recrimination, and the immaturity of the partners in early marriages may lead to hasty decisions.

Some couples may enter marriage with the expectation or at least the anticipation of the possibility of the break-up of the marriage. Pre-marital contracts by which each partner intends to protect him- or herself against financial losses in the event of divorce create the impression that the partners doubt the durability of their union although lawyers may be inclined to defend such measures as commonsense precaution.

Acceptability of Divorce

In a survey undertaken by the Prime Minister's Office in May 1984, 33.1 per cent of the women (married women 32.5 per cent) considered divorce acceptable while the ratio was 26.8 per cent for men (married men 25.5 per cent). About 30 per cent of all pollees had no objection to divorce while 65.5 per cent thought that, in general divorce should be avoided. Only 16.7 per cent were totally opposed to divorce.

In an earlier Japanese survey, 8.6 per cent of the women replied 'yes' to the question whether they would divorce if they were dissatisfied with their marriage, and 18.2 per cent answered that they would probably do so. The readiness of women to resort to divorce if they felt disappointed was even more telling in other countries. Compared with a total of 26.8 per cent for Japan, the ratios were 79.9 per cent in West Germany, 79.1 per cent in Britain, 67.8 per cent in Sweden, 67.7 per cent in the United States, and 41.2 per cent in the Philippines.

Factors in Break-Up of Marriage

The variations in the parting of couples are innumerable. In some cases, the commonness may have been weak from the start, in others, physical attraction may have been the decisive factor for the marriage and with the decline in sexual passion, life in common loses its meaning. Married life may move into a rut and its triteness may mean boredom and sterility. A development particularly pronounced in the United States is the increase in divorces for which it is difficult to find a concrete reason. The wife suddenly announces that she wants to be free and discover her own identity. She feels unfulfilled and aspires to do something more meaningful. Not only have divorces of older couples become more numerous but in about 70 per cent of all divorces, the wife initiated the divorce. Often such divorces are not the result of dissatisfaction with the husband or the environment but they are prompted by intellectual or idealistic convictions or abstract desires. In Japan, the emptiness of some women's daily lives seems to play an important role in divorces where women between 30 and 50 leave the economic security provided by a hard-working husband who, totally absorbed in his job, does nothing to relieve the dullness of everyday life. In West Germany, three out of four divorces are sought by women. There are two reasons for this, one psychological and the other financial. The psychological reason is the higher happiness expectation, the financial reason the possibility of being awarded support even if she lives together with a new lover (as long as she does not remarry).

There have always been marital problems, but in today's 'open society' couples are more inclined to resort to divorce than in former times. Divorce no longer carries a social stigma, and the stronger emphasis on personal happiness disposes people to call a marriage quits if it fails to fulfil their expectations. Women, in particular, are more ready than before to initiate a divorce.

External conditions can become of critical importance for the inner development of the marriage partners. The feeling of togetherness may weaken if the husband's job requires long absences. In a society providing a strong framework for family life, the force of habit or social pressure may offset individual factors so that, for example, the families of seamen remained together although they were away from home for weeks and months. In today's society, however, the framework of the social order is weak and the changed views on sexual morality and the nature of marriage admit divorce as a possible alternative to a marriage that has become meaningless. Moreover, the sexualisation propagated by the media raises high expectations of sexual excitement and gratification which the life with the marriage partner seems unable to fulfil. Finally, it cannot be denied that sexual experiences happen which not only stir sexual lust but also shake an individual's love life to its very foundations and create the conflict between duty and desire so often depicted in literature.

Such phenomena have become the object of systematic research in recent decades but they have always occurred in human society and divorce may be as old as marriage itself. At any rate, the old civilisations had rules on divorce just as they had regulations for the conclusion of marriage.

Divorce in the Bible

The Mosaic law provided that a man could dismiss his wife by giving her a 'bill of divorcement' (Deut. 24,1), and even before Jesus' condemnation of divorce (Matth. 19,7-9), Malachy, one of the last prophets, had announced the Lord's disapprobation of divorce: 'For the Lord, the God of Israel, saith that he hateth putting away;' and the reason for God's disapproval is the repudiation of the solemn conclusion of marriage: 'Because the Lord hath been witness between thee and the wife of thy youth against whom thou hast dealt treacherously: yet is she thy partner and the wife of thy covenant' (Mal. 2, 16 14).

Some years ago, a Catholic professor of exegesis contended that the texts in the New Testament prohibiting divorce and remarriage (Matth. 5, 31-32; 19, 3-9; 1Cor. 7,10-11) do not contain an immutable moral rule but a dynamic norm of conduct expressing an ideal. His view has not found acceptance in the recent revision of Canon Law. The word of Jesus 'What therefore God hath joined together, let no man put asunder' (Matth. 19,6; Mc 10.9) certainly supposes that marriage as an institution is from God, but logic does not warrant the inference that every couple is brought together by God. In many instances, it seems more appropriate to attribute a marriage to human folly rather than to divine wisdom.

Historically, Church discipline has not been uniform. The fathers of the Church declared remarriage after divorce contrary to Scripture and the Church imposed penalties to force the dissolution of a second marriage. But it was impossible to compel the strict observance of this rule, particularly in Gaul and the Germanic kingdoms. Roman law and the *leges romanae barbarorum* recognised divorce by mutual consent, unilateral repudiation on certain grounds, and divorce on account of guilty conduct of one party which allowed the innocent party to remarry. Germanic law also acknowledged divorce by agreement and in case of certain legal grounds, unilateral dissolution, first only by the will of the husband, later also at the instance of the wife. The Church admitted some exceptions to the prohibition of remarriage after divorce.

An Anglo-Saxon penitential compiled around the year 700 AD recognised divorce and remarriage. A man could dismiss his wife if she committed adultery and marry another woman if it was his first marriage, and the adulteress could remarry after five years of penance.

In his book, *Life After Marriage: Love in the Age of Divorce*, A. Alvarez comes out strongly in favour of the Roman system. Roman marriage was a civil contract, he says, and it could be dissolved as any other civil contract. . When the mutual affection which had prompted the parties to conclude the contract perished, they could decide to scrap the agreement. The Church fathers, Mr Alvarez contends, ruined this sensible arrangement by elevating a simple civil contract into an immutable spiritual sacrament. He quotes the scriptural injunction. 'What therefore God hath joined together, let not man put asunder' and concludes 'When marriage became holy, divorce became damnable.'

Divorce in Roman Law

Mr Alvarez has a point. For the Greeks and Romans, marriage was a contract like any other contract. Marriage was a legal arrangement, but so was concubinage and even slaves who, in Roman law, were neither things nor persons, could enter into a kind of legal arrangement called *contubernium* which could be used by slaves and free people. A written contract of marriage or official registration was made obligatory for persons belonging to certain classes by Justinian in 538 but for others, marriage required no particular formality nor did divorce. Roman law distinguished between divorce by mutual consent (*divortium*) and unilateral dissolution by one spouse (*repudium*), but even when lawful and unlawful reasons for divorce were introduced, divorce was not made subject to a judicial procedure.

Divorce was possible at the instance of the husband in marriage with *manus* (in which the wife was under the power of the husband). In marriage without *manus*, either party was free to put an end to the relationship at will. Usually, a formal letter announcing the divorce was drawn up but the intention to divorce made clear to the other party and accompanied by actual parting was all that was legally necessary. The Christian emperors imposed penalties on those who divorced without good reasons but the parties retained power to end their marriage by their own act.

The religious views of antiquity did little to enhance the sanctity of the marital union. The Olympian gods were married but marital fidelity and restraints on sexuality were scorned. The gods mixed with mortals and immortals, married and unmarried. Naturally, society had rules on the validity of marriages, the legitimacy of children and the right of succession, but the main factors supporting the continuity of marriage were social and economic rather than legal and religious.

Divorce in Germanic Law

In many of the old European systems in which females were legally and economically dependent, marriage implied the transfer of the woman from the control of her family to the control of the husband, and divorce meant the repudiation of the woman and her return to the power of her family. According to Germanic law, marriage could be dissolved by mutual consent as well as unilaterally by the will of the husband, and later also by the will of the wife, but divorce on the part of the wife required certain legal grounds while divorce on the part of the husband without cause entailed payment of a penalty. But Germanic and Frankish law did not provide for the intervention of public authority in divorces.

Protestant churches generally allow divorce and remarriage and in 1981 the Synod of the Church of England decided that divorced Anglicans could marry in the Church. But the Greek Orthodox Church protested strongly against the revision of the Family Law by the government of Prime Minister Papandreou which introduced civil marriage, decriminalised adultery, allowed marriage of adulterers and gave civil courts authority to grant divorces (until then, Greek law had recognised the exclusive jurisdiction of the Greek Orthodox Church over marriage and divorce).

Divorce in Islam

The *Qur'an* distinguishes divorce before and after the consummation of the marriage (see particularly Sura 2, 226-238 & 241-245; 65,1-7) and fixes a period of waiting of four months and ten days (three menstruations; the period is three months for women after the termination of menstruation or prior to its start) before remarriage (this also applies to remarriage after the death of the husband). Divorce from the same woman is allowed twice; a third divorce is only permitted if, in the meantime, the woman had been married to another man. Although divorced, mothers should continue to feed their babies for two full years. In case of a rupture between husband and wife, a reconciliation should be attempted for which each family should appoint an arbitrator (Sura 4, 39).

According to Islamic law, a divorce may be effected simply by mutual agreement of the spouses which is known as *khal* if the wife comes to some financial arrangement with her husband to pay him for her release (this is based on Sura 2, 229). A wife may obtain a judicial decree of divorce on the ground of some matrimonial offence committed by the husband, such as, cruelty, desertion or failure to maintain (not in Hanafi law). The husband alone has power to terminate the marriage unilaterally by repudiation of his wife (*talâq*). *Talâq* is an extra-judicial process. The husband may repudiate his wife at will and his motive in so doing is not subject to scrutiny by a court or any other official body. Repudiation repeated three times constitutes a final and irrevocable dissolution of the marriage, but a single pronouncement may be revoked at will by the husband during the three months following the repudiation or, if the wife is pregnant, until the birth of the child.

Britain's House of Lords has ruled that oral pronouncements of divorce sanctioned by the Sharia are valid in British courts.

In Egypt, a law decreed in 1975 by the late Anwar Sadat without the consent of parliament declared that polygamy was harmful to the first wife and gave her the right to divorce her husband when he took a second wife. The law, often called Law Jihan because its adoption was largely due to the efforts of Jihan Sadat, the late president's wife, required that all divorces must be legally registered and that the wife must be informed of the divorce. It gave the wife the right to keep young children and to retain the family dwelling after the divorce.

The law was ruled unconstitutional but a new law passed in 1985 reaffirmed certain basic rights for women although the government declared that no encroachment on a man's right to polygamy was implied.

Divorce in Japan

In feudal times, the Japanese husband could divorce his wife by a 3½-line letter (known as *mikudari-han*). Because this curt notice was written on a single sheet of paper, many Japanese insert an extra sheet of paper with a short letter even today in order to avoid the impression of unpleasantness.

Japan had her highest divorce rate a hundred years ago (1883: 3.39 divorces per 1,000 population), but the divorce rate had been rising in recent years. In 1983, the number of divorces rose to 179,160 (up from 163,992 in 1982), bringing the divorce rate to 1.51 per 1,000 population. Marriages numbered 762,553, or 6.4 per 1,000 population. There was, therefore, one divorce for every 4.3 marriages. In 1984, the number of divorces came to 178,758, corresponding to a divorce rate of 1.5. It was the first decline in the number of divorces since 1963. Marriages numbered 739,993, equivalent to a rate of 6.2 per 1,000 population, the lowest level since the government began compiling statistics. The ratio of divorces to marriages rose to one divorce for every 4.1 marriages.

Preliminary statistics estimate the number of marriages in 1985 at 735,000 (6.56 per 1,000 population) and the number of divorces at 165,000 (1.47 per 1,000 population and one divorce for every 4.45 marriages).

In 1983, 70.0 per cent of the couples who divorced had children who were minors and in 71.8 per cent of the cases, the mother was given parental rights over them. The average duration of the marriages which ended in divorce had been 9.9 years; 7.4 per cent of the divorces occurred in the first year of marriage, 7.2 per cent in the second year, and altogether 32.2 per cent in the first five years of marriage. The second five years (6-10 years of marriage) accounted for 23.2 per cent of all divorces and 20.2 per cent happened in the third quinquennium (11-15 years of marriage). The number of divorces after ten years of marriage has doubled in the last ten years and accounted for 44.6 per cent of all divorces in 1983.

The largest number of divorces, 90.3 per cent of the total, were based on consent, 8.6 per cent on mediation, and 1.1 per cent on court sentences (in contested divorce suits) or judgements (in voluntary proceedings). Of the couples who divorced in 1978, 62 per cent had come together in love matches, 40 per cent had no children, and 30 per cent had been living together with the parents of one of the spouses. The number of children affected by their parents' divorce has doubled in the period from 1950 to 1982 when it exceeded the 200,000 mark. According to a report of the Ministry of Health and Welfare, in 1983, the initiative for seeking a divorce was taken by the wife in 55.3 per cent of the cases, by the husband in 35.2 per cent, and by parents or other relatives in the rest of the cases.

A noteworthy trend was the proportionally larger number of divorces in higher age groups. In 1950, men between the ages of 25 and 29 accounted for the largest percentage of divorces, 29 per cent, and the share of this age group was 30 per cent in 1960. In 1982, however, the largest number of divorces occurred in the 30 to 34 age bracket. In 1950, divorces were proportionally most numerous among women between the ages of 20 and 24 (34 per cent); in 1970, the 25 to 29 age group accounted for the highest proportion of divorces (30 per cent), and in 1982, the 30 to 34 age bracket was leading with 26 per cent of the total number of divorced women.

Some Japanese sociologists blame the overprotection of boys by their *kyôiku mama* for the failure of many marriages. Mothers who plan a 'dream' career for their sons leave them no time for playing with other children so that the boys, especially if they are only children, grow up isolated and unable to relate to others. As young men, they do not know how to handle their wives and to make the adjustments necessary for a life in common.

Among the older divorcees were housewives who had suffered long years of abuse from tyrannical and insensitive husbands but who did not want to break up the family for the sake of the children. Since the children had completed their education and had married, they felt that they had done their duty and wanted to shake off the yoke of male selfishness.

In recent years, the expression *katei-nai rikon* (divorce in the home) has gained currency in Japan. It refers to couples who continue living together despite the break-down of their marriage. They no longer trust each other, have suspended marital relations, sleep in different rooms and hardly talk to each other. Most of these couples are in their 40s when the financial burden of raising children reaches its peak. In her book with the title *Katei-nai Rikon,* Iku Hayashi relates the case of a woman who put off a divorce because of her concern for the upbringing of her three teenage children and the husband's sick and senile parents living with the family. When she learned that her husband had an affair with another woman, she pressed for a divorce but her husband told her that he had no intention of divorcing her until after the death of his parents. It would be too hard for the new wife who had not been married before to take care of the old parents.

Divorce Rate

The divorce rate has been going up almost everywhere in the world. It was 1.78 per 1,000 population in West Germany (1983), 2.55 in Sweden (1983), 2.93 in England and Wales (1978), 1.59 in France (1983), 0.18 in Italy (1978), 2.56 in Denmark (1978), 2.38 in Canada (1977), 3.21 in Australia (1977), 3.48 in the Soviet Union, and 5.1 in the United States (1982). Naturally, even in the same country, the divorce rate is different for different groups or regions. In the United States, divorce is unknown among the Amish who do not permit it, and low among the Mormons who marry under the sacred vows of the Temple. The divorce rate is high in California which, in 1981, had 133,578 divorces, 11 per cent of the national total. This reflects the fractionalisation and diversification of life-styles. The divorce rate of teenagers who married is 80 per cent. For blacks, the ratio was 233 divorces per 1,000 married women in 1981. This was up from 104 divorces per 1,000 in 1970. For Hispanics, the rate went up from 81 in 1970 to 133 in 1980, and for white women from 56 in 1970 to 110 in 1980.

The number of divorces in the United States fell from 1.21 million in 1981 to 1.18 million in 1982, bringing the rate down from 5.3 to 5.1. The decline was attributed to the recession. The number of divorces in 1981 was exactly one-half of the number of marriages (2,438,000),so that the divorce rate was half the rate of marriages (10.6). In 1981, the medium length of marriage of couples being divorced was seven years while most divorcees had been married two years. About half of the divorcing couples were between the ages of 25 and 34, while 22 per cent of the wives and 13 per cent of the husbands were under age 25. About 32 per cent of the wives and 42 per cent of the husbands were 35 and older. The divorces involved an estimated 1.18 million children. In 1982, 30.4 per cent of all first marriages of women between the ages of 15 and 44 had ended in divorce, and nearly 4 per cent within the first year of marriage. For white women, the divorce rate was 28.9 per cent while it was 45.6 per cent for black women.

In Britain, the divorce rate doubled between 1970 and 1981. In the latter year, divorces numbered 146,000, two-and-a-half times the 1970 figure. The most dangerous time for British marriages was between the third and fourth wedding anniversaries. Many divorces involved women who had married in their teens or whose children were conceived before marriage.

In the Soviet Union, one out of three marriages ends in divorce. With a population of 270 million, the country has between 2.6 million and 2.8 million marriages a year and close to 950,000 divorces. In the European part of the USSR, the divorce rate is almost 50 per cent. One-third of the divorces occurs before the couple celebrates its first wedding anniversary and 16 per cent within three months after the wedding. The divorce rate has tripled in the last 20 years and this increase coincided with a decrease in the birth rate despite a three-fold increase in the financial incentives paid to large families in the same period.

Causes of Divorce

Alcohol is said to be responsible for about half of all divorces. Nearly one-third of the women blame their husbands' drunkenness for the break-up of the marriage. Infidelity ranks second as the cause of divorce, followed by lack of housing, medical problems and the inability or unwillingness to have children. Young people are often psychologically unprepared for marriage since, on average, they marry two years earlier than they did in 1965.

An important factor responsible for divorce in the Soviet Union is the oppression of women. The Second World War almost wiped out an entire generation of Russian men and the country has taken a long time to recover from the carnage. Male life expectancy is declining mainly as a result of alcoholism, and women outlive men by about ten years. In 1960, there were 170 single women for every 100 single men, but a high male birth rate in the 1970s has almost equalised the ratio. The problem was largely confined to the Slavic population while the Asiatic and Caucasian areas preserved a more normal sex balance.

Soviet women prefer to stay single and pursue careers rather than marry a man who drinks, is lazy and doesn't help at home. 'What do you need a man for?' is one of the most frequent utterances of young

Moscow women. Women want a more independent life-style. They are ahead of men in education; 59 per cent of those with secondary and higher education in the country are women. Sociologist Yuri Ryurikov expressed the fear that marriage as an institution would not survive in the USSR. Russian women have changed their ideas while men have not, and women are unwilling to submit to male chauvinism.

A special case of divorce is the dissolution of fictitious marriages. In Singapore, paper marriages were arranged for securing government flats (married couples got preferences) and obtaining cheaper company housing loans. Once these objectives had been achieved, the marriage was annulled on grounds of non-consummation.

Why does a marriage end in divorce? Just as it is impossible to give a universally valid answer to the question why people get married, there is no common denominator explaining the phenomenon of divorce. Two people who have been partners for 20 or 30 years find themselves forgetting what brought them together. Small irritations are nursed into rankling resentments. Spouses trade insults and blame each other for the poisonous atmosphere in the once happy home. The togetherness which used to be a source of blissful joy becomes an unbearable burden.

A Japanese marriage counsellor thinks that divorce is inevitable once a wife develops a dislike for her husband. 'It is a matter of feeling, not of reason,' he says. Everything connected with the husband becomes disagreeable, from his face and his smell to handling his underwear and washing his rice bowl.

In a ten-day period, the typical problems of 519 persons, mostly women, using a Tokyo telephone counselling service, were the husband's infidelity, dissatisfaction with family life, financial troubles, discongruity of character, wife-beating, sexual incompatibility and mother-in-law problems. Over 40 per cent of the callers were wives in their 30s, and many found their lives empty and meaningless. A common problem preventing most of them from seeking a divorce was what to do with the children. Women in their 40s and 50s, whose children had left home saw no point in going on living with their spouses since the loving feeling that once joined them had gone.

Reasons Given in Court Proceedings

Although the grounds on which divorces are granted by the courts often constitute *a-posteriori* rationalisations of the outcome rather than a disclosure of the genesis of the split, they provide some hints. In 1983, according to data published by Japan's Supreme Court, women filed 36,566 of the 49,293 petitions for the intervention of the family courts in disputes between husbands and wives. The reasons for which people applied to the courts for divorce were as follows:

Share in reasons alleged by men %		*Share in reasons alleged by* women %
3.2	Violence	36.4
58.4	Incompatibility	42.5
23.8	Marital infidelity	30.8
1.4	Failure to support	22.9
2.5	Drunkenness	17.5
15.6	Desertion	16.8
10.5	Mental cruelty	17.2
11.6	Prodigality	18.8
20.1	Difficulties with relatives	11.2
13.4	Abnormal character	8.6
22.7	Refusal of cohabitation	5.4
9.5	Sexual dissatisfaction	4.8
3.9	Illness	1.9

Note: Up to three of the alleged reasons per case have been tabulated.

The frequency pattern emerging from these statistics is in conformity with the general experience and with the particular situation in Japan. Incompatibility is alleged most often by men as well as women but men find it more difficult to get along with their wives than vice versa. The prevalence of violence among the reasons alleged by women seems to correspond to the actual state of many marriages but somewhat surprising in view of the Japanese tradition is the large share of marital infidelity in the reasons alleged by men. The disruptive role attributed by men to difficulties with relatives reflects Japanese conditions and this may at least partly apply to the refusal of cohabitation. The higher rates of charges of failure to support, mental cruelty and prodigality on the part of women seem in conformity with general conditions. Noteworthy are the almost equal rates of desertion in the motives of men and women.

The courts approach divorce as a legal problem but divorce is primarily a problem of human relations. Marriage counsellors frequently urge couples thinking of divorce to sit down together, weigh the plusses and the minusses of their relationship and then decide whether they should make a fresh start or tear up their marriage contract. In most cases, it is too late to solve the conflicts leading to divorce when the courts get involved. The legal approach may be appropriate for settling the financial problems arising out of the divorce but the basic disagreements would have to be detected and resolved before the parties appeal to the law.

The declaration of one party that he or she is going to seek a divorce may bring long-smouldering feelings of discontent or anger into the open. When a wife who had filed for divorce told her husband that she wanted to keep the house for herself and the children, the man obtained a demolition permit, leased a bulldozer and wrecked the family's $85,000, three-bedroom home. The wife was out of town and the couple's three children were not at home. A policeman called to the scene by neighbours let the husband continue his work of destruction when shown the demolition permit.

Genesis of Disintegration of Marriage

In many cases, the genesis of marital discords can be traced to attitudes rather than conduct. In Japan, the initiative for divorce has shifted from men to women. Young women have a very strong consciousness of the equality of sexes while young men still harbour the old patriarchal tendencies. Because of the atomisation of urban society, the acquaintance leading to marriage is often shallow which makes marital relations fragile. Social mobility, change of residence, occupation and social environment cause tension and unrest. Economic and social factors have altered the position of women in society and upset traditional sex roles. Many divorces result from economic conditions. Women often have to earn money because their husbands' income is low, and an increasing number of women who had been working outside the home have sought a divorce.

The social and attitudinal factors related to divorce have been summarised by W. J. Goode in the following table (Family Disorganisation, in: Merton-Nisbert, *Contemporary Social Problems,* New York 1961, pp. 425-6):

greater	*Probability of divorce*	*less*
Very early marriage (15-19 years of age)	Average age (US men 23, women 20 years of age)	
Short period of acquaintance before marriage	Long period of acquaintance (two years and longer)	
Short or no engagement	Long period of engagement (six months or longer)	
Couples whose parents' marriage was unhappy	Couples with happily married parents	
Religious indifference or belonging to different religions	Both parties belong to the same denomination	
Disapproval of marriage by relatives and friends	Approval of marriage by relatives and friends	
General dissimilarity of origin and cultural and social environment	Similarity of origin and cultural and social environment	
Different view on role and mutual obligations of husband and wife	Agreement on roles and obligations of husband and wife	

Many divorces start with a communication gap. In the beginning of the marriage, spouses may discuss everything with each other and are ready to yield in order to preserve the harmony of their common life. But maintaining the initial level of communication and compromise in the face of the attenuating influence of everyday life may require uncommon efforts.

Another frequent precursor of divorce is depression. The causes of depression are manifold, but disappointment with the way in which the marriage has worked out often leads to its break-up. The husband's absorption in his work somehow shrinks his consciousness of other matters, including the state of his marriage. A man may become depressed if he fails in his career but his depression rarely results in divorce. In men, depression related to marriage more frequently seems to arise from the break-down of the marriage than to cause it. For women, on the contrary, depression often induces the dissolution of the marriage.

Marriage is not the main emotional support of men. Marital problems may disturb and upset a man, but they rarely drive him to despair. Unless a woman is strongly involved in a career, marriage and family are essential for giving meaning to her life. If marriage does not fulfil her expectations and if she can no longer be sure that her husband loves her, she can easily fall a victim to depression. Women realise how little they mean to men after marriage, and this realisation frequently brings on the lonely teens and early twenties of young wives.

It may be that a woman prefers the misery she knows to the vacuum of a separation or the uncertainty of a new beginning. She may fear the loneliness of an ostracised divorcee more than the wretchedness of an unhappy wife.

Incompatibility

Of the other reasons allegedly causing divorce, incompatibility sounds most like an *a-posteriori* rationalisation of a great variety of factors that may have contributed to the failure of the marriage. There certainly are marriages where the couple's relatives or friends say 'These two should never have married.' Character and temperament undoubtedly influence man's behaviour, and what is often called instinctive aversion does exist. But man's behaviour is not necessarily determined by his likes or dislikes, his inclinations or antipathies. Perfect harmony between two human beings is an impossible dream. Differences are a question of degree, but people may discover that they are more different than they thought or that their differences are harder to overcome, to overlook or to forget than they expected. Habits acquired in long years of growth cannot be discarded like ill-fitting clothes.

The basic precept of early Greek philosophy, 'Know thyself' (inscription on the temple of Apollo at Delphi attributed to Pythagoras and others), is hard to obey in today's society in which life-style and education are hardly conducive to self-discovery. Cicero already wrote: 'Everyone is least known to himself, and it is very difficult for a man to know himself.' People seldom try to seriously examine their values, principles, convictions and ideals, but they may be aware of their interests, preferences, fancies and tastes or their hates and aversions. If they would reflect without prejudice on their clashes with other people, they might find out who they really are, but few people are objective enough to judge themselves without bias and still fewer are wise enough to draw the consequences. Marital quarrels could help to get along better if the parties could hold a dispassionate inquest on their disagreements and probe together what they could do to avoid these clashes. But such a counsel of perfection may be beyond the virtuousness of the ordinary mortal.

In Japan, incompatibility often was and sometimes still is not a question of the relations between husband and wife but between wife and mother-in-law. It is still fairly common that the husband's parents live with him if he is the eldest son, or rather that the eldest son continues to live with his parents after he gets married. When the old Confucian morality held sway over the Japanese and the rules laid down by Ekiken Kaibara (Confucian scholar, 1630-1714) in his *Onna Daigaku* (Great Learning for Women) dictated the education and behaviour of women, a wife would return to her family if the going became too rough but would usually suffer silently and patiently the vile treatment meeted out by her mother-in-law. She might have been comforted by the expectation that, some day, she could take it out on the woman her son would marry.

But today's young women are a new breed and they are not prepared to submit to the mother-in-law. On the contrary, they are very much conscious of their position as the mistress of the house and brook no interference by relatives. The husband is torn between his obligation to his mother (the traditional *kôkô*, filial duty, derided by his wife as 'mother complex') and his affection for his wife, and often his sense of filial duty will prevail. Due to the difficulties between wife and mother-in-law, incompatibility is relatively more often alleged by men seeking a divorce than by women.

Money Troubles

Money troubles are frequently associated with the disagreements leading to divorce. The husband complains that the wife spends too much or that she uses the household money for buying cosmetics or jewellery. The wife frets because the money she gets for running the household is not enough and she has to work for her own clothes.

There are two points which may aggravate disputes over money. First, money is not an ephemeral affair but a permanent problem and the economic situation of a family does not change overnight. Secondly, money easily leads to recrimination. Monetary problems can be caused by outside constraints, the impossibility to find work, to improve one's position or unexpected and unavoidable expenditures, but they may also result from the spending habits of either or both of the spouses or, occasionally, of their children.

Infidelity

Marital infidelity is not only one of the legal grounds of divorce but also a major factor in the actual breakdown of many marriages. There are, however, enormous differences in the attitudes and reactions of spouses to the sexual misconduct of the partner, and these attitudes are influenced by the mores of society or a particular class as well as by individual views on sexual behaviour.

Historically, the double standard of morality sanctioned one code of conduct for men and another for women. Men were permitted considerable sexual freedom not only before marriage but also afterward whereas strict chastity was required of women before marriage and fidelity thereafter. Men were allowed to have concubines or mistresses, and brothels were frequented by married men just as freely as by bachelors. In the upper classes of some societies, liaisons of men or women raised no eyebrows, and nowadays, cohabitation may take the form of a *ménage à trois*. In modern society, the question sometimes is not whether extra-marital relations will lead to divorce but at what point the parties will call it quits.

There is no universal pattern in which marital infidelity evolves. Some people go back to the habit of sexual promiscuity they indulged in before marriage because they never accepted the restraints of a monogamous marriage. People may be unwilling to break off relations with a lover with whom they were intimate before getting married. Others get bored with what they call the monotony of the same sex partner and hanker after sexual adventure. The temptations associated with meeting attractive and willing individuals at the place of work seem particularly hard to resist for middle-aged men and women. A wife may become suspicious if half-explained or over-explained latenesses increase, and if latenesses become absences, her suspicions will be confirmed. The lives of the great and not-so-great are full of accounts of how casual encounters blossomed into friendships and stirred irresistible passions.

Here again, there is a noteworthy difference between the old and the new Japan. In the old Japan, only the official wife belonged to the 'house' but concubines still held an official position at the court of Emperor Meiji. Up to this day, mistresses are kept not only by those who can afford it but also by men who have to resort to all kinds of crookedness to pay for their fancy. Many Japanese wives, however, no longer silently tolerate the waywardness of their mates. Some wives put up with the sexual misconduct of their husbands for the sake of social appearances and at best retaliate by having affairs of their own.

Many Japanese wives do not leave their husbands because they are unable to support themselves. They are disadvantaged and cannot expect to find a suitable job. They never contemplated a career and even if they worked before their marriage, their skills are outdated and they have little or no seniority. Nevertheless, many wives now choose an uncertain future rather than continue living with an unfaithful husband and they often take their children with them when they move out. In some of these cases, the separation is only *de facto* and neither party bothers to make it legally valid. Sometimes, this is done later, particularly if either party finds it necessary to regulate a new marriage.

A young Japanese writer whose first novel propelled him to fame and riches married his college sweetheart but the marriage broke up after eleven months. The wife charged that her husband had had affairs with ten women after their marriage and had claimed that it was a writer's privilege to sleep with other women. His latest novel had a fashion model as its heroine and he contended that he had to consort with models, designers and stylists to obtain background material for his book. He maintained that he did not have sexual relations with any of them but conceded that he had changed rapidly during the year following his marriage and that his wife could not keep up with him.

Divorce Brokers

An enterprising Japanese divorcee started the business of 'divorce broker.' Just as a go-between has traditionally been used for arranging marriages, so it seems easier to attempt a reconciliation or to arrange a divorce by a neutral party. Because Japanese law allows divorce by mutual agreement, there is no need to have recourse to the courts. But direct negotiations between the parties may be difficult, especially if a property settlement or children are involved or if the parties are already living separately.

Effects of Divorce

A divorce may have devastating effects on the social life of the divorced. Even old friends may shun a divorced husband or wife, contacts are cool and invitations to parties are not forthcoming. The reason may be not so much the condemnation of divorce as the wish to avoid awkward situations. People would feel embarrassed meeting somebody whose position has radically changed. They might possibly have to take a stand on the merit of the divorce and the responsibility of the partners and do not want to blame one or the other. Immediately after the divorce, therefore, friends and acquaintances try to keep out of the way of the separated parties, but there may be a renewal of social contacts once the dust has settled and the new status of the parties has become accepted.

An American research project studying the effects of divorce at a point ten years after the break-up of the marriage found that about two out of every three people who had initiated the divorce were happier than ten years ago. Living conditions had improved for only 10 per cent of both of the former partners and both were in a worse situation in 20 per cent of the divorces. Nevertheless, 90 per cent of the women and 70 per cent of the men were still convinced that the divorce had been the right decision. When the marriage broke up, 44 per cent of the women and 20 per cent of the men had felt intense anger and this feeling remained about the same after ten years. Women under 40 were better able to embark on a new life, either in the form of a career or another marriage, than older women, and 70 per cent of the women under 40 had improved their financial situation. None of the older women remarried and 40 per cent of the women over 40 were financially worse off than before the divorce. More than half of the women felt that they had not been responsible for the failure of their marriage while 30 per cent of the men took the blame for the divorce. About 20 per cent of the women and 25 per cent of the men admitted that they had been partly at fault.

The study discovered some differences in the way boys and girls react to the dissolution of the family. Earlier research had pointed out difficulties experienced by young boys of divorced parents in behaviour, discipline and learning but new findings suggest that divorce may have a 'sleeper effect' on girls who have difficulty establishing and keeping relationships with men when they progress into adolescence and adulthood. They experience a fear of betrayal connected with the divorce of their parents.

19

Divorce Law and Morality

Legal Effects of Divorce in Japan

FROM A LEGAL POINT OF VIEW, marriage comes to an end by death, annulment or divorce. Divorce means that the marriage bond is dissolved and that the marriage ceases to exist. In its strict sense, annulment means that the marriage never existed and that a putative marriage is declared invalid. But in Japanese law, annulment (*torikeshi*) is not retroactive (Civil Code, Art. 748, Par. 1), and although there was a flaw in the conclusion of the marriage, it is considered legally valid until the time of the annulment so that, as far as the marriage bond is concerned, the Japanese annulment is the same as a divorce.

The legal effects are very different in the case of death and divorce. In the case of death, the surviving spouse who changed her (his) name at the time of marriage can but need not resume her (his) old name (Art. 751, Par. 1). Relations with relatives remain the same but the surviving spouse can declare her (his) intention to terminate these relations (Art. 728, Par. 2). In the case of divorce, the partner who changed her (his) name at the time of marriage resumes her (his) old name (Art. 767) and relations with relatives cease automatically when the divorce takes effect (Art. 728, Par. 1). As mentioned above (ch. 7), retention of the marriage name is possible by sending a notification to the registry office within three months after the divorce. Contracts concerning property concluded between the divorcing spouses become invalid but obligations already in existence, including joint obligations, remain in force.

The right to divorce has taken many different forms. In patriarchal systems, the husband had the unilateral right to divorce his wife. As mentioned above, the husband's right to repudiate his wife was found in the Old Testament, in Roman Law and in the *Qur'an*. The right could be unqualified so that the husband could discard his wife at will, or it could be conditioned so that the husband could dismiss his wife only for specific reasons.

Until the Meiji era, the Japanese husband had the unilateral right to divorce his wife; his only obligation was to give his wife the document called *mikudari-han* (mentioned above) which entitled the wife to remarry. This system was abolished by the *Dajôkan* (Great Council of State) in 1875. The head of the 'house' also had the right to send away the wife

of any member of the house. During feudal times, the wife had no right
to divorce; she could only flee to a temple. Originally, every Buddhist
temple connected with a nunnery had the right to mediate a divorce for
a woman taking refuge in the temple, but in the later Tokugawa era,
this right was limited to two temples (known as *enkiri-dera*, divorce
temple), the *Tôkeiji* of the Rinzai sect in Kamakura, usually referred to
as Matsugaoka, and the *Mantokuji* in Nitta (in today's Gumma Prefecture).
The temple would call together representatives of both parties and try
to arrange a divorce; if the negotiations failed, the wife would be kept
for three years in the temple; after this period, she was free to remarry.
A feudal lord whose wife disappeared would rush his retainers to the
enkiri-dera and block the gate. But if the wife succeeded in throwing one
of her geta through the temple gate, she was considered to have entered
the temple and was safe from her husband.

The Meiji Civil Code sanctioned divorce by mutual agreement;
otherwise, the husband could divorce his wife only for adultery or other
serious marital misconduct. For the first time in Japan, the wife was
given the right to sue for divorce; she could appeal to the courts in case
of cruel treatment, desertion or other grave wrongdoing, but not for
infidelity.

Divorce by Agreement

Divorce by agreement is another form of divorce without the intervention
of public authority. In Japan, divorce by agreement is established by the
same formality as the conclusion of marriage: an oral or written
notification attested by two witnesses and accepted by the family
registration office (Art. 764). But while a minor requires parental consent
for contracting a marriage, no such consent is necessary for divorce —
which is consistent with the rule that upon marriage, a person is
considered an adult (Art. 753) and also more appropriate in view of the
nature of divorce. There is no way to ascertain whether the divorce
agreement was really free and voluntary on the part of both parties. It
happens that a divorce notification is sent and accepted without the
knowledge of the wife. There are also no guarantees for the wife's support
after the divorce and the protection of the children. The law simply state
that, in case of divorce by agreement, the parents must determine who
will have parental rights (Art. 819, Par. 1).

A divorce must be unconditional and unlimited, which means people
cannot divorce for a certain purpose or a certain time. If the divorce is
not absolute, it is considered fictitious and invalid. Japanese law requires
that the date of the discontinuance of cohabitation is entered into the
notification to the family registry office (Family Registration Law, Art.
57, Par. 1, No. 5). This does not mean that the divorce is null and void
if cohabitation does not cease but it creates the suspicion of a fraudulent

divorce. In many cases, divorce notifications have been held invalid if the spouses did not actually separate. A divorce to which consent is given under duress can be declared invalid.

In a divorce by consent, each party can demand the partition of the property. If the parties cannot agree on the partition or negotiations on the partition are impossible, the parties can ask the family court to carry out the partition. This request must be made within two years after the divorce. The court must take into consideration the amount of property acquired by the cooperation of the parties and all other circumstances in deciding whether a partition should be made and what the amounts and method of payment should be (Civil Code, Art. 776).

Legal Reasons for Divorce

Although divorce by mutual agreement involves disturbing possibilities of abuse, it is best suited to the nature of marriage and the actual conditions of most marriages. But only few countries recognise this system. In many other countries, divorce requires the intervention of the courts which can grant a divorce if the conditions laid down by law are fulfilled. In the main, the legal grounds for divorce can be divided into two categories, grounds based on the guilty conduct of one party and grounds based on the break-down of the marriage. Not all conduct incompatible with the duties of marriage constitutes a ground for divorce; on the other hand, crimes not related to marriage can support an action for divorce. Some of the grounds related to guilty behaviour on the part of one of the spouses are adultery, bigamy, pregnancy at marriage, cruelty, violence, indignities, failure to provide, desertion, alcoholism, drug addiction, felony conviction, felony committed before marriage. Due to the double standard of morality, the man's adultery was often not recognised as a ground of divorce, and the situation was practically the same when the wife had no right to sue for divorce. In Japan, discord with the ascendants of the spouse constituted a ground for divorce.

Under a law passed by the Iranian parliament in March 1983, women have been given the right to apply to the courts for divorce on moral and ideological grounds without the husband's consent. Islamic law does not require specific grounds for men divorcing their wives.

The second group of reasons for divorce are based on the break-up of the marriage. Among these reasons are some that relate to the conduct or condition of the party from whom divorce is sought, but others have no such connection. Insanity, imprisonment, absence and loathsome disease appear among the reasons for divorce. The so-called Enoch Arden law provided for annulment of marriage upon showing that the other party had been absent for five consecutive years (the period is different in different jurisdictions) and that diligent search had failed to produce evidence that such other party was living.

Judicial Separation

In legal systems not recognising divorce, separation is possible (that is cessation of cohabitation either by mutual agreement or, in the case of 'judicial separation,' under a decree of a court). *Separatio a mensa et thoro* (separation from board and bed) is also recognised in Canon Law for some of the reasons that, in secular law, would justify a divorce, notably adultery (c.i.c., can. 1151-1155). If one party commits adultery, the other has the right to separation for life, the bond remaining, unless he or she consented to the adultery, or was a cause of it, or expressly or tacitly condoned it, or committed the same crime. If one party lives a criminal or infamous life, gravely endangers the other's soul or body, or makes life unbearable, separation is allowed but the parties must live together again when such cause ceases.

Annulment

Although the Catholic Church does not permit divorce, she grants annulments. Actually, an annulment presupposes that the marriage for which the annulment is sought was not really a marriage. This means that either consent to marriage as understood by the Church was missing due to essential defects of understanding or will, that the marriage was not celebrated in the form prescribed by the Church, or that it was concluded despite the existence of an impediment making the marriage invalid.

Bigamy, incestuous marriage, impotence, marriage under duress, intention of a spouse never to have children, psychological inability to enter into a marriage contract and marriage under age (16 years for men and 14 for women) are some of the reasons for which annulments are granted. Nymphomania or satyriasis are grounds for annulment only if the condition existed at the time of the wedding. In June 1983, the Sacred Roman Rota (the highest tribunal of the Church) ruled that a husband's latent homosexuality at the time of the marriage did not constitute a ground for annulment because it did not exclude the possibility of a happy marriage. However, the Rota annulled a marriage on the ground of ignorance of the nature of matrimony because the bride believed that a couple could have babies just by sleeping side by side. An annulment used to be a very complicated, time-consuming and expensive procedure, and in order to disprove the charge that annulments were just for the world of the rich or well-connected, the Church, in 1970, simplified the procedure for the United States and Australia and also introduced less onerous procedures for Belgium, England and Scotland.

The simplified procedures resulted in a sharp increase in annulments, particularly in the United States where, in 1979, about 30,000 marriages were pronounced invalid on the basis of the 'American' norms. Rome found that annulments were given too easily and quickly; the late Cardinal Pericle Felici, then head of the Roman Rota, said that the ease with which marriages were annulled in the United States amounted to church-sanctioned divorce. The liberalised procedures were superseded by the new code of Canon Law which came into effect in 1983. Annulment requires a judicial procedure normally comprising two instances and, different from the former procedure, the case need not be brought before the Rota for the final decision (although each party can still appeal). The court of first instance is the court of the diocese in which the marriage was contracted, or in which the domicile or quasi-domicile of the defendant is located, or the court of the domicile of the plaintiff if both parties live in the region of the same episcopal conference, or the court of the diocese in which most of the evidence is to be collected. The tribunal of the metropolitan see is the court of second instance. Each tribunal is made up of three judges. Lawyers are not required but in all instances, the so-called 'defender of the bond,' equivalent to a public prosecutor, must argue the case for the validity of the marriage. It is the duty of the plaintiff to submit the names of his or her witnesses, all relevant documents and other evidence to sustain his (her) claim that the marriage is invalid.

If there is indisputable documentary proof of the nullity of the marriage, it can be declared void without a formal judicial proceeding and the annulment can be pronounced if the court of second instance confirms this sentence by decree. Otherwise the case goes to the court of first instance and its judgement is submitted to the court of second instance which can confirm this judgement or start a new examination. If the nullity of the marriage is confirmed by a decree or a sentence of the court of second instance, the parties are free to contract a new marriage. If the tribunal cannot be convinced beyond a reasonable doubt that the marriage is invalid, the parties remain married.

One of the latest cases of annulment concerned the marriage of Princess Caroline of Monaco to Philippe Junot for which Pope John Paul II appointed a special commission. The princess remarried in a civil ceremony without waiting for the outcome of the inquiry.

The new annulment procedure seems to have enabled the Church authorities in the United States to deal efficiently with the actual situation. In 1984, the marriages of over 50,000 American couples were pronounced invalid by Church tribunals, and Vatican officials became worried. One of the measures taken into consideration to stem the torrent of Church-sanctioned marriage break-ups was to take jurisdiction over annulment cases away from the diocesan chanceries, establish regional tribunals and reserve the final decision to Rome, thus undoing the most significant reform of the new code.

Judicial Divorce in Japan

The present Japanese law stipulates that a party can sue for divorce on five grounds: 1. unchaste conduct of the spouse; 2. wilful desertion; 3. if the other party has been missing for at least three years and it is unknown whether he or she is alive or dead; 4. if the other party is suffering from a serious mental disorder which is deemed incurable; 5. if there is any other grave reason for which it is difficult for a spouse to continue the marriage (Civil Code, Art. 770, Par. 1). But 'irreconcilable differences' generally accepted as reasons for the dissolution of the marriage in the West are not considered grounds for a divorce in Japan.

The granting of a divorce is left to the discretion of the court. Even if the grounds for a divorce are present, the court can refuse to allow the divorce if, in consideration of all circumstances, the continuation of the marriage seems appropriate (Art. 770, Par. 2). (When Spain's new divorce law enacted in 1981 was debated, an amendment which would have given judges the right to deny a divorce was defeated.) In actual practice, the court suggests an attempt at reconciliation. In order to prevent hasty and ill-considered divorces, the old law provided that for divorce, persons under 25 needed the consent of the same persons whose consent was required for marriage. The reconciliation procedure provided by law often is ineffective because the persons charged with this procedure do not necessarily enjoy the confidence of the parties.

The Japanese courts adhere to the principle that the party responsible for the break-down of the marriage is not entitled to a divorce. In February 1983, the Supreme Court upheld the decisions of the Fukuoka District Court and the Fukuoka High Court denying a divorce to a man who asserted that his wife's egocentric personality and sloppy housekeeping had turned him to other women. The court reaffirmed the long-standing rule that the request for a divorce by the party whose culpable conduct caused the failure of the marriage will not be granted.

In May 1985, however, the Osaka High Court upheld a controversial decision of the Osaka District Court approving the divorce of a man who had committed adultery and had filed a forged divorce notice with the family registry office. The couple got married in 1972 but in the following year, the husband started a love affair with a bus conductress and left his wife to live with his lover. The wife once agreed to a divorce by consent and received alimony but she changed her mind and refused a divorce. The district court granted the husband's request for a divorce on the ground that the wife was partially to blame for the husband's adultery because she was too jealous and kept him in 'mental custody.' — 'He had good reason to flee from his wife,' the judge said. The High Court upheld the ruling. On principle, the court explained, the divorce should not be approved because the husband's adultery was responsible for the break-up of the marriage. But the divorce should be allowed because the couple had been living apart for over 10 years and the husband insisted on a divorce. The court's reasoning is rubbish and only a pretext for a decision the court wanted to reach on human grounds.

The Supreme Court has ruled that a 16-year separation was no ground for divorce. The husband had first filed for divorce in 1970 because his wife had left him and went to live with her parents. The husband's attachment to his mother who was living with the couple under the same roof and the wife's infatuation with a religious group led to the break-up of the marriage but the husband's divorce suit was turned down by the Tokyo District Court in 1973. He tried again in the court which had jurisdiction over the wife's place of residence and in 1982, the Takaoka Branch of the Toyama District Court granted a divorce because the separation had made the marriage meaningless. But on appeal by the wife, the Kanazawa Branch of the Nagoya High Court overturned the verdict of the lower court and scrapped the divorce. Although the wife was not without fault, the court said, and her attitude towards her husband left much to be desired, the husband had been lacking in love and compassion, neglected his family duties and had been overindulgent to his mother. The husband then appealed to the Supreme Court but lost his appeal because there was no legal ground for a divorce.

Japanese divorce law applies only to a marriage between a Japanese husband and a Japanese or foreign wife. A foreign couple or a foreign male married to a Japanese wife can sue for divorce in a Japanese court if the court has jurisdiction over the case based on domicile or residence but the court must apply the substantive law of the husband's home country. (Article 16 of the Law Concerning the Application of Laws says: 'Divorce shall be governed by the law of the home country of the husband at the time of the occurrence of the fact constituting its cause.') But in 1981, the Kyoto District Court granted a divorce in a case involving a Filippino man and a Japanese woman. The court based its decision on a 1980 precedent and, among other reasons for applying Japanese law, cited the fact that a divorce is impossible in the Philippines.

The same law provides that foreign law should not apply if its provisions contravene public order and good customs. In a 1984 decision, the Supreme Court upheld the lower courts' ruling that a Korean woman was not entitled to a share in her husband's property because South Korean law does not provide for the partition of marital property in the case of divorce. The absence of such a provision, the court ruled, did not make South Korean law incompatible with Japan's public policy. The stipulation that, in determining the indemnity to be paid by the guilty party, the contribution of the other spouse to the family property during the marriage should be taken into consideration had substantially the same result as the partition of property, the court said.

German Divorce Law

Under former German law, an action for divorce could be brought on the ground of adultery and other sexual crimes, attempted murder, wilful desertion, serious violation of the duties of marriage (which included cruelty), destruction of the marriage by infamous or immoral conduct, and a psychosis which had lasted three years during the marriage, had made a spiritual community between the spouses impossible and allowed no hope for restoring this community.

The new German law (First Law for the Reform of Marriage and Family Law, 1976) stipulates that a divorce can only be granted by a court and that the basic reason for every divorce is the break-down of the marriage. Culpable conduct of one party is no longer mentioned in the law. A divorce can be granted if: 1. the marriage has broken down and the spouses have been living separated for one year; 2. the marriage has broken down and the spouses have not separated or have lived separated for less than a year but for reasons related to the other spouse, the continuation of the marriage would be an unjustifiable hardship (*unzumutbar* for the spouse asking for a divorce.

A marriage is considered to have broken down if the community of life does no longer exist and the spouses cannot be expected to restore it. The judge is not to inquire into the reasons why the marriage has broken down. Under certain circumstances, the break-down is assumed to be irreparable. This is the case if: 1. the spouses have been living separate for a year and both apply for a divorce; 2. the spouses have been living separate for a year, one of them applies for a divorce and the other agrees to it; 3. the spouses have been living separate for three years.

In order to prevent irresponsible divorces, the law includes a so-called 'hardship clause' which provides that a divorce should not be granted despite the break-down of the marriage if: 1. special reasons demand the continuation of the marriage in the interest of minor children, and, 2. a divorce would impose an extraordinary hardship on the spouse opposing the divorce on account of special circumstances. But after five years, a divorce must be granted also in cases covered by the hardship clause.

The provisions of the new German law making the break-down of the marriage the sole ground of divorce has led to 'automatic' divorces and the German Constitutional Court, in 1980, declared the 'hardship clause' unconstitutional because the absolute possibility of divorce after the lapse of a certain period of time was incompatible with the protection of marriage and the family in the Fundamental Law. Divorce should be an exception to life-long marriage — a postulate not met by the divorce law in its present form.

The experience with the new divorce law has revealed serious shortcomings, particularly egregious injustice in individual cases. The change in economic conditions has made it very uncertain that a divorced partner can find employment which can impose an enormous burden on a party which, under the old law, would have been innocent. Another sore point is the duty to supplement the income of a divorced partner if there is a difference between the old and the new standard of living — which may assure a comfortable standard of living for the rest of his or her life to a divorced partner who actually was responsible for the collapse of the marriage. The new law has too many irrational consequences. The Federal Constitutional Court has decided that a partner whose demand for support is grossly unfair (for example, remarriage immediately after divorce with the partner in adultery) is not entitled to support merely because he (or she) educates a common child.

As the English Divorce Reform Act, the German divorce reform was a dogmatic attempt to exclude any consideration of guilt from the divorce proceedings and to abolish the right of the innocent party to oppose a divorce which was branded as 'marriage by legal coercion' and unlawful interference in individual freedom. Basically, the present divorce law denies the character of marriage as an institution and reduces it to the status of a mutually rescindable contract.

Law tends to be behind the times. In the balance between stability and progress which is essential for the well-being of every society, law represents one of the most important factors ensuring stability. The result is the tensions between the existing legal order and social reality which, in periods of rapid social change, may turn into incongruity. This is what has happened to the law on marriage in general and the divorce law in particular. The law was based on the principle that marriage was a union for life and that divorce, if allowed at all, should be restricted to a few exceptional cases.

Divorce in the US

In the United States, the generally recognised causes for divorce were six: adultery, bigamy, conviction for certain crimes, intolerable cruelty, wilful desertion for two years and habitual drunkenness. In all cases of absolute divorce, remarriage was permitted, but in a few states that right was denied to the guilty party. In none of the states could marriage be ended by mutual consent. All divorce proceedings assumed that one of the parties opposed the suit brought by the other. Hence, where 'collusion' came to the notice of the court, that is to say, when it became evident that the party against whom the action was brought was somehow cooperating with the plaintiff, the court generally refused to grant the divorce.

One of the characteristics of the divorce situation in the United States was that women filed for divorce much more often than men. Possibly, the husbands were more often to blame than the wives for the situation which represented legal grounds for divorce. But another reason may have been that a man who appeared as defendant in a divorce suit was far less compromised than a woman so that the husband generally permitted the wife to institute divorce proceedings.

No-Fault Divorce

A notable trend in the divorce reform was the abandonment of the notion of matrimonial fault as the basis of divorce and the shift to make the break-down of the marriage or mutual consent grounds of divorce. Divorce no longer involved an adversary procedure and thus became less traumatic and also more open and honest. Generally, the new laws enabled one spouse to have the marriage dissolved even over the objections of the other. The length of time an unwilling spouse can prolong a marriage varies from six years in France and five years in Britain and West Germany to six months in California. Since the reform of 1976, Australia has only one ground for divorce, the irretrievable break-down of the marriage which either party can claim simply by proving twelve months' separation from the other. Secret hearings are held in a family court. In 1977, Brazil made marriages soluble after three years of legal or five years of actual separation, and Italy's civil divorce introduced in 1970 requires a minimum of five years' separation. In most cases, however, the partners agree to part; what they do not agree upon is who should pay for what.

This is the Achilles heel of the divorce reform. The no-fault divorce reduces marriage to a mutually rescindable contract between two equal partners and implicitly denies the institutional nature of marriage. The controversies now surrounding the division of property, the duty of maintenance and the custody of the children stem from the fact that these problems are alien to the nature of marriage and therefore cannot be settled on principles based on the nature of marriage. Under the old law, divorce implied redress for a tort inflicted by the guilty party on the innocent party and the main objective of the consideration of what had happened during the marriage, in particular the contribution of the wife to the household and the family property, was assessing the seriousness of the tort and the compensation to be paid. The obligation to support a wronged wife could impose a crippling burden on the husband and even on his heirs, and a wronged husband could refuse maintenance and deny custody of the children to his guilty wife. In short, divorce entailed the application of retributive justice.

The philosophy of the no-fault divorce formed the basis of the Divorce Reform Act enacted for England and Wales in 1969. If there is mutual consent, a divorce can become effective in eight weeks (but not within the first three years of marriage). Under the procedures for do-it-yourself divorce, the problems of child custody and financial maintenance of wife and child were not resolved. The Matrimonial Causes Act of 1973, therefore, tried to clear up the financial problems incidental to divorce and under the instructions of Section 25 of the act, judges were to put parties so far as possible in the financial position in which they would have been had the marriage not broken down.

In the 1970s, courts in Britain and elsewhere began to attach greater weight to the contribution of wives to the economic situation of married couples. Lord Denning greatly increased the right of the wife over the matrimonial home even if it was in the husband's sole name. In a bewildering decision, he allowed a former mistress to retain occupancy of a council house while the owner had to find somewhere else to live. In the case of Wachtel v. Wachtel, Lord Denning's appeal court ruled in 1973 that, where a marriage has lasted a reasonable time, where children have been born, where the wife has looked after the home and the husband has worked, the wife should have one-third of the capital and the husband should have the continuing duty to pay for both her and the children.

Given the premise of no-fault divorce, the wife's conduct should have no bearing on her right to maintenance. If there is no guilt, there is no blame. But for a man who has to move out of his house, going on paying the mortgage on the matrimonial home his ex-wife shares with a series of lovers, the law does not make sense. Men see themselves as the victims of the new philosophy of divorce. To support a wife for life places a heavy burden on any man and if he has to pay as much as 45 per cent of his gross monthly income, he can hardly think of entering a second marriage. Many husbands, therefore, default on their maintenance payments and those who do not consider it an injustice that they are forced to pay life-long maintenance to an able-bodied ex-wife on the basis of a marriage that does no longer exist. Few men can support two families, and second wives may have to work and even forego children of their own to help sustain her husband's first family.

In most divorces, it's the man who pays. Both man and woman pay in anguish; the man also pays financially and often pays with a broken career. Prisons filled with men who haven't paid their alimony and welfare rolls loaded with divorced mothers unable to provide for their children give a hint of the social costs of divorce.

Child Custody

Child custody is another matter in which men feel cheated. Why should women get custody more than nine times out of ten? Men can be as good with small children as women; so why are they discriminated against? That was the burden of the film Kramer v. Kramer.

In the United States, the number of 'single fathers' has increased significantly. The US Bureau of the Census reported that, as of March 1984, 799,000 single fathers were raising their children. Although there can be no doubt that, generally speaking, fathers are able to rear children without the help of a woman, the number of fathers awarded custody in divorce proceedings has not been rising. Men often fight to retain custody of their children or obtain visiting rights, and numerous clubs and associations of single fathers offer help in solving the problems arising from the absence of a mother. Judges, however, stick to the old stereotype that a woman is better qualified than a man to take care of children. In a noteworthy case, the wife was a career woman who went to the office every day while the husband stayed home and raised the kids. When they divorced, the mother was given custody of the children and the first thing she did was to go out and hire a nanny.

Support

In England, under instructions of the Lord Chancellor, Lord Hailsham, the Law Commission recommended four changes in the rules regulating the levels of support after divorce: 1. courts should abandon the unrealistic goal of leaving the parties financially as if there had been no divorce; 2. financial support for children should take priority over the support of the wife; 3. ex-wives should be encouraged to become financially self-sufficient; 4. the obligation to support an ex-wife for life should be ended; courts should be able to dismiss a woman's claim to alimony against her will.

Scotland has a separate legal system and adopted no-fault divorce only in 1976. Soon, the Scottish courts were facing the same problems that had been vexing the courts south of the border: on what principle should matrimonial property be allocated upon a divorce which is neither party's fault?

In a report published in 1981, the Scottish Law Commission proposed that, barring special circumstances, women should have the same responsibility of paying their own way after divorce as men. The report proposed fair shares in the division of property, including sharing of property accumulated during the marriage. The reform drawn up by the commission would allow not only for the care of the children and for those otherwise unable to provide for themselves but also for the economic handicap suffered by housewives attempting to re-enter the labour market. To this end, the proposal suggested a rehabilitation period of three years after which payments to the divorced person should cease.

Divorce in Ireland

In the Republic of Ireland, divorce is prohibited by the constitution. Civil law allows judicial separation but a civil divorce is impossible. Separation is granted on the basis of marital fault so that a guilty wife is not entitled to maintenance payments from her husband. In actual judicial practice, however, courts grant allowances not only to deserted wives but also to women who have been the guilty party in separation proceedings.

Due to the relaxed practice of the Catholic Church in granting annulments, there are couples who are free to remarry as far as Canon Law is concerned but who, if they would marry in the Church, would be bigamists (and whose children would be illegitimate) in the eyes of the civil law.

Due to the legal situation, about 70,000 men and women were trapped in marriages that had broken down or unable to regulate their relations and to legitimise their children. Efforts to amend the legitimacy laws or to permit civil annulments were unsuccessful. Civil recognition of marriage annulments granted by the Church has been ruled out because it would go against the constitutional separation of church and state which is upheld adamantly in view of a possible reunion with Northern Ireland.

In April 1986, the government announced the plan to hold a national referendum on a constitutional amendment which would allow divorce in certain cases, including the break-down of the marriage for at least five years. But in the referendum held on 26 June, 1986, the majority of Irish voters sided with the Catholic hierarchy against Prime Minister Garrett FitzGerald and rejected the proposed amendment by ratio of 63.5 per cent to 36.5 per cent.

Malta and San Marino are the only other European countries not permitting divorce, but Malta recognises valid divorces secured abroad.

The Greek Family Law of 1983 introduced divorce by consent. The old law limited divorce to strictly defined grounds such as bigamy, adultery and desertion; under the new law which was strongly opposed by at least part of the Orthodox Church, divorce can be obtained almost automatically if husband and wife have been living apart for four years.

California's Pro-Per Procedure

In California, the Divorce Reform Bill signed into law in 1969 by the then Governor Ronald Reagan replaced the former grounds of divorce based on the guilt of one party by the catch-all clause of 'irreconcilable differences.' One of the results of the reform has been the growing number of 'do-it-yourself' divorces, involving couples filing dissolution forms without consulting attorneys. This, in turn, has led to the appearance of non-attorney marriage consultants and companies selling marriage dissolution kits — a package of forms, samples and instructions for completing the divorce procedures. The so-called 'pro-per' procedure (acting as one's own attorney) works if couples have no small children and can settle community property division amicably. Its chief attraction is the low cost.

In South America, divorce is legal in some countries such as Brazil and Uruguay but it is not permitted in others such as Argentina.

In the People's Republic of China, the first marriage and divorce

SM-T

law was enacted in 1950. It was intended to expunge all vestiges of feudal marriage customs and banned compulsory, arranged marriages, concubinage, child betrothal and interference in the remarriage of widows. Divorce was permitted only when mediation and counselling had failed and marriage clearly could not go on. A new marriage law went into effect on 1 January, 1981. It still requires mediation but stipulates 'In cases of complete alienation of affection and when mediation has failed, divorce shall be granted.' One party can apply for divorce even against the wishes of the other.

The authorities, however, became alarmed at the growing number of divorces (about 400,000 a year). In order to stem the flood of divorces, the courts charge fees ranging from 10 to 50 yuan ($3.60 to $18) in divorce proceedings. The courts decide whether one or both parties will have to pay the fees. Incompatibility, mostly because of hasty or unhappy arranged marriages has been the most often alleged reason for divorce but Communist publications blamed 'third parties' (meaning extra-marital relations) for many divorces.

In Burma, divorce or separation can be effected with the consent of both parties. The wife can ask for a divorce only on the grounds of the husband's cruelty or dereliction of duties but not for taking a second wife. The wife's infidelity, on the other hand, is sufficient ground for divorce.

Absolute civil divorce does not exist in the Philippines but legal separation is possible and so is annulment. But the Muslims in the Philippines can observe their own religious marriage laws which allow divorce.

Child Custody in Japan

Japanese law provides that in the case of divorce by agreement, the parties must also determine who shall have parental rights and decide on other matters related to custody. If the parents cannot reach an agreement or if no consultation is possible, the family court makes the decision. The family court can also appoint a replacement for the custodian agreed upon by the parents (Civil Code, Art. 766; 819; 771). If the parents divorce before a child is born, the mother has parental rights; but after the birth of the child, the parents can agree that the father should assume parental rights (Art. 819, Par. 3).

If the father becomes the custodian of the child or children, he will be solely responsible for their upkeep and education, and vice versa: if the mother gets parental rights, the father has no longer any obligation for the support of the children. If, however, on account of illness, unemployment or any other reason, the parent responsible for the support of the children is unable to fulfil this duty or can only partly live up to his obligations, the child (not the parent) has the right to claim support from the other parent. This claim for support can also be made against grandparents, brothers or sisters who are financially able to support the child. If the mother has remarried, the child has no right to demand support from the mother's second husband.

Children and Divorce

In November 1982, West Germany's Constitutional Court declared the provision of the Civil Code 'parental care is to be assigned to one parent alone' (Art. 1671, Par. 4) unconstitutional and therefore invalid. The child should not be forced to renounce one parent despite the changes involved in divorce. This decision, without explicitly referring to it, agrees with the experience that the traditional arrangements do not work. Many boys and girls are left with mothers responsible for everyday life but unable to cope with their responsibilities and fathers who appear only as occasional visitors or do not appear at all. 'Positive divorce' asserts that each parent must provide a home for the children who should have two homes and two families where they equally belong — a scheme hard to put into practice and probably unsuitable in many cases.

As mentioned above, under the Japanese family system, the wife returned to her own family if her husband died or if she was divorced and she had no longer any relation with her children. In today's Japan, the problems are very much the same as in the United States and Europe. The wishes of the divorcing parents may collide with each other as well as with the wishes of the children and the problems of custody may be complicated by the problems of support. The old European rule of thumb that the father takes care of the boys and the mother of the girls is no longer valid. The father may consider his former wife unfit for educating the children but may not be in a position to educate them himself. The mother has to earn a living after the divorce and will be away from home most of the day. Sometimes, the parents of either husband or wife may be able to look after the children. The children often do not want to be separated from one another. In a recent American divorce trial, the judge allowed the children to intervene in the suit through an attorney and state their preferences for custody. There are many cases in which the situation created by the remarriage of the parents after their divorce is hardly conducive to the education of the children.

Many of the authors have expressed the opinion that children contribute to the stability of the marriage. Aristotle already wrote: 'children seem to be a bond of union (which is the reason why childless people part more easily), for children are a common good to both and what is common holds them together' (Nicomachean Ethics, bk.8, ch.12). But there seems to be little conclusive evidence for this view. In Japan, 60 per cent of all divorces affect children and almost half of the children in institutions which, in the old times, took care of orphans now are there because their parents disappeared or divorced. Children brought up in institutions find family life difficult because they never experienced that kind of life.

It has often been said that parents who divorce while they have small children are irresponsible but the problem is far from simple. While it is true that children growing up in a one-parent family are in many ways handicapped, the situation in a family in which the parents stay together only on account of the children may be unwholesome. The strained relations between spouses who have become estranged cannot but affect the family atmosphere and may also influence the treatment of the children. They will live with parents who, at best, ignore each other, but are more likely to be more or less openly hostile to each other. Children normally love both parents and feel a great deal of emotional distress and anguish when they have to witness the lack of love and harmony or even open antagonism. To live with parents who hate and despise each other may create more pain and unhappiness than the separation from one of the parents. Children are afraid to show their affection for one of the parents if they know the other will be offended. If the parents separate, the children may still feel loved and cared for by both parents. Father and mother are divorcing each other, not their children whom both love.

Small children may not receive the warm affection they need from parents who regard them as obstacles to seeking their own happiness and older children may find it difficult to trust parents who do not trust each other. The situation will be particularly difficult if extra-marital relations are involved. If a woman says that she does not want a divorce because of the children, it may be just a way of saying that she is frightened as much for herself. Parents may attempt to gain the loyalty of their children even before their actual separation. While children tend to side with the parent who is given custody, they may maintain relations with their other parent. Boys, in particular, who are brought up by their mother may choose to live with their father when they grow older.

Child psychologists maintain that the effects of divorce are different for different age classes. Babies are exclusively oriented towards their mother and the departure of the father has only an indirect influence, for example, through the emotional state of the mother. The father starts to play a more important role for children of two or three years, but divorce begins to affect children more strongly when they are four or five. They imagine that they might have done something to cause the separation, that it was their fault. Children between six and eight are old enough to understand that the relations between their parents have gone wrong but they do not know what to do about it and feel neglected and rejected. They sometimes try desperately to replace the missing parent. The tendency of nine-to-twelve year-olds is to be ashamed of their parents and to hate the parent they consider guilty. Such a reaction is less common among teenagers who, however, are inclined to side with one or the other of the parents and experience conflicts of loyalty.

Parents should prepare their children for the split in the family and not wait until the actual separation. To give children the necessary information, including information on the future arrangements, is part of the parents' responsibility for limiting the emotional damage of the break-up as much as possible.

In his book, *The Boys and Girls Book About Divorce,* Dr Richard A. Gardner stresses the child's right to know the truth about divorce. Many parents, he says, make the mistake of hiding from their children things they ought to know, things which would make life less painful and less confusing if they were brought into the open. Children can get caught up in the whirlpool of anger, hate and fear associated with divorce or in the loneliness and sadness created by the break-up of the family. The important thing, Dr Gardner tells his readers, is that having a parent leave you or having a parent not love you does NOT mean that there is something wrong with YOU. Children should be made to understand that their parents' divorce is not their fault, and that parents do not stop loving their children if they stop loving each other.

Children often evince an intense longing for the missing parent; the yearning of boys of 6 to 8 for their father has been found to be particularly strong. But visiting fathers often do not know what to do with their children. If visits are infrequent because of geographical distance, the emotional damage may not be great, but if father and mother live in the same neighbourhood, children often feel abandoned or cast aside.

Visits may be a stress on adults because they revive the memories of anger, frustration or jealousy felt before the separation. Mothers who have custody of children sometimes discourage visits or try to sabotage them. If the parent who has custody of the children attempts to prevent visits and all contacts with the absent parent, it may become a destructive experience for children who have strong emotional ties with the absent parent.

Rather ingenious arrangements have sometimes been worked out to lessen the impact of the separation of the parents on the children. In the United States, some states allow joint custody. Instead of moving the children each month to a different household, a Michigan court decided that the parents might go their separate ways but that their three teenage boys would stay in the family home and the ex-mates would move in and out each month.

The separation from father or mother may not be the only effect of divorce on the children. The changes in living conditions may have an even more serious impact. If a parent moves out of the house with a child committed to his or her custody, the child, by moving out of the neighbourhood, loses friends and play-grounds and may have to go to another school. Money may become scarce, causing a decline in the standard of living. Mothers must go out to work and can no longer devote themselves fully to the care of their children.

Generally, girls overcome the impact of a divorce better than boys. Girls can show their emotions, they can weep and express their distress whereas boys are supposed to bear everything 'like a man.' A German study found that twice as many boys as girls suffered from difficulties related to divorce: problems in school, physiological and psychological growth troubles, depression, phobias and speech defects. Children from broken families are more likely to become juvenile delinquents, drug addicts and suicides.

Economic Effects of Divorce

Divorce terminates the legal obligations incidental to marriage. The duties of cohabitation, cooperation, support and fidelity cease to exist. The parties are no longer obliged to share the household expenses and assume joint liability for all legal acts related to ordinary domestic affairs. The spouses lose the right to void mutual contracts and their property contracts become invalid.

But divorce may create new financial obligations between the separating parties. The heart of the matter is the social and economic security of the former partners and their children. In view of the difficult problems involved in the financial aspects of divorce, the provisions of the Japanese Civil Code are almost laconic. In case of divorce by consent, one party can ask the other for a partition of their property. If no agreement on this matter is reached or no agreement can be made, the parties can ask the family court to make the division (the right to apply to the court lapses in two years from the time of the divorce). The court must take into account the amount of the property acquired by the cooperation of both parties and all other circumstances in deciding whether there should be a partition and in fixing the amounts as well as the manner of the apportionment (Civil Code, Art. 768). The same rules apply to a divorce granted by a court (Art. 771).

Actually, the party responsible for breaking up the marriage pays a sum meant as 'heartbalm' (isharyô) in addition to the share of the property and the total is called tegirekin (solatium for severing connections).

No more than 10 per cent of divorcing Japanese couples reach any kind of settlement in court. Payments may come to about ¥5-¥10 million which is meant to include housing, maintenance, schooling, medical costs and sundries. It is a clear lump-sum payment intended to settle all claims.

Although the law provides for the partition of the property at the time of the divorce, 60.7 per cent of the wives who had jobs received no property but 57.8 per cent of the wives were without a job. The divorced wife procured her living expenses by herself in 56.4 per cent of the cases of divorce in 1978, parents or other relatives supplied the necessary means in 25.4 per cent and husbands paid support to their former wives in 2.7 per cent of the cases. The wife shouldered the entire living expenses of the children in 54.8 per cent of the cases, the husband in 22.4 per cent, both husband and wife contributed in 6.7 per cent and others took care of the children in 16.1 per cent of the cases. The monthly income of the wife after divorce was between ¥40,000 and ¥80,000 in 45.7 per cent of the cases, between ¥81,000 and ¥120,000 in 29.1 per cent, between ¥121,000 and ¥180,000 in 12.2 per cent, below ¥40,000 in 8.4 per cent and over ¥180,000 in 4.7 per cent. In 1983, average earnings of divorced women amounted to ¥1.77 million a year, and only 21.4 per cent of the divorcees received financial support from their former husbands for raising their children.

Since couples in their 30s now account for the largest group of those getting divorced, about 70 per cent of the divorcing couples have children. In 1984, 223,000 children under the age of 20 were affected by the divorce of their parents, and in 70 per cent of all divorces, the children were supported by their mothers. Because most divorced women taking care of the children do not receive child support from their ex-husbands, a growing number of divorced mothers must rely on public welfare.

In a recent case, the Japanese Supreme Court decided that the claim of a divorced wife takes precedence over the claims of the creditors of the bankrupt husband. The couple divorced by consent shortly after the husband's business failed and the husband ceded to the wife a piece of land which was the only substantial property he owned. A creditor sued to have the transfer of the property voided because it was prejudicial to the interests of the creditors. But the Supreme Court upheld the sentence of the High Court which had turned down the demand of the creditor. The indebtedness of the husband constituted only one factor to be considered but did not by itself require to cancel the transfer, the Supreme Court said. The payment to the wife comprises three elements: 1. the partition of the common property; 2. support of the wife after separation; 3. the solatium to be paid by the party responsible for the divorce. It happens that the transfer of property to a divorced wife defrauds creditors, but in the present case, the wife had not only worked for the husband's business but also took over the couple's two children and was entitled to a special solatium because the husband had a lover with whom he had a child.

Under Japan's welfare legislation, a woman without a husband who has to take care of a child under the age of 18 is entitled to a monthly allowance of ¥32,700 if her yearly income is below ¥3.61 million, regardless of the income of her former husband; if her income is higher, no allowance will be paid. Under a revision which went into effect in November 1984, the monthly allowance is ¥33,000 if the mother's income is below ¥1.51 million; the allowance is ¥22,000 if the yearly income is between ¥1.51 million and ¥3 million; no allowance is paid to a mother earning more than ¥3 million or whose former husband's income exceeded ¥6 million at the time of the divorce.

Two phenomena illustrate the changed situation in Japanese society. The first is the rising number of wives paying a solatium to the husband from whom they separate. In the agreements worked out through conciliation proceedings in Japan's fifty family courts or the verdicts pronounced in these courts, the percentage of women paying *tegirekin* rose from 8.9 per cent in 1968 to 11.1 per cent in 1979. This reflects the growing number of women who are financially independent and still young enough to contract another marriage. The second phenomenon is the payment of a solatium by the wife's lover to the injured husband. Japanese law has no action for alienation of affection but in 1981, the Sapporo District Court ordered a company executive to pay a solatium of ¥2.5 million to a carpenter who had divorced his wife because of her affair with the executive. In another case, a woman who fell in love with a customer at a snack bar where she worked to contribute to the household expenses was sued by her husband for child support and her lover agreed to pay ¥60,000 a month to settle this claim.

Although divorce is nothing new in Japan, many young couples seem completely at a loss when they discover that they are heading towards a divorce. Not infrequently, a reconciliation is worked out when they visit a lawyer. Until it reached the stage of divorce, they had never sat down and discussed together what they were both feeling. Japanese women are rarely prepared either spiritually or materially to take on divorce. Although they may be working, they do not earn enough to support themselves. If they had taken stock of reality, they would, at least in some cases, have thought about preserving their marriage instead of thinking about divorce. While the husband is usually blamed for the divorce, it is often the wife who wants a divorce because she feels unhappy with the present marriage.

A divorce consulting firm was denounced by the Tokyo Bar Association for engaging in business reserved by law to lawyers and its staff were arrested. The high fees demanded by lawyers are one of the reasons for the popularity of non-professional divorce consulting. Clients must pay lawyers a retainer of ¥335,000 if the solatium sought is ¥3 million and a fee of the same amount must be paid later. For a solatium of ¥10 million, the retainer amounts to ¥850,000. Court costs are extra. Many women wanting a divorce don't have this kind of money. By comparison, the consulting service that was closed down demanded an entrance fee of ¥50,000 and a retainer of ¥50,000.

Financial Settlements in the US

According to a survey of the US Bureau of the Census, 17 million women had been divorced or were currently separated in 1981, but only 782,000 were entitled to alimony payments under court orders or legal agreements. Only 340,000 women, however, were receiving the full amount of the alimony payments, another 187,000 were getting partial payments but the remaining 255,000 were getting nothing. Payments averaged $3,000 a year. Of the 8.4 million women with children under 21 whose fathers were absent, about 4 million were supposed to receive child-support payments under court orders or legal agreements. But only 1.9 million were receiving the full amount, one million more were receiving only part, and the remaining 1.14 million received nothing. The average yearly payment was $2,106. The bureau calculated that total or partial default cheated the children out of nearly $4 billion a year in support. Nationwide, the total owed by fathers under court orders or legal agreements amounted to $9.9 billion, but only $6.1 billion was actually being paid. A California study found that many of the delinquent fathers had substantial incomes. While the wife's income had typically dropped by 73 per cent a year after divorce, that of the husband had risen by 42 per cent.

For most women, pursuing a recalcitrant ex-mate is expensive and usually a frustrating process. Courts have huge backlogs of child-support cases and even if a judgement is won and arrears are collected, payments may soon cease.

The American courts have virtually ignored the conduct of either party and there is little uniformity in the extent to which behaviour of a spouse is taken into account by courts in determining the financial settlement at the end of a marriage. Congress has drafted a law that will give divorced wives a share in their husbands' military pensions. Noteworthy, however, are the attempts of the courts to work out settlements that will effect an equitable distribution of the assets created in the course of the marriage. In a California case, the wife had been working during the ten-year marriage to make it possible for her husband to become a doctor. Shortly before the husband set up his urology practice, the marriage broke up and in addition to standard items, the wife claimed an interest in the money her ex-husband would earn as a urologist. The wife was not awarded alimony because her salary enabled her to maintain the standard of living she had while married. Her support of her husband was only taken into account in the apportionment of the property. The court rejected the wife's contention that her husband's degree was 'community property' — which, in California, is split equally — but conceded that the wife's investment in her husband's education entitled her to at least part of its value.

Generally, the wife has only been reimbursed for what she contributed to help her husband get his degree but the assertion that a supporting spouse should be compensated by giving him or her a larger share of the couple's property or higher alimony has found some acceptance. By statute or court decisions, 14 American states have recognised the principle that a professional degree obtained by a spouse while being supported by his or her partner constitutes marital property which must be taken into consideration in the division of property incidental to a divorce. In December 1985, the New York State Court of Appeals upheld a lower court's decision ruling that the medical licence earned by the husband during his marriage was marital property and that the ex-wife who supported them both while he studied and trained to become a doctor was entitled to a portion of its value. The husband filed for divorce two months after obtaining his licence to practise medicine. The wife had sacrificed her education and career opportunities to further those of her husband which, the court noted, represented the kind of 'joined effort' mentioned in the state's 1980 divorce law as having to be considered in the division of property.

While divorce laws require a fair division of property, judges often do not include intangible assets such as future earning capacity, professional education or medical insurance. In her book *The Divorce Revolution,* Professor Lenore Weitzman of Stanford University maintains that the no-fault divorce legislation has resulted in the impoverishment of divorced women and their children. The long-term alimony under the old laws has often been replaced by short-term maintenance support to enable the former wife to find work by which she can support herself. But courts fail to consider that after long years of marriage, women do not possess the job skills required for maintaining their former standard of living. Professor Weitzman found that in 114 California divorces, the women on average suffered a 73 per cent decline in their living standards while the men achieved a 43 per cent upturn. Another factor in the 'feminisation of poverty,' Professor Weitzman contends, is the burden of young working women with custody of small children because only half of all fathers comply with court orders to pay child support.

Alimony in Muslim Divorce

In India, the Supreme Court has enabled Muslim women to obtain alimony from their former husbands. The court's decision resulted from the complaint of a 69-year-old woman, Shah Bano, who, after 43 years of marriage, left her home to escape quarrels with her husband's second wife. For the next two years, her husband voluntarily paid her about $17 a month but then payments stopped. Shah Bano appealed to the local magistrate, citing an Indian law providing that a man must maintain his indigent wife unless he himself is destitute.

The husband retaliated by divorcing Shah Bano. In accordance with the Sharia, he repeated *talâq* three times in the presence of witnesses and paid his ex-wife the $250 dowry he had deposited with the court when he married her. But the magistrate found this insufficient and when the case reached the Supreme Court, the husband was made to pay $15 a month in alimony and $870 in legal fees.

The decision roused the anger of conservative Muslim men who contended that it violated the constitutional guarantee of freedom of religion. Shah Bano, who had been ostracised by her community and brainwashed by the Muslim clergy, asked the Supreme Court to cancel the judgement. But unless superseded by legislation, the decision stands and it has already been followed by the Rajasthan high court. Prime Minister Rajiv Gandhi avoided comment but promised to issue a white paper on the application of the Sharia.

After consulting various Muslim groups, the government introduced a bill in Parliament that would except Muslim women from the alimony provisions in India's Code of Criminal Procedure. The law states that divorced women who are destitute have the right to alimony while other women have to sue for alimony. The proposed bill would limit the right to alimony of divorced Muslim women to the three-month period called *iddat* fixed by the *Qur'an* for ascertaining whether the divorced wife is pregnant (Sura 2,228). If the woman has children under 18 years, she could claim support for two years. The woman would also be entitled to the dowry settled at the time of the marriage and to all property given to her by relatives or friends during the marriage. If the woman were unable to support herself after the *iddat*, she could ask a magistrate to have her relatives take care of her and if they failed to do so, the magistrate should order the board administering Muslim property to support her.

The bill, far from solving the problem, caused new storms of protests. Opponents of the bill argued that, on the one hand, it failed to reflect the provisions of the *Qur'an* (interpreted differently by different Muslim scholars) while, on the other, it was incompatible with India's secular constitution by setting up special regulations for some citizens on the basis of religion. Members of Gandhi's Congress (I) Party and even members of his Cabinet opposed the measure.

Palimony

The most controversial contribution of American jurisprudence to the rules on property settlement in the case of divorce is the 'palimony doctrine.' In 1976, the California Supreme Court, in the case of Lee Marvin v. Michelle Triola Marvin, held that cohabitants who split up must abide by any prior arrangement on how to apportion income and property. The contract is enforceable even if it is simply oral, and in certain cases it need be no more than a pattern of conduct that implies such an agreement. The decision did not say that cohabitation is the same as marriage but it applied the rules governing the property settlement in a divorce to the break-up of a *de facto* relationship.

The implications of the Marvin v. Marvin case are far-reaching. It underlines the change from the institution of marriage in which the rights

and duties of the partners are based on status to a contractual relationship
which effectively forces rights and duties of marriage on couples who
chose not to marry precisely in order to be freee of these obligations.
Although the ruling maintained that an implied or oral contract can be
as valid as a marriage contract, it also put the burden of proof of the
existence of such a contract on the party claiming a share in the property
and thereby reinstating the messy procedure the shift to no-fault divorce
had attempted to end. Only that cohabitants have to drag the details of
their private lives into open court to prove the existence of an oral
agreement to pool assets and to work for each other's benefit and to
disprove that theirs was not an implied contract for prostitution — his
money for her sexual favours — may be even more disreputable than
the old contested divorce cases.

The devastating social effects of the palimony doctrine were
exemplified by a suit brought by a California woman, Vicki Morgan,
against the estate of the late Alfred Bloomingdale, heir to the
Bloomingdale department store fortune and long-time friend of the
Reagans. Miss Morgan who claimed to have been Bloomingdale's
'travelling companion, confidante and business partner' for 12 years
alleged that Bloomingdale had promised her 'lifelong support.' Since
Mrs Bloomingdale was her husband's sole heir, the suit pitted mistress
against widow. The court found that the relationship between plaintiff
and decedent was nothing more than a contract for prostitution between
a wealthy, older married paramour and a young, well-paid mistress and
dismissed the claim. Miss Morgan lost on appeal.

It certainly is a legal anomaly that people who reject the
responsibilities of marriage want the law to give them its benefits.

William Donner Roosevelt, grandson of Franklin D. Roosevelt, was
the respondent in a palimony suit brought by a New York woman who
claimed that he had agreed to support her for life. Another case which
received much publicity was the suit brought by Mrs Marilyn Barnett
against tennis star Billie Jean King. While Mrs King conceded that she
had had a lesbian relationship with Mrs Barnett, she denied that she or
her husband had made any promise of support and the suit was dismissed.
A palimony suit brought by a male dancer against pianist Liberace was
likewise thrown out of court.

Problems of No-Fault Divorce

The assumption of the no-fault philosophy that both parties can stand
on their own two feet after divorce is obviously wrong. Economic
equality between the sexes does not exist. As long as women have babies
and take time off to look after them, they will fall back in their professional
careers. For childless women under 30 who continued working after
getting married, divorce with no reciprocal obligations may be bearable

but for a woman who withdrew from the labour force for childbearing and stayed at home to enable her husband to devote all his time to his work, the clean break is not a workable idea.

Since one salary can rarely support two families, the suggestion has been made that no man should be legally obliged to maintain more than one wife and one set of children. In other words, the former wife and her children should receive state allowances without regard to the maintenance payments that her former husband may or may not make. Such a proposal is in accord with the welfare state philosophy but would further increase an already unbearable burden, shift payments that should be made by individuals to the public, and encourage even greater irresponsibility in divorces.

Another proposal to solve some of the financial problems connected with divorce envisages divorce insurance. One of the 'family guarantee' plans would provide temporary child support. The main purpose would be to give the partners one or two years of financial relief at a time of economic and emotional stress, protect the children from becoming public charges, save unemployable divorcees from hasty remarriage and help fathers from avoiding children because of delinquent payments. Insurance experts, however, think that such insurance would be unsaleable. To be insurable, an event must be of sufficiently low frequency so that the risk can be spread among many persons, all persons must be exposed to the risk more or less equally, and the event must be beyond anyone's control. On all three conditions, divorce does not qualify as an insurable event. Furthermore, fraud would be a very difficult problem. A burned-down house stays burned down, but a divorced couple may simply go on living together.

German Law on Financial Settlements

The financial settlement incidental to divorce has become the subject of a fierce controversy in the Federal Republic of Germany. In the bad old days before the divorce reform, each divorce had to have one innocent and one guilty party. But the rules adopted in the revision of the divorce law abolished the consideration of guilt and therewith the former basis for regulating support. The new regulation lays down that the economically strong party shall be obliged to support the weaker party irrespective of guilt or innocence. A special ordinance regulates arrangements for the family home and furniture. But claims for support or alimony are reduced to a few typically defined cases: if on account of the care for or education of a common child, one party cannot be expected to earn a living independently, or if on account of age or sickness, one party is unable to take up a suitable occupation. A claim for support is also recognised if training, retraining or reeducation make it impossible to earn a livelihood. Otherwise, each party is responsible for his or her maintenance.

This regulation which makes the claim to support largely independent of the conduct of the parties has aroused vehement criticism. A husband may be willing to support his children but resents having to subsidise the promiscuity of his unfaithful wife because she has taken charge of the children and is not required to work for her living. A wife may be upset because she is forced to stand on her own feet after having given her best years to her husband and the husband's lover will enjoy the fruits of a career made possible by the wife's sacrifices.

Just as West Germany's Constitutional Court held the 'hardship clause' unconstitutional, the court, in 1981, condemned the new regulation of alimony and support as unconstitutional because it fails to sufficiently and equitably do justice to individual cases. The Constitutional Court also declared the provisions of the tax law unconstitutional which disregard the fact that the economic situation of single parents who have to work and are responsible for the maintenance and education of children is weaker than that of a married couple. The court held that the present tax law imposes an unjustified extra burden on widowed, divorced, separated or unmarried parents who are solely responsible for educating at least one child. In order to avoid a further worsening of the situation by simply invalidating the unconstitutional provisions, the court imposed on the legislature the duty to enact a suitable regulation by the end of 1984.

West Germany introduced a new institution called *Versor-gungsausgleich* (benefit apportionment). It intends to apportion the pension claims or other prospective old age or disability benefits of a divorced couple. In the present social security system, a spouse who is not or only partly gainfully employed during the years of marriage will be in a disadvantageous position if divorced. As a rule, a wife who takes care of the household and the children and does not work will be worse off because she has no independent social security claims of her own. The new marriage legislation tried to mitigate this inequity by providing for the transfer of part of the prospective social security claims of the spouse with higher eventual benefits to the spouse with no or lower claims. The details of this arrangement are rather complex (BGB Art. 1587-1587p).

France

In France, divorce reform was instituted in 1975. The financial settlement depends on the financial situation of the family. For families who own no property which could be divided, traditional alimony payments are the rule. For families with property, the common property is divided equally (or according to the terms of the marriage contract). In order to rectify any imbalance in the financial position of the parties to the divorce, a sum called *prestation compensatoire* is set aside. This sum is assessed by a judge by taking into account future needs and past non-financial contributions to the family assets. The actual size of the payment depends on the court and individual circumstances. It is an alternative to alimony and designed expressly to be a once-for-all severance of financial ties between husband and wife. If it cannot be paid all at once, which is very common, it may be paid in instalments. Heirs must honour the obligation. But the sum is never changed. Alimony is index-linked but not the *prestation compensatoire.*

Pensions after divorce are divided between spouse No. 1 and spouse No. 2 according to their years of marriage to the deceased pensioner.

In most countries, the rule has been that alimony payments cease upon remarriage or that there shall be a mandatory revision of payments.

Divorces involving the Anglican clergy have increased and recently numbered about 80 a year. When a clergyman leaves his wife, he invariably resigns his post and moves away. His wife is then forced out of her church-provided home to make way for a new vicar. She is seldom offered accommodation, receives little or no financial help, and no church pension in old age.

Catholic Position on Morality of Divorce

The question of the morality of divorce divides Catholic moralists from almost everybody else. According to Catholic teaching, unity and indissolubility are essential properties of marriage which make it incompatible with polygamy and divorce. A perplexing point for the theologians was that polygamy as well as divorce seemed to have been sanctioned in the Old Testament. Perfect indissolubility, therefore, was asserted as a postulate of divine law for a marriage contracted and consummated (*matrimonium ratum et consummatum*) between Catholics of which the old code of Canon Law said that it could not be dissolved by any human power and for any cause whatever and could only be ended by death. Theologically, this position was based on the sacramental character of the Christian marriage which, in accordance with the Epistle to the Ephesians (5, 31-32), is described as a consecration making the union of husband and wife as indissoluble as the mystic union of Christ and his Church. A marriage validly contracted between two baptised persons or between a baptised and a non-baptised person that is not consummated is dissolved by solemn religious vows (that is, if one of the spouses with special dispensation enters a religious order and pronounces solemn vows) and can also be dissolved by special dispensation.

According to the law of the Greek Orthodox Church, religious profession also dissolves a consummated marriage. A marriage contracted by two unbaptised persons even if consummated can be dissolved if one of the parties becomes a Christian and the other will neither convert nor live in peace with the Christian. This dissolution is not an automatic effect of baptism but takes place when the Christian contracts a new marriage. This is called the Pauline privilege because this practice relies on the teaching of St Paul (1Cor 7,12-17).

Catholic moral philosophy holds that the marital bond is indissoluble by natural law and can only be dissolved by divine authority. What is forbidden by natural law is intrinsically wrong (in other words, wrong and evil by its very nature). Such a position, of course, clashes with the licitness of divorce in the Old Testament so that the Scholastic authors asserted that divorce was only against the secondary precepts of natural law (those derived from the general principles) or that divorce is intrinsically wrong not in an absolute sense but only conditionally.

Divorce is said to be so contrary to the fundamental purposes of marriage that it can never be permitted by merely human authority but only by the authority of God. Suarez explains it as follows: 'The dissolution of marriage upon the authority of the persons involved is not permissible, because private individuals may not, on their own authority, do anything that works against nature. In the case of the precept in question, however, an exception is made with respect to the authority of God, as the Author of nature; and therefore, when God prescribes that the situation be otherwise, this does not constitute a dispensation but the observance of the precept in accordance with the condition included therein' (Suarez, De Legibus, 1.2, c. 15, n. 28).

Suarez here lapses into a completely voluntaristic conception of natural law in which its contents as well as its binding force are derived from God's will — a position more in line with William of Occam than with the premises of Suarez himself. He holds that natural moral law is a judgement of reason which presents actions as commanded or forbidden by the Author of reason, because the light of reason shows them to be in agreement or disagreement with man's essential nature; and at the same time reason judges that God wills that which accords with nature: essential being ought to be realised. In its essence and intellectual content, natural law is absolutely dependent upon the divine intellect, in its real existence, on the divine will. This latter proposition is true in the sense that without God's creative will, there would be no actually existing order, but it is not true in the sense that the obligation of natural law depends on God's will. Man's inner ordainment to act in accordance with the essential order of human nature, that is to say, to develop himself by his free actions in conformity with his own nature, is the reason of the obligation to observe the natural law. Man is bound to live towards his end because he is ordained by his nature for this end and this end is to be attained by his own free actions.

In a similar lapse into voluntarism, St Thomas, responding to the objection that natural law can be changed because God commanded the prophet Osee to take to himself a 'wife of fornication' (Osee 1,2) although adultery is against natural law, wrote: '. . . intercourse with any woman, by the command of God is neither adultery nor fornication' (S. theol., 1-2, q. 94, a. 5, ad 2).

The Case for Indissolubility

Just as hard cases make bad law, so invidious problems make bad philosophy. The indissolubility of marriage is postulated on the exigencies of what was traditionally (but no longer) considered as the primary purpose of marriage, the generation and education of children. This purpose, it was argued, requires the certitude of paternity and the cooperation of both spouses. Accidentally, divorce may be better for certain individuals but it is ruinous to mankind in general. Laws are made for the common good and they may occasionally result in personal disadvantage. The possibility of divorce would undermine conjugal relations and marital love, threaten the steady, sedulous and lasting care for the family, and would create unequal conditions for husband and wife: it would be relatively easy for the husband to find a new wife but the wife, especially if she is no longer young and attractive, would face great hardships.

The medieval Scholastics had no reason to discuss civil divorce because it did not exist; in the nineteenth century, Catholic moralists generally stressed that the government had no authority to interfere with the marriage bond but authors admitted that civil divorce might sometimes be necessary for protecting an innocent party from the other party. People who intend only a separation and have no intention of marrying again may sometimes be obliged to secure a civil divorce in order to obtain support and custody of the children, or to effect a civilly valid distribution of property.

The principle that the morality of divorce must be judged on the basis of the nature of marriage is correct, but many wrong conclusions have been deduced from this principle because of a warped view of the nature of marriage. Marriage, as explained above, is the personal union of man and woman for a life in common. What is required in view of the nature of such a union is a postulate of natural law. Spouses have a moral obligation to live up to their marriage vows, which means they must fulfil the duties inherent in marriage. These are not only negative duties, for example, abstaining from what is incompatible with marriage, but also positive demands such as mutual esteem, trust, support as well as guidance, admonition, warnings and reprimands. Although many catalogues of conjugal and domestic duties have been compiled, the need for positive action results largely from concrete situations which bear on the common life of husband and wife. Love is not inconsistent with duty and can be the most effective inspiration for fulfilling one's duties, but duties remain also when love has faded. However, the duty to live a common life and to adhere to the requirements inherent in marriage can, like all moral obligations be disregarded and the neglect or repudiation of marital and domestic responsibilities can and usually will lead to the break-down of the marriage.

Moral Guilt

The disintegration of a marriage is not a natural disaster and not a necessary development; it is attributable to the conduct of the parties and involves their responsibility. Usually, however, the failure of a marriage cannot be traced to one act, one event, or one decision. The no-fault legal divorce does not settle the question of moral responsibility. Morally, both parties may be responsible for the disruption of the marriage.

But that somebody was responsible for the break-down does not change the fact that the marriage is on the rocks, and the consideration that marriage should be for life is of no use. What has happened cannot be undone because it was morally wrong. The condemnation of the effect of a moral wrong does not change its reality.

The problem of the indissolubility of marriage has been complicated by an obscurity in the notion of natural law. The basic reasoning in the conception of natural law asserts that something can be just and right 'out of the nature of the thing' (*ex natura rei*) so that the nature of the thing becomes a norm of human action (which is what law means). Commonly, natural law is explained on the basis of human nature. Because human nature does not change and man cannot cease to be a man, the duties inherent in and imposed by human nature do not change. The nature of marriage does not change in the abstract — although it must be conceded that the concept of marriage is not necessarily the same — but marriage as an actually existing human relationship can change.

The duty of husband and wife to live a common life and to do what is required for their common life is based on the nature of marriage, not on human nature, and not on the nature of marriage in the abstract, but on the nature of their own marriage, the marriage which they are living.

In a static conception, the unity (or rather unicity) and indissolubility of marriage appear as its essential properties, but in a dynamic consideration, they are tasks implied in the personal nature of the marital union, postulates resulting from the exclusiveness of conjugal relations. It is not on account of the principle that marriage as a personal union should be indissoluble that husband and wife are bound to keep their marriage intact but because their marriage exists as a personal union. If marriage ceases to be such a union, the postulate also ceases. A marriage that has failed becomes a merely formal relationship and is no longer a union that demands the unconditional mutual surrender inherent in a personal union. There is no moral obligation to preserve a marriage that is a marriage only in name, and the continuation of a marriage that has broken down may be irreconcilable with personal dignity.

During his visit to Germany, Pope John Paul II said: 'It is impossible to live only on trial and it is impossible to die only on trial. It is impossible to love only on trial and to accept a human being only on trial and for some time.'

Marital faith is an expression of the indefeasible dignity of man because a marriage with reservations is against human dignity. But to be forced to live together with somebody whom one does not care for or even hates is also against human dignity.

In some cases, one can escape physical togetherness by separation of bed and board but this does not abrogate the bond with a person with whom one does not want to have anything to do. It also seems hardly compatible with human dignity to condemn two people to abstain from sexual relations on account of a failed marriage.

It has often been argued that the possibility of divorce in itself favours marital discord and disruption. But the togetherness of marriage requires more than a common name, a common dwelling and a common household. The sincerest intention in contracting a marriage does not nullify the possibility that attitudes and conduct can become mutually unbearable, and everything can happen from verbal savagery to mistreatment and a life of crime and exploitation.

Avoid Divorce for the Sake of the Children?

A question which looms large in many divorces is the moral obligation of the parents to their children. For parents who love their children the question arises whether they should, in conscience, place the needs of their children first and prevent the damage that a divorce would inflict on their children. The basic obligation of parents is the care for the physical and spiritual well-being of the children. Although the presence of both parents constitutes the 'normal' framework for the children's education, it is not absolutely necessary and one parent alone can provide whatever is required for rearing a child.

Parents may decide that they should stay together for their children. This may be possible in exceptional cases. If parents can manage to live together without exercising their conjugal rights ('like brother and sister') and maintain civilised relations with each other, such an arrangement may succeed. The danger is that parents may become bitter and frustrated. They resent having to wait for their children to grow up before they can resume their own lives.

Different from the question of the strict moral duties of the parents is the question of the desirable environment. A home that is a battlefield is not very conducive to the rearing of children. Divorce imposes a great emotional stress on all parties but children, particularly older children, can adjust better to a divorce than to a household in constant turmoil.

In an attempt to soften the feelings between divorcing couples, the

United Methodist Church developed a ritual for ending the marriage in which the former husband and wife 'release' each other with vows of forgiveness and charity and gratitude for good times. Although divorce has become socially more acceptable, it is a sad and painful experience for most couples. Few former partners preserve respect and understanding for each other, with each party trying to put the blame for the break-down on the other. They not only take a negative view of each other but also want their relatives and friends to share this view. Generally, the husband may retain his contacts related to his professional interests but often friends and acquaintances greet divorce with little more than silence.

Mass weddings have found their counterpart in mass divorces. A Dallas lawyer persuaded a family-court judge to consolidate the no-contest procedures for his clients. Under normal procedures, applicants must state that the divorce is uncontested and that the marriage produced no children. In the consolidated rite, Family Court Judge, Linda Thomas, said a few words, 108 people raised their right hands in unison, and seconds later all of them were divorced.

20

Remarriage

REMARRIAGE MEANS ANOTHER MARRIAGE after the dissolution of a preceding marriage by death or by divorce. Remarriage after death has been socially acceptable if a decent interval was observed between the death of the former partner and the new marriage. Remarriage after divorce has been a controversial step in much of the western world.

The Church and Remarriage

One of the famous romances of the twentieth-century was the *affaire de coeur* between Edward VIII and Mrs Wallis Simpson. The fact that Mrs Simpson had been divorced made her unacceptable as queen and Edward abdicated as king of England in December 1936 to marry the woman of his choice. That Mrs Simpson had been divorced twice was only one of the reasons why the British establishment was upset by Edward's choice but the Prime Minister, Stanley Baldwin, and the Archbishop of Canterbury, Cosmo Gordon Lang, agreed that the ban of the Church of England on marriage with a divorced person constituted an insurmountable obstacle to the union.

The Anglican Church has since changed her position on remarriage but the Catholic Church still forbids remarriage of a divorced Catholic. Because, in the eyes of the Church, a civil divorce does not solve the marriage bond, a civil marriage contracted by partners of whom one is divorced is invalid and such people cannot be admitted to the sacraments. In recent years, the Church has shifted her emphasis from the denial of the sacraments to retaining contacts and having the couple take part in church services. In most cases, it will be impossible to restore the first marriage.

At the conclusion of the Roman synod of bishops in 1980, Pope John Paul II stated that in order to be readmitted to the sacraments, the new partners would have to observe complete continence, that is, abstain from all acts reserved to husband and wife. Such a demand seems to reduce marriage to its sexual contents and treat marital eroticism and sexuality as some kind of consumer good from which man can refrain in the same way in which he can abstain from alcohol or cigarettes. Such a distorted partnership would have a detrimental effect on family life.

The Greek Orthodox Church tolerates remarriage after divorce on the possibility that the sacrament of marriage was not originally received with the consciousness and responsibility that would have made it fully effective. The second marriage, however, is celebrated in a kind of penitential rite.

After 15 years of agonised debate, the Church of England decided to allow divorced Anglicans to remarry in the Church. By a vote of 284 to 143, the synod of the Church of England, in July 1983, formally accepted the principles and procedures for a second marriage in church outlined in a special committee report. Ten bishops voted against the proposals and 33 voted in favour, including the Archbishop of Canterbury, Dr Robert Runcie. The General Synod provisionally approved the process of remarriage in November 1983 but sent the proposals back for discussion in each of the 43 dioceses. Although remarriage had become standard practice of many Anglican priests, the Church's historic position that marriage is indissoluble had prevented official recognition of the practice.

Remarriage will not be permitted automatically and a first reform proposal required a three-stage procedure. An initial report of the local vicar was to be reviewed by a special regional panel and the final decision was to be given by the local bishop. The procedure was scheduled to go into effect Easter 1984 but the parish clergy rejected the procedure as too cumbersome and a new proposal limited the review by a special regional panel to extraordinary cases. After the initial consultation of the couple with the vicar, permission will be given by the competent diocesan bishop. The general synod voted to rescind the prohibition of remarriage proclaimed in 1938 but the new procedure has still to be approved by the dioceses and the bishops of the Church of England.

Motives for Remarriage

The motives for remarriage are varied but the two most important considerations are companionship and economic security. In the traditional family, the loss of the wife creates a vacuum not only in the personal relations of the husband but also in the management of the household, and the loss is particularly upsetting if the husband is left with small children. For a wife, the death of her husband often means economic insecurity, but according to an American estimate, three quarters of widowed and divorced women are the sole supporters of their families. Naturally, social security and life insurance may shield the family from starvation but in many cases, these resources are insufficient to allow the wife to maintain the former standard of living or to give her children the education she wants them to receive. This does not mean that the loss of her mate creates less loneliness and emptiness for a wife than for a husband, but that economic factors may play a relatively more important role in her decision to remarry.

According to Japanese law, a waiting period of six months must intervene between the dissolution of the marriage (by death or divorce) or the declaration of nullity and the remarriage of the wife (Civil Code, Art. 733, Par. 1). If the wife gives birth to a child conceived before the dissolution or nullification of the marriage, she is free to remarry from the day of the birth ón (ibid., Par. 2). If the woman remarries before the expiration of the prohibited period and she bears a child, the new husband can appeal to the courts if he thinks that the child is not his (Art. 773).

Many years ago, an American life insurance company carried out a survey on the marriageability of single, widowed and divorced individuals. This investigation found that for both sexes and age for age, chances of marriage were greatest for those who had been married and divorced, next highest for widowed and poorest for single people. American estimates put the chances of remarriage at about 30 per cent for divorced women and at 40 per cent for divorced men. Another American survey carried out in 1982 found that 60 per cent of the women whose first marriage had ended by divorce or the death of their spouse had remarried. More than half of those remarriages had taken place within three years after the end of the first marriage. On the other hand, divorce is a bitter experience and divorced people may be unwilling to risk another marriage. In countries or regions with a high divorce rate, the rate of remarriage also tends to be high, and young people remarry more frequently than do the old.

Attitudes Towards Remarriage

According to a survey of the Japanese Ministry of Health and Welfare conducted in 1978, there were considerable differences in the attitudes of divorced men and women to remarriage. Below are some of the results of the survey (per cent of respondents):

	Men	Women
Intention to marry again in the future	52.3	28.6
No intention of remarriage	24.5	56.0
Remarriage already fixed	12.5	5.5
Undecided	10.7	9.9

Among the reasons for the relatively greater number of men who contemplated remarriage after divorce, the following were the most frequent: 1. Men need somebody to take care of the household; few men are willing and able to do their own cooking or other household chores. Feminists consider this an instance of the male way of thinking in terms of the 'functional constraints' on women. 2. The wish for companionship and particularly for a sex partner is stronger in men than in women. 3. Men find it easier to approach women and to take the first step towards a new marriage than women. 4. Relations and acquaintances are concerned about the problems of a man living alone and try to find a suitable partner. As a result of the solicitude of third parties, men receive many more proposals for remarriage than women. 5. A middle-aged man, say of 40 or 50, is not considered too old to remarry while remarriage is often ruled out for a woman of the same age.

Women are not only less inclined to venture on a new marriage but also encounter greater handicaps. Although man's dream to lead a virgin home as his bride may belong to a past age, many men feel an emotional aversion against a woman who has been 'used' by somebody else. Women more often than men have children, above all small children, they have to care for, and their chances of remarriage are smaller than those of 'unencumbered' women.

Reasons for Rejecting Remarriage

Many women who reject the thought of remarriage have been hurt by the psychic trauma of their first marriage. They cite the experiences in their first marriage as the reason for their negative attitude. It is understandable that a woman who has been brutalised by her husband regards all men as animals and does not want to put herself again in jeopardy. For a woman who divorced her husband because he was an abominable creature whose attitudes and behaviour were unbearable, the risk of having the same experience again is a potent deterrent against remarriage. Women get a divorce when their attitudes change or their attitudes change when they get a divorce, and in both cases, their views on men, women and marriage are different. Before their first marriage, they were naïve and single-hearted, but they have since become critical and demanding. They have definite ideas on what a man should be and what he should do. A man should listen to his wife and respect her wishes. The wife is not her husband's servant or valet; the husband should take care of his own things himself. If they do not find a man who is superior to the man they divorced in character, behaviour and achievement, their divorce would have been meaningless. Many women hate being again fettered to the house, they do not want to give up the job they found after their divorce or renounce a career they built up. On the other hand, the life of a single woman may be trying, not only economically but also psychologically.

In Japan, men marrying for the first time numbered 691,448, equivalent to 89.0 per cent of the 776,531 marriages celebrated in 1981; 85,083 men remarried. First-time marriages of women numbered 702,259 (90.4 per cent of the total), 74,272 were remarriages. In 1980, the largest number of remarrying women was in the age groups from 25 to 34 while the number of remarrying men was already high in the 20- to 24-year group and increased further in the age groups from 25 to 34. Marriages in which both husband and wife married for the second time were relatively numerous in the 30- to 34-age group.

It seems that people who remarry choose partners who themselves have been previously married more often than the statistical probability would indicate. This may be a special case of 'assortive marriages.' Because they have gone through the same experience, they have something in common which distinguishes them from other people.

Success of Second Marriage

A closed society imposes great restraints on personal behaviour whereas the anonymity and lack of cohesion of modern urban societies favour divorce and remarriage. Not only have divorced people a good chance of remarriage, but their second marriage may be more successful than their first. The reasons for these two phenomena are partly overlapping. The failure of the first marriage may have been a chastening experience so that people approach the second marriage with lower expectations and reduced demands. The disaster of a wrecked relationship may lead to self-reflection so that people may become less selfish, less egocentric, more patient and more indulgent. They may have less illusions and be better prepared for the pitfalls of marriage. In this sense, the risk of a second marriage may be smaller than that of the first. A woman who has been married before may be a better housewife than a woman without this experience.

Difficulties in Second Marriages

Second wives have a 60 per cent chance of being last wives. A man marrying for the second time will often ask less and give more but, on average, the learning experience of the previous marriage seems less effective for men than for women which may be attributable to the greater plasticity of women. On the other hand, a woman will have to make a careful assessment of the economic implications when she marries a divorced man. If he has to support his first wife and children from his first marriage, life may be difficult. No man can afford two families unless he is well off. Most second wives, therefore, have to work.

Young people are often unwilling to make sacrifices; if they feel dissatisfied, they quit. In a repeat marriage, the will to make the marriage a success may be stronger. The second marriage may be contracted with less haste and more deliberation than the first, and more thought may be given to the prospects of the marriage and the chances that it will succeed. These considerations do not apply to marriages in the entertainment world in which marriage seems to have lost its institutional stability.

It has, also been claimed however, that, on average, second marriages run a greater risk of ending in divorce than first marriages. People who have found it difficult to live with someone else the first time may find it just as difficult to do so the second time. A new husband may be compared with a former husband or, still worse, with the deceased husband — who, for this purpose, is spoken of in accordance with the old injunction *de mortuis nil nisi bonum* (concerning the dead, nothing but good shall be spoken — attributed by Plutarch to Solon).

One of the hazards of a new marriage is the possibility that the remarrying partner will still be emotionally attached to the former partner. This danger may be greater in the case of remarriage after the death of the former partner than after divorce. The worst thing a second wife could do in such a case would be to compete with the first wife (the danger hardly exists in the case of men). She has to be true to herself and build up emotional bonds that have value and strength of their own. There is, however, also the risk that a second marriage is contracted only for social or economic reasons.

There may be certain differences depending on the reasons of the divorce. If the first marriage was dissolved because of marital infidelity, the partner in the affair may become the spouse in a subsequent marriage if he or she is free to marry. Otherwise, the lovers may give up the idea of getting married. In a society in which marriage is only one form of more or less permanent relations between the sexes, the impossibility of marriage will be considered only a minor inconvenience. If the break-down of the first marriage had nothing to do with extra-marital relations, the choice of a new partner may be made with greater circumspection. It usually is not love at first sight and the choice is less influenced by emotion. With greater maturity, people often have a better judgement on the personality of the partner and base their choice on factors that really count in marriage.

In the United States, divorce lawyers now speak of 'regulars' who contract 'serial' marriages. In their search for relief from the pain resulting from divorce, people may turn to alcohol, drugs, promiscuity or sweets but also to remarriage. Some of these consolatory marriages soon turn sour and end in redivorce after about 2.5 years. Often, the complications of previous marriages lead to the break-up of the new marriage. The wife doesn't want her money to be used for alimony or child support and is resentful when the husband's salary goes to sustain his former wife.

Changes in Views on Marriage

Some years ago, the late Margaret Mead expressed the opinion that divorce and remarriage would become the common pattern of marital life. 'In the past,' she said, ' a man and a woman could be married 30 years and still have something to say to each other. But this is not the way life is today and it's reasonable that married individuals should have recurrent choice in their marriage.'

There is no denying that marriage has become more negotiable and more temporary. The increase in divorce and remarriage has been enormous in almost all countries in which it is possible. In a society in which the notion of the sanctity of marriage has got lost, marriage has sometimes become an arrangement of convenience of the parties. But many of the young people who dropped out of society and tried to find happiness in alternative life-styles have been disappointed. Too many psychopaths joined communes and other anti-establishment groups, and psychopaths being almost without exception egocentric, the idealism of the groups was soon destroyed by the vicious in-fights of disappointed visionaries.

The failure of the counter-culture has resulted in a greater responsiveness to personal values and lasting commitments. Although protest movements and drug abuse are filling the headlines, the desire to find a life with a personal meaning, emotional security and spiritual satisfaction is animating a growing number of people. This does not mean the return to the traditional marriage with its fixed roles of husband and wife but the quest for a marriage in which the creative energies of man and woman can interact.

Remarriage and Children

For children, remarriage of the parent with whom they have been living may bring a new home, a new standard or a new style of living, a new school, new teachers and new friends. Above all, it will bring a step-father or step-mother. A step-parent may be up against a handicap from the very start. The role of a step-father seems to be somewhat less odious than that of a step-mother but the wife and her children may get together and make the new husband an outsider who is allowed to provide for them but is never accepted as a member of the family. If he gains the affection of the wife, the children may resent it as stealing the mother from them. The change in parent will bring changed feelings and changed behaviour. There is always the danger of poor communications between parents and children, resulting in a loss of affection and inconsistent discipline.

It is unreasonable to expect that a child will accept the new father or mother as a replacement of the person who was yanked out of the child's life without regard to his preferences and affections. Children may be more inclined to regard the newcomer as an intruder and even if they outwardly adjust to the new situation, the inner rejection may create more conflicts than the parents imagine. For the divorced spouses, the ex-husband or ex-wife belongs to the past, but children have no ex-father or ex-mother. The natural relationship cannot be changed at the pleasure of other parties. But it may happen that a child forgets or even rejects the natural parent from whom it is separated.

If the children live with their mother, the father's second wife may become a weekend step-mother. The situation will sometimes be delicate and it would be too much to expect instant mutual love. It requires a discriminating outgoing friendliness and prudent restraint. While the wife may try to correct her husband's treatment of his children if she thinks that he is making mistakes, criticism of their mother would, under normal circumstances, be the worst thing she could do.

If some time has intervened between divorce and remarriage, the children may have built a special relationship with the parent with whom they have been living. This relationship may be threatened by re-marriage. They may have tried hard to replace or compensate for the missing parent and now see their efforts slighted. They may blame the intruder but may also feel betrayed by the parent whom they trusted but who they feel has let them down. In such a situation, the remarried parent is caught between two loyalties and it depends on the personality of the step-parent to find a solution to the conflict. To gain the trust of the step-children while convincing them of his or her affection for their parent may be the most decisive element in building a new family. It is important to have achieved a certain degree of cohesion and understanding before the new family has offspring of its own. Relations between half brothers and half sisters are, as a rule, relatively simple as long as they are young but may become more complicated when they grow older.

The American study on the effects of divorce ten years after the dissolution of the marriage mentioned above reported that it took children of school age an average of 4.5 years to adjust to the new family situation. The relations between husband and wife in a 'blended' family have a different influence on boys and girls. The relations of girls with their step-mothers worsened the better the relationship between husband and wife while that between step-son and step-mother improved. Step-daughters have less difficulties in accepting step-fathers and the step-father's relation with step-sons as well as step-daughters becomes more satisfactory when the relationship between husband and wife becomes smoother.